The Conservative Party and the Destruction of Selective Education in Post-War Britain

The Conservative Party and the Destruction of Selective Education in Post-War Britain

The Great Evasion

Piers Legh

BLOOMSBURY ACADEMIC
LONDON • NEW YORK • OXFORD • NEW DELHI • SYDNEY

BLOOMSBURY ACADEMIC
Bloomsbury Publishing Plc
50 Bedford Square, London, WC1B 3DP, UK
1385 Broadway, New York, NY 10018, USA
29 Earlsfort Terrace, Dublin 2, Ireland

BLOOMSBURY, BLOOMSBURY ACADEMIC and the Diana logo
are trademarks of Bloomsbury Publishing Plc

First published in Great Britain 2023
Paperback edition published 2024

Copyright © Piers Legh, 2023

Piers Legh has asserted his right under the Copyright,
Designs and Patents Act, 1988, to be identified as Author of this work.

For legal purposes the Acknowledgements on p. viii constitute
an extension of this copyright page.

Cover image © Grant Faint/Getty Images

All rights reserved. No part of this publication may be reproduced or transmitted
in any form or by any means, electronic or mechanical, including photocopying,
recording, or any information storage or retrieval system, without prior
permission in writing from the publishers.

Bloomsbury Publishing Plc does not have any control over, or responsibility for,
any third-party websites referred to or in this book. All internet addresses given
in this book were correct at the time of going to press. The author and publisher
regret any inconvenience caused if addresses have changed or sites have ceased
to exist, but can accept no responsibility for any such changes.

A catalogue record for this book is available from the British Library.

A catalog record for this book is available from the Library of Congress.

ISBN:	HB:	978-1-3502-5463-3
	PB:	978-1-3502-5464-0
	ePDF:	978-1-3502-5465-7
	eBook:	978-1-3502-5466-4

Typeset by Integra Software Services Pvt. Ltd.

To find out more about our authors and books visit www.bloomsbury.com
and sign up for our newsletters.

To my mother for her loving encouragement.

Contents

Acknowledgements		viii
Introduction		1
1	A piecemeal development	5
2	The start of the slide 1951–8	27
3	Acceleration into destruction 1959–64	59
4	A proclaimed opposition 1964–70	85
5	A minister under siege 1969–74	119
6	Opposition from 1974–9	147
7	Thatcherism in education 1979–90	155
8	The Major years 1990–7	165
9	New Labour 1997–2010	173
10	A door half opened under Cameron and May 2010–present	185
11	A need for honesty	197
Notes		200
Bibliography		224
Index		232

Acknowledgements

My thanks to Jonathan Smith, Archivist of Trinity College Library, Cambridge; Chris Collins of the Margaret Thatcher Foundation; and Andrew Riley, Senior Archivist of Churchill College, Cambridge. I am also grateful for the help of Anabel Farrell, Conservative Party Archivist, Oliver House at Bodleian Libraries Oxford, and Anna Towlson, Archives and Special Collections manager at LSE Library. Special acknowledgement goes to Emily Drewe, Editorial Director at Bloomsbury Academic, and to Abigail Lane and Megan Harris for their assistance. In addition, I am grateful to Kumaraguru Elangovan, Project Manager at Integra Software Services. I would also like to thank Richard Murray for his advice.

My thanks also to Sir Graham Brady MP, George Walden and Conor Ryan for taking the time to speak to me.

I would also like to show my appreciation for Professor Kevin Morgan and Professor Andrew Russell who supervised my PhD dissertation at the University of Manchester from 2006 to 2010, which forms the basis of this book.

Introduction

In December 2017 the Archbishop of Canterbury Justin Welby, during a debate in the House of Lords, stated that 'the academic selective approach to education' made a statement that was 'contrary to the notion of the common good'.[1] Welby was quick to add that approaches that did not give fullest opportunity to those of higher ability also produced this. Yet the comments of the old Etonian Welby, himself a product of one of the most selective independent schools in the country, are not untypical of those in the British establishment. An approach that is at best lukewarm about selective education in the maintained sector has been the norm at the higher levels of British debate for several decades. Yet the reasons why Welby and so many others at the top of British public life offer such an equivocating position on this issue are rarely explored.

In Britain, the dominance of independent schools in gaining places at the leading universities and the most prestigious posts in society remains a source of great tension and earnestly felt concern, particularly at the political level. Politicians of all persuasions constantly claim that they are tackling the problem and that the gulf between the independent and state sectors will be closed. As a result, according to them, we will become a land of equality of opportunity with wealth and class irrelevant in regard to accessing quality education. Universities are now pressured to admit state pupils based on 'contextual' factors that favour those considered 'disadvantaged'. Yet despite these policies, there are little signs of any break with the long-standing situation, namely of a massive divide in relative achievement and prestige between the independent and state sectors.

In late 2016 the new Prime Minister Theresa May made grammar schools into a signature policy as part of a raft of new education measures, and suggested that a significant number of new ones were to be created. Yet following the catastrophic result for the Conservative Party in the June 2017 general election that lost her overall majority, May's grammar school policy was abandoned and appears distinctly unlikely to be revived in the near future. Thus there is little sign of any root and branch reform of the non-selective state comprehensive system that the vast majority of British people have been educated within for the past fifty years.

It is a commonly made assumption that the Labour Party are opposed to selection and grammar schools in the interests of equality, while the Conservatives very much believe in meritocracy and back grammar schools to the hilt with committed fervour. However, I shall show in this book that the truth historically has not been so simple.

In fact, comprehensive schools developed rapidly in spite of many years of successive Conservative rule during key periods of post-war educational development. Indeed, the specific role of Conservative governments in the development of comprehensive schooling in Britain in the middle to latter half of the twentieth century has not been properly explored. I seek to uncover the arguments, justifications and evasions used at the time that allowed it to mushroom in the way that it did. What was left unsaid was often as significant as what was. In addition, the actions and standpoints of key figures were often at odds with our popular perceptions of them, most notably in the case of Margaret Thatcher. In short, the Conservative Party has been much more ambiguous regarding selective state education than is commonly supposed. This book seeks to unmask this.

It starts with a history of educational developments from the beginning of the twentieth century that laid the bedrock in terms of institutional practice, attitudes and prejudices that resulted in the 1944 Education Act. This summary and discussion of events thus provide a foundation for the subsequent chapters.

From Chapters 2 to 5 it analyses the record of the Conservative Party, both in government and in opposition, in response to the pressure for comprehensive schooling and egalitarianism from the Labour Party and the British left. Through examination of Hansard debates, Conservative Party publications and personal correspondence, it looks into the Conservative Party elite's attitudes, prejudices and machinations and shows that they were not merely passive actors in comprehensive schooling's advance. The roles of education ministers Florence Horsbrugh, David Eccles, Quintin Hailsham, Geoffrey Lloyd, as well as Edward Boyle and Margaret Thatcher under Edward Heath, are all considered. Within this period between 1951 and 1974, I engage in detailed analysis of internal debates as well as question educational historians' portrayal and interpretation of them. This forms the 'core' section of the book's analysis.

I then examine events since comprehensive education's triumph as the majority form of secondary schooling in Britain, including the Thatcher and Major governments who, while advancing policies such as grant maintained schools, did not fundamentally reverse the comprehensive nature of the system. From there it considers the ambiguous stance of David Cameron's Coalition government, which included the allowance of an 'annexe' in Kent as well as Theresa May's subsequent approach from 2016 to 2019. It also assesses more recent developments under Boris Johnson's leadership, as well as any hints of change under his successors.

Secondary sources dealing with post-war British educational history in depth have shared certain characteristics. For example, in the case of Brian Simon's *Education and the Social Order 1940–1991* (1991), Roy Lowe's *Education in the Post-War Years* (1988) and Ken Jones' *Education in Britain: 1944 to the Present* (2016 latest edn.), all three academic authors portray Conservative governments of the 1950s, 1960s and 1970s as staunch defenders of grammar schools and selective state education. This is despite all three authors inevitably being forced to acknowledge that many comprehensive schemes, including the famous Leicestershire experiment of 1957, were enacted under Conservative ministers David Eccles (in both his two periods as minister), Quintin Hailsham and Geoffrey Lloyd between 1957 and 1962. At most such authors have acknowledged an occasional pragmatism on these ministers' part. Nevertheless, they seek to actively present their ministerial actions as a Conservative ploy to conserve and strengthen the selective 'tripartite' system and undermine comprehensive schools' development. Such portrayals by these and other academic authors have dominated the way this subject has been explored for several decades. It has produced a consensus of outlook that I wanted to be free from when researching and writing this book.

The book's theme is timely, given recent debates over 'privilege', private schools and university admissions criteria that now emphasize 'contextual' factors of social background. It is therefore relevant to current debate and concerns in the media and wider society. In doing so, I hope to contribute to a greater understanding of the Conservative Party's policy approach towards secondary education and academic selection, including its recurring patterns and tendencies over several decades.

1

A piecemeal development

The first chapter examines the early development of Britain's secondary education system that culminated in the 1944 Education Act. It explores the thinking underpinning this process, including marked tendencies by the education establishment towards discouraging pupils from embarking on technical and vocational education at a young age. The curriculum and overall purpose of the secondary modern school were never properly defined during these years, with technical schooling under-developed and its progress envisaged only in limited terms. It examines other tendencies in thought by the Board of Education and those key figures behind the eventual Act, including their notably open-ended approach towards selection at 11 by examination as well as towards the 'multilateral' school, the precursor of the comprehensive. These ambiguities and anomalies would pave the way for future controversies.

The beginnings of a system

The English education system has long developed in an essentially piecemeal fashion. Grammar schools existed from the sixteenth century, while the leading independent schools, or 'public schools' as they later became known mainly, with a few exceptions such as Eton and Winchester, developed from the late eighteenth century onwards. However, it was not until the late nineteenth century that we can clearly say that the beginnings of a modern, rationalized education system took shape. This occurred within an atmosphere of Victorian philanthropy. Under W.E. Forster, the head of the Education Department under William Gladstone, school boards were created that were directly elected by the particular district they were situated in. The 1870 Elementary Education Act accompanied a whole raft of public legislation passed at this time encompassing public health and factories, road and bridge building, the reform of the Civil Service, as well as law, penal and electoral reform.

A first major step towards the centralization of British schooling occurred with the publication of the Bryce Report in 1895, which recommended the creation of a unified central authority. This highly significant step was carried out by the Act of 1899 that set up the Board of Education, which took over the work previously carried out by the Charity Commission. With Arthur Balfour taking over from Lord Salisbury as Prime Minister in 1902, and amid the promise of early legislation on education, the 1902 Education Act was passed.

This was the first comprehensive education Bill to reach the Statute book. At this time, it was claimed that the local school boards were too small, for the most part, to carry out their necessary responsibilities in secondary education. It was also felt that there was a lack of co-operation between existing authorities and agencies, and therefore insufficient harmony of purpose. As a result, under Part III of the Act, the county and county borough councils, which had been created in 1888, became the new local education authorities. These were now to be responsible for organizing secular instruction. Within a given district, there would be one authority for all types of education – technical, secondary and primary – and it would be the rating authority for the district area. Church schools, although continuing to be run by voluntary bodies, had a provision for their maintenance put onto the local government rates. This created much religious controversy, particularly among Nonconformists.

As a result of these changes, there was concern expressed at this time, one that would recur many times in the future, about the threat of 'uniformity'. However, the sense of a need for unified control of primary and secondary education had clearly become manifest by the beginning of the twentieth century. Nevertheless, it is striking that this major act of educational centralization occurred under a Conservative government.

It was also during this time that a major extension of grammar school facilities occurred, with a marked increase in the number of free places and scholarships offered. The Board's Secondary School Regulations for 1905–6 required that a secondary school must offer at least a full four years' course for their pupils. Furthermore, in 1907 it became a condition that any school receiving grant from the Board must offer 25 per cent of its places free of charge. In 1926, a directive issued by the Board of Education required schools to choose a single source of grant, either directly from central government or by being 'grant-aided' by their local authority. A list was set up on this basis comprising the schools that chose the former route. This led to the emergence of the direct grant schools, which ultimately occupied a mid-position between the maintained and independent sectors. Even at this stage of relative infancy in the development of Britain's education system, the opportunities for obtaining a grammar school education were growing steadily.

Other types of school were also developing during this period. The Junior Technical or trade schools existed in limited numbers by the beginning of the twentieth century. These were designed to both continue the pupil's general education and also to provide a special training for future entry into particular industries or trades. The normal age of admission was 13, and the course usually lasted for two to three years. However, they were restricted by the need to not turn out more pupils than could be absorbed by the local industries, and were thus envisaged in essentially limited terms. The development of technical education was therefore hampered even at this early stage.

Apart from the grammar schools and the meagre number of junior technical schools existed an even smaller number of 'central' schools that started to develop at this time. Usually based in large cities, their ultimate intention was practical and commercial, yet without being vocational in any narrow sense. They therefore lay in an intermediate position between the secondary grammar school, on the one hand, and the junior technical school, on the other. In addition to its lower leaving age and less academic curriculum, it was significant that the central school did not in any sense aim at providing technical training for any particular trade or business. It would form the basis for what would later be known as the 'secondary modern' school.

However, the effects of war were changing the mood of the country. The First World War served to increase the desire for the extension of public education, with industrial workers increasingly regarded as citizens. Within this atmosphere, the 1918 Education Act proposed a further act of educational centralization. Named the 'Fisher Act' after H.A.L. Fisher, the President of the Board of Education in Lloyd George's war-time coalition government, it abolished fees in elementary schools, as well as all exemptions from the leaving age of 14, and extended the range of ancillary services that the local education authority could provide. In addition, it emphasized the development of courses of advanced instruction within elementary schools for older and more intelligent pupils. In spite of this, a sense of a lack of correlation between the different parts of what was gradually becoming an education 'system' remained. This led in 1926 to the publication of the first and most important of a series of reports by the Consultative Committee of the Board of Education that would be produced over the next twenty years.

Entitled *The Education of the Adolescent*, its deliberations were presided over by the Board's chairman Sir Henry Hadow, and would later become popularly known as the Hadow Report. It was this report that defined the ideal of diversified post-primary schools to cater for different types of pupil. The concept of secondary education was now to be officially broadened out beyond that of grammar school education (that was academically oriented) in order to fully acknowledge the less academic pupil, with secondary schools to be developed that carried a 'practical and realistic bias.' At this time, approximately 90 per cent of children received elementary education up to the age of 13 or 14, with older children being catered for by senior departments within the same schools as much younger children. The small minority who entered grammar schools or the tiny number of central schools usually transferred at the age of 11.[1]

The Hadow Report took the view that all the different types of secondary education should ideally begin at the age of 11. Indeed, there was unanimity among the Report's authors on this. They justified the age of 11 because it was already the tendency of schools to treat it as the 'natural turning point' up to which primary education led and from which post-primary education began.[2] It was of course the established age at which pupils normally sat for the free place examination for the secondary grammar schools. Therefore, the Report's authors were in fact suggesting that the structure of the new secondary education for the majority of pupils should be grafted onto existing practice. The consensus about the suitability of the age of 11 was therefore a judgement derived more from the needs of practicality and administrative convenience than from principle. This seems altogether more convincing than what the Report otherwise claimed to be the authority of psychologists and 'educational theory' that this age gave an adequate indication of the differences of interests and abilities amongst pupils.[3] As they admitted, the arguments deriving from educational theory were reinforced by 'practical considerations.'[4]

In terms of the proposed curriculum for what would later be known as the secondary modern schools, it was not to be merely 'vocational or utilitarian.' Instead, it was vaguely considered that the schools should use 'realistic' studies as an instrument of general education. This, the Report's authors felt, would connect the school work 'with the interests arising from the social and industrial environment of the pupils.'[5] Therefore, while the intention was for a broadly similar curriculum to that of the grammar schools during the first two years, a 'practical' bias was to be introduced in the third and fourth years.

In order to give a sense of direction to the modern or 'senior' schools as they were then known, the Report proposed that a leaving examination be introduced for pupils to take at the age of 15. It was felt that otherwise 'the schools themselves may become uncertain in their aim and vacillating in their methods, if they have no suggestion of a definite standard to guide their work.'[6] And yet, strikingly, the Report also emphasized that the presentation of pupils for any such leaving examination should be wholly optional, in respect of both the individual pupil and the school as a whole.[7] The fear was that a compulsory examination would 'cramp' these schools' development, resulting in a 'general loss of the freshness and elasticity' which it claimed presently characterized many of them.[8] As we can see, one sentiment thus contradicted the other.

As a result, from the outset the curriculum and ultimate intention of the modern schools were defined in terms that were essentially vague and ambiguous. Indeed, even the courses of instruction during the final two years were not to be fully vocational. Instead, the bias was only to be of a 'general' kind, and only practical in the 'broadest sense,' unlike the specific vocational teaching given in many Junior Technical Schools and Junior Art Departments. Many of the problems that afflicted the intended 'tripartite' system of secondary education thus had their roots in the ambiguities of the Hadow Report that formed its basis.

Similarly, the Report's approach towards the junior technical schools was obscure. In regard to the issue of lowering their age of admission to 11, as it was proposing with the other types of school, it nevertheless thought it 'highly inadvisable' that a boy or girl should be placed at so early an age as 11 in a school planned to give a course of definitively vocational education.[9] Again, there was a recurring sensitivity within the Hadow Committee about pupils being guided down a vocational or technical route at an early stage. Furthermore, junior technical schools were treated as a completely separate category from the other types of school within the Report, with their desired numbers still related to their necessity for specific local industries within their immediate areas as before. Indeed, the Report effectively batted away the idea of a wider extension of such schools. While stating that junior technical schools were doing 'admirable' work and that 'it is hoped that that they will continue to develop,' it added:

> Their principal function has been hitherto to give a preparation for industries requiring somewhat specialised technical qualifications; and the areas in which they can develop in any number are, therefore, those in which such industries exist on a considerable scale.[10]

Technical schools were therefore envisaged on an essentially limited, ad hoc basis.

Nevertheless, the Report emphasized the differences of ability between pupils. There had to be diversity of educational provision, as equality 'was not identity.' As more children received post-primary education, 'the more essential it is that that education should not attempt to press different types of character into a single mould.' The system of education was to provide a range of educational opportunity to appeal to varying interests and cultivate powers which differed widely, 'both in kind and in degree.'[11] The terms of the Hadow Report thus formed the basis for subsequent development within secondary education over the next decade. However, the assumption by the Hadow Committee of 'parity of esteem' between the different types of school was not shared by the Board of Education.[12] Revealingly, the new modern schools would be governed under the Code for Public Elementary Schools, while grammar schools retained the inevitably higher status of being governed under the more prestigious 'Regulations for Secondary Schools.'

The proportion of free places provided at grammar schools grew substantially during this period. In 1924, the Board of Education made awards of up to 40 per cent of free places permissive for local authorities. By 1932, the percentage of children holding free places was 46.3 per cent in England and 67.6 per cent in Wales. Furthermore, seventy-nine schools were entirely free. By 1937, the percentage of those paying full fees in England had decreased from 54 per cent in 1932 to 49 per cent.[13] The system, at least regarding the provision of grammar school education, was becoming increasingly generous. Indeed, the future discontinuation of fees was now being regarded as a future prospective policy.

The next major report on secondary education produced by the Board was published in 1938 under the Chairmanship of Sir Will Spens. While concerning itself with secondary education generally, it focused particularly on the grammar and technical schools. The Spens Report was significant in that, unlike the Hadow Report, it recommended the expansion of the technical schools, as well as the continued development of the other types.

The junior technical schools, whose age of entry was still at age 13, had long been disadvantaged by the fact that the more intellectually able pupils had been selected for the grammar schools at age 11. The Report's key recommendation was that a number of the existing junior technical schools that provided a curriculum based on the engineering industries should be converted into Technical High Schools with an age of entry set at 11. This was in order for them to be accorded equality of status with schools of the grammar school type. A distinction was made between junior technical schools based on the engineering and building industries that were felt suitable for this, and junior commercial and home training schools that were not considered adequate for the uplifting of their status. In addition, the Report noted how approximately 85 per cent of junior technical schools were housed in technical colleges or institutes, with only about 16 per cent of these schools having more than 200 pupils, while 54 per cent had fewer than 100.[14]

Yet in spite of the fact that the Spens Report bemoaned the tendency for the curricula of the newer types of school to be overly influenced by that of the grammar school, it still desired that the curricula of all the different types of school be broadly the same within the first two years of secondary education from the age of 11 to 13. Furthermore, according to the Report's authors, in regard to small grammar schools which incorporated modern (senior) schools, the advantage of leaving final transfer until the age of 13 was that 'it often enables a juster estimate to be formed of the capacity of a child to benefit by a grammar school education than did the examination at the age of 11.'[15] However, the more pertinent question of whether in that case a better universal age for starting all secondary education was 13 rather than 11 was simply not addressed. This omission would carry major implications for the future.

The issue of multilateral schools was also briefly considered. The concept of the multilateral school involved all three types of secondary education being offered in the same school. It was in fact the precursor to the modern comprehensive. However, the Spens Report stated, 'with some reluctance,' that they could not advocate the adoption of multilateralism as a policy.[16] It was felt that the key difficulty with multilateral schools was the necessary size of them. However, somewhat cagily, they added that they 'did not wish to deprecate experiments in multilateral schools,' and that, 'the various difficulties may be surmounted in sparsely populated rural areas where a grammar school and a modern school may be formed into a multilateral school.'[17] Intriguingly, the door was thus being left open for the possibility of multilateral schools in the future. However, it was assumed the different 'types' of education would remain distinct and separate within them.

The Spens Report also broached the issue as to what the overall percentage of provision for grammar and technical high schools should be. The region of approximately 15 per cent nationally was considered sufficient as a standard by which local authorities might plan their provision of grammar school education having regard to the particular needs of their areas. Nevertheless, the Report was at pains to point out, regarding an issue that would constantly reverberate in the future, that the amount of provision that would be desirable could not be laid down for the country as a whole to any precise extent, as it would depend in each area on the character and traditions of the population, the prevailing industrial conditions and the future careers of the children.[18]

Nevertheless, the Report was sanguine about the chances of technical schools being likely to enjoy 'equal prestige' with grammar schools in the future. There would be 'little difficulty in transferring such pupils, when the alternative is a Technical High School.'[19] Similarly, in regard to the emerging notion of 'modern' schools, it stated that:

> the more general recognition of the parity of schools will induce parents to choose a modern school at the outset, if they are persuaded that it is more suited to the aptitudes and actual requirements of their children.

And yet it added:

> There is much greater necessity for transfers from a modern school to a grammar school or technical high school than in the opposite direction ... *the kind of transfer which we consider to be undoubtedly of highest importance and of most frequent occurrence is that from modern schools to grammar schools or technical high schools.*[20]
>
> (my emphasis)

As a result, the intention was that once a child had been admitted to a grammar school, subsequent transfer to a modern school 'will, therefore, as a general rule, remain rare.'[21] This approach inevitably reinforced the difficulties regarding the modern school's sense of status.

The three types of pupil

The third of the major key reports published by the Board of Education during this period was the Report by the Committee of the Secondary School Examinations Council entitled *Curriculum and Examinations in Secondary Schools*. The Committee, appointed by Sir Cyril Norwood in 1941, published its recommendations two years later in 1943.

Ultimately, the Norwood Report saw its goal as being to 'reconcile diversity of human endowment with practical schemes of administration and instruction.'[22] The differences of ability between pupils and thus the necessity of different types of education in order to cater for it were recognized more explicitly in this report than in the others. In turn, it set out in an altogether more detailed fashion the essential nature of the intended 'tripartite' system of education.

The Norwood Report memorably defined three essential types of pupil: the pupil interested in learning for its own sake, who could grasp an argument and follow a controlled line of reasoning, 'who is interested in causes, whether on the level of human volition or in the material world,' and who was regarded as the grammar school type of pupil.[23] By contrast, technical schools were suited for those of similar ability but whose abilities and interests lay in the field of applied science and art, the control of material things, and who would take up certain crafts, including engineering and agriculture. The third type of pupil was defined as one who dealt more easily with 'concrete things' rather than with ideas. His point of view was essentially practical. As they explained:

> He may see clearly along one line of study or interest and outstrip his generally abler fellows in that line; but he often fails to relate his knowledge or skill to other branches of activity ... abstractions mean little to him.[24]

For this type of pupil it was felt, in these terms that appear so unfashionable today, that he must have 'immediate return for his effort.'[25] By contrast, the grammar school curriculum would treat the various aspects of knowledge as intended for coherent and systematic study 'for their own sake apart from immediate considerations of occupation.'[26] The Norwood Report was certainly not shy of outlining differences between pupils and noting their implications for future roles in the wider society.

Like the other reports, the Norwood Committee was somewhat optimistic about the existing situation, stating that the junior technical schools, while 'inadequate' in number and equipment, provided 'varied opportunities.'[27] Meanwhile, the senior 'modern' schools were vaguely described as 'still in the process of formulating their aims and methods' in order for them to 'gain the scope necessary to them to fulfil the promise which they already show.'[28] It was already noticeable within this verbiage what little progress had been made in regards to these two types of school since the Hadow Report had proposed them seventeen years earlier.

Notably, the Norwood Report reinforced the age of 11 as being the ideal age for starting secondary education. As noted earlier, there was inevitably a sense that secondary schools were being organized to fit an existing structure, a constant tendency in Britain's piecemeal educational development. According to the Report, and somewhat conveniently:

> The evidence placed before us and study of the views of those who have already considered similar evidence convince us that special interests and abilities do in fact often reveal themselves clearly by the age of 10 plus or 11 plus.[29]

It also reiterated that the curriculum of the three types of school should be generally similar, albeit with some variation, between the ages of 11 and 13. This would constitute the 'lower school' for all three types of institution. During these years, 'the special interests of the child would be studied and, if desirable, transfer would be recommended.'[30] Thereafter, a pupil would then pursue a course of study suitable to him in the correct type of school to offer it. This need for a two-year period of further assessment somewhat contradicted the fixing of 11 as the ideal starting point. Yet this was not considered.[31] According to the Report's authors:

> It is not for us to say exactly what form the curriculum of the Lower School of a secondary Modern school or a secondary technical school might take, but we think we can safely assume that the curriculum of either would furnish good evidence of a pupil's need of secondary Grammar school education, and certainly we should expect the Lower School of the Grammar school to detect special aptitude for Technical or Modern School Education.[32]

The Report was thus notably optimistic and indeed complacent about the potential success of this somewhat vague means of catering for all types of pupil.

War-time developments under Butler

This last report had been commissioned under a new President of the Board of Education. Richard Austen 'Rab' Butler had been appointed President on 20 July 1941. Serving alongside him was James Chuter Ede, a Labour Member of Parliament, as his Parliamentary Under-Secretary. Butler, who would turn out to become one of the most significant Conservative politicians of the post-war period, already saw with his canny eye the opportunity that education gave him, personally and politically, within Britain's post-war reconstruction. He therefore saw it as being vital for the Conservative Party to be associated with 'progressive' reform. In his memoirs, Butler would tell of how he was urged to get involved in education by John G. Winant, the American Ambassador who had told him that Britain would 'go socialist' after the war, and that at education Butler could therefore 'influence the future of England.'[33] In short, Butler saw it as his great opportunity to make his political mark.

His goal was to formalize the education system fully into primary and secondary stages, involving the assumption of the different types of school provided at age 11. He also sought to increase the school leaving age to 15, with the ultimate intention of raising it to 16 at some point in the future.[34] As Butler would later put it, given the mood for change associated with war, the 'time was ripe' for major reform. As he observed:

> Amid the suffering and the sacrifice the weaknesses of society are revealed and there begins a period of self-examination, self-criticism and movement for reform.[35]

In spite of the educational developments over the previous twenty years, Butler was nevertheless keen in his memoirs to paint the educational picture at the time in decidedly negative terms. Grammar schools were, he claimed, 'restricted to a small minority of children.'[36] By contrast, he added, the 'vast majority' of pupils still spent their whole period of education in elementary schools, which 'still suffered from the blight of poverty and inferiority associated with the traditions of the past. Thus, through sheer lack of opportunity, much human potential was wasted.'[37] Secondary modern schools had not of course been properly developed. It was felt that 'two nations' still existed in England a full century after Disraeli had used the phrase. Indeed, in distinctly un-conservative language, Butler later wrote of the need for the 'reconstruction' of the social system, with the goal of the 'realisation of a full democracy – an order of society free from the injustices and anomalies of the pre-war period.'[38]

Notions of greater class equality were in the air at this time, along with a general dissatisfaction with the past. At the end of 1940, the Archbishops of Canterbury and York, the Roman Catholic Archbishop of Westminster and the Moderator of the Free Church Federal Council wrote a letter to *The Times* on 21 December under the heading, 'Foundations of Peace.' They argued that extreme inequality of wealth and possessions should be abolished, and that every child, regardless of race or class, should have equal opportunities for education, suitable to the development of his particular capacities. Within this altogether more socialistic atmosphere, a key question to ask is how much Butler really favoured this type of thinking that appeared radical in its implications. A 'Green Book' was then published in June 1941 which encouraged a further stimulation of thinking about educational reform and criticized the existing anomalies between the different types of secondary school provision.

One of the three espoused aims that Butler had at this time, along with instituting greater industrial and technical training, as well as resolving long-standing anomalies between denominational schools and those that were fully state-run, was the 'public schools question.' This was concerned with the issue of how to bridge the gap between these leading independent schools and the maintained system, within this atmosphere of greater social concern about lack of equal opportunity. A long-standing question, however, is whether Butler was really committed to this objective at this key opportunity for change.

Significantly, the Prime Minister Winston Churchill himself was wary of highlighting the public schools as an issue. Indeed, in response to correspondence from Butler stating his three objectives, Churchill was emphatic that it would be a 'great mistake to stir up the public schools question at the present time.' Furthermore:

> We cannot have any party politics in war-time, and both your second and third points raise these in a most acute and dangerous form.[39]

Butler would later relate in his memoirs how, in regard to achieving his goals for the maintained education system, 'I knew that if I spared him the religious controversies and party political struggles of 1902 and side-tracked the public schools issue, I could win him over.'[40] This was essentially Butler's attitude towards the public schools issue from as early as September 1941 during his tenure at the Board of Education. It surely suggests that he never really intended to do anything particularly radical regarding the public schools, partly in order to achieve his other aims.

Butler's noted biographer Anthony Howard claims that the issue of the public schools 'preoccupied' the Board of Education in the early months of 1942, and further asserts that Butler was disposed towards ending 'the great divide' in British education by incorporating the independent fee paying sector into the reconstructed secondary education system.[41] This included a proposal for at least 25 per cent of the public schools' annual admissions being taken up by state primary pupils or 'bursars.' Howard is notably keen to emphasize Butler's progressive and meritocratic credentials, claiming that Butler had an 'agnostic' attitude towards the public schools' eminence.[42] However, this does not seem to have been borne out in practice.

While substantial progress was being made regarding the core issue of the maintained education system, the public schools question was instead handed over to a Committee appointed in July 1942 under the Chairmanship of a Scottish judge, David Pinkerton Fleming, then Senator of the College of Justice in Scotland. Anthony Howard himself admits how striking it was that Butler, instead of conducting 'bilateral agreements' with the Governing Bodies Association in the more interventionist manner that he was approaching the denominational problem, 'chose the easy way out and plumped for an independent committee of inquiry' concerning the public schools' integration.[43]

The resulting publication, which would later become known as the Fleming Report, was published in 1944. Indeed, it would be somewhat contemptuously described by Butler as that 'sensationally ingenuous report' that 'tended only to confirm the view of my old Corpus mentor, Sir Will Spens, that there was no practical solution to the problem of public schools, since they were sui generis.'[44] Even more revealing was the manner in which Butler then further described the aftermath in his memoirs:

> Though Labour members breathed a certain amount of ritual fire and fury about social exclusiveness and privilege, the appointment of the Fleming Committee had

temporarily removed the fuse. Or, in a railway metaphor, the first-class carriage had been shunted onto an immense siding.[45]

This suggests, if nothing else, a significant amount of expediency and political sleight of hand at work on the issue. Only a very reduced version of the Fleming scheme would in fact be put into practice. The public schools issue had been effectively sidelined.

In his biography, Howard is notably defensive of Butler's negation of the issue and seeks to portray his actions in the best possible light. Apparently, Butler was imperilled enough already on the religious issue affecting the maintained schools and could not 'risk' a second major battle at the same time. In addition, he claims that Butler had received 'warning shots' from the public school lobby as well as the Anglican establishment connected to them, 'that in tackling it head on he might well imperil the gains he was seeking to make elsewhere.' Therefore, Butler had preferred to fight on one issue at a time rather than become mired in both.[46] It is essentially suggested that Butler's political nerve failed him, thus stopping him from doing what he otherwise sought to achieve. As a result, according to Howard, he 'may not have made a particularly courageous decision', but 'characteristically, however, he probably made a sensible one, at least in terms of his immediate objectives.'[47] Never is it even suggested by Howard that Butler had no real intention of doing anything very fundamental about the public schools question in the first place. Quite apart from anything else, in spite of what Howard claims to have been his 'agnostic' attitude towards the public schools and his self-proclaimed desire to democratize the structure of British society, Butler sent all three of his sons to Eton.

Indeed, Butler seems to have been adept, on the one hand, at retaining certain established interests such as the public schools in their present form, while at the same time maintaining favourable relations with such distinctly un-conservative organizations as the National Union of Teachers who, having received an early version of his plans for educational reconstruction on 9 April 1942, described them as the most 'progressive' ever outlined by a President of the Board of Education. Furthermore, Butler emphasized that it was the Labour Party who were most concerned about the future pattern and structure of British education in a way that the Conservative Party did not appear to be. As he noted in private correspondence: 'I find in education that much of the drive towards a vaguely progressive future comes from Labour.'[48]

The basis for the 1944 Education Act

Matters proceeded rapidly under Butler, with a memorandum on educational reconstruction sent to the Cabinet in April 1943, and a White Paper published in July of that year. To analyse the White Paper is key, for it discussed the different types of school envisaged. (By contrast, the Education Bill published later that year, which would become the 1944 Education Act, would not in fact mention the different types of schools directly.)

However, the White Paper did not give clear statements about the process of academic selection for the three types of school. Instead, it appeared to contain different points of view fitted expediently into one. At the outset, it stated that:

> The new educational opportunities must not ... be of a single pattern. It is just as important to achieve diversity as it is to ensure equality of educational opportunity.

And yet the following line offered a corrective to the previous statement:

> But such diversity must not impair the social unity within the educational system which will open the way to a more closely knit society and give us strength to face the tasks ahead.[49]

Clearly, vague concerns about social unity and equality weighed against the desire for freedom and diversity of educational provision. This balancing of sentiments would occur throughout the White Paper.

Strikingly, in addressing the mode of assessment for secondary education, it stated that:

> There is nothing to be said in favour of a system which subjects children at the age of 11 to the strain of a competitive examination on which, not only their future schooling, but their future careers may depend.[50]

It further claimed that:

> It is obvious that a final selection at the age of 11 makes no allowance for the child who develops later than the majority of his fellows. Spasmodic attempts are made here and there at a further re-sorting of children at the age of 13, but they are the exception rather than the rule.[51]

The White Paper was staunchly critical of the way in which the system of assessment and selection normally took place. This was of course done through the Special Place examination, usually taken at age 11. According to the White Paper, it was clear that there was 'urgent need for reform.' Following on from these sentiments, it stated that in the future, children of age 11 should be classified:

> Not on the results of a competitive test, but on an assessment of their individual aptitudes largely by such means as school records, supplemented, if necessary, by intelligence tests, due regard being had to their parents' wishes and the careers they have in mind.[52]

There was to be a review at age 13, or even later and therefore facilities for further transfer if the original 'choice' proved unsuitable for the pupil. However, as we have seen, these sorts of sentiments had in fact been expressed several times before, going back to the Hadow Report nearly twenty years earlier.

At the end of the White Paper, within the summary of principal reforms, one of the changes to be effected by 'administrative action' as opposed to legislative change included:

> The abolition of the present Special Place examination and the adoption of other arrangements for the classification of the children when they pass from primary to secondary schools.[53]

Correspondingly, the question of how far teachers' assessment of their pupils' school records could be incorporated into the process was not laid down in any detail. After all, the whole question of how far the system could possibly move away from competitive examination and then add a further review at 13 was unclear as secondary education would continue to begin at age 11. And so the issue remained obscure.

The White Paper further expressed the long-standing concern that too many of the nation's children were attracted 'into a type of education which prepares primarily for the University and for the administrative and clerical professions; too few find their way into schools from which the design and craftsmanship sides of industry are recruited.'[54] But the White Paper had to admit that the junior technical schools' progress in increasing their numbers had been slow and their chances of attracting the most able children were adversely affected by the fact that they still normally recruited at age 13. Yet there remained little sign of any constructive proposals in this area. The senior or modern schools continued to be vaguely described as offering 'a general education for life, closely related to the interests and environment of pupils and of a wide range embracing the literary as well as the practical.'[55] Their ultimate purpose was still not being outlined in 1943.

Even more strikingly, the White Paper even added that it would be 'wrong' to suppose that the three different types of school would remain separate and apart. Different types of school, it stated, could be combined in one building or on one site as considerations of 'convenience and efficiency' would suggest.[56] Thus the possibility for experiments with multilateral schools was being kept open, as in earlier reports. However, it is clear that the White Paper still strongly assumed that the principle of different types of secondary education for different types of pupil would remain. Despite this, with the benefit of hindsight Butler would later disingenuously claim that this passage 'forecast the comprehensive idea.'[57]

These sentiments thus formed the basis of the 1944 Education Act. As we can see, its thinking did not indicate any great degree of originality. Most of these sentiments had been expressed for over two decades. Nevertheless, the 1944 Education Act instituted a greater degree of formality within the education system. The County and County Borough Councils were made responsible for all stages of a pupil's education. Tuition fees at all fully maintained schools were forbidden, and the school leaving age to be raised to 15 with this legislative change carried out in 1947.

The Act also revised the terms of the direct grant to operate alongside local authority-maintained grammar schools. Under the new direct grant scheme, those schools receiving it were to provide 25 per cent of their places free of charge to children who had spent at least two years in maintained primary schools, with a further quarter to be paid for by the local education authority if required. The remaining places would be funded through the payment of fees. Yet all pupils would have to show sufficient merit through their performance in the examination taken at 11. Thus, 164 direct grant schools continued in a 'mid-position' between the fully maintained and independent sectors.

In spite of the growing powers of central government, there was a marked degree of emphasis upon the notion of 'partnership' between the Ministry of Education, the teachers and the local authorities. In short, running education was to be seen as a co-operative effort. As a result, as we shall see later, the Minister's actual powers in relation to the education service, particularly the local authorities, would often be downplayed during the immediate post-war period. In fact, they were considerable in nature.

The Minister's powers were outlined within Section 68 of the Act. It stated that, in respect to local authorities who were acting 'unreasonably' in wielding their educational policies for their respective areas:

> He may ... notwithstanding any enactment rendering the exercise of the power or the performance of the duty contingent upon the opinion of the authority or of the managers or governors, give such directions as to the exercise of the power or the performance of the duty as appear to him to be expedient.[58]

The notion of local authority freedom, on the one hand, and ministerial power and responsibility, on the other, would in future often be cited or minimized as either of the relevant actors within the educational process saw fit to suit their own purposes.

Meanwhile, the recommendations of the Fleming Report regarding the public schools were never incorporated by the Ministry of Education. As Butler would later put it, the 1944 Act was certainly an example of 'our inveterate prejudice for fragmentary and gradual legislation.'[59] As a result, 'it did not, as some would have wished, sweep the board clean of existing institutions in order to start afresh.'[60] Indeed, it built on from what had preceded it in the past.

Deliberations within the Conservative Party

An important insight into the thinking within the higher reaches of the Conservative Party during this period can be gained through examining the deliberations of the Central Committee on Post-War Problems, which focused upon the Party's approach to a wide range of policy areas during the war years. In spite of the fact that their work would ultimately play little part in the formulation of the Conservatives' 1945 election campaign, it provides an important insight into their approach towards the rapid developments taking place within secondary education. Most of the deliberations of the particular sub-committee on education took place at the same time that the 1943 White Paper was being formulated. Therefore, one can see how the Conservative sub-committee's thinking paralleled that of Butler at the Board of Education.

The sub-committee was in fact critical of the rapid nature of some of the developments in secondary education taking place. These included the raising of the school leaving age to 15 immediately after the war was over, with the intention of it being eventually raised to 16. This of course meant a massive proportion of extra pupils that would now have to be accommodated by the existing school system in a context of severe shortages of provision. The sub-committee was essentially sceptical, both at the level of practicalities and that of principle, as to whether this accommodation of extra pupils was in their best interests. They felt this concern in particular because the vast majority of these extra pupils would be those who had not been selected by the Special Place examination at age 11.[61]

Teachers would thus need to have a clear idea of what they were hoping to achieve for these pupils. There was of course the associated difficulty, given the fact that the secondary modern school was still in its infancy and with its aims still unclear, of providing for older children whose bent was practical rather than of a literary or academic nature. There was still a need to develop a type of general education based around a core of varying practical interests. All in all, it was feared that raising the school leaving age would create a whole set of new difficulties.

The attitude taken by the Conservative sub-committee towards selection for the secondary schools was markedly similar to that of the White Paper. As they noted, the process was almost entirely through a formal competitive examination at the age of 11. According to the committee, this method was 'indefensible' and needed to be 'drastically altered.' In a manner again strikingly similar to that of the White Paper and so many of the major reports issued over the last two decades, the examination was felt to 'distort' primary education and subject children to unnecessary rigidities.[62] Yet somewhat contradicting their earlier sentiments, they also admitted that, 'by and large it does pick out those children who are best capable of profiting by the "Grammar School" type of education.'[63] It was therefore not apparent quite where they stood on the desired method of selection.

Regarding the children within secondary grammar schools, they noted how these pupils were composed of a mixture of those who had gained a place through the 'Special Place' examination or because of their parents' willingness and ability to pay fees. According to the sub-committee, 'the combination of these two methods of selection is probably much more efficient than the dependence upon one method alone would be.'[64] Furthermore, in terms that showed how they defended fee-paying in relation to secondary education:

> We are resolutely opposed, on deep grounds of principle, to any alteration of the system which would make it impossible for any parent to procure for his child the kind of education he wants the child to have. So far as we are concerned, this is a vital position, that nothing would persuade us to abandon.[65]

Thus the Conservatives' attitude towards selection was somewhat altered by their preferred emphasis on parental choice that was inevitably associated with fee paying and independent schooling. This in fact militated against meritocracy and the open and transparently competitive selection process. Revealingly, the committee felt in addition that the trade schools and junior technical schools that still selected their pupils at 13 through varying methods achieved their intakes, 'by a more sensible procedure than that of written examination.'[66]

The Committee emphasized that there needed to be an expansion of the junior technical schools to an extent 'far beyond anything envisaged in 1939,' and that therefore they must be a central part of the immediate post-war programme. As they rightly and prophetically stated:

> Not until this expansion is sufficient to enable the Junior Technical schools to take their full share in post-primary education, alongside of the fully reorganised Senior (or Modern) schools, shall we be in a position to say that the machinery of post-primary education is properly assembled.[67]

These sentiments advocating that all three prongs of the tripartite system be properly established first before the raising of the school leaving age would instead be lost amid the post-war messianic spirit for rapid and instant provision.

The Green Book, which had been published by the Board of Education in 1941, had suggested that all pupils could spend a transitional period of two years between the ages of 11 and 13 in the secondary modern schools before being transferred to the three different types of school at age 13.[68] Therefore, even in 1941, the Board was advocating the idea of the common school, if for a limited period, in order to encourage 'parity'. In prescient fashion, the Conservative Committee's Chairman Geoffrey Faber could readily see the implications of this type of thinking. As he put it, 'nothing' could possibly put the modern schools on a level with the selective schools except getting rid of selection, or the merging of all secondary schools into multilateral schools. In his words:

> To keep back children, who are up to selective standards, in schools primarily designed for children below selective standards, for the sake of 'parity,' doesn't seem sensible to me.[69]

Therefore, albeit in these distinctly low-key terms, Faber was honest about what could happen if this preoccupation with 'parity' was taken to its logical extreme. Of course, he wrote, the grammar schools naturally 'would fight bitterly' against their submergence in a multilateral system, adding (somewhat naively, given later events) 'I don't see how they could be brought into it.' Therefore, Faber counselled against widespread adoption of the multilateral school plan that was being advocated in London. It was therefore the view of Faber that the Board of Education's policy 'ought to preserve the principle of selection as more important than that of parity.' Local authorities could decide for multilateral schools as long as it did not undermine the established semi-independent schools' freedom (such as the direct grant schools) to remain outside.[70]

Unlike the official reports, the sub-committee was also keen that the education for most pupils provided within the secondary modern schools should be based specifically on technical and practical skills, rather than abstract knowledge. This type of training was felt to be better adapted to the needs of the majority of children than the academic and literary discipline of the grammar schools. The education given in the modern schools, they felt, should have 'a strong technical bias'.[71] Yet this rather obvious intention for the modern schools would never fully develop at the official level.

Nevertheless, the concluding section of the report shows the direction of political consensus and accommodation that the Conservative Party was heading in at this time. They were at pains to point out how opposed they were to all attempts, from whatever quarters, to convert the rate of educational progress into 'a party issue'. It thus complained of 'people with pre-war minds' trying to make a partisan issue out of matters that were essentially common sense. According to the Conservative sub-committee, most problems regarding education had 'passed out of the field of political controversy'. Instead of partisan argumentation or voting, they favoured 'plain, sensible, direct thought about the best way of actually doing the things about which we are all generally agreed'.[72] Nevertheless, this begs the question of whether this approach by the Conservative Party was commendably high-minded or rather, loftily naive and even dishonest about the inevitably politicized and contentious nature of organizing a national education system. This approach that was so desirous of consensus encapsulated a meandering approach to politics at this time that the Conservative Party, far more than Labour, took to heart.

Events following the 1945 General Election

As has been noted already, the deliberations of the Conservatives' Post-War Problems Committees did not in fact have any great influence ultimately on the Party's general election campaign. Secondary education was not uppermost in the Conservative Party elite's minds at this stage, with greater concern being felt about the threat of Labour's plans for the nationalization of industry along with the rapid growth of the welfare state. Clement Attlee's famous Labour general election victory in 1945, which deposed the war-time leader Churchill, appeared to herald a new Britain geared towards the common man. Public education was being portrayed as an issue, at least officially, on which there was a degree of consensus between the two main parties. Any underlying principled disagreement on the nature of secondary education was not to be officially acknowledged.

Yet in 1945 the Ministry of Education still viewed the secondary modern's goals and curriculum as something for individual schools to work out for themselves. Evidently, few hopes were in fact held for what constituted the clear majority of pupils. As they revealingly put it at this time:

> It has to be remembered that in these schools will be a considerable number of children whose future employment will not demand any measure of technical skill or knowledge.[73]

Furthermore, the Ministry of Education was noting favourably how multilateral schools avoided the 'problem' of selection at age 11 and that they offered the 'great social advantage' of bringing together children of different types, 'thus providing a common background for them in later life when they will be occupying different positions.'⁷⁴ Therefore, largely because of such social considerations, the door was already effectively being left open for the multilateral school being adopted in certain cases. While noting their excessive size, the Ministry added that,

> when opportunity offers, there is much to be said for bringing together separate schools of different types on the same site, or in close juxtaposition.⁷⁵

In addition, there was a marked lack of enthusiasm shown by the Ministry for the idea of further transfer at the age of 13 taking place frequently as this militated against the formal commencement of secondary education at 11. As the Ministry revealingly described it:

> There are great advantages for a child if he can spend his secondary school life at a single school and avoid a break at 13, and administrative convenience should not lead to a break at 13 becoming the rule for the generality of pupils.⁷⁶

As before, there was never any real debate as to whether the age of 11, for this very reason, was in fact ideal in the first place.

Nevertheless, dissent was starting to grow within the Labour Party, with the drive towards comprehensive schooling being urged by organizations such as the National Association for Labour Teachers. However, Ellen Wilkinson, the first Minister of Education under the new Attlee government, remained protective of the Labour tradition that defended the grammar school as the passport of social mobility for working-class pupils. In 1947, Wilkinson issued a pamphlet entitled *The New Secondary Education*, which defended the existing tripartite system and argued that it needed time to settle down in order to take proper effect.

But while defending the central notion that the majority of children learnt most easily by dealing with 'concrete' things and following a course rooted in their own day-to-day experience, the pamphlet was keen to emphasize common ground between the different types of schooling.⁷⁷ And of course the curriculum of the secondary modern school was still not being defined with any precision.

In regard to technical schools, where a great deal of special equipment such as modern engineering tools were required, the Ministry considered that it would be 'uneconomical' to establish a secondary technical school too small to use them fully. As it put it:

> The majority of towns in England and Wales are too small to provide for a single-stream secondary technical school of any one particular kind without drawing pupils from a wide area.⁷⁸

And then, as it further revealed:

> One way of meeting these difficulties would be to make, where all the necessary conditions as set forth in this pamphlet can be satisfied, some kind of bilateral

arrangement. A technical course might be planned alongside a grammar or modern school course, if the head of the school understood and was in sympathy with the character and objectives of the technical course and if the appropriate staff and equipment were provided.[79]

At age 16, there could be possible transfer to a full-time course in a college for further education, adding how 'a much greater degree of vocational specialization will at this stage be justifiable.'[80] Therefore, the Ministry of Education was even now proposing secondary technical 'courses' rather than schools. It was now clearly suggesting that there would be difficulty in building a significant number of new technical schools and was already providing rationalizations for slow future progress.[81]

Meanwhile, the Conservative Party hierarchy was clearly aware of the shortages and difficulties for the system in terms of it coming properly to fruition as intended. As we have seen, they were already cognizant of ultimate socialist intentions regarding 'multilateral' schools. In 1949 the Conservative Research Department, in a brief prepared for members of the Conservative Parliamentary Backbench Education Committee, noted that more attention needed to be paid to the secondary modern curriculum. The headmasters, they noted, simply decided the course to be followed, and inspectors would inform them, 'if they so desire,' of the methods used in the other schools that they had visited. They also noted that 'the Minister does not give guidance in this matter.' They acknowledged that this was a subject which required more research, yet added the qualifier that 'it must be remembered that these schools have only been in existence for a very short time.'[82] This was in spite of the fact that, as we have seen, discussion of the secondary modern school at the official level had been taking place for decades.

There was also concern that the most able pupils would be held back by the growing ideology of the day. As Hugh Linstead, the Conservative Member of Parliament for Putney who had been Chairman of the Party's Education Committee, stated at this time:

> As a nation we cannot afford to rely upon the wasteful Socialist practice of holding back the intelligent in the fear that the less intelligent may thereby be discouraged or discontented.[83]

For Linstead, 'leaders' were to be encouraged in all areas of life, in opposition to the 'levelling' tendencies that socialism was depicted as threatening. Indeed, Conservative Party publications at this time expressed a fear of standardization that would entail the conformity of the individual to the system. Linstead noted how 'the socialists' were keen on building 'educational factories.' Citing developments coming from the London County Council, he noted how 'the Socialists seem to prefer them in order to make sure that the grammar school does not outshine any other type of secondary school.'[84]

In this manner, the Conservative opposition's 1949 statement of policy at this time, *The Right Road for Britain*, showed a marked concern at the totalitarian nature of socialism and its potential subordination of the individual to the mass system. In addition, it expressed concern that the Christian faith was being replaced by secular materialist ideologies and a generally mechanistic approach to life.[85] Socialism would create a 'uniform and standard society in which the best is levelled down and success is the target of envious attacks,' with the dignity and value of the individual in danger of being subsumed.[86] It is difficult, of course, to know how deeply felt this sentiment was, or whether it was merely a form of political rhetoric designed to influence the public against the rise of social democracy that appeared to be in the ascendancy. Yet the rhetoric was vivid in nature. In answer to the 'forces of totalitarianism' would be instead an emphasis on individual liberty that would encourage enterprise and initiative.[87] Through education, the people would be equipped to 'withstand the onslaught of materialist ideologies and to bend science to the aid of mankind.'[88]

On a more practical level, they acknowledged the dearth of technical schools and colleges, as had been done so many times before. They therefore claimed that:

> A Conservative Government will give first priority to increasing the number and status of technical schools and colleges, which must be fully equipped and staffed.[89]

They also stated:

> We regard with suspicion the tendency to create enormous and unwieldy multilateral schools. Under certain circumstances, variations of the multilateral idea may well be adopted. But we shall not allow them to become so big that individual attention and a sense of community cannot be given to the children.[90]

In spite of their criticisms of the size of the intended comprehensive schools that were being carried out at that time, most notably under the London School Plan, the inevitable impression to be drawn is that they were holding back from taking any stronger position on whether comprehensive education was actually bad in principle. There was a degree of circumspection and pragmatism from the Conservative Party regarding the issue even at this stage.

Further difficulties

By the time of the 1951 General Election, there was increased general awareness of the impact the parlous state of the country's finances was having on the education service and in particular the ability to carry out all the aims of the 1944 Act. The rise in the birth rate immediately after the war was putting untold strains on the burgeoning social services. There was now a 'bulge' in terms of the number of children coming into the schools as well as the extra numbers caused by the raising of the school leaving age. Difficulties had also inevitably been created by the displacement of pupils to the new housing estates. Already, there were muted suggestions about possibly either lowering the school leaving age, which had of course been raised to 15 in 1947, or raising the age at which children entered the primary school. Currently, this was fixed at age 5, a comparatively young age compared with other European countries. In addition, by 1951 there was already disappointment being expressed at the lack of progress made with technical education.

Under the Attlee government, the Ministry of Education inevitably made little progress in terms of providing the necessary spending for technical schooling. The increase in the birth rate and the problems of providing adequate buildings which that increase had brought, alongside great existing shortages within the teaching profession had created, as the Labour Minister of Education George Tomlinson admitted, 'a situation in which the implementation of the 1944 Act has had of necessity to take second place.'[91] Tomlinson even admitted publicly that the Ministry was actually holding back on spending on this type of education, with alleged cuts in technical college building now being made against him. Tomlinson's reply to searching questions about cuts in this area was simply that the size of the programme 'will not increase quite as rapidly as we would have liked.'[92]

By this time, approximately 20 per cent of all maintained pupils in England and Wales by the age of 13 years were in grammar schools or grammar school streams. However, the key difficulty with the intended tripartite system lay in the fact that wide disparities of grammar school provision now existed between different local education authority areas. For example, while the proportions in Cardiff and Cardiganshire were 32.4 per cent and 48.1 per cent, respectively, in Gateshead the proportion was a mere 9.3 per cent. Plainly, the concept of local authority freedom lacked credibility when confronted with such stark discrepancies between different areas of the country. It was difficult to see how the goals of the 1944 Act could be achieved with this situation existing. According to the historian Rodney Barker, the 'unsatisfied demand' for grammar school education was a key part for the campaign for reform.[93] The need for greater grammar school provision was thus of burning importance to those who wished to defend the tripartite idea.

By this stage, the Labour Party's position on comprehensive schools was becoming clear. At the 1951 Labour Party Conference, there was resounding support for a motion stating that the comprehensive system of education carried the basis for educating the next generation to form a socialist society. Furthermore, Labour's education spokesman Alice Bacon appeared to give credence to these sentiments during her speech on behalf of the National Executive at the same Labour conference. In addition, the Labour Party pamphlet, *The Policy for Secondary Education,* published in 1951, further made it clear what their intentions for secondary education were.[94]

Meanwhile, the London County Council had begun a policy of instituting comprehensive schools within the London area. The Chairman of its Education Committee in fact stated that the policy of instituting comprehensive schools, in the opinion of the majority party on the LCC, was the only possible way of implementing the 1944 Act. At this time, a notable grammar school, the Strand, was being threatened as a result.

In a similar vein, there were concerns expressed at this time by Conservative MPs about the future of the independent 'public' schools. Their future, particularly the minor ones, was somewhat precarious, as in many cases their running costs were too high for them to be adequately maintained and their fees increasingly expensive for the parents to meet. In 1951, before the Conservative general election victory later that year, there was concern about what the Labour Party's ultimate intentions towards them were.[95] Indeed, there appears to have been more concern expressed at this stage by the Conservative Party elite about the future of the public schools than that of the grammar schools, in spite of the encroaching comprehensive developments within urban areas.

Both in debate within the House of Commons and outside, the Labour Party were becoming increasingly open about their dislike for the selective examination at age 11 and the tripartite system for its general effect of stratification. Their arguments were rarely made in terms of concern for educational quality or standards. But unfortunately, their position was often strengthened by criticisms of examinations made by Conservative Members of Parliament as well at this time. Much was said on both sides of the Commons about the negative effects on pupils due to the importance of the examination. Indeed, Kenneth Pickthorn, a Conservative MP who would shortly become Parliamentary Secretary to the Minister of Education, himself stated that while he could accept advantages stemming from an 'accident of birth,' added that 'if I knew that…manifest superiorities over me were wholly due to merit, I might find it beginning to be a little difficult to bear.'[96] Alternative methods, such as teachers' overall assessment, continued to be spoken of in altogether more positive terms.

On the eve of the 1951 General Election, the Conservative Party obviously understood that Britain was orientating itself towards an altogether more socialdemocratic future. The signs that the future of the selective system of secondary education was far from secure were therefore already obvious before the 1940s ended, with the ultimate intentions of comprehensive school campaigners on the left becoming clearer. The reluctance by the educational establishment to plan provision, including those of grammar schools, in an actual 'system,' along with 'bilateral' arrangements already being favoured rather than separate technical schools, alongside a lack of clarity about the appropriate age of selection, pointed towards future weaknesses. Having achieved its unexpected victory in the 1951 General Election, the Conservative Party elite could hardly have failed to be aware of these omissions and the potential fuel it gave to those campaigners. Yet because of their desire not to regard education as an issue of partisan politics, these key ideological battles were something that they, unlike the left, sought to avoid.

The opening chapter has shown how a combination of a lack of clarity regarding the purpose of the secondary modern and an insufficient value accorded to technical education amid long-standing discrepancies over the provision of grammar schools between local areas represented key omissions on the part of the Ministry of Education. The Conservative Party was by now clearly aware that the seeds of commitment to the comprehensive principle were germinating within the Labour Party. The need for the selective process to be both transparent and yet sufficiently flexible would have been readily apparent to even the most casual of observers. These omissions should be borne in mind as we turn to the next chapter, as they constituted key problems that the Conservative government of 1951 needed to address if they had really been the keen defenders of selection that they have subsequently been presented as being.

2

The start of the slide 1951–8

The Conservative governments of this period were fully aware of key challenges presenting themselves to the selective secondary education system. Yet in spite of what has been commonly portrayed by educational historians, successive Conservative education ministers, along with their Ministry of Education officials, did not seek to confront these difficulties and strengthen the selective process. Instead, core issues became enveloped in an atmosphere of expediency and cynicism, with selection at 11 allowed to become a political bogeyman. By contrast, there was a marked desire to deter any proposed reform of the independent 'public' schools. This approach culminated in the White Paper *Secondary Education for All* in 1958, which symbolised the desire by the Conservative government to avoid an outright commitment to selective state education. This opened the door further to the development of comprehensive schools in a greater number of local authority areas.

Early controversies

The Conservative government that took office in October 1951 inherited an economy that was in deep financial straits. The crisis in the country's economic condition meant that Britain was heavily reliant on Marshall Aid from the United States. Within this situation, with Churchill as the first post-war Conservative Prime Minister and Butler the Chancellor of the Exchequer, the government was desperately seeking to make any economies that they could. This meant cutbacks in civil expenditure, including education. For the post of Minister of Education, they were therefore looking to appoint an individual who they thought would be compliant and would easily accept spending restrictions on their department.

The choice of Florence Horsbrugh reflected this. At age 62, she was unlikely to have a significant future as a minister. Indeed, education would prove the pinnacle for her. Horsbrugh had been the Member of Parliament for Manchester Moss Side since 1950. Having previously served as the MP for Dundee from 1931 until 1945, she had held ministerial office in the wartime coalition governments as Parliamentary Secretary to the Ministry of Health and to the Ministry of Food. In the former post she had been notable for arranging the evacuation of schoolchildren from major cities during the war, and had long been known for taking an interest in social welfare issues, including introducing as a private member the Bill which became the Adoption of Children (Regulation) Act in 1939. She would turn out to be only the third woman to be appointed Cabinet minister in Britain's history, and the first woman to hold a Cabinet post in a Conservative government. Yet there was little indication that Churchill and others rated Horsbrugh highly, and she had not been a particularly notable figure previously. This suggests that in spite of the significance of the 1944 Act, the position of Education Minister was not held in high esteem and was patronizingly felt to be a 'woman's post'. (Ellen Wilkinson had of course previously served in this position under the Attlee government.)

Horsbrugh therefore arrived at the Ministry of Education in a highly unenviable position, with the Chancellor Butler looking to make whatever savings in civil expenditure that he could. A year after Horsbrugh's appointment, by October 1952 Butler was anxious for economies in departmental expenditure to be implemented, given the existing balance of payments deficit.[1] Horsbrugh was pledged to cut her investment programme by £90 million over the next seven years. Similarly, she was being pressured to raise the rate of contribution for teachers' superannuation, since the scheme was now in deficit.

The important question to consider is whether Horsbrugh was put under greater relative pressure to make economies in her department compared with other ministers during this period. For her part, Horsbrugh could only tell Butler that she could not find any real economies that could reasonably be made.[2] In terms of extreme measures, she was forced to consider two options: of either raising the school entry age to 6 years of age, or alternatively, and even more radically, lowering the school leaving age again to 14. She was also forced to give consideration to the re-imposition of school tuition fees as well as charges for ancillary services such as school milk.[3]

School expenditure had risen rapidly due to the heavy increase in the birth rate immediately after the war. But at this time the Exchequer was seeking to claw back all that it could, with Butler even proposing greater charges on prescriptions, as well as desiring cuts in food subsidies.[4] Furthermore, Horsbrugh had a noticeably tougher time from Butler in regard to making economies in her department in stark contrast to that of Harold Macmillan, the Minister of Housing and Local Government, who had already embarked upon notably high spending policies of housing expansion. In spite of the massive demands of building that this entailed, this policy was stoutly defended by both Macmillan and David Eccles, the Minister of Works. Indeed, the Conservative Party had already pledged a policy on housing of 300,000 houses a year.[5] It was surely also significant that while Macmillan was safely ensconced in the Cabinet in his respective post, Horsbrugh, despite being in charge of the nation's education, would not be made an official member of the Cabinet until 1953.

There was only one reasonable possible economy that could be made: of increasing the rate of contribution under the Teachers' Superannuation Act from 10 to 12 per cent. Yet here there was great opposition, with pressure coming from the Burnham Committee to substantially increase teachers' salaries. Furthermore, Butler wanted to put a bigger share of educational expenditure onto the rates, with Horsbrugh desperately cautioning against this. And yet in spite of all this, Butler continued to be determined to squeeze whatever administrative economies he could out of the Ministry of Education.[6]

As well as trying to cope with this, Horsbrugh was facing growing pressure from the Labour opposition to approve comprehensive school schemes in London. By 1953, the comprehensive principle had become the basis of the Labour Party's programme for secondary education. Their policy was now clear and unambiguous. In their June 1953 statement on policy entitled *Challenge to Britain*, they announced that when next in office Labour would begin an attack on 'educational segregation.' They would 'abolish' the 11 plus examination, because they were 'convinced that all children would benefit if, between the ages of eleven and fifteen, they shared the facilities, both social and academic, of one secondary school.'[7] Their intended 'high schools' would have classes not only for those intending to go to a university, but also for technical and commercial students. It also added that once they had reduced sizes in primary schools and created the new secondary schools, their aim would be to take over the best of the 'public' schools and independent day schools as high schools for children who stayed on after 15.[8] There was thus no secret of what their ultimate intentions were by this stage.

Yet Horsbrugh could not reasonably have been called a die-hard opponent of comprehensive schools at all. Of the twelve comprehensive schemes so far submitted in London, she had approved no fewer than ten. Horsbrugh's rhetoric was in fact largely pragmatic and moderate on the issue. She emphasized 'flexibility' and experiment with comprehensives in certain areas. In addition, she was reported as being particularly interested in the 'variety' of selection procedures that were being worked out by local authorities at this time.[9]

Labour, by contrast, was becoming increasingly aggressive. In the Committee on the Education Bill in February 1953, the Labour opposition proposed a clause demanding that, in examining the development plans of local education authorities, the Minister should 'endeavour to secure an adequate number of comprehensive schools in the various areas.' In response to this action, Horsbrugh merely asked the Opposition to withdraw the clause on the grounds that it was 'undesirable' to write prescriptions for types of schools into the Act.[10] In fact, Labour's clause was defeated by twenty-one votes to seventeen.

In a similarly moderate spirit, in remarks that were reported in the *Manchester Guardian* newspaper, Horsbrugh was quoted as saying at this time, 'The eleven plus examination is an ordeal immensely stiffened for the child by the anxieties of parents.' She stated how she recognized the need for 'ample opportunities' for rectifying mistakes, not just at 13 or 15, but as soon as a serious error was noticed. There was therefore always an awareness shown by her about the difficulty of the 'borderline' cases under the system of selection.[11] However, she also pointed out that comprehensives simply represented an easy solution to these inevitable difficulties.

The Labour Party then confirmed their allegiance to the comprehensive ideal in resounding fashion at their annual Party Conference in Margate in October 1953. At the Conference, an amendment was added by the National Association of Labour Teachers that called for the abolition of the current 'segregation' of pupils under the existing system.[12] Under the amendment, local authorities would be asked to put forward new development plans for secondary education, 'utilizing existing schools along comprehensive lines.'[13] The Party membership overwhelmingly voted in its favour. Also at this time, much of educational opinion, including the editorial of the journal *Education*, the mouthpiece of the Association of Education Committees, was now in favour of moderate 'experiments' with comprehensive schools and felt that this was the 'reasonable attitude'.[14]

Many notable educational historians have taken the conventional view that the Conservative governments of the 1950s were keenly and ideologically supportive of grammar schools and the tripartite system and were grimly determined to shore it up during this period. For instance, Brian Simon wrote that the defence of the grammar school was 'a major issue of policy' for these governments and was held to 'firmly' throughout the decade. He also claimed that a policy of 'obstructing' the move to comprehensive education was carried through 'equally relentlessly,' by Horsbrugh's successors David Eccles, Lord Hailsham and Geoffrey Lloyd.[15] Similarly, Ken Jones wrote of how the Conservatives invested 'much political capital' into the grammar school and that in doing so they acted as an 'apologist' for the secondary modern. He even asserted that the 'centre-piece' of their post-war educational policies was the defence of the tripartite system.[16] Roy Lowe, in somewhat more measured terms, nevertheless gave the impression of Eccles and the Ministry being 'committed' to both the grammar school and the secondary modern, and that there was an 'out and out' defence of selective education taken by them in this decade.[17] Other authors such as Gary McCulloch and Michael Sanderson echoed this tendency, with McCulloch portraying their secondary modern policy as a tool to protect the 'cherished' grammar school, while Sanderson claimed that technical schools were neglected due to Conservative governments favouring the liberal academic education that grammar schools offered.[18] Yet as I will show, the actual events show a much more nuanced and politically expedient approach taken by Conservative ministers during this period.

In her speech at the annual Conservative Party conference in Margate that year, Horsbrugh was at pains to point out that she was not trying to set up a 'rigid framework' for education. She proudly highlighted the speed of educational building in the two years since taking office, while making comparisons of cheapness of cost with the record of the previous government. At this point, Angus Maude was one of the few notable figures in the Conservative Party who was prepared to describe Labour's pro-comprehensive policy as 'revolutionary,' while Mr R.J. Fulford, the Chairman of the Conservative Teachers' Association (CTA), emphasized how the Americans were now starting to realize the deficiencies in standards and other social problems resulting from the 'neighbourhood school' that was the norm in the United States.[19]

However, circumstances were now militating strongly against Horsbrugh being able to take decisive action in secondary education without facing mounting political campaigns of protest. A considerable controversy occurred in relation to the plans of the London County Council for the creation of a new comprehensive girls' school, named Kidbrooke, that was to involve swallowing up Eltham Hill, a notable girls' grammar school. On 26 October 1953, Horsbrugh made a speech at Caxton Hall to the London Conservative Women's Conference telling them of the London Council's plans that would affect Eltham Hill, and informing them of their right to send objections to her as the Minister. In addition, she was reported as being critical of the size of the proposed comprehensive schools under the London School Plan.

It is important to note here the key aspect of the 1944 Act detailing the Minister's powers in this area. This was contained within Section 13 of the Act. In regard to the proposed enlargement or discontinuance of a maintained school, the local education authority concerned was obliged to give public notice after which there was a statutory period of two months within which public objections could be made. At the end of this period, the Minister would then make the decision of whether or not to approve the proposed scheme. Eltham Hill had not in fact been originally intended within the London Schools Plan and was the only girls' grammar school existing in the area. The key issue was that the Minister was being pressured to authorize the closing down of existing schools in order to 'feed' the comprehensive schools that were intended.

It was claimed by pro-comprehensive campaigners that the London County Council had first produced a report indicating its intention for Kidbrooke to include Eltham Hill as early as October 1952 and that it was on 16 February 1953 that the suggestion that notices were necessary had been made.[20] Yet Horsbrugh had not made her supposedly propagandist speech against it until October 1953. The accusation was that she had waited all this time in order to suddenly derail proceedings. The Minister thus stood squarely accused of abusing her ministerial powers and undermining local authority freedom.

As a result of her ultimate rejection of the Council's plan, Horsbrugh was further accused of meddling in and obstructing the plans of the London County Council regarding comprehensives, with the original plans having been known over a year earlier. The inevitable claim was that Kidbrooke would not be able to go ahead properly without the inclusion of the more academically inclined girls of Eltham Hill, and would suffer as a result of not being a 'proper' comprehensive. According to the Labour MP Arthur Skeffington, the comprehensive policy had been 'hotly and consistently attacked by Conservatives,' with constant opposition exhibited by them to the plan's 'constructive advance.'[21]

However, as Horsbrugh explained in her defence of her actions, the actual notices for the closure of Eltham Hill had not in fact been published by the London Council until 25 September 1953. And as she pointed out, according to the terms of the 1944 Act, it was only after notices had been published that a period of two months could begin during which statutory objections could be made. She had therefore only been informing local inhabitants of what their rights were under the Act, which as Minister she was at liberty to do. She added that she was not against experiments with comprehensive schools, only that she was against development plans with comprehensive schools only. Eltham Hill was therefore being left the option of its girls being able to choose to go to Kidbrooke or to remain.[22]

However, this argument carried little weight with the increasingly intransigent proponents of comprehensive schools on the left. The attack left its mark on Horsbrugh and showed just what a Minister of Education could potentially face regarding the defence of grammar schools as early as 1954. These sorts of disputes, with the notion of local authority 'freedom' being used in deliberately selective fashion, would be replayed constantly in the future.

It was not just within London that developments were leading in the direction of comprehensive schooling. The West Riding Education Committee was now seeking to extend their current scheme of enabling pupils at 15 and over who wanted to become teachers to enter grammar schools to those seeking to enter other professions.[23] Meanwhile, the Liberal Party's Educational Advisory Committee were advocating at this time that the lower 'B' and 'C' streams from the grammar schools be provided within the modern schools so that the latter type of school could retain academic pupils, with the status of the secondary modern schools being thought to be strengthened as a result.[24] This type of thinking would have distinct repercussions for the future.

The Conservative Teachers' Association, whose committee advised the Parliamentary Party on educational matters, was gravely concerned by recent events.[25] In a report on the future of secondary education published in February 1954, it claimed that the natural differences between pupils were being deliberately minimized by those seeking to impose the comprehensive school universally. By contrast, pupils needed to be placed with those who were of similar aptitude to themselves. It stated that its report

> will be found to have nothing to do with comprehensive schools except to condemn them since they render themselves unable to make adequate provision for the vital differences between pupils.[26]

The CTA stressed the important, if obvious, fact that 'the most urgent need of the moment' was for a vigorous and convinced development of the secondary modern. However, they also highlighted the still paltry proportions of both grammar and technical schools.[27] They also suggested that the controversies regarding the examination taken at 11 would be eased somewhat if pupils were given two opportunities for taking it. For the CTA, there would ideally be grammar school places for at least 20 per cent of the child population at the age of 13 under all of the local education authorities.

The great difficulty that the Conservative Teachers emphasized was that the position of the technical school remained so weak. Indeed, they noted how a number of areas in fact possessed no technical schools at all. There remained particular difficulties of provision for this type of school within rural and small urban areas, owing to the small number of children that were felt to require this type of education. While they allowed that in certain cases this problem might be surmounted by having technical 'sides' within grammar or modern schools, they emphasized that this should only be in particular circumstances, and not be regarded as a replacement for the technical school. In their eyes, the technical school would ideally stand alone. Therefore, the Conservative Teachers counselled against the idea of a 'bipartite' system within one particular school.[28] However, in practice this was what was already often happening, with technical streams instead being provided in grammar and modern schools.

In terms of the secondary modern, even the Conservative Teachers were defining its role in vague terms. While the modern school was to be valued for its 'variety and adaptability,' the direction in which its curriculum should ultimately point was not defined. According to the Conservative Teachers, 'local conditions ... must decide to what extent the Modern School should experiment without encroaching on the Technical Schools.' Employing further generalities, it was felt that the secondary modern school's overwhelming need was to build a 'tradition.'[29]

A key issue concerned the ease of transfer for the late developer. As the Conservative Teachers noted, the advocates of the comprehensive school were making an effective case that this type of school would enable pupils to be transferred from one kind of curriculum to the other within the school with a minimum of disturbance, without the difficulties of the selective process at age 11. Under the existing system, there was inevitably a chance of a certain proportion of pupils being allocated to the wrong type of school. As they noted, it was of course in the pro-comprehensive campaigners' interest to highlight the alleged deficiencies and unfairness of the existing system.[30]

A further problem for both grammar and technical schools at this time was the extent of early leaving by pupils before the age of 16. This was a particular problem for the technical schools with the lure of many boys towards early employment. A large problem in fact lay in the attitudes of industry. Very few firms were often willing to apprentice boys after the age of 16 who had obtained the General Certificate of Education (GCE) at ordinary level. According to the CTA, the Trade Unions were 'not yet helpful' in the matter of allowing boys to take the GCE at 16 and over and then start a trade apprenticeship, thus compounding the problems for the technical schools generally. An outdated age limit of age 16 was still being adhered to.[31]

Because of all these factors, urgent implementation was needed on three fronts: the greater and more even provision of grammar schools, a marked increase in the number of technical schools and the development of the secondary modern schools, ideally with their own kind of leaving certificate in order to give them a sense of status and overall objective. It was vital that the tripartite system addressed these issues in the early and mid-1950s if it was to work properly. However, the influence of those such as the CTA was decidedly limited on ministers, even with a Conservative government now in office.

And the pressure on Horsbrugh from Butler to make economies regarding civil expenditure continued. In 1954, Horsbrugh was in the midst of passing the hugely unpopular Teachers' Superannuation Bill before Parliament that sought to curb teachers' salaries. Furthermore, the Swinton Committee was then formed, which sought to exert further pressures for economies on ministers, not least Horsbrugh at education. At this time, it was suggesting cuts of 5 and even 10 per cent in budget estimates for the Ministry of Education.[32] Other measures being proposed were an increase in charges for school meals and restricting free meals to those children who were considered undernourished. This policy obviously carried dire political consequences if enacted.[33]

Much of this problem had resulted from the raising of the school leaving age to 15 in 1947, as the Conservatives' Post-War Problems Committee had correctly prophesized. As noted earlier, Horsbrugh's problems regarding the escalating costs for the education service amidst a lack of existing provision, given the strains being put upon it, were being exacerbated by Macmillan's housing policy. As a result of so many houses being built in such a short space of time, hundreds of thousands of families had been swept into new housing estates where no schools existed. This of course furthered the practical and expedient case for comprehensive schools being built in those areas.

By 15 July 1954 Horsbrugh was able to tell Stephen Swingler, the pro-comprehensive Labour MP for Newcastle under-Lyme, that of the thirteen proposals made to her for the establishment of comprehensive schools since taking office she had deferred decision in two, approved six in full and four in part, and refused the approval of one because she did not consider it educationally advantageous.[34] This was hardly the record of a staunch anti-comprehensive campaigner.

Yet in the midst of rows over the Teachers' Superannuation Bill, Horsbrugh was sacked from the post of Minister in October 1954. She had been shabbily treated, and was given little support by either Churchill or Butler in occupying an extremely difficult role at a time of enforced 'cheeseparing' of public expenditure on education. She had been forced to labour under a brief that maintained a ban on work to relieve overcrowding and replace bad premises and end all-age schools and had therefore effectively lost out to Macmillan's housing policy. It is difficult to avoid concluding that Horsbrugh had been used as a scapegoat for unpopular policies. With a general election looming in the coming year, she was by now clearly regarded as an electoral liability.

A desire for overlap

By contrast, her successor in October 1954 David Eccles would not labour under any such sense of limitation. One of the group who had drafted the Party's Industrial Charter in 1947, he had of course played a key part in the Conservatives' housing drive at the Ministry of Works, and was known amongst his colleagues for possessing no lack of self-assurance. From the outset, he was able to obtain an ending of minor restrictions on rural reorganization and building works from Butler. Eccles felt the Government could bring into education 'some of the feeling of expansion and success which has been the mark of our housing drive'.[35] The list of minimum improvements would cost £300,000 in 1955–6, with a rise to an estimated £3 million by 1958–9. Eccles was thus able to make more promises about the greater provision of technical education in future. It was obvious that Butler was giving Eccles far greater leeway than he had ever given Horsbrugh. Meanwhile, the issue of teachers' pensions was kicked into the long grass by the existing scheme being scrapped and an alternative plan of protracted negotiation advanced instead. Furthermore, Eccles firmly dismissed any suggestion, as Horsbrugh had done, of altering the duration of schooling. As he noted in a memorandum a month after taking his post, 'If we, who mostly send our children to boarding schools, encouraged early leaving from county secondary schools, we should present the Opposition with a first class Election issue'.[36] This shows the degree of class consciousness with which he viewed these issues.

Upon attaining his new post, David Eccles was in fact strikingly opaque on key aspects of secondary education. As evidenced by his internal communications with his officials at this time, Eccles rightly considered the secondary modern school curriculum and its ultimate purpose to be unclear. There of course remained no overarching definition of what it was meant to consist of. But in spite of his ostensible emphasis upon technical education, it appeared his main concern was in fact to shore up the secondary modern curriculum in essentially academic terms. In particular, he keenly asked his officials what alternative there was for the child who 'just' failed to get into the grammar school.[37] Eccles, a graduate in philosophy, politics and economics at Oxford, was particularly struck by the importance of the teaching of English and arts subjects for pupils in secondary moderns. The notion that the secondary modern school was to be valued for a different type of education from the grammar school, and should not to be measured in the same terms, did not figure within his approach from the beginning of his ministership.

Furthermore, Eccles was against wholesale transfers occurring a second time from secondary moderns to grammar schools at the age of 13. This was currently the case within certain local authority areas in order to ameliorate the effects of the 11 plus examination. Yet in his view, this further reallocation of pupils was to be avoided other than in the case of obvious 'misfits.' As evidenced from his notes before a meeting with his officials in the Ministry in February 1955, he preferred the idea of 'overlapping' between grammar schools and secondary moderns.[38] This meant providing a similar curriculum for those in both the lower streams of the grammar school and the upper tiers of the secondary modern. If possible, moderately academic pupils were to be kept within the secondary modern in order, he felt, to boost its status. Logically, this led towards smaller grammar school provision overall, and certainly not any policy to substantially increase their numbers. This was in spite of the fact that the overall national shortage of grammar school provision as well as the often massive discrepancies in provision between different local authority areas was a major attack point for pro-comprehensive campaigners. This key weakness was therefore not going to be addressed.

The atmosphere was one of expediency above all else. As Eccles commented, 'I like the idea of overlapping between grammar schools and the secondary modern. But this can hardly be general unless Secondary Moderns are pretty large.' After all, the argument for transfers was inevitably a strong one as long as the secondary modern schools remained small and therefore less able to accommodate the more academic pupils. Therefore, his notes at this time reveal how he was keenly considering the question of 'how important to a secondary modern is it to keep a few bright children?'[39] One can also see how his chain of reasoning was leading him to consider the altogether larger comprehensive school in at least certain cases.

This mind-set thus characterized the discussion that took place between Eccles and his officials the following day on 23 February. Those assembled included the Chief Inspector of Schools Sir Martin Roseveare and his colleagues. At the beginning of the meeting the ostensible aim was set out that, rather than trying to produce a small elite, they were seeking to try to produce in everyone 'the values hitherto characteristic of the middle classes.' It was added that 'the Minister rather favoured the latter view.'[40] This ambiguous standpoint led to a discussion that inevitably sought to boost the secondary modern school's academic status by seeking to encourage academic courses within it as much as possible.

From examination of the minutes of this key meeting one can see that there was a noticeably settled consensus among the participants that, like Eccles, opposed wholesale transfers out of modern schools other than in extreme cases.[41] Instead, the emphasis was on increasing the number of pupils in modern schools taking the GCE 'O' level. Inevitably, it led the officials away from any serious consideration of substantially increasing the number of grammar school places. Indeed, in the view of one of the school inspectors present, 'the higher the percentage of selective places, the greater the sense of failure among the children not selected'.[42] The long-held confusion regarding the purpose of the secondary modern school alongside insufficient recognition of its need for a separate and distinctive purpose thus remained.

The officials' opposition to a second transfer at 13 was made plain. Indeed, the school inspectors present claimed that local education authorities 'loathed' their 13 plus transfer arrangements. The matter was largely being viewed in terms of practical convenience for local education authorities given the existing arrangements. At this point in the meeting, Eccles summed up by saying that 'it seems that we should kill the idea of the desirability of general arrangements in modern schools for 13 plus transfers'.[43] Therefore, one of the core weaknesses in the existing system, of insufficient grammar school places alongside the under-development of a system of second transfer at 13, was to be deliberately submerged.

Those present were also keenly aware that a number of local education authorities at this time were abolishing their 11 plus arrangements, or were alternatively using them to allocate places in comprehensive schools. Yet they were already prepared to envisage this as long as 'geographical considerations' suited comprehensives, such as in the case of rural areas with small grammar schools.[44] While adding the caveat that the wishes of the schools and local opinion should be in favour, they were clearly opening the door of possibility for future comprehensive school developments. Those assembled assumed that the differentiation of the three kinds of education would remain while being fully aware of how difficult it would be to adequately provide the sufficient range of grammar, secondary modern and technical courses within the comprehensive system. Yet astoundingly, no fundamental objections to the comprehensive school were mentioned in the minutes beyond its potentially excessive size.

Regarding the provision of technical education, it was strikingly asserted by one of the school inspectors present that 'we would not agree that there is a "kind of boy or girl" with identifiable technical bent anyway at the age of 11 to 13'.[45] Naturally, this sort of sentiment further undermined the whole basis of the tripartite idea and militated against the furtherance of technical schools. It was added by this inspector that many children went to them simply because they were better than the other available option of the secondary modern.[46] As a result, it was stated that 'there is much to be said against the general adoption by local education authorities of technical secondary schools'.[47]

They noted favourably how the Isle of Wight authority was at this time scrapping its grammars and turning them into grammar/technical (high) schools. They therefore preferred grammar and technical arrangements as part of what was known as a 'bilateral' notion instead. They would thus 'discourage' the provision of small (i.e. 1 form entry) selective schools.[48] Clearly, practical considerations rather than principle were paramount in the minds of those present.

Eccles then held a second meeting on 9 March to consider the development of external examinations for secondary modern schools. Similar tendencies of thought were again displayed that showed a striking complacency among the administrative elite. The long-standing intention behind the establishment of external examinations for secondary modern pupils was of course to give them an aim to work towards and offer the schools a defined purpose. Yet astoundingly, the consensus taken by the assembled group was to be firmly opposed to this. It was felt, adopting a sentiment that had been expressed so many times before, that the secondary modern schools and staff would become 'cramped' in their aims and that this would be 'virtually certain if external examinations became common'.[49] Yet this was in spite of the fact that at the same time Eccles was of course encouraging secondary modern schools to have more of their pupils take academic 'O' level courses. In response, one of the Ministry officials present pointed out the incongruity of this approach given what they were proposing for the modern schools and the GCE. However, this observation was instantly dismissed by the school inspectors who repeated that further external exams would be a disrupting influence. Eccles therefore committed himself to being 'firmly opposed' to allowing any external examination other than GCE 'O' level to be taken by pupils under the age of 16.[50] However, it was felt expedient that, rather than express outright opposition to specific external exams for secondary moderns, the issue should be 'soft-pedalled' at the next meeting of the Secondary Schools Examinations Council on 21 March.[51] A distinct condescension towards the secondary modern was evident among those at the top of the official education tree.

Eccles' sentiments in his speech at the National Union of Teachers Conference in Scarborough on 13 April thus sought to bolster this approach. Along with platitudes about how greater expansion was taking place and more money being spent, as well as the replacement of slum schools and the reorganization of all-age classes, his sentiments were markedly populist and egalitarian. In front of the NUT, he praised what he claimed to be the fading of distinctions between grammar schools and the rest. In doing so, he caricatured a past where it had only been the grammar schools that mattered, while the majority were forgotten and sunk. By contrast, he described how in the present day 'we are all coming closer together', and that, 'in a sense we are all working class now'.[52] People would all now be living increasingly similar lifestyles, he continued, in this modernist, technological age of higher living standards.

He intended to have, rather than selection for a few, 'selection for everybody'. Using a somewhat strained railway analogy, he claimed that while previously only a few had travelled along the grammar school track, now everybody could be carried and accommodated. Yet this was in fact being employed as a means of justifying his stance of not enlarging grammar school provision:

> The question is therefore posed, shall we double or treble the grammar school railway, or shall we develop other forms of transport alongside, with opportunities to change from one system to the other? I am definitely for the second proposal.[53]

Eccles was therefore presenting the situation as an 'either or' between establishing greater grammar school provision, on the one hand, and providing for the other types of secondary education, on the other. They were being portrayed as mutually exclusive. But this of course was disingenuous. Both were needed urgently to be developed in parallel with each other.

Furthermore, he told the NUT that he was quite prepared to consider comprehensives, while adding that 'practical considerations' might limit experiments with them. However:

> On the other hand there are no objections to a comprehensive on the score of wasting existing assets where an area needs both a new grammar school and several new secondary moderns. In such a case, if the local people really want one, I would agree to a comprehensive ...[54]

While opposed on the grounds of size to a whole new series of comprehensive schools being created, the potential ground for future schemes was nevertheless being laid.

In regards to technical education, Eccles' stance was to distribute technical 'courses' over as many schools (grammar and modern) as possible. According to him, there would only be 'rare cases' where 'the local need is so strong as to call for a new technical school.' Nor did Eccles want to talk about ideal national percentages for grammar and technical places. Modern schools were to be vaguely encouraged to develop 'extended courses.' This would apparently create many and various secondary modern and technical 'streams.'[55] It all had a tinge of the opaque about it. The question to ask is whether Eccles foresaw what would happen as a result of not rectifying the omissions that lay in the current system, and where the logic of it would ultimately lead in the future.

Ultimately, Eccles saw the alleged controversy felt to be aroused by the 11 plus examination as a potential election issue and was worried by it. A memorandum circulated by him to the Cabinet in April 1955 on the eve of the general election that year reveals the extent of his feelings. According to Eccles, in spite of the 1944 Education Act, the 'disappointment and jealousy' among parents about their children not winning places at grammar schools were very much apparent, while parity of esteem between the different types of school had not been established, 'and the resentment appears to be growing.' Furthermore:

> Although the comprehensive school is certainly not the right answer, we cannot leave the 11 plus examination where it is. The anxieties and jealousies are too easy to play on.[56]

As we have seen however, Eccles and his colleagues had already of course been considering the wider possibility of the comprehensive school for future developments. Indeed Eccles had, by April 1955, already approved two new schools of this kind.

As Eccles further revealed, 'we have to build something like three quarters of a million new secondary modern places and can, therefore, influence the pattern of schooling without disturbing what exists.'[57] This pragmatism was emblematic of Eccles' whole approach. He looked to spread courses with a vocational interest over as many secondary schools as possible and claimed that 'where this is already happening, local education authorities are finding that complaints from parents about the selection procedure are strikingly reduced.'[58] It was looking more and more like a short-term patchwork solution. With the work of the secondary modern to be merged at both ends with the grammar and the technical school, the rationale for retaining the three separate types of school as the basis for policy was already being undermined. Its ultimate logic led in the direction of the comprehensive school.

Other Conservative MPs shared this approach when making their contributions to the debate. For example, James Pitman the MP for Bath and Commander Sir John Maitland representing Horncastle were particularly prepared to countenance comprehensives in low-density population areas, with the Eton-educated Pitman claiming that the difficulties of comprehensives only arose in high-density areas compared with areas such as his own constituency.[59] Maitland, meanwhile, claimed to agree with the comprehensive principle and would only deplore those with a 'rigid and doctrinaire' attitude towards enforcing them everywhere. Strikingly, he added that education should not be approached in a 'party spirit'.[60] The contrast between Tory MPs' often tempered and cautious flexibility and the vehement pro-comprehensive commitment of the Labour side could not have been more marked.

Indeed, Eccles himself admitted that:

Hon Members opposite want to get rid of the 11 plus examination and we very well understand the reasons. The difference between us is how to get rid of it.[61]

As the pro-comprehensive Labour MP Arthur Moyle then observed later on in the debate:

The Minister is committed to the comprehensive school, just as we are on this side of the committee. I have not yet heard the Minister turn down the principle of the comprehensive school.

The only difference between the parties is as to the extent to which the comprehensive school should be applied.[62]

(my emphasis)

There was no subsequent rebuttal from the Conservative side of the House to this striking assertion.

Nevertheless, on 11 May 1955 the Joint Committee of the Four Secondary Associations, a body of some 35,000 teachers representing a range of schools, wrote to Anthony Eden, the Prime Minister, warning of the threat posed by the comprehensive school to the country's education. They expressed concern about its associated swamping of the gifted individual who was in danger of becoming 'only a unit in a vast scheme,' with an accompanying loss of high scholarship:

In spite of the great progress made in the last ten years, in spite of greater equality and widening opportunity, we see these aims imperilled by the hasty and wholesale adoption of schemes, particularly that of the comprehensive school, which are intended to create still greater equality, but may well have the opposite effect.[63]

However, the Prime Minister's carefully worded reply would only venture carefully about his government seeking a 'variety of schools.' Grammar schools would be 'preserved and strengthened' but he did not of course mention any planned increase in their number. According to Eden, they were prepared to see 'experiments' with comprehensives where all the local conditions were 'favourable' and 'no good schools swallowed up.' Noticeably, their opposition was again restricted to their 'hasty and wholesale' adoption.[64] Eden's reply was of course an exercise in trying to neutralize such concern.

Indeed, Eccles considered educational expansion to be an astute means of associating the Conservative Party with a key part of the welfare state in the public's mind. As he noted, 'a political party aiming to poll more than half the votes at future General Elections, must be clearly identified with one sector of the sprouting welfare state.'[65] He therefore urged the Prime Minister for greater support for the reorganization of rural areas. This was intended to be achieved within the next five years. He further warned Eden that a 'half educated electorate' would be 'fodder for the class war and a menace to free institutions.'[66] Such key aims as forestalling inflation, preventing and settling strikes and abandoning restrictive practices would only be solved, he claimed, through better education. Such expansionary instincts were inevitably fuelling a view of British education as a mass-oriented system to be conceived in populist and consumerist terms for electoral gain.

And Eccles was determined to achieve his expansionist aims, even to the extent of alienating Butler. An exchange of terse correspondence in November 1955 shows the Chancellor's exasperation with Eccles. As in the past, Butler had emphasized to all spending departments the need for economies as a result of rapidly spiralling inflation in the summer of 1955. All departments were being asked to seek reductions in their estimates or keep them to the lowest possible level for 1956-7. This of course would have affected Eccles' expansionary policies. Eccles replied that it would be 'impossible' to keep his estimates from rising, particularly given the increase in the school roll and the expansion at the top of secondary schools and in further education.[67] He would simply do his best to keep his estimates as low as possible. Tension would also flare between them in November when Eccles appeared to instruct local authorities to go ahead with their spending projects in spite of Butler having emphasized to them the need to exercise restraint. According to Butler, local authorities were to be free to defer education projects, including rural reorganization.[68] However, Eccles made a statement to the press that gave the impression local authorities were to be free to proceed. He then defended himself against Butler's admonition by saying that local authorities could 'not square' the message of reducing expenditure to the 1954-5 level with maintaining the educational programmes that they had been promised.[69]

In short, Eccles was a resolute and indeed wilful Minister of Education and, unlike Horsbrugh, was given a relatively free rein throughout most of his tenure by Butler. He would become renowned as a key figure in Britain's educational expansion and his general approach suited the 'consensus' spirit of the day. However, in the crisis following the resignation of Anthony Eden in 1957, the new Prime Minister, Harold Macmillan, sent him to the Board of Trade, a post he had long coveted.

Developments under Boyle

Eccles' successor as Minister of Education would be Lord Hailsham. A peer who had enjoyed a brilliant career in law, Hailsham had been strongly influenced by the thinking that lay behind the Beveridge Report, *Social Insurance and Allied Services* in 1942. He had quickly acquired a reputation as a left-wing Conservative by forming the Tory Reform Committee in 1943. This organization became known for developing what many senior members of the party regarded as policies of an almost socialistic nature. He had also become widely recognised for his writings on politics. In 1947, *The Case For Conservatism* was published, which expounded the case for a 'progressive' conservative ideology. Then known as Quintin Hogg, he had succeeded to his father's viscounty in 1950. Having served as first Lord of the Admiralty, Hailsham was appointed as the new Minister of Education by Macmillan on 13th January 1957. It would, however, turn out to be a tenure of a mere eight months.

His Parliamentary Secretary was Edward Boyle. This key figure would, more than anyone else, come to personify the Conservatives' approach to secondary education over the next decade. A corpulent baronet with markedly liberal attitudes, he was considered to be the colleague who most shared the outlook of the future Conservative leader and Prime Minister Edward Heath. He had served various political apprenticeships during the 1950s, including Economic Secretary to the Treasury in 1955. This new appointment, given Boyle's well-known 'moderate' tendencies on social issues, including immigration, would be highly significant for the future direction of the education service.

By 1957, the key issue of the discrepancies in grammar school provision existing between different local education authorities was an even more obvious point of attack for pro-comprehensive campaigners than ever. It even led the Labour MP Sydney Irving on 24 January to suggest that Boyle call for a conference of local authorities to be established to institute a 'pooling' of places in order to mitigate the effects of the lack of uniformity between them. Boyle simply replied that adjustments were being made through the school building programme, but that differences would remain because authorities suited their policies to the needs of their areas. Furthermore, 'in a locally administered system, uniformity would be neither possible nor desirable.'[70] (This emphasis on preserving local authorities' autonomy would form the basis for his stance on comprehensive schools' development over the next ten years.) Characteristically, in response to pressure from Labour members accusing the Government of dragging their feet on comprehensive schools, he sought to reassure them that the issue would not be approached in a 'doctrinaire' spirit.

In March 1957, twelve local authorities had grammar school provision for 30 per cent and over of their children (with nine of those in Wales) while thirty-eight local authorities had grammar school places for 15 per cent or less. Boyle was notably reluctant, in spite of entreaties by Labour's Alice Bacon, to publish this information in the Official Report. Yet while claiming to agree with Bacon, 'that this is the most important aspect of our educational policy at the present time', Boyle would only lamely repeat the recurring sentiment that it could not be expected that there would be a high degree of uniformity of provision between local authorities due to the great variety of local circumstances.[71]

Nor would Boyle be drawn to give any fundamental answer on the issue of late grammar school transfers. The Conservative MP for Darwen Charles Fletcher-Cooke pleaded with Boyle to take the problem of late transfers 'really seriously,' asking, 'Is he aware that many of us believe that the only way to save the grammar schools is to make their intake by late transfers not only more readily available but more readily available to all parties?' To this key question, Boyle merely replied that he would pass on his suggestion to 'his noble friend.'[72] In fact, Fletcher-Cooke's desire would have meant reneging on Eccles' earlier policy of discouraging these sorts of transfers. Already, there was evidence that both Hailsham and Boyle were unwilling to do very much to defend the selective system against the increasing attacks being made upon it at this time.

In the House of Commons on 14 March, Boyle revealed that in the last year of 1956 approximately 8,500 candidates from 600 secondary modern schools, comprising about a quarter of the secondary modern school roll, had been entered for the GCE. About half of these candidates had turned out to be successful. The fact that such a paltry proportion of the overall secondary modern school population was successful in fact suggested that the existing system worked fairly, if not entirely, accurately. Yet the political obsession with secondary modern pupils being given the opportunity to take the GCE was now very much in abundance. Furthermore, Boyle could not answer questions from Reginald Moss the Labour MP for Meriden about which courses had been introduced in secondary modern schools that led to certificates other than the GCE. He could only vaguely reveal that 28,000 pupils had stayed on at secondary modern schools beyond the age of 15 to take 'extended courses.'[73] Clearly, these less academic courses were not a priority and were of course, as seen earlier, still not officially recognized.

At the same time, the influence of left-wing sociologists on the manner in which education was being viewed was growing. An influential work, *Social Class and Educational Opportunity* by Jean Floud, was published that emphasized that 'social selection' occurred within the grammar school and that working-class children were significantly less likely to stay on into the sixth form due to environmental factors.[74] Such research findings were now being used as a form of ballast by those such as the Labour MP Alice Bacon for their pro-comprehensive campaigning.

Nevertheless, Floud conceded that neither subjective bias nor diversity of performance in attainment tests, relative to intelligence, was in fact prejudicing the chances of working-class children. The differences in proportion of the various occupational classes to the grammar school intake could be explained 'almost entirely in terms of the unequal distribution of measured intelligence.'[75] In spite of this, Floud continually emphasized the influence of the home environment and the need to tackle the question of the 'interaction' of homes and schools.[76] Another influential book, *Comprehensive Education: A New Approach* by Robin Pedley, emerged that urged for greater experiments to be made in the field of secondary education based upon comprehensive schemes in Leicestershire.[77] These highly politicized works played a vital role in influencing both ideological and expedient-minded politicians and undermining selection.

Increasingly deterministic arguments were now being made that the UK needed to vastly increase its 'output' of university graduates in mathematics and science, with negative comparisons made between Britain and Russia. Such sentiments inevitably fuelled a push for greater numbers of pupils to stay on at school. Indeed, there was expected to be a peak in terms of the number of secondary school pupils by 1960. Along with the constant accusations of insufficient education spending, the political debate about the education service was increasingly being drawn up in producer-driven and expansionist terms that inevitably put the Conservative government on the defensive.

The Labour opposition was now increasingly kicking against the validity of the 11 plus examination. On 5 April 1957, as notable a figure as Chuter Ede was claiming in the House of Commons that the failure to get into a grammar school was now regarded 'as an intellectual and social stigma,' and staggeringly, downplayed the validity of exams in general.[78] And Edward Boyle's responses suggested that the Conservative government's education spokesman was essentially seeking to appease those trying to discredit the existing system. Boyle openly admitted that he saw much of it as being at fault himself. He 'entirely' agreed that the 'present system of selection causes a great deal of anxiety in many quarters,' and that 'it would be both foolish and wrong simply to remain content with it.'[79] The significance of these sentiments cannot be overstated.

The 11 plus examination, Boyle claimed, cast a 'shadow' over the primary school curriculum, 'often with a rather evil effect.' He welcomed the more flexible arrangements, such as those giving weight to teachers' opinions, that had been introduced in certain local authorities. He added that 'quite apart from the feelings of parents, I should be the last to wish to skate over the wider social implications and disadvantages of our present system.'[80] Through these public sentiments, he was effectively damning the system himself. While acknowledging the central criticism of the divergences in existing grammar school provision, he stated that building programmes were framed with a 15 to 25 per cent selective provision in mind. (Technical school provision was being included within that figure.) Nevertheless in regard to the discrepancies, he merely claimed that the Ministry had taken notice of this and would do what they could.[81]

Boyle also opened the door further for the possibility of rural comprehensives being created through amalgamation where there were small grammar and secondary modern schools already existing. As he said, 'I can well believe that a school of this kind might make a better contribution to the needs of a country district than a series of smaller schools.'[82] He also considered comprehensive schools to be feasible for the emerging housing estates, of which so many had sprung up in the last decade. Like Eccles' officials, he appeared to be viewing the matter through the prism of administrative pragmatism and convenience.

In any event, according to Boyle, it all ultimately lay in the hands of the local education authorities who should simply be left to make decisions for their areas. The role of central government was increasingly being downplayed. As he put it, 'I should be very sorry if any central authority tried to force them to adopt one solution or the other as a matter of principle.'[83] He was increasingly portraying himself as not being wedded to any particular conception of how the secondary education system should be structured. Given the vehemence of those who were pro-comprehensive, this apparently reasonable approach was distinctly flaccid, and did not stake any core position on the issue.

Indeed, inside the Conservative Party they were in fact now starting to move away from a defence of the existing system that carried academic selection at 11, without going as far as openly stating that comprehensive schools should be universally substituted in their place. The Conservative Research Department astutely noted in confidential papers in May 1957 how certain local authorities were adopting increasingly informal arrangements. In the notable experiment in Leicestershire, all pupils could move forwards to the grammar schools there at age 14 simply on the basis that their parents undertook to keep them there until they reached 16. Academic selection was being taken out of the whole process and simply replaced with the wishes of parents.

Boyle himself regarded what was happening in Leicestershire as 'an important new experiment,' and encouraged further experiments in this field where a local education officer and his committee were so inclined. Tellingly, the Conservative Research Department now felt that the Party should be seen to further move with this tide. Having described these experiments, it noted:

> One is left with the impression of a need for reconsidering the Party's policy, not only on the 11 plus examination, but on secondary education as a whole.[84]
>
> (my emphasis)

The same confidential document by the Conservative Research Department expressed concern about the escalating fees of the independent schools and the effect upon their clientele at this time. Indeed, their whole attitude towards the public schools' situation was markedly protectionist, in stark comparison to their increasingly pragmatic approach towards selective schools within the state sector. As we shall now see, it was in fact the future of the public schools that was weighing on the minds of those in the upper echelons of the Conservative Party throughout 1957.

The public schools question again

Upon his appointment as Minister in January that year, Hailsham had received a letter of congratulation from the Headmaster of Eton, Robert Birley. Along with the expected platitudes, Birley expressed his concern to Hailsham, a former pupil, about what he regarded as the lack of positive direction within the Conservative government. As a result, he was concerned about what Labour would do when next in office:

> It seems true that the Conservative Party is sadly lacking in a positive educational policy. What worries me is the very prevalent view that if the Labour Party take up some line or other in Education, it is bound to come off in the end, just because they will be in office eventually.

To Birley, the Conservative government's appeasement of Labour's stance regarding maintained schools for fear they might do something worse in office might be repeated with the public schools, 'unless the Conservative Party work out a policy about them.'[85]

For his part, Hailsham replied that he was 'very open to new ideas' and welcomed the proposed visit.[86] The correspondence further shows that Birley arranged meetings with Hailsham to discuss the 'public schools question' over the period of February and early March 1957. This clearly indicates the degree of concern felt by the Eton headmaster over this topic. The issue of the public schools' place in British society was now rearing its head again at a time of great unpopularity for the government in the aftermath of the Suez crisis. Those within the Conservative Research Department were asking in May 1957 how, given the high cost of education for fee-paying parents, the independent schools were to survive. Rhetorically, they asked, 'Are we prepared to sacrifice them to Reform, or can we save them by Retrenchment?' They added, with a notable air of concern, that 'what seems certain is that the prevailing policy of "peaceful coexistence" cannot have a happy ending for the independent schools.'[87]

At this time, the Conservative Research Department noted recent remarks made by the Labour MP Michael Stewart published in the *Daily Express* on 6 May 1957, which stated that the next Labour government, having 'improved' the state sector, would throw open the public schools to 75 per cent non fee-paying pupils. The Research Department therefore warned that the Party could expect the independent schools to be a 'major issue' at the General Election. Therefore, they emphasized the importance of an answer to Labour's planned pamphlet on education due to be published in the summer of 1958.[88] Nevertheless, they continued to reject the Fleming policy of opening up the public schools to pupils from the maintained sector. Hailsham himself was completely against the adoption of the Fleming proposals and informed a group of public school representatives of this in March 1957. They, along with Birley, were clearly concerned about safeguarding their long-term future.

In an interview on 27 March with John Cole of the *Manchester Guardian* on the relationship between the independent and state sectors of education, Hailsham was keen to downplay the value of any such policy of integration. In so doing, he sought to minimize the significance and prestige of the independent schools. The thinking that lay behind the Fleming scheme was dismissed, with Hailsham asserting that it subscribed to a 'romantic' notion of a 'two nations' idea of the country that he claimed no longer existed in modern circumstances. He added, staggeringly, that the Fleming proposals rested on a 'false premise' that the public schools disproportionately produced leaders in the country. Instead, Hailsham claimed in the interview that it was in fact universities that now did this and that Britain was now heading, he assured Cole, towards an 'aristocracy of achievement.'[89] In retrospect, these sentiments by Hailsham surely appear ironic given that he and Boyle were already assisting developments within the maintained system that were encouraging the elimination of the grammar schools that had long been the public schools' main rivals. The sense of double standards between how the Conservative Minister was viewing the independent and state sectors was now palpable.

He added that it would be a misuse of public funds to supply a minority of pupils from the maintained sector with places in public schools. According to Hailsham, the Ministry was not to 'go over the heads' of local authorities by independently providing the money to send boys to them, and added that he did not want to make the Minister 'a court of appeal' from the local democracy. The fact that there had always been a notable lack of pressure in Parliament for the implementation of the Fleming Proposals was 'naturally' taken by Hailsham as a sign of a lack of public enthusiasm for it. A father, to use the analogy in his conversation with Cole, was just as entitled to buy his son Latin Grammar as he was to buy him 'lollipops'. It would, however, be necessary to establish a case for 'privilege at the public expense'.[90]

At a Cabinet Home Affairs Committee meeting on 19 July at which Butler was also present, Hailsham stated that it was 'essential' for the Government to have a coherent policy on the public schools before the next General Election, but that the Fleming Plan 'did not provide any adequate basis for such a policy'. The provision of boarding places for 'certain classes' of children was to normally be made within the maintained system, and not by acquiring a proportion of the places available at the public schools. The description of the meeting then notes how 'there was a considerable measure of agreement ... that the Fleming Plan would not form the basis for a satisfactory policy'.[91] Interestingly, it then describes how the Cabinet Committee then had a 'general discussion' on the Government's policy towards the public schools which was not recorded. There was obviously a great desire for discretion on the issue. It appears the eventual decision was to mask the issue for the time being. One can see therefore how Hailsham weaved and side-stepped the issue at this time.

Polls taken at this time suggested that the Conservatives would lose the next general election. As a result, morale in the party was low. Over lunch with Macmillan at the Turf Club in September 1957, Hailsham accepted the office of Lord President of the Council and to also serve as Chairman of the Party. In fact, Hailsham had had little to show for his eight months at education other than instituting a lengthening of the training period for teachers to three years. He had also given a sense of reassurance to the teaching profession, in particular the National Union of Teachers, by pushing for added educational spending from the Exchequer where he could. He would go on to become a renowned Chairman of the Party over the next few years. However, the fact that he was replaced at this time confirms once again that education was hardly a priority from Macmillan's point of view.

The loss of faith

The new Minister of Education appointed by Macmillan was Geoffrey Lloyd. Having been Parliamentary Private Secretary to Stanley Baldwin from 1931 to 1935, he had been a leading figure in Midlands Tory circles for two decades. He had represented Sutton Coldfield as MP since 1955 as well as serving as Minister for Fuel and Power during those years. His appointment, on 17 September, came at a difficult time for any Minister to defend a high-spending department. As ever, economic difficulties continued to abound, with constant threat to the value of the pound sterling from inflation. Peter Thorneycroft, the Chancellor of the Exchequer, was anxious to allay this through measures of economy.

It was therefore decided by the Cabinet in September that investment in the public sector in 1958/9 and 1959/60 should be restricted to the 1957/8 level. Inevitably, Lloyd expressed concern that, on top of an earlier government measure of a block grant, such a cut in educational investment would 'revive' doubts about the Conservatives' commitment towards the education service.[92] Yet in spite of Lloyd's protestations, Thorneycroft wanted him to make a cut of £20 million over those two years that would inevitably further affect school building programmes. All the while, Thorneycroft claimed that education was already receiving preferential treatment compared with other forms of capital expenditure.

At this point, the minutes reveal how Macmillan stepped in to defend Lloyd at the Cabinet meeting on 15 October by arguing for £15 million of savings rather than £20 million. In so doing, he stated that the policy should be presented not as a reduction in capital expenditure, but as an attempt to 'spread' that expenditure over a slightly longer period.[93] This divergence over educational capital expenditure clearly indicates the tensions existing between Macmillan and his chancellor Thorneycroft over expenditure at this time. It is reasonable to speculate as to what extent this degree of parsimony by the Conservative government affected their ability to respond to the need to build more grammar schools and further develop the secondary moderns in order to build their public esteem.

At the Conservative Party Conference in October 1957, delegates were becoming increasingly restive on the issue of comprehensive schools. Mrs Josephine Cook of the Bradford Education Committee noted the recent developments in her Labour-controlled city. An increasing number of mergers of existing grammar schools into comprehensives were now taking place. She noted, perhaps more naively than she realized, how it was 'nothing short of unadulterated impudence that these plans are going on right under the very noses of this Conservative government.'[94] But in marked contrast to these sentiments coming from the floor, Lloyd, in his first Conference speech as minister, would only confine himself to emphasizing his opposition to comprehensive schemes based on 'political motives' rather than for 'educational reasons.' This of course implied that there was an easy means of separating the two.[95] As noted earlier, the Conservative Party elite was in fact opening itself up more and more to the comprehensive idea under the heading of practical-sounding 'experiments.'

All the while, the Conservative Party's Parliamentary Education Committee, which comprised backbench MPs, was now becoming increasingly ready to listen to pro-comprehensive arguments from outside experts. The Committee was chaired by Gilbert Longden, the MP for South West Hertfordshire, and included members such as James Pitman and John Maitland, whose pragmatic tendencies have been noted earlier, as well as Enoch Powell. On 23 June 1958 they were addressed by R.G.K. Hickman, the Assistant Secretary to the Education Department of the National Union of Teachers. In his remarks to the Committee, Hickman sought to minimize the difficulties regarding comprehensive schools' potentially huge size, claiming that the problems of comprehensive schools lay mostly in terms of their receiving inadequate staffing.

Hickman then informed the Committee that the tripartite system had 'clearly served its turn,' and that he was in favour of 'bilateral' schools providing technical education, in contrast to it being provided in separate technical schools.[96] (This of course was already happening.) However, 'bilateralism' was in fact the first step in the merging tendency for the different types of education. All the while, Hickman played down recent information about comprehensive schools in the United States, where reports of their inferior standards had caused anxiety. It was surely significant that the Conservatives' Parliamentary Education Committee appeared receptive towards those who believed that the future lay with bilateral and comprehensive school arrangements.

In June 1958, the Labour Party's policy statement on education, entitled *Learning to Live*, was published. This document, which would later be submitted to the Party's annual conference in October, confirmed that the next Labour government would 'require' local education authorities to prepare secondary education development plans that adopted the comprehensive principle 'with all reasonable speed.'[97] Yet, in spite of what many in the Conservative Party had feared, it also revealed that upon gaining office they would do nothing to threaten the public schools. They were not in favour of the state taking over their running, nor did they intend a policy of ensuring a significant percentage of places for local authority pupils as the Fleming Plan had envisaged fourteen years before. They defended their change of heart on the grounds of the excessive cost involved, as well as the practical difficulties of selecting the required state pupils to take up places. As it stated:

> Labour concludes that at present no scheme for 'taking over' or 'democratising' the public schools shows sufficient merits to justify the large diversion of public money that would be involved.[98]

Instead, their vague conclusion was simply that under the comprehensive system the maintained schools would be firstly improved greatly, and that measures to tackle the independent schools could possibly be taken up again at some stage in the future. The sheer irony, and the resulting sense of opportunity, was certainly not lost on the Conservatives' Parliamentary Education Committee.

At its meeting on 7 July, with Gilbert Longden in the chair and Edward Boyle as Parliamentary Secretary in attendance, Lloyd was by now noticeably wavering on defending selection for the maintained sector, in spite of his public utterances that officially defended grammar schools. From the outset of the meeting, he wanted to know 'whether we were right to make a major issue of defending them politically' and how much of a 'liability' the Party undertook by 'standing out in favour of selection.'[99]

Yet in spite of Lloyd's lukewarm stance, many of the others present in fact contradicted the increasing fatalism displayed by Lloyd and Edward Boyle by relating their own more positive experiences with selection in their constituencies. Richard Hornby claimed that the 11 plus was less of an issue due to the greater prestige of the secondary modern schools and the improved quality of their buildings. He felt that most people were in fact satisfied with how the selective system was applied. However, Hornby emphasized that the question of later transfer remained important. In addition, Tom Iremonger the MP for Ilford North considered it 'vital' for the Party to set out to be champions of the grammar school, and warned that one bad case of a lack of flexibility in transfer could be 'very damaging.'[100] Others present at the meeting stated that it was in fact insufficient grammar school places that were arousing parental indignation in certain quarters, so that it was crucial that transfer should be easier and on a larger scale. The general sentiment from the Committee therefore was in fact fairly hopeful about the system but felt that it needed to be strengthened, particularly in terms of added flexibility and ease of transfer. Even Lloyd then agreed that the Government should take more of an active part in transfer policy as it was 'politically important.'[101]

Lloyd therefore appeared to accept the mainly upbeat reports of those present, stating that the Labour Party's threat had 'given us a strong position as the champions of the grammar schools.' However, despite what had been said he thought nevertheless that 'we must try to make selection at 11 plus both less unpopular and more efficient.'[102] And as we have already seen, his Parliamentary Secretary Boyle had already been critical and indeed opposed to the examination at 11, and also towards selection at 11 generally.

The Committee members generally agreed that the age of 11 was premature for selection and far from ideal. Nevertheless, it was decided that it should be publicly defended by arguing that it was necessary to allow sufficient time for secondary education afterwards. Indeed, Boyle claimed that the postponement of selection in maintained schools until even age 12 would militate against the reduction of primary school classes and the ensuring of four years of secondary education. This underlined, of course, the essentially 'piece-meal' process by which the maintained secondary system had developed over recent decades.

Lloyd seemed to think that secondary modern schools having new buildings were crucial to their future prestige. Meanwhile, the Chairman Gilbert Longden, while claiming to have faith in secondary moderns, suggested they 'drop' the name 'secondary modern' from their titles in order to boost their public esteem.[103] This type of condescension was hardly a vote of confidence on their part for the secondary modern schools' future. The key question to ask from these episodes is whether Lloyd privately had much faith in their future even at this stage.

In stark contrast to the scarce number of committee members at the discussion concerning the maintained schools' future, the meeting held by the Conservatives' Parliamentary Committee the following week on 14 July for the Headmaster of Eton Robert Birley to discuss the future of the public schools was packed. The attendees included both Kenneth Pickthorn and Dennis Vosper, who had both been former Parliamentary Secretaries to the Minister of Education. The meeting was taking place in an atmosphere of relief, given the Labour Party's recently published policy statement that they would tolerate the public schools when next in office.

Birley called the Labour Party's recent statement 'extraordinary.' As he noted, it meant the public schools would be 'reprieved,' while at the same time it carried the 'proposed extinction' of the public schools' greatest rivals, the grammar schools. Nevertheless, he told the assembled throng (many of whom were former pupils at his school) it would be unfortunate if they were 'lulled into a false sense of security.'[104] He remained cautious, being concerned that fringe elements in the Labour Party would still succeed in agitating for a radical policy instead of the position outlined in *Learning to Live*. In particular, he mentioned the Victory for Socialism group's recent publication *Equality in Education*, which had called for the public schools' total integration. Birley was reluctant to put forward a policy merely, as he put it, as a 'sop to Cerberus.' However, he thought that the Conservative government should adopt a policy that would enable the public schools to better serve the society, otherwise they were in danger of becoming an 'anachronism.' He therefore wanted the Conservative government to embark upon a constructive scheme to broaden their social basis for admission. This would 'serve the interests' of the public schools and thus safeguard their long-term future survival.[105]

Birley's recommendation was that the government make the public schools accessible to pupils from a wider social background by subsidizing 'assisted places' in them, as opposed to making direct subvention to the schools themselves. (Tellingly, Birley regarded the idea of a tax concession in regard to public school fees as politically impossible.) In addition, Birley considered that it would be 'fatal' for the independence of the public schools if they became in any way maintained or aided.[106]

In fact, Birley could see an optimistic future for the public schools and clearly thought such pragmatic action would lead to a greater degree of security for them in the long term. After all, as he told one of the assembled members, while it was conceivable that there might be a shift of opinion by middle-income parents leading towards greater use of the state education system in the future, as had occurred with the National Health Service, he could see little signs of this at present. On the contrary, it seemed more likely to Birley that the 'wholesale' comprehensive type of secondary education advocated by the Labour Party, in the words of the minute, 'insofar as it deprived them of the grammar schools as an alternative, would mean that more, not fewer, middle-income parents would aspire to send their children to Public Schools.'[107] It appears that Birley could clearly foresee where developments would lead in the future. In regard to his proposals, Birley affirmed that the Governing Bodies Association representing the public schools, of which he was the head, would give 'sympathetic attention' to any positive Conservative proposals for their future. A canny operator and strategist was thus at work.[108] Yet like his predecessors, Lloyd considered it politically wise to defer consideration of any proposals in relation to the public schools that involved government assistance. The Home Affairs Committee agreed with him.

A 'drive' in state education

On 14 July 1958, the very same day as Birley's meeting with the Education Committee, a Cabinet memorandum for a 'drive' in education intended for the maintained schools was published for its perusal. Introducing it, Lloyd argued that there would be major political benefits in a new five-year building programme for maintained schools. It would involve improving or replacing out-of-date secondary schools, starting with grammar and technical schools, and then the secondary moderns. Through enacting this building policy, according to Lloyd, 'we can do so without spending much more money than will be spent simply to continue existing policies.' As a result, 'the general public will give us credit.'[109]

The intended five-year programme was to cover the period from 1960 to 1965 with the intention that the total annual expenditure of the local education authorities in England and Wales would rise substantially. To Lloyd, whose concern appeared primarily to showcase the Conservatives' spending and expansionary policies, it was 'the best possible corrective' to the suspicion that the Conservative government was not interested in the maintained system of education.[110]

It was claimed that the new programme would offer scope for 'local initiative and experiment,' as well as being instrumental in raising the quality of all secondary schools. Lloyd added tellingly:

> We should thus take the sting out of the 11 plus examination and, by offering opportunities rather than by compulsion, we should reconcile national need with individual choice and achievement.[111]

Thus with such banalities did Lloyd introduce his policy. Incredibly, he added with almost stunning complacency how meanwhile, 'the Labour Party's policy of "comprehensive schools for all" is never likely to be widely accepted, quite apart from other objections to it.' Through somewhat general polices involving major teacher recruitment, with the expansion of teacher training colleges and a five-year school building policy, the government would improve all secondary schools and pupils would apparently be more likely to attend schools that would be 'suitable' to them. The ostensible aim, as Lloyd put it, was to make a reality of secondary education for all within the quickest possible time.[112] Thus, it was felt that this 'moderate' approach would win the Conservative government future electoral benefits.

At the Cabinet meeting on 24 July, with no less than Butler, Hailsham and Eccles all present, there was general agreement with the course that Lloyd was taking towards greater 'social investment.' Revealingly, Lloyd remarked as part of his justification for his policy that the majority of secondary modern schools were in many respects 'little better' than the old-style elementary school.[113] The current criticisms of the secondary modern school would be allayed, in his view, if the secondary modern school developed on more 'progressive' lines, leading to a greater number of pupils voluntarily staying on beyond the school leaving age. Nothing, however, was mentioned at the Cabinet meeting about the need to defend the existing selective system itself, particularly the grammar schools.

Over the summer of 1958, while the White Paper for the 'drive' in education was being formulated, Lloyd's Parliamentary Secretary Edward Boyle made a number of visits to Newport, where the council was considering comprehensive developments that potentially threatened the established grammar schools there. As a result of this intervention, the Newport local education authority ultimately had to submit a revised plan that did not affect notable selective schools such as the Newport High schools and St Julian's. The revised plan, which encompassed two new comprehensive schools but did not now include the established grammars within it, was then allowed to proceed in October. Nevertheless, there was much protest by the Council's education committee as a result of its plans for a full comprehensive scheme being thwarted. It thus reserved the right, while accepting this 'interim' scheme, to consider the matter further.[114]

On 31 July, Boyle was then forced to make an embarrassing admission when answering questions in the House of Commons. He admitted that the proportion of thirteen-year-old pupils attending grammar schools or 'similar courses' in other secondary schools excluding comprehensives had in fact decreased from 20.9 per cent in 1953 to 20.3 per cent in 1957. In answer to particular questions from the Labour MP Stephen Swingler concerning the proportions for Newcastle under Lyme, the percentage had in fact declined from 19.5 per cent in 1954 to 15.4 per cent in 1958.[115] This represented a key failure by the Conservative Government in terms of increasing the proportions in local areas that badly needed them if the political attacks against grammar schools were to be withstood.

Boyle could only feebly claim that they had adjusted building programmes to help those local authorities that were most short, notably Nottingham and Salford. He added, 'I believe that in general in recent years there has been a great improvement in the average level over the country.'[116] In reality, very little had actually been done in this regard. Overall, the combination of the increased number of secondary school pupils that had been caused by the rise of the birth-rate in the post-war years, along with the insufficient provision of corresponding extra grammar school places to meet this, had served to depress the overall grammar school proportion. Instead, the burden of grammar school-type pupils was increasingly being shifted onto the secondary modern schools' 'advanced courses'.[117]

Boyle was questioned further about the number of grammar schools that had been joined with other schools since the war. Boyle revealed that fifty-five grammar schools had been amalgamated with schools of other types by January 1958. In answer to further questions from the MP for Dorset North Colonel Richard Glyn, he revealed that three more were being amalgamated in the Dorset area, affecting Bridport, Gillingham and Beaminster. All of these proposals, Boyle claimed, would be 'considered carefully on their educational merits,' in contrast to what he termed the 'preconceived doctrine' of the Labour opposition on comprehensive schools.[118] The Conservatives' education spokesman was increasingly using the rhetorical tactic of depicting a great contrast between the Labour opposition's approach to comprehensives and their own. In reality, it was only a matter of degree.

Meanwhile, the Conservatives' 1958 policy statement *Onward in Freedom* showed the extent to which their tone was shifting and sliding on the issue. Their section on education stated that experiments in school structure were to be 'followed with interest.' Any degree of criticism was merely expressed by adding that 'we believe it would be utter folly to put all our eggs in one comprehensive basket, or to mis-shape education in order to re-shape society.'[119] These banalities camouflaged the fact that the goal-posts within their position were now moving.

At the Labour Party Conference in Scarborough in October, the Party's policy statement on education, entitled *Learning to Live*, was adopted by the delegates by 5,176,000 votes to 1,336,000. (However, a composite resolution by the MP Fred Peart that called for the abolition of fee paying and the 'integration' of all independent schools into the maintained system in turn produced 3,067,000 votes against *Learning to Live*, with 3,544,000 remaining in favour.) As before, arguments emphasizing practicality and cost were produced against any policy of immediate abolition of the public schools.[120] From observing these events, the public schools strategists' relief must have been palpable. Birley's prediction was coming true.

The following week, the Conservatives held their own Party Conference at Blackpool. In the debate on education, Donald Moore, the Chairman of the National

Advisory Committee of the Conservative and Unionist Teachers' Association, which was disproportionately made up of grammar and technical school teachers, called on the Party to 'resist the attack on the grammar schools.' Of the fifty-five comprehensive schools that had been approved in the country, with twenty having originated under a Conservative government, he felt that 'surely that is experiment enough.'[121] In addition, he emphasized the socialist and egalitarian intentions lying behind the idea of the comprehensive school.

Furthermore, Wickham Partridge, also of the National Advisory Committee of the CTA, called for more to be done:

> We must ask the Minister to look at the anomalies in the widely different percentages of grammar school places provided by different local authorities, to see if he cannot persuade the low percentage authorities to build a few more proper grammar schools.[122]

Those assembled, he reminded them, should not forget that the 11 plus examination was the poor man's 'Open Sesame' to the grammar schools and the university.[123]

Another delegate, Councillor Martin Henry of Accrington, while more critical of the system, echoed the point that the Party could not plausibly claim to represent equality of opportunity while these wide discrepancies of grammar school provision between different local areas still existed. The comprehensive school, he continued, was a 'telling weapon' in the socialist armoury as part of the exploitation of public concern and dissatisfaction at the alarming anomalies existing throughout the country.[124] It was thus imperative that in order to justify the tripartite system, that the necessary places were found in grammar schools. The message to Lloyd was obvious.

Nevertheless, other types of perspective were strongly expressed as well. In particular, Lady Lewisham of Lewisham West, who would later be known as Raine Spencer, claimed that the secondary modern schools were suffering, partly through under-funding, but also because they had 'the cream' taken away from them by the selective process. This was a view that of course militated against further transfer and inevitably saw the secondary modern in the academic shadow of the grammar school. Secondary moderns, she argued, also required more graduate teachers.[125] Clearly, the views held within the Conservative Party continued to be somewhat mixed in this respect.

However, Lloyd's conference speech did not address any of these concerns. As the *Education* journal later reported it, 'if Mr Partridge and others like him expected the Minister to explore or even to touch on the bread and butter issues they raised, they waited in vain.'[126] Instead, Lloyd waxed vaguely about the new technological age, and Britain's need for more technicians, engineers and 'highly qualified men.' There was very little that was actually specific. While he referred to grammar schools as 'one of our great democratic institutions,' Lloyd emphasized more secondary modern children staying on to take the GCE, a matter of 'very great importance.' It was an open question, he claimed, as to whether it was better for a particular child to be in the lower forms of a grammar school or in the top forms of a good secondary modern. However, this latter position, in his view, would ideally grow. This, he continued, was what would ideally be found in areas with successful secondary modern schools. As a result, the whole subject of 11 plus selection would become 'almost a side issue.'[127] Thus, the 'good' secondary modern school, according to Lloyd, was intrinsically bound up with providing academic courses at GCE 'O' level.

He confirmed his approval of local authorities embarking upon experiments, welcoming in particular the recent ones in Reading and Southampton. In these more compact towns and cities, secondary moderns were coming together with each specializing in certain academic areas. The modern schools undergoing these experiments were praised by Lloyd as reaching a very high 'and indeed a grammar school standard.'

Moreover, Lloyd referred to the recent Leicestershire experiment, in which entry to the grammar school simply depended upon parents deciding to let their child stay on at school until 16, in distinctly favourable terms. He claimed that it gave teachers and parents more time 'to make up their minds' about the particular qualities of the children. However, this experiment of course did not measure objective measurement of pupils' actual abilities, but rather parental aspiration. The process was subjective, and inevitably hinged on social and cultural factors. Regarding comprehensive schools, Lloyd described having seen 'some very, very fine schools,' while noting potential problems with excessive size in some cases. He continued to emphasize their flexible approach in contrast with what he described as the Labour Party's dogmatism on the issue. It was not until the end of the speech that Lloyd then announced his new Five Year Plan for the building of more and better quality schools with the emphasis to be upon secondary modern school building.[128]

Meanwhile, educational opinion continued to shift among those in influential circles. In the journal *Education*, the official organ of the Association of Education Committees, its general secretary William Alexander was suggesting that the 'party political controversy on this subject could with advantage be dropped.' His view proposed pragmatic acceptance and a purely administrative approach, with local authorities' flexible arrangements to be supported by the government. To Alexander, the issue of secondary school type should be left for each LEA to work out for itself, with the solution considered particular to each authority. The local education authority would therefore tackle the problem of the secondary schools, 'in the way which it thinks will be most acceptable to the parents and best for the children.' All that was important, in this notably weaselling spirit, was to simply enable all the secondary schools to be 'good schools.' There was a distinct whiff of wanting to opt out of any hard debate and to fudge the issue.

For Alexander asserted that:

> *To achieve these ends there is a limit beyond which selection for grammar schools should not be allowed to go since it must adversely affect the possibilities of the development of the modern school.*
>
> (my emphasis)

The 'common sense of this problem,' according to Alexander, was simply to emphasize the adequate supply of decent buildings and appropriately trained teachers.[129] Thus, this supposedly apolitical approach enveloped itself in a deliberate naivete about the plainly political designs of many local education authorities. The educational establishment's 'moderate' approach thus neutralized the arguments of those opposing comprehensive schemes outright and effectively ripped the ground from under their feet. And it was a road that Lloyd was of course already set upon. While not actively in favour of comprehensives becoming the norm in the future, it effectively counselled a lack of opposition to their advance. Indeed, this type of pragmatism and opacity sought to effectively slough off all the fundamental issues at stake and reduce them to the need for the adequate supply of buildings and money.

Other well-connected figures in the education world outside the Conservative Party were also critical of secondary modern schools for political purposes during this key period. In 1958, Professor Harold Dent, the editor of the *Times Educational Supplement*, published a notable study of the development of the secondary modern school between 1945 and 1957. Dedicating it in fatalistic spirit, 'to all the secondary modern schools that tried,' it effectively, while purporting to be balanced, undermined the secondary modern school through a constant emphasis on its difficulties.[130] Dent acknowledged that many secondary modern schools had been creative and inventive in their provision of courses for their pupils. Yet under the pretext of supposed concern, Dent argued that there was now a vast gulf between those secondary moderns providing GCE 'O' level courses and those that did not. By 1956, almost 17 per cent of secondary modern schools were entering pupils for the GCE, with a rapid growth of this trend during the mid-1950s. As a result, he felt that they would inevitably become split into GCE and non-GCE secondary moderns. In addition, he continually emphasized the disappointment felt by a vocal minority of parents whose children had not gained grammar school places.

Dent's central claim was that the secondary moderns still lacked an overall purpose. Yet while appearing at first to be supportive of the concept of the modern school, Dent implied throughout that not enough was being expected academically of their pupils beyond advanced elementary work. He emphasized that one of the 'crying needs' of the secondary modern was to have 'recognized avenues of progression' from school to further education.[131] Yet in spite of this and somewhat suspiciously, he claimed that Eccles' decision not to introduce further external examinations for secondary modern schools had been the right one. In fact, Dent was a firm believer in constantly exploring the academic capacity of children of low or modest ability, suggesting priorities that tended towards levelling. Significantly, he felt that none of these disadvantages occurred with bilateral, multilateral and comprehensive schools.[132] Underneath it all, Dent did not want to buttress the secondary modern school as it stood. And inevitably, given his position, these opinions carried significant weight. Such sentiments from influential figures put doubts into the minds of both the intelligentsia and the public about the secondary modern.

The White Paper

Within this atmosphere, the Conservative Government's White Paper was finally published in December 1958. As expected, it symbolized the Government's retreat from the hard questions with its notable meandering and evasion throughout. In all, the 'merging' tendency between the different types of education was to be encouraged even more. It of course wholeheartedly supported the idea of as many secondary modern pupils staying on beyond the school leaving age as possible. In particular, it praised the fact that there had been a large increase in the number of pupils competing successfully in the examinations for the GCE examination at 'O' and 'A' level. Yet in doing so, it inevitably found deep fault with the current system in place:

> The fact is that there are too many children of approximately equal ability who are receiving their secondary education in schools that differ widely both in quality and in the range of courses they are able to provide.[133]

These sentiments echoed those of figures such as Dent. The selective system was portrayed as being unjust in relation to borderline pupils and that pupils were not receiving sufficiently 'good opportunities' in academic terms that they deserved. For this reason, a sizeable proportion of the secondary modern schools were portrayed as not performing their function adequately.

Going further than Conservative governments had hitherto, comprehensive experiments were to be regarded as having a substantial case in country districts where the population was correspondingly sparse. Comprehensive schools were also considered to be suitable in areas of extensive new housing, 'with no existing schools with a "well established tradition" of grammar and technical or modern schools.'[134] (This notion of 'well established tradition,' however, gave a large scope for flexibility of definition.) By the same token, comprehensive schemes were deemed unacceptable when a local authority sought to bring an existing grammar school with 'a long and distinguished history' to an end in order that a new comprehensive could monopolize the brighter pupils in the area.

Within this tentative approach, it could only half-heartedly defend those local authorities that continued to maintain a straightforward distinction between pupils' capacities without embarking on educational experiments. In a key note of defensiveness, which almost begged the suggestion in advance, it added that:

> it would be entirely wrong to abandon the grammar schools, of whose achievements in educating the ablest of our children and in providing the nation with increasing numbers of highly trained citizens, there can be no doubt.[135]

The White Paper confirmed its support for existing tendencies, such as advanced technical courses being provided in grammar schools alongside 'more traditional courses.' In addition, there was further support for secondary moderns developing academic 'specialisms.'

On the all-important question of transfer, it stated that there should be arrangements for a pupil who would obviously progress better in another type of school to transfer as early as possible. Nevertheless, it added:

> ...but such transfers can never be anything but exceptions to the normal rule and there must be –and be seen to be – opportunities in all the secondary schools, and not just in the grammar and technical schools, for boys and girls to go forward to the limits of their capacity.[136]

Continuing in these vague and open-ended terms, it stated that:

> *there must be full recognition of the fact that, where separate grammar and modern schools exist, there will be an overlap in the capacity of the pupils and that therefore the courses offered must overlap also.*[137]

(my emphasis)

In order to rectify the '11 plus problem,' the merging tendency between the grammar and modern schools was being increased further.

The White Paper further claimed in this unspecific manner that the schools would avoid the two opposing errors that each must do 'everything,' and that each type of schools 'must have a fixed and self-contained territory in to which no other must enter.' Different needs were to be met in different ways, with 'ample opportunity for healthy development between these two extremes.'[138] It was all to be noted for its studied opacity and fudge.

The Government's actual policy in practical terms was a continuous building programme for primary and secondary schools covering the five years from 1960/1 to 1964/5 that aimed to get £300 million worth of projects started within that period. In addition to the programme of capital expenditure, there was to be a marked increase in annual expenditure to allow for a substantial increase in the number of teachers. All secondary school buildings were to be brought up to modern standards, with the issue of building quality seemingly regarded as more important than anything else. Revealing its central emphasis at the end, it claimed for young people and their parents that:

> As the plan takes shape, they will certainly discover that the school to which a boy goes at the age of 11 need not finally determine the educational goal which he will be able to reach.[139]

This of course effectively conceded that this was the case at the present time.

The minutes of the Cabinet meeting a few weeks earlier on 25 November reveal the level of concern felt by the Cabinet about paragraphs in an earlier draft of the White Paper concerning comprehensive schools on the eve of publication. There had been some degree of consternation about the potential 'political embarrassment' caused by them. However, as the minutes also reveal, it was felt that the balance of advantage lay in keeping them in, albeit in a redrafted form. The published version would be noticeably more circumspect about the case for rural comprehensives and those within areas of new housing. Macmillan emphasized the need for publicity, given the 'moderate' terms in which the White Paper had been drafted and the 'empirical' approach that they felt had been adopted.[140]

However, the American academic Max Eckstein, having analysed the White Paper, could not have put it better:

> In a somewhat contradictory fashion, there are signs ... of a movement towards unilateralism. If ones notes the supremacy of the academic standard above all,

the avoidance of discussion of the technical school, the widespread interest in the Leicestershire experiment, a trend is revealed which may be highly significant.

As he further noticed, the White Paper stated priorities for improving physical conditions, 'while at the same time it avoids the broader social and philosophical problems.'[141]

As 1958 ended, it was already becoming clear that the White Paper policy would not have the desired effects that Lloyd and others claimed for it. Indeed, as Lloyd admitted to Macmillan at this time, the actual expansion of the schools was not intended to be as great as they were publicly making out. Expansion was in fact to be at only a 20 per cent rate of increase and kept under control. Essentially, the White Paper was urging the continuation of existing policies, albeit at a somewhat quicker rate. Lloyd confidently prophesized to Macmillan, 'A good deal is therefore already going on which will be readily accepted by the general public as covered by the White Paper umbrella.'[142] But the evasions and ambiguity contained within the White Paper would have far-reaching consequences. This soft-pedalling approach by the Conservative Party would soon be exposed for its lack of principle. And events would soon begin to spin out of their control.

This chapter has shown how the tendencies of thought noted earlier within the Ministry of Education were replicated by the Conservative governments of the 1950s. Administrative convenience and pragmatism, rather than educational principle, were at the forefront. As the decade wore on, it became apparent that the issue of secondary school reorganization, including comprehensive 'experiments,' was increasingly to be treated as matters for local authorities, rather than central government being fully involved. This characteristic of viewing maintained secondary schooling in terms of political expediency rather than overarching vision was particularly displayed by the education ministers David Eccles and Geoffrey Lloyd. There was thought to be short-term political benefit gained by avoiding the core task of strengthening the process of selection by ability. Instead, a 'merging policy' was undertaken in relation to grammar, secondary modern and technical schools. Allowances for comprehensive schools in certain local cases opened the door for their future increase in numbers. Finally, the publication of the 1958 White Paper embodied the long-standing Conservative party desire of avoiding the issue becoming 'party-political' by evading key philosophical questions surrounding selection versus egalitarianism.

3

Acceleration into destruction 1959–64

The third chapter shows how the White Paper policy unravelled in the latter stages of Conservative government in the late 1950s and early 1960s. The Conservatives' approach led in fact to local authorities refurbishing plans for comprehensive schemes as well as seeking to undermine selection at all ages. It thus shows how the Conservatives inadvertently laid the groundwork for the Labour Party's ultimate assault on selection when they took office in 1964. A clear and unambiguous line on what was ideal was never firmly expressed in the Conservative government's policy. The chapter concludes by considering key examples of how educational historians have not explored these ambiguities in the Conservative government's approach towards selection during this crucial period.

A line of least resistance

In spite of the White Paper's optimistic rhetoric, by late 1958 the core issue of the grammar and secondary modern schools' future was being fudged. Regardless of the pressure of certain Conservative backbenchers such as Paul Williams for Sunderland South, who urged Lloyd at the Parliamentary education committee meeting on 8 December to put a stop to further comprehensive school experiments until the present ones had been assessed, no straightforward answer was given. Instead, Lloyd was now noticeably keen to stress that the Minister's powers in regard to intervention in local education authorities' schemes were limited. His powers, he emphasized, were essentially confined to school closures and cases of new building.

He claimed to those who were representing constituencies in the North East, where grammar school provision was particularly low, that he was adopting a 'positive approach'.[1] Opportunities for transfer to grammar schools would be made for those who had successfully completed secondary modern school 'careers', which meant delaying any transfer in most cases until the age of 15 or 16. Tellingly, Lloyd stated that the tripartite system had been found 'wanting' and was 'out of favour' with the educationists. He now looked for a new parity of esteem between the grammar schools and the 'High' Schools, which he felt the modern schools would now become. Furthermore, Lloyd felt that the decision to raise the amount devoted to school building would rebound to the Conservatives' credit at the General Election after next.[2]

The Prime Minister Harold Macmillan himself expressed sentiments that sought to bolster the Government's position. In a speech at Newcastle Upon Tyne on 19 January he described how too many children in secondary modern schools were receiving a 'second best education,' and that 'in too many places, that is at the moment true.'[3] The White Paper plans would change all this, he claimed, and it would be much less the case in future.

The feeling within the Ministry of Education, as the Private Secretary to Lloyd put it in private correspondence to the Prime Minister's Private Secretary at this time, was that Britain would now be taking the education of the 'average child' seriously, as the Americans had with their High School system.[4] Yet this was happening, ironically enough, against a background where the Americans were increasingly concerned that their largely non-selective high school system did not cater sufficiently for the exceptional pupil.

Both Lloyd and Boyle were clearly adopting the strategy of emphasizing local education authorities' freedom to organize education as they saw fit. The role of the Minister, the Department and their potential scope for intervention in local authorities' schemes was increasingly downplayed as being out of their hands. Their predecessor Lord Hailsham was ably assisting at this time by increasingly emphasizing the Minister's role in public comments as one of 'functus officio,' as he would put it.[5] According to this portrayal, the Minister of Education was to merely perform his limited statutory duty and had no remit that would enable him to intervene.

Edward Boyle symbolized this approach. In a speech at Gillingham in Dorset on 14 January, he defended the decision to merge the small grammar and secondary modern schools there to form a comprehensive. Yet the controversy surrounding this key decision affecting a Conservative-run local area soon reared itself. A week later on 21 January the MP for the area, Colonel Richard Glyn, angrily wrote to Lloyd claiming that his Department's decisions bore no relation to the approach outlined in the White Paper's section on comprehensive schools. He protested that the result of the Gillingham decision would mean that parents in the area would now be deprived of choice between the grammar and the secondary modern school there. While Glyn 'entirely' upheld the principles outlined in the White Paper, 'experience shows that these bear no relation to the way in which your Department is actually operating.' Furthermore, in regard to the forthcoming debate taking place on the White Paper, he added that:

> This conflicts so utterly with paragraph 16 of your White Paper that, with the knowledge of what you have actually approved, I cannot listen to what I think you are going to say in the debate.

He therefore demanded to know, and partly also, as he put it sardonically to Lloyd, to 'inform yourself,' of the number of grammar schools that had been merged into comprehensive schools in this way since the Conservatives had taken office in 1951.[6]

It was only after another letter to Lloyd and two further ones to Edward Boyle that Glyn finally received a reply that answered his enquiries. In a letter dated 10 February, Boyle revealed to Glyn that fifty-four grammar schools had either been merged into comprehensives and similar schools or been closed by February 1959. In addition, there were three more proposals at this time, of Gillingham and Lyme Regis in Dorset, and one case in the West Riding, that had been approved but not yet carried out. Only two proposals of this kind had in fact been refused.

In his reply, Boyle reiterated the distinction that the Conservative government was making between country areas with scattered populations compared with urban areas of dense population as to their suitability for comprehensives. He claimed that in the case of Gillingham, the grammar school had effectively been a 'bilateral' school on account of the rural area it was situated in. According to Boyle, it had therefore contained 'a considerable number of children who would not have got a grammar school place in many other parts of the country'.[7] By splitting hairs in this way, Boyle thus rationalized the decision that had been taken.

But tensions were not just being aroused among Conservative supporters in the South West. Also at this time, Herbert Lee, the Chief Agent for the Bradford Conservative Association, wrote to William Urton at Conservative Central Office informing him of the mood amongst Conservative members on Bradford City Council's Labour dominated education committee. Many were now threatening to resign as a result of what they considered to be Lloyd's vacillating approach that was undermining them in their efforts to oppose the city council's plans for comprehensive schools in the city. Instead, they claimed that the Minister was 'following the socialist line'.

The plan involved the extension of four existing secondary modern schools carrying a five form entry to form 4 (10 form entry) comprehensives. Furthermore, three new grammar-technical 'bilateral' schools were apparently being planned as the first instalments of comprehensive schools. All of these proposals came within the Minister's remit to intervene under the 1944 Act. Two Conservative Members of Parliament, William Taylor and Arthur Tiley of Bradford North and West, were now seeking a meeting with the Minister. As Lee further pointed out:

> They are aware, of course, that a public denunciation of the Minister could be detrimental to the Party's interests at this time, but there is no telling when the storm could break … If he persists in this attitude then I feel that serious consequences could follow.[8]

Lee also informed Urton that the Conservative committee members felt that ultimately, given their dissatisfaction with Lloyd and his Ministry officials, 'the whole case should go to the Prime Minister'.[9]

Lee, in his turn, handed the letter on to Michael Fraser at the Conservative Research Department for his advice on how to reply. For his part, Fraser, while sympathetic to their 'understandable' feelings, was nevertheless keen to dampen the issue down. He instructed Lee to reply that it would come within the Minister's scope for decision, and that 'it is far from being a foregone conclusion that the Socialists would get their way'.[10] According to Fraser, both Taylor and Tiley had met Boyle at the Ministry on 4th February. Urton then dutifully copied out Fraser's diplomatic reply to Urton word for word and sent it off.

But this was still not enough for Lee, who wrote back to Urton on 14 February. He revealed that the Chairman of Bradford's Labour-dominated Education Committee had claimed that Lloyd's Ministry of Education officials had already approved the intended building programmes in principle. In addition, those Ministry officials had been fully aware that the three new bilateral schools were intended to be the first instalments of comprehensives. And all the while, the socialists on the Education Committee had been claiming that the programme was in line with the Conservative government's recent White Paper. Those on the left were clearly exploiting the White Paper's vague terms in order to aid their moves towards comprehensive schemes.

Further emphasizing the problems caused by the White Paper's lack of clarity, Lee argued that the areas affected by the proposed comprehensive developments did not fall within the White Paper's description. Therefore, contrary to what Fraser had told Urton, Bradford City Council was in fact already making formal proposals to the Minister about their plans.[11] Ironically, in spite of Lloyd and the Ministry officials' hope that the White Paper would submerge the comprehensive issue, it was in fact now rebounding on them. Certain local councils were deliberately interpreting the White Paper in ways that suited themselves.

There was now a growing feeling among backbench Conservative MPs that the Minister was not treating these local secondary school proposals sufficiently rigorously. Yet to further emphasize the gulf in perspective between different strands of the Party, Lord Hailsham, now Lord President of the Council, was quoted in the Lords as stating that there ought to be no overriding of local education authorities unless it could be shown that they had forgotten the interests of the children and teachers in the interests of 'political dogma'. When defined like this, the instances for when the Minister was required to intervene remained suitably vague as well as rare. Hailsham was further quoted as saying that the comprehensive school had an honoured place within the educational system, and that there would be 'many' areas where it would be best.[12]

On 8 March, Macmillan sent a minute to Lloyd on the situation regarding comprehensive schools, noting that he had heard 'sounds of disquiet' on the issue.[13] In Lloyd's reply, he claimed that he had been able to reduce the tension, while at the same time being forced to admit that the White Paper policy was causing confusion. While it had heightened local interest, he told Macmillan, some Labour councils were clearly 'refurbishing' long-standing plans to organize comprehensive schools in their areas. 'And some of them have undoubtedly been giving the impression locally that I had already approved these plans.'

He then noted the recent controversy in Gillingham, but airily claimed to Macmillan that it was opposed by certain local interests more because it disturbed the status quo than from 'any real understanding of the issues involved.' While he stated that he would seek to reassure people concerning his ministerial powers under the 1944 Act and his opposition to 'sweeping' socialist plans, nevertheless, he wanted to 'steer them away from adopting a position which might make our education policy seem as doctrinaire in one way as the Labour policy is in another.'[14] Such 'moderate' sentiments, however, were increasingly satisfying no-one.

This irresolute approach was borne out by the school building plans that Lloyd was agreeing to during this time. In spite of the controversy that had occurred at Gillingham, Lloyd was set on more proposals of this kind that would establish additional rural comprehensive and bilateral schools for 1961 and 1962. And this was despite the fact these cases usually involved a grammar school being submerged in the process. New comprehensive proposals included the case of Romford in Essex in which the proposed school, having originally been approved as a grammar, was now to open as a comprehensive without the Minister's approval.[15]

Many of the proposals, which often affected the older parts of towns, clearly went beyond the White Paper's terms of suitability. But Ministry of Education officials were viewing these matters largely in terms of practical organization. They felt the new proposals would shore up secondary school provision in certain areas in the name of administrative convenience. The Ministry, in this ultra-pragmatic spirit, was set on this path. In the words of one official:

> Some of these proposals might, with a mere shift of emphasis, turn out to be in effect proposals for large and properly ambitious modern schools.[16]

The Ministry was therefore largely resolved on an inevitable comprehensive path. Private minutes reveal however that Boyle was concerned about one of the proposals at Chipping Campden in Gloucestershire that involved a rural bilateral scheme similar to the one at Gillingham. Boyle was worried about the controversy in Dorset repeating itself, warning an official of the strong local feeling and cautioning that 'we must walk warily if we are to avoid another Gillingham.'[17] Difficult and controversial cases were to be handled carefully, and referred to Boyle so that he could 'prepare the ground' with MPs and others concerned over difficult cases in their constituencies.[18] There was a sense of carefully contriving to push it all through. It is clear that more were planned for implementation after the General Election later in 1959.

Indeed on 8 October, the Conservative Party won a landslide general election victory, aided by a 'give-away' budget from the Chancellor Derick Heathcoat Amory. The government now held a majority of over a hundred. David Eccles was returned to the post of Minister of Education for a second time on 14 October and would remain for another three years, while Boyle returned to the Treasury as financial secretary, with Kenneth Thompson replacing him as parliamentary secretary to the Minister.

A reluctance to confront

From early on in his second period as Minister, Eccles was put under increasing pressure to accept the findings of a major report by the Central Advisory Council for education under the chairmanship of Sir Geoffrey Crowther. The report focused on the education of pupils of average and below-average ability between the ages of 15 and 18. It reaffirmed the principle of compulsory full-time education up to the age of 16 as well as part-time education up to 18 for those not at school. The Chancellor Heathcoat Amory balked understandably at the expense involved in the degree of expansion envisaged for the education service.[19] Eccles was now under constant pressure in the House of Commons from the Labour opposition to live up to the high-spending policies that the Crowther Report was calling for.

Meanwhile, the growing controversies regarding comprehensives did not abate one iota in spite of the election victory, with the Minister appearing more impotent than ever. In response to a request by Eccles, the Ministry official Ralph Fletcher prepared a brief summarizing his remit as Minister in the law as it stood in March 1960. By this time, Eccles had been back in the post for only five months. Yet he was clearly worried about the extent of his ministerial powers in relation to the growing number of comprehensive schemes now being submitted by local authorities. Conservative ministers would long claim that the Minister's powers under the law did not extend far enough to enable them to intervene more at this time. However, if one looks more closely, one can see the extent to which it in fact centred on whether those at the top of the education service really wanted to fight or not.

In most cases the Minister had ample powers to stop comprehensive schemes under his powers contained in Section 13 of the 1944 Education Act. If an authority wanted to introduce a new school or close an existing one, or enlarge the size of an existing school to the extent that the Minister considered it to amount to the creation of a new school, the Minister had the authority to intervene. The proposed scheme would therefore have to gain his approval. However, according to the ministry officials outlining his powers, he did not have the power to 'insist' that the education be of a particular type (i.e. selective), that the age range remain unaltered, or proscribe in terms of the sex of the pupils. The authority could introduce changes of this kind without his approval as long as they did not at the same time make the school larger or open or close another school.[20]

In practice, because comprehensive schools were usually much bigger in size than grammar or modern schools, the Minister could usually intervene in schemes for new comprehensive schools for this somewhat accidental reason. In fact, much depended on the particular standpoint of the Minister and his personal readiness to 'get tough' with the local education authorities and use the powers at his disposal.

The cases of difficulty were where local authorities sought to introduce comprehensive schools without making them larger than the schools that previously existed. Therefore, the danger occurred with proposals for changes of type (such as from grammar to comprehensive) without a change of size or age range, or simply through an alteration of the age range alone. An authority with large grammar schools, for example, could potentially turn all of them into comprehensives without consulting the Minister. Alternatively, a local education authority could, if it was so determined, simply abandon selective entry for its schools and let them wither away as undersize comprehensives or secondary moderns until the Minister was driven to allow them to be closed. This latter course had not been attempted by a local authority in its entirety. However, local authorities such as Rotherham had embarked upon reducing their selective places which had resulted in the discontinuation of the technical school there. This had been done partly as a response to the refusal of their earlier comprehensive scheme proposal.

Academic selection was not therefore recognized in the law and local education authorities had no duty to undertake it. It was felt by Fletcher that it would be impossible to impose such a duty by legislation, ironically enough, 'without enacting a rigid system quite contrary to the flexibility recommended in the White Paper.' As he then added:

> This would be highly undesirable and it seems better to accept the risk, which is not a serious one at present.

Incredibly, Fletcher felt, regarding those local authority schemes that were possible without ministerial approval, that:

> The Minister may well feel that on the whole this is as well as it enables sensible but unpopular things to be done without his taking the blame.[21]

This shows the degree of political cynicism and expediency being shown in the Ministry at this time regarding the increasing number of comprehensive schemes being mounted.

They were only now starting to recognize the particular danger related to changes of age range. According to Fletcher, the state of the Minister's powers meant there was nothing he could do about the so-called 'Leicestershire scheme.' As noted before, in this case the age range of the schools had been altered so that all pupils attended the junior (comprehensive) schools from age 11 to 14, with 'grammar schools' provided that took those at 14 based merely on their parents' assurance that they would keep them there until at least 16. Those whose parents did not undertake to keep their children at school beyond the minimum school leaving age simply remained in junior high schools. This scheme had been launched under Conservative auspices in Leicestershire and was soon to be carried out in Derbyshire as well as under Labour local authorities. It was being defended by two highly articulate Chief Education officers, Stewart Mason and Robin Pedley, both of whom were determined to get rid of selection above all else. Findings about the Leicestershire scheme were, according to Fletcher, 'not reassuring.'

The Ministry was now fully aware of what the ultimate intention of the scheme's supporters was. The Leicestershire scheme was effectively a fig leaf for full-scale comprehensive schools. Based on a recent conversation between H.M. Inspectors and the area's Chief Education Officer, the latter had admitted that once the national school leaving age was raised to 16, everyone in the junior high school in their fourth year would automatically go onto the senior 'grammar school,' and therefore the whole system would become comprehensive in any case. The Chief Education Officer at Derbyshire apparently had the same intention. Eccles, Hailsham and the Ministry officials had therefore long had the wool pulled over their eyes with what they had considered to be merely 'moderate' schemes for simply getting rid of the 11 plus examination.

It is a measure of the gravity of the situation that even an official with Fletcher's attitudes saw the future risk of the comprehensive school taking over. He therefore did not think it would be difficult to devise an amendment of Section 67 (4) of the 1944 Act that would enable the Minister to determine when an alteration in the age range or perhaps in the case of the sex of the pupils amounted to the establishment of a new school. While, Fletcher added, this would be an 'extreme' measure, 'it cannot be said in this case that the risk is a small one'. The number of grammar schools potentially threatened in this way in Leicestershire and Derbyshire numbered between twenty-five and thirty, according to his calculations. 'The only alternative,' he added, 'is to let matters take their course.'[22]

The ultimate approach being displayed by the Ministry officials was one of fatalism. They appeared loath to acknowledge that the ultimate end of the comprehensive vision lay, namely, in all schools becoming forced to conform in their make-up. All other types of school would inevitably be absorbed rather than simply be allowed to remain alongside. A sense of defeatism mixed with cynicism was pervading the Ministry.

Private notes within the Ministry at this time also show how their general view continued to be opposed to any policy of higher percentages of selective places for grammar schools, with the idea of a second 'creaming' at age 13 felt by Ministry officials to give the secondary modern school, in losing its more academic pupils this way, 'a grievous blow.'[23] This tendency had been hugely reinforced by the White Paper policy that desired a lower percentage of pupils of between 15 and 20 per cent, rather than 25 per cent or above, being admitted to grammar schools. As an official himself recommended:

> I would hope that we could discourage schemes involving selective schools which admitted more than 20 per cent of the secondary pupils, because we want the other secondary schools in the area to have the material with which to develop 'overlap' courses on White Paper lines.[24]

Regarding the threat emanating from the Leicestershire scheme, the Ministry of Education officials were generally loath to do anything to increase the Minister's powers. In March 1961, the Permanent Secretary at the Ministry, Mary Smieton, wrote to Eccles warning against any public discussion of the merits of secondary school organization, including the Leicestershire experiment. The issues that affected secondary education were to be played down, as she put it, in the interests of a 'period of calm'. Any 'overt action' by the Ministry to draw attention to the disadvantages or indeed dangers of schemes being introduced in other areas, she continued, 'would bring the whole thing prominently into party politics'. It was feared that there was a greater likelihood of the scheme spreading rather than being diminished 'by precipitate action now'. Effectively, the recommended response was to sit it out and wait and see what would happen. They favoured a policy of inaction and clearly wanted to avoid a fight with the local education authorities more than anything else. Thus, an approach of expedient-minded passivity prevailed, with Smieton minimizing the seriousness of the matter by adding that 'it is very unlikely, except in Leicestershire itself, that anything would get very far without our hearing about it.'[25]

Yet even those at the helm could not dismiss the threat of the Leicestershire scheme spreading as a precursor for widespread comprehensive schools. Edward Boyle, now at the Treasury, wrote at this time to Kenneth Thompson, the Parliamentary Secretary, regarding its development. Boyle was clearly extremely interested in current proceedings at his former post. Yet strikingly, his main concern about the Leicestershire scheme lay more in the junior 'high school' losing its more able pupils to the 'grammar school' through its operation of parental choice, rather than from any apparent concern about the spread of what was known to be the first stage in the development of universal comprehensive schools nationally. In fact, Boyle confirmed to Thompson his continued support for authorities in country areas introducing medium-sized comprehensives that did away with what he termed 'tiddler'-sized grammar schools.[26]

Thompson replied by informing Boyle that his concern about the 'rump' of 14-year-olds left in the junior schools was ultimately going to be answered by Stewart Mason's admission that once the school leaving age was raised to 16, all pupils would be transferred to the grammar school, thus turning the whole scheme into nothing but a system of junior and senior comprehensive schools. He also informed Boyle of how the schools inspectors' view of the Leicestershire scheme was generally unfavourable. Nevertheless, Thompson, like Smieton, instead drew the same blithe conclusions from these developments:

> Moreover despite the favourable publicity, the idea has not caught on generally. On the whole therefore we do not think the situation will get out of hand and we are not contemplating anything in the nature of legislation to strengthen the Minister's powers. If opinion hardens against the idea it may in the end come to very little.

Meanwhile, Thompson confirmed his support for turning rural secondary schools into country comprehensive schools, being 'convinced' that small rural secondary schools 'are likely to be unsatisfactory' and that rural authorities were partial to 'forming rather larger units.'[27]

On 5 July Eccles was forced to reveal in the House of Commons, in answer to questions from Frederick Willey, that the number of new entrants being admitted to grammar and direct grant schools was markedly declining. The number had reduced from 147,000 in 1958 to 130,000 for the last year of 1960, with it being estimated to further decline to 120,000 in 1962, a loss of 27,000 in four years.[28] It was also revealed that a mere 228 technical schools now existed, with most local authorities now providing technical courses within secondary modern schools. Regarding this however, Eccles merely said that he would 'rather leave to them (local education authorities) that freedom of choice.'[29]

Increasing attention was being devoted towards the development of academic education for less able pupils. Eccles was now in talks with the Secondary Schools Examination Council about the introduction of external examinations for pupils below GCE-level ability that were felt to be a stimulus to the schools. These examinations were to be centrally supervised, something that Eccles had notably been against six years earlier. This would turn out to be the Certificate of Secondary Education, or 'CSE.' Similarly, the Central Advisory Council for Education was now meeting under the chairmanship of Sir John Newsom in order to focus upon the education of children of average and below-average academic ability. This was the increasing emphasis at the time.

Correspondence shows that the Conservative Teachers' Association raised concerns to Eccles about a notable 'alternative' scheme for the West Riding area of Yorkshire in November 1961. This authority had in recent years steadily embarked upon a bipartite system of secondary school selection by teacher recommendation rather than through formal examination. They also expressed caution about any extension of the earlier Leicestershire scheme to other areas, as well as opposition to the increased programmes for very large schools that many local authorities appeared set upon. In addition, they repeated their criticism of the continuing under-provision of grammar schools in many local areas.[30] Inspection of the correspondence today shows the handwritten annotations by Ministry of Education officials in the margin of the CTA's letter to Eccles. They display a marked degree of condescension, and even contempt, for the CTA's point of view. Yet this was an attitude that appears to have been shared by Eccles himself. In his reply, he was keenly defensive of the experiments occurring in West Yorkshire, and stated that he 'personally welcomed it' and that it was 'encouraging.' This was partly based, he explained, on the lesser number of complaints that had been received from parents and teachers about the selection process since that system had been adopted. This again suggests what his ultimate priorities were.

In regard to the core issue of grammar school provision, Eccles justified his stance in terms of the White Paper policy. As he put it:

> It follows I think from what is said in the White Paper about encouraging variety in the organisation of secondary schools that it would not be appropriate for the Minister to seek to impose some uniform amount of the grammar kind of provision.[31]

Similarly, he claimed that, as Minister, he could not undertake to withhold approval from proposals for secondary schools larger than an 8 form entry simply on the grounds of size. Yet this was in spite of the fact that, as we have seen, the issue of size did very much come under the Minister's powers when potentially rejecting local authority schemes. Nevertheless, he claimed that in many areas where there was a heavy concentration of population, 'I could not dispute that it makes perfectly good sense for authorities to provide schools for over a thousand children.'[32] Inevitably, schools of such size tended overwhelmingly to be comprehensives. The CTA's concerns were clearly inconvenient to Eccles and were therefore to be dismissed.

Throughout this time, the rate of educational expenditure was growing rapidly. This was particularly due to the expanding number of teachers and the cost of maintaining and operating the buildings provided by the investment programme. Local authorities' future expenditure was estimated at this time to rise from £694 million in 1961/2 to £830 million in 1965/6. The Chief Secretary to the Treasury Henry Brooke stated anxiously that the rate of expenditure was growing faster than the national product. Because of the claims upon the system, he therefore considered it to be reckless to embark upon a new wave of educational expenditure. On present policies, the rate of increase was 4.6 per cent a year, and now the Treasury wanted to reduce this to within 3 per cent.[33] From their perspective, educational spending had to be reined in.

Eccles' reaction, given the pressure he was under at this time from the Labour Party for greater expansion, was predictable. He claimed that any reductions would result in a wastage of pupils' talent, particularly within the 15 to 18 age group. He thus sought to defend his spending corner by claiming that there would be a massively negative reaction from parents at any slow-down in expansion that would affect their children's educational chances. In spite of what was clearly happening to the economy, Eccles remained firmly within the welfare-expansionist mode of thought at all costs. As he stated, 'It may be said that the balance of payments has to be our priority, but this has little appeal for the working man and his family.'[34] Eccles was always a doughty fighter when it came to defending his department's spending levels.

Amidst the strains on the economy, comprehensive reorganization continued rapidly. In the summer of 1962, the Labour-controlled Newport Education Committee successfully persuaded Kenneth Thompson of the merits of their plan to rehouse the High School in new premises at Bettws on the outskirts of the city. This was in spite of the concern expressed by Conservative members on the education committee that the move ultimately heralded it being changed into a comprehensive school, and that this was merely the first step. An incensed party supporter wrote to the Conservative Party Chairman Iain Macleod, by way of attaining influence with Eccles, to express his concerns. In anticipation of the familiar defence by Conservative Ministers of Education, he added, 'You may reply that you have no jurisdiction over the decisions of this Education Committee, but on the other hand you do have very considerable influence in that you control the purse strings.' Furthermore:

> I frankly do not enjoy seeing a Conservative Government supplying the money for the implementation, in this case, of a purely political decision by the Labour Party.[35]

Another supporter wrote to Macleod about the degree of opposition to the move on educational grounds coming from the Headmaster and the parents, teachers, pupils and the governors at the school. He tellingly revealed that:

> One of the most disappointing factors in the campaign against the Socialist-controlled Education Committee to remove the school, is the complete lack of support from the Conservative Minister of Education.[36]

Kenneth Thompson visited Newport in early July. In subsequent internal correspondence, he then claimed that the buildings currently being used were of insufficient quality. Stating that they ought to 'strip off' the 'sentimental considerations' that naturally arose when institutions faced change, he claimed that he was fully satisfied with the local authority's plans. Apparently, the authority had assured both Boyle and himself that grammar school education would continue on the same basis at the new site at Bettws. Somewhat loftily, he pronounced that a Minister could hardly decide such a disputed matter on the assumption that the 'solemn undertaking' of a public authority was 'suspect or worse.' Therefore, 'I am prepared to accept in toto the good faith of the Authority and I put full weight in their assurances.' Furthermore in similarly insouciant spirit:

> If this is acceptable, and I think it must be, it seems to dispose altogether of everything but the sentimental remains of the objectors' case.[37]

But the fears of Conservative supporters in the Newport area were not dissipated by these assurances about the Newport Borough Council's intentions. Letters continued to be sent to Macleod warning that if the opportunity arose, these assurances would soon be forgotten by the Newport Council.

A shifting emphasis

Meanwhile, Edward Boyle was appointed the new Minister of Education in July, replacing Eccles whom Macmillan considered to have been agitating for the leadership. Boyle was of course by now an experienced figure within the Ministry. It is crucial to ascertain his mentality at this time. It appears that in spite of what he now knew about the ultimate intentions of those behind the Leicestershire scheme, Boyle was set to allow it to continue.

Given this context, his remarks to the Conservative Parliamentary Education Committee in November 1962 were surely significant. It was a good thing, he claimed at the meeting, to get away from the 'sharp categorization of secondary schools.' He stated that too high a proportion of grammar school places affected both the secondary modern and any neighbouring comprehensives negatively. Furthermore, comprehensive schools should have 'a strong grammar element' rather than, as he somewhat dismissively put it, 'being glorified secondary modern schools.'[38] This clearly shows that Boyle was already subscribing to an egalitarian mode of viewing the maintained education system well before the Labour victory in 1964. Directly or indirectly, Boyle's thinking was moving in the direction of feeding comprehensives as a desired form of school organization.

In December 1962 the Conservative Teachers' Association submitted a report to Boyle on the state of secondary education, laying particular emphasis upon comprehensive schools and the Leicestershire scheme. They expressed further warnings about the potential spread of the scheme, and counselled that it should be confined to Leicestershire until such time as it proved to be of educational value. In their view this would be 1967 at the earliest. They again warned that the scheme was being expanded, both in Leicestershire and in other areas, 'for administrative and social reasons rather than on educational grounds.' They added:

> It is obvious that the Scheme could be exploited by a left wing local education authority for political motives, and its spread to other parts of the country must be watched with vigilance.[39]

The annotations of the Ministry official Miss Wilma Harte, who read the Conservative Teachers' letter in preparation for the Minister's perusal, again reveal an obvious contempt for their point of view. In subsequent correspondence with her fellow officials, she called this, 'a feeble production by the Conservative teachers', adding that, 'there is nothing really for the Minister to comment on.' There was no point, in her view, in engaging with their advice about not allowing other authorities to proceed with the Leicestershire experiment. As she put it:

> Generally speaking, we cannot stop them and when the Authorities concerned are sensible and open minded it would be wrong, I think, for the Minister to seek to be an obstacle to new developments.

Furthermore, in this expedient-minded vein, she added:

> In so many ways, the world is moving too fast these days for a Minister of Education to say that nobody is to change anything until he is sure that it will be safe.[40]

A suitably emollient and diplomatic ministerial reply was then suggested by Miss Harte, which of course claimed at the outset how interested the Minister was to read the Committee's conclusions.

In Boyle's reply, he stated that the 'Leicestershire-type' schemes did not require his approval unless they specifically involved the closing down of an existing school or the establishment of a new one. There was not necessarily anything, he continued, to stop other local authorities experimenting on these lines. Boyle, Eccles and other ministers along with the Ministry itself had of course chosen to do nothing to rectify their lack of powers in this area.

Regarding the motives of Stewart Mason, the originator of the Leicestershire scheme, Boyle stated, 'I have no doubt that the driving force behind the plan has been a genuine desire to promote a worthwhile educational experiment.' He merely told the CTA that he would keep close watch on any further experiments that might be carried out elsewhere. The Conservative line was to be 'resolutely opposed' to any proposal which positively *required* authorities to reorganize their systems of secondary education in such a way that removed selection. However, he added, 'I think our posture ought in general to be sympathetic to experiment in this field.'[41] In regard to a school that was truly comprehensive with the full range of ability, an increasing number of parents 'will make that school their first choice.' Boyle was gradually shifting the goalposts of possibility all the time.

The Conservative Party's public statements on education started to show an increasingly egalitarian emphasis upon pupils of average and below-average ability at this time. The Party now claimed to be aiming to give a 'square deal' to the majority of pupils, rather than simply the most able. This sentiment of course inadvertently conceded that those pupils had been neglected until this point. In suitably vague terms, all were to travel along the 'educational road' as far as their ability and perseverance would take them. Meanwhile, they were keen to emphasize that 'We believe in a diversity of secondary schools, and a rigid adherence to the "11 plus" is not part of Conservative policy.'[42] Increasingly, they wanted to be dissociated from any public position that supported academic selection by examination for secondary school entry.

Yet, extraordinarily, in the very same public statement the Conservative Party also acknowledged how the Americans were continuing to warn about the deficiencies in their own 'high' school system that was based on the comprehensive idea. Indeed, it described how Vice-Admiral Hyman Rickover, in a recent official report to the United States Congress, had urged America to adopt the English system of separate secondary schools for brighter children, and quoted his remarks that had appeared in *The Daily Telegraph* on 3 September 1962.[43] Yet, incredibly, the Conservatives' policy statement drew no deductions from this within the context of Britain's increasing move towards comprehensives.

As a public programme, education was now second only to defence in terms of expenditure, with spending rising on it at a rate of about 10 per cent a year. The Conservative government's thinking was now heavily influenced by the view that increased spending on education would lead to greater economic growth. This way of thinking had also been encouraged by Macmillan's National Economic Development Council. In addition, the recently published Robbins report was encouraging a major expansion of higher education within the universities and technical colleges.[44]

Then came a moment of great symbolic importance. The London County Council decided at this time to do away with the 11 plus written examination. In a subsequent speech to the Association of Education Committees in Belfast on 5 July, Boyle declared his true feelings more than on any previous occasion. He stated that he himself had long wanted to move away from formal methods of selection and welcomed the decision. The time had come, as he put it,

> to make an end of the absolutely strict neutrality which the Ministry has maintained in public towards local selection methods ... I have no doubt that the status of the old written examination as a means of 11 plus selection has been dealt a mortal blow.

Characteristically, Boyle added that it would be quite another thing, however, to suggest that 'discretion' in this matter should be suddenly removed from local education authorities. Nevertheless, he continued with his indirect support for greater egalitarianism, adding that:

> I certainly would not wish to advance the view that the bipartite system, as it is often called, should be regarded as the right and usual way of organising secondary education, *compared with which everything else must be stigmatised as experimental.*

(my emphasis)

The Party's 1963 pamphlet *Educational Opportunity*, which quoted Boyle's speech, added that one of the outstanding achievements of the last decade had been the progress made in developing the secondary modern school, and it was 'unfair to write them off as failures.'[45] But this latter point was hardly supported by the earlier statements. Taken with what Boyle had been saying about the selective system of examination overall, the general thrust of his remarks had hardly suggested a great deal of faith in the secondary modern schools, and thus the existing system as a whole.

Similar sentiments were echoed in his speech to the Party Conference in Blackpool later that year, stating that:

> if we as a Party say that we believe – as we do – in an opportunity state, *then this must mean that we want every child to have the same opportunities for acquiring intelligence* (my emphasis). I think that we can all too easily forget just how much the scales are still weighted against children from many homes, however potentially gifted they may be, in our society.[46]

The key question to ask is what Boyle did in fact envisage for the future of the maintained secondary system. Given his predilection for a vaguely merging effect between the grammar and secondary modern schools, along with an abandonment of formal written examinations for selection purposes, his position was now effectively advocating comprehensive schools by the backdoor.

Shortly afterwards in the House of Commons on 11 July, Boyle engaged in a curious exchange with his former Parliamentary Secretary Kenneth Thompson. Adopting a markedly different emphasis now that he was no longer in post, Thompson asked what advice should be given to local education authorities about the maintenance of standards in grammar schools given that many were contemplating changes in their selection procedure. Boyle was noticeably quick to refute the tenor of the question, stating that there was no reason to suppose that recent changes in the formal methods of selection had 'in any way' affected grammar school standards. When Thompson then reinforced his question by emphasizing the importance they should attach to grammar schools and to the selection of children 'appropriate for what they have to offer,' Boyle noticeably took issue with the use of the term 'appropriate' for those concerned. The responsibility of the grammar schools, he stressed, was 'as great to those children with not quite such a high level of attainment, who none the less can gain very much from working in a grammar school atmosphere.'[47] Again, Boyle's sentiments were all moving in the same egalitarian direction without ever actually declaring it outright. Something else was clearly being envisaged for the grammar school in future.

The Newsom Report

A seminal report was now published that encapsulated the current state of thinking on secondary education. In March 1961, Boyle's predecessor Eccles had given a reference to the Central Advisory Council for Education in England to advise him on the education of pupils aged 13 to 16 who were of average and below-average ability. Strikingly, this Council included Alec Clegg, the Chief Education Officer for the West Riding of Yorkshire, who had been behind the experiments in secondary school selection in that area. Their deliberations ultimately produced the Newsom Report *Half Our Future* that was published on 7 August 1963. In its introduction, Boyle emphasized that there needed to be new ways of thinking and a change of heart in regard to these pupils, 'on the part of the community as a whole.'[48]

The resulting report, based upon a survey of 6,202 fourteen-year-old boys and girls in secondary modern schools, highlighted throughout that a great degree of untapped potential lay dormant among such pupils. It therefore argued that teachers should be specially trained in order to teach them more effectively. Among its principal recommendations was a programme of new techniques for teacher training, 'to help pupils whose abilities are artificially depressed by environmental and linguistic handicaps,' which was to be instituted by the Ministry.[49]

Yet the Report's emphasis led inescapably towards a spirit that was opposed to differentiation between pupils to any obvious degree. It stated that:

> Excessively fine gradings of ability groups should be avoided. More than three broad groupings is probably unnecessary, and groupings in the final years at school should be largely based on subject or course choices.[50]

All schools were to look ahead to a situation in which all pupils would remain in full-time education until the age of 16. They were to be increasingly designed to compensate for the handicaps of pupils from backgrounds characterized by cultural and linguistic shortcomings. Their role was being expanded, with teacher training methods increasingly geared towards the less able.

Indeed, the Report carried assumptions of a very particular nature about intelligence and ability. In its words:

> Intellectual talent is not a fixed quantity with which we have to work but a variable that can be modified by social policy and educational approaches.

Furthermore, in the Report's view, intelligence was 'largely an acquired characteristic' that was greatly influenced by the social and physical environment.[51] Inevitably, there was much emphasis on the influence of home conditions, particularly for working-class children, and the problems experienced by schools in underprivileged areas that made their work difficult. The Report sought policies that included financial incentives to encourage teachers to work in areas of relative deprivation and emphasized the existing inadequacies of resources and facilities between schools. It was thus increasingly held to be the schools' responsibility to alleviate a range of social ills. Until this problem was rectified, the Report claimed, 'large numbers of boys and girls, including many of those with whom we are directly concerned, will continue to be penalised by the accident of their environment.'[52] Given this emphasis on the less able and the disadvantaged, the Report inevitably approved of a type of positive discrimination.

Nevertheless, the Committee was against the idea of specific posts for teachers of below-average ability pupils, 'which would tend to create a separate class of teachers.'[53] Instead, the intention was that all teachers were to be increasingly trained in courses designed to teach pupils of average ability and below. Inevitably, this spelt major implications for the future of teacher training, particularly given the background trend towards comprehensive schools.

Teacher training was to include courses in sociology, psychology and child development, with pupils' social difficulties increasingly acknowledged. Indeed, it added that student teachers, as part of their training, 'may need to examine their own social preconceptions.' In regard to those teaching pupils from similar social backgrounds, it stated how:

> In so far as the teachers' own educational progress may have been untypical of others in their circumstances, they may have even less sympathy with environmental difficulties.[54]

Teachers were therefore intended to become significantly more sociologically aware and understanding of their pupils' familial and social disadvantages in a way that they had never been expected to before.

Allowances were to be increasingly made for children from working-class families. Schools were 'to provide the background of conversation and exchange of information which an educated family offers, and they have to coax their pupils to take part in it.'[55] It was not considered whether such an emphasis might in fact serve to depress standards and expectations of the working-class child and his family if teachers were to take such an approach to an excessive degree. Nor was it asked whether such sociological 'understanding' might in more radical teachers' hands ultimately militate against trying to transmit the educated culture to the working-class child in the first place. This well-meaning focus on the less able, with an increasingly sociological role for maintained schools, inevitably evoked a form of condescension. It would have major implications for British state education in the future. And Boyle, the Education Minister who approved it, stood squarely in the middle of this vanguard of educational progressivism.

This was illustrated by the kind of support that Boyle received for the published Report and the quarters from which it came. A notably positive reaction came from the Central Council of the Trades Union Congress (TUC), whose General Secretary George Woodcock wrote to Boyle in November 1963 enclosing the Council's views on the report. In particular, they praised Boyle and the Newsom Report's general view that the 'qualities defined as intelligence may be acquired through education.' In particular, they supported the Report's emphasis against 'fine gradings' of ability quoted earlier.

Inevitably, the Report's sentiments led to the TUC urging Boyle that only the organization of secondary education on a comprehensive basis would give effect to the Advisory Council's 'more progressive methods' in secondary schools. Boyle, for his part, promised that he would 'take your Council's views into account.'[56] In fact, his current policies of expanding the teacher colleges and increasing the school building programme were already in harmony with the Report's recommendations. In essential terms, Boyle and the Newsom Report had set the egalitarian ball rolling. It could now be pushed further leftwards by the encouragement of those such as the TUC.

In February 1964, Boyle was forced to admit to the Conservative Parliamentary Education Committee that the White Paper of 1958 had been 'overtaken by events.' This was in spite of the fact that it had been clear what could happen with such an open-ended policy at the time. In response, Boyle was planning on running with the tide. He re-asserted that he was 'not happy' about children of roughly equal ability being selected for different types of school, a view that in fact went well beyond what the White Paper had, in its ameliorative spirit, advocated. Unbelievably, in almost socialistic terms, Boyle then claimed that 'segregation,' in his view, intensified the 'bias' in favour of middle-class children that already existed in society.[57]

However, given the rush by local authorities towards ending selection and the number of comprehensive schemes now being proposed in urban areas such as Liverpool and Manchester, Boyle admitted that the Minister's present powers in this area 'needed strengthening.' Nevertheless, in trying to play down the magnitude of what looked increasingly likely to happen to the grammar schools, he claimed that 'no conservative and indeed few socialists would want them all to come to an end.' He offered up the crumb that if parents did not wish their children to go to an 'experimental' type of school, 'they could always appeal to the Minister.'[58] Given the situation, this was surely scant reassurance.

The changed attitude of members of the Parliamentary Education Committee was further evident when they received a deputation from the increasingly beleaguered Conservative Teachers' Association on 16 March. The Conservative Teachers were particularly concerned about the recently proposed schemes in Liverpool and Manchester that they felt were effectively abolishing parental choice in those areas. They revealed to the Committee that they had invited Boyle, who was not present, to discuss these proposed schemes with them, but that he had claimed to be unable to do so since no final proposals had been put to him. In addition, they were concerned about a proposed scheme at Cardiff that was on the lines of the Leicestershire Plan. As they had earlier expressed in their concerns to Boyle, they were worried that these experiments would be used over the whole country. Comprehensive schools were continuing to be introduced through 'backdoor methods,' often through manipulation of the age of entry.

It is clear that certain members of the Parliamentary Committee such as John Jennings, the MP for Burton, clearly recognized that the Leicestershire scheme could ultimately destroy the status of the grammar school. At this point, Raymond Gower, the MP for Barry, who had been educated at Cardiff High School, informed the Committee that he was sponsoring a private member's bill, albeit seriously belatedly, to strengthen the Minister's powers in relation to secondary school reorganization.[59] Yet strikingly, it was the Chairman of the meeting, Enoch Powell, who effectively threw a spanner in the works.

Powell pointed out how, if the minister's powers were indeed increased, 'we would find ourselves up against the problem of defining in reasonably precise terms the type of secondary education which we favoured.' In this notably pragmatic and cagey spirit, he reminded the Committee that in the new and expanded towns, 'we were unlikely to see the bilateral system established.' There was also the additional problem, he added, of the effect of the school leaving age being raised to 16, as this was bound to have repercussions on a number of the schemes now in operation or pending. Incredibly, Powell, the former Birmingham grammar schoolboy, was therefore counselling them in a plan of studied inaction in the face of the potential destruction of the grammar schools.

Furthermore, David Renton, the MP for Huntingdon, warned that the Conservative Party 'must be careful not to let itself get into the position of defending the 11 plus exam,' and claimed the comprehensive school had 'a good deal to be said for it as it' as it was able to offer a wider choice of courses to pupils.[60] In stark contrast to these sentiments, the Deputation from the Conservative Teachers' Association felt the main reason for the unpopularity of the 11 plus was because of the low percentage of grammar school places persisting in many areas. This shows the clear contrast in position now between the Deputation and the assembled MPs. However, the Conservative Teachers' Association's view ultimately carried little clout.

Studied inaction

In February 1964, the Prime Minister Alec Douglas Home decided that the Ministry of Education should have a single minister with total responsibility over the whole educational field. From 1 April the Ministry became known as the Department of Education and Science. It was to be a single unit but with two separate administrative parts, with one responsible for schools and the other for science and higher education. Having renounced his peerage, Quintin Hogg (formerly Lord Hailsham) was appointed the new Secretary of State for Education and Science. Edward Boyle was appointed Minister of State for Education (with a seat in the Cabinet) along with a second minister, Lord Newton.

Shortly after this major development, Raymond Gower, the Conservative MP for Barry, stood up in the House of Commons on 21 April to introduce his motion that any local education authority proposal to change the status or nature of a secondary school should require the Minister's approval. He noted the potential destruction of a large number of grammar schools as well as other secondary schools of 'long-established merit,' and argued that his proposed modification would provide 'some ultimate safeguard' from what was now happening.[61] He added that the current ministerial powers of Section 13 and Section 68 did not extend far enough, and therefore the Minister did not possess sufficient powers to deal with proposals which circumvented the terms of the 1944 Act. The intention was to thus modify and change them 'in one small particular.'[62] Gower could plainly see the desperate nature of the situation.

Speaking for the opposition, Harriet Slater, the Labour MP for Stoke on Trent North, made the inevitable claim that Gower was trying to take responsibility away from local authorities and thus undermining their 'freedom to experiment.'[63] In this highly significant moment that was never given the recognition it deserved, Gower lost this key motion by 176 noes to 152 in favour.

Strikingly few key figures in the Conservative Party ranks tuned out to vote on this occasion, with no members from the front bench present. Those who did support Gower notably included the former Education Parliamentary Secretaries Kenneth Thompson and Kenneth Pickthorn, as well as Nigel Birch and Tufton Beamish. By contrast, among those voting against the motion, all the key Labour members for the comprehensives movement were out in force. They included Anthony Crosland, Barbara Castle, Michael Foot, Jennie Lee, Tony Benn, Alice Bacon, Roy Jenkins, Reg Prentice, Michael Stewart and Denis Healey. Yet none of the parliamentary big players from the Conservative government had made themselves available. At this key moment, the Conservative elite chose not to intervene to strengthen the Minister's powers despite holding a large majority in the Commons. Instead, the rhetorical subterfuge of 'local freedom,' even if it meant the potential destruction of all the grammar schools, continued to be deployed in high Tory circles.

Quintin Hogg, in his new role as Secretary of State, proved to be no less fatalistic than Boyle when it came to secondary school reorganization. Despite socialist authorities putting forward more comprehensive schemes, with the Government being criticized by many Conservative party supporters for not having overruled them, Hogg professed himself to be uncomfortable about a Conservative Secretary of State being able to 'override' the local democracy.[64] In many cases, according to Hogg, the Minister had no power to intervene. Yet as we have just seen, the Conservative government was not taking any steps to rectify this state of affairs.

As Hogg noted at this time to the Conservative Parliamentary Committee, it was clear that a significant number of local authorities were submitting schemes simply in order to get rid of the 11 plus examination. In particular, many were trying to devise schemes which avoided the closure or the opening of a school so that they would not have to seek the Minister's approval under the 1944 Act. In notably lame fashion, Hogg merely stated that the Conservative Party 'must try and insist' that the change of a school in this way was properly discussed with the Ministry and the Inspectorate.

Nevertheless, in spite of having recognized the inadequate state of the Minister's present powers, Hogg felt that the Party 'should avoid getting caught on an anti-comprehensive hook.' There were many good comprehensives, he went on, and such schools were the best solution in many areas. The Party should not criticize the socialists of being dogmatic, he went on, 'if we were also dogmatic in the other direction.' A clear determination to do nothing of consequence continued to be the order of the day. Instead, he was keen to assure Joan Quennell, the MP for Petersfield, that people were entitled to contract out of the state education service to the private sector if they wished, 'and he would fight to the death on this matter of principle.'[65] Hogg's different attitude towards independent schooling was always noticeable.

Perspectives allied to the Conservative Party were constantly shifting. In January 1964, the Bow Group, a research group for younger Conservatives, issued a publication entitled *Strategy for Schools* that was published by the Conservative Political Centre. While not formally connected to the Conservative Party itself, the Bow Group was influential as a breeding ground for ideas to 'merit consideration' by the Party and a wider audience.

It advocated a 'broad curriculum' for all pupils until the age of 15 and aimed to replace the GCE 'O' level examination with the CSE for all pupils. According to the Bow Group authors, the 'narrowly conceived education' of practical, technical or classical categories 'must disappear from our educational system.'[66] They advocated comprehensive schools in new areas, as well as a policy of substantially enlarging the ability intake of grammar schools to further their objective of a 'common curriculum' for all. Indeed, they claimed that it was the differentiation of schools that was responsible for the lack of emphasis traditionally given to technical and vocational education.

According to them, there was 'no doubt that the tripartite or bipartite system existing over most of the country today, needs to be swiftly and critically overhauled.'[67]

Throughout the report comprehensive schools were praised, while the existing system stood accused of encouraging a 'wastage of talent.'[68] Concerns about comprehensive schools were dismissed throughout. It is surely significant that such a report was published by the Conservative Party at this crucial time. This type of thinking had clearly extended beyond any core left-wing interest to encapsulate the thinking of even supposed moderates within the teaching profession. Crucially, all of these recommendations came from Conservative-supporting teachers in the early stages of their professional careers.

On 25 March, Lord Newton, acting under Hogg and Boyle, introduced a short Bill in the House of Lords to enable local authorities to engage in experiments with the age for secondary school entry other than the usual transfer age of 11. Having been read for a second time in the Lords on 9 April, with Newton claiming that the proposed Bill would merely allow a 'strictly limited number of educational experiments' not presently permissible under the law, it was then introduced by Hogg in the Commons on 1 July.[69] They appeared to have hoped that such a moderate policy of greater flexibility for local authorities, which might include 'middle' school experiments from 9 to 13, would defuse the tension surrounding selection at 11.

While both Hogg and Newton mildly termed it to be an 'enabling' Bill, it was clear that it would in practice further the impetus for comprehensive reorganization. Amazingly, rather than strengthening the Minister's powers, Hogg and Boyle, together with Newton in the House of Lords, were handing even more latitude to the local authorities. As Frederick Willey, the Labour member for Sunderland North, noted, the Bill legitimated the actions of local authorities that had been taken in defiance of the Minister and the 1944 Act and was thus removing an obstacle in the way of local authorities wanting to reorganize on comprehensive lines. As he put it:

> However much the right hon. and learned Gentleman may seek to disguise this, the Bill is a capitulation by the government.

As Willey further pointed out, Hogg would be aware that once the Bill became law there would be 'considerable pressure' on him from many education authorities to provide for schools that would bridge the 11 plus gulf.[70] The Bill would effectively regularize what, as has been seen, was already happening.

Another comprehensive proponent, Horace King, seized on what was being proposed, noting how in the relevant section of the Bill:

> In Clause 1, the party opposite are adding another nail to the coffin of tripartism and already the Secretary of State, chief of many Ministers of Education, is converted – or seems to be.[71]

Other Labour members were similarly exultant. Merlyn Rees noted the contrast between Lord Newton's measured description of the proposed bill in the Lords that it would merely 'allow experimental bridges to be thrown across the gulf,' with Boyle's earlier statement in 1963 that such schemes should not be 'stigmatized' as mere experiments. Rees thus exposed the incoherency and lack of clarity from the two Ministers of Education both on the issue of what the proposed bill would mean as well as their position on educational experiments generally.

Those Conservative MPs who took a principled stance on the future of grammar schools were inevitably alarmed. John Jennings, the Member for Burton, stated that he was 'frightened' about Clause 1.[72] Yet all the while, despite Jennings' further questions to him, Hogg would not admit the potential implications of such a Bill for the selective system's future. Robert Cooke, the Conservative member for Bristol West, also saw the possibility for the misuse of the Bill as a vehicle for the hastening of the extinction of the grammar schools. Local freedom, he continued, could be used for 'dangerous political purposes.' He therefore sought Hogg's assurance that it would never be his wish to see the sort of 'wanton destruction' that he feared was being planned in Bristol at this time, 'under the cloak of a Measure of this kind.'[73] Strikingly, Hogg said nothing in response to this as well. As the Labour MP for Flint East Eirene White revealed, ninety local education authorities were already actively considering schemes of secondary reorganization. The Government, she claimed revealingly, 'have not awakened early enough to see what has been happening in education.'[74]

In a manner similar to that of Boyle, Hogg was also having recent remarks that he had made used against him. Less than two months earlier, he had revealed in the Commons that he had considered the tripartite system to have 'broken down' seven years earlier when he had first served as Minister of Education in 1957.[75] The fact that both Hogg and Boyle had made recent personal statements undermining the selective system was now being skilfully used by the pro-comprehensive Labour side as ammunition to prove the Conservative government's incoherence on the issue and their lack of faith in the present system.

All the while, Hogg was ever keen to downplay the extent of his ministerial powers and thus underline their limited nature. His interpretation of his duties was laissez-faire to say the least. If a local authority chose an 'educationally viable' scheme:

> it is not my duty to substitute my own judgment for that of the local authority *even where my judgement would not coincide with its judgment.*[76]
>
> (my emphasis)

It was to be a very high threshold indeed before Hogg would consider a local authority to be acting unreasonably. Indeed, he almost seemed to want to invalidate his own role as Secretary of State in the matter.

Instead, Hogg simply mentioned the need for the 'desirability' of consultation on these schemes with the Department, teachers, inspectorate, parents and local electors.[77] Defending the lack of action taken by himself and his predecessors in tackling the age of secondary school transfer in previous years, he claimed that he and his colleagues had been more concerned about ensuring 'secondary education for all' by getting rid of the remaining all-age schools. In any event, he continued, they should wait for the publication of the report currently being chaired by Lady Bridget Plowden before determining the ideal age of secondary school transfer for future national policy.[78] Thus, the whole issue was being devolved even further.

Three months later in the General Election on 16 October, despite the Chancellor Reginald Maudling's best efforts to reign in public spending and correct for an overheating economy, the Labour Party with Harold Wilson as leader gained a wafer-thin majority. Nevertheless, the incoming Labour government was clear and decisive about what it planned to do in office. And one of those aims of course involved transforming the whole nature of the country's secondary education. Shortly afterwards, Michael Stewart, the new Labour Secretary of State, was announcing that the reorganization of secondary education was to become 'national policy.' In contrast to the attitude taken by Hogg and his Conservative predecessors, this was a government with no qualms about not appearing 'bipartisan' whatsoever. The situation for selective schools was more desperate than ever.

A selective portrayal

As noted earlier, educational historians have tended to portray the Conservative governments of this period as if they were ideological defenders of the tripartite system, with the underlying goal to protect the grammar school at all costs. For example, Brian Simon attacked the Conservative governments for obstructing comprehensive reorganization because they did not allow all-encompassing schemes that would have included all schools within a given area.[79] Thus, the actions of the Conservative government have long been portrayed according to a pro-comprehensive standpoint with an inevitably distorting effect.

In his own portrayal, Ian Fenwick claimed that the Conservative government was attempting to uphold a politically unsustainable defence of selection. This is despite his noting the contrast between their 'fluid' stance and that of the Conservative and Unionist Teachers' Association, who tried to exert a pro-selection pressure on ministers by counselling against comprehensive experiments.[80] In fact, Fenwick himself acknowledged that the Conservative government, rather than being combative on the issue of selection and school type as the CTA would have preferred, often tried to direct these competing pressures and demands into 'uncontroversial channels.'[81]

In their respective works on this period, both Simon and Fenwick released official information that showed how during this period of a huge increase in the secondary official school population, the overall percentage of grammar school pupils in relation to the secondary school population in fact decreased from 28 per cent of pupils in 1954 to 24 per cent in 1959, and stayed at that level until 1963.[82] Concentrating on the proportion of 13-year-old pupils in each type of secondary school, Simon showed that the percentage of pupils in selective grammar and technical schools (including grammar and technical streams) remained static, slightly decreasing from 23.0 per cent to 22.9 per cent between 1950 and 1961. By contrast, the proportion of 13-year-olds in comprehensive schools increased markedly, albeit from a very low base number, from 0.4 to 5.3 per cent. If those pupils at 'other' schools (mostly bilateral) are included, the figure increases to 11.2 per cent.[83] Simon's own work thus showed how little the Conservatives concentrated on building more of the two types of selective school during this period in order to forestall the pro-comprehensive critics.

Simon maintained that the policies pursued by Eccles, Hailsham and Lloyd were a 'last-gasp defence' against comprehensive reorganization. Nevertheless, he acknowledged that the Conservative government's 1958 White Paper *Secondary Education for All* aimed to build a hugely increased number of secondary moderns with an extended curriculum in areas of new housing with no existing schools. In doing so, he added that this was an option that was preferred to that of building new grammar schools.[84] This was despite many areas still severely lacking them. Roy Lowe also noted in his respective work that new comprehensives were considered more popular in middle-class 'dormitory' towns or new housing areas that lacked grammar schools.[85] This does not sound like the actions of a Conservative government ruthlessly shoring up a tripartite or bipartite selective structure. One would surely expect a government that was ideologically determined to defend the selective system to have strengthened all the different parts of it.

Lowe also noted a meeting that apparently took place in 1955 between David Eccles and Robin Pedley, the progenitor of the Leicestershire experiment, that suggested that Eccles was giving a tacit nod to such proposals. This forced Lowe to briefly consider that Eccles was not in fact 'supine' on comprehensive reorganization coming from local authorities but actively approving certain types of scheme.[86]

Gary McCulloch also stated that Conservative ministers sought to defend the 'status quo,' particularly grammar schools, from the comprehensive idea with the strategy of reinforcing secondary moderns.[87] Yet he portrayed Eccles feeling a sense of dilemma about 11 plus selection, and described Eccles entertaining the possibility of non-selective schemes for 11 to 15 year olds involving all secondary schools as a 'compromise' in 1956.[88] Indeed, Eccles was considering precisely this in September that year in a paper whose purpose was to 'save the public schools.'[89] Alongside seeking to make entry to the independent schools easier by adding to the direct grant list, he was envisaging the maintained secondary education system being 'completely recast,' in the words of one of his officials, with both grammar and secondary modern buildings used as non-selective 'senior' schools for pupils until the age of 15.[90] He claimed that the grammar schools' sixth form work could then be supposedly provided in sixth form colleges. Strikingly, Eccles was warned of the 'unending storm' that such a proposal, in which the grammar schools would be 'truncated,' would result in.[91] Indeed, the grammar schools would have been irrevocably altered under these plans.

McCulloch also identified another meeting between Eccles and Pedley at this time to discuss 14 plus selection.[92] This took place one month after Eccles' deliberations on recasting the secondary system. At the meeting, Eccles acknowledged certain misgivings about Pedley's non-selective proposals that involved pupils transferring at 14 to another school or remaining based merely on parental preference. However, Eccles signalled his interest and approval for Pedley's ideas in areas with smaller grammar schools, which he thought could not provide proper sixth form work without a 'grossly inefficient' use of the best teachers.[93] This hardly suggests that Eccles was a staunch upholder of the existing selective system. McCulloch also did not fully pursue the issue of Eccles' position regarding further transfers to the grammar school from the secondary modern at age 13. While he described Eccles agonizing somewhat over this, he did not acknowledge that Eccles and his officials ultimately came down against such transfers.[94] A keen ideological defender of selection would surely have sought to increase such later transfers, as it would have strengthened the selective system in the face of the attacks coming from its egalitarian critics that centred on the age of 11.

More recently, Peter Mandler has asserted that the 11 plus and academic selection was manifestly unpopular with the general public. However, he has also claimed that the Conservative governments of the late 1950s and early 1960s were 'wedded' to tripartite or bipartite systems, including the long-term protection of grammar schools, as part of their support for the social order and middle class interests.[95] Yet Mandler goes on to describe how the Conservatives sanctioned the 2 tier Leicestershire schemes advocated by Pedley throughout this period. As just noted, these involved fundamentally altering many grammar schools' academically selective status, although Mandler does not acknowledge this. These Conservative governments are nevertheless portrayed as having been instinctively keen to defend the existing system but were forced to accept local authorities' experiments in the face of supposedly widespread public hostility towards academic selection in favour of 'grammar schools for all.'[96] Events are thus rationalised as part of an inevitable path towards universal comprehensive schooling.

Dennis Dean was more perceptive in his notable article on this period. He described how in the late 1950s Geoffrey Lloyd was influenced by those who felt that the system had catered too much for the more able, and that more should be focused on those who were less so.[97] Dean showed how a distinct air of political expediency and calculation pervaded, with education increasingly viewed by Eccles, Hailsham and Lloyd as an 'investment' that would yield both economic success and electoral dividends.[98] Dean suggested that they considered middle-class parents could be wooed with 'grammar-type' education in secondary modern schools, rather than through the inevitably restricted route represented by selection at the age of 11 to the grammar school.[99] This militated against building more grammar and technical schools, and instead encouraged a vague and all-encompassing role for the secondary modern. Technical, vocational and academic courses were therefore to be spread over all types of school. Eccles had promoted the Colleges of Advanced Technology (CATs), yet these were intended for school-leavers and envisaged in regional terms. This institution, viewed as a possible goal for all types of pupil, inevitably militated against technical schools being built in large numbers for pupils at an earlier stage. It also meant an increasingly unclear identity for both the secondary modern and the grammar school, which were being tacitly merged through this emphasis which resulted in them undertaking increasingly similar courses.

Dean observed that while Florence Horsbrugh's approach had been straightforwardly conservative, her successors, while speaking the language of academic excellence, diversity of school and selection by ability, encouraged trends of merging schools that operated against selection.[100] By not targeting the anomalies of the existing system, the Conservatives therefore played into the hands of a Labour opposition determined to exploit them. This was despite the fact that comprehensive schooling and its egalitarian ideals were of limited public appeal. Dean noted this in terms of Mark

Abrams' opinion survey findings and subsequent advice to the Labour Party to play down the ideological intentions that lay behind comprehensive schooling. A Labour strategy of concentrating on the irregularities of the existing system and emphasizing individual opportunity through comprehensives was thus considered to be more likely to be successful against a Conservative government losing its nerve due to a mixture of lack of faith and political expediency that had backfired. Instead, the government appeared to be at the mercy of those who had a stake in educational expansion and who deliberately manufactured public demand for it, when it in fact had 'little support' among the groups supposed to benefit from it.[101]

The chapter has therefore shown how as the late 1950s wore on into the early 1960s, Conservative ministers of education increasingly portrayed the issue of secondary school reorganization as a matter out of their hands. It begs the question as to whether the 1958 White Paper was deliberately made ambiguous in order that the government would not have to define what system it did in fact believe in. Along with ministerial ambiguity, it appears that officials largely viewed the matter in terms of what was considered to be better practical organization of secondary education within certain local education authority areas. No steps were taken to strengthen existing anomalies within the ministerial powers from the 1944 Act, particularly in relation to the Leicestershire scheme. Noticeably, it was relatively lower-ranking Conservative MPs such as Raymond Gower who made efforts to attempt to rectify this, rather than the party leadership. Indeed, rather than strengthening ministerial powers, the Conservative government gave even greater latitude to local authorities with their 1964 legislation allowing greater experiments with age ranges. Tellingly, Quintin Hogg would not admit to the potential consequences of such a Bill in terms of its enabling local authorities to go even further with what they were already doing.[102] Against a backdrop of increasing egalitarianism and concentration on the pupil of lesser ability through the Newsom Report and the development of the CSE exam, both Hogg and Edward Boyle expressed a notable defeatism and lack of faith in the existing system and downplayed the extent of their ministerial powers during this period. It is therefore my contention that regardless of whether the Conservatives had won the 1964 general election, comprehensive reorganization would have continued and become the main form of secondary school organization under their leadership, given that they continued to defend the Leicestershire scheme and similar local authority experiments.

4

A proclaimed opposition 1964–70

This chapter describes the degree of radical and far-reaching change in secondary schooling that the Labour government undertook with the issuing of Circulars 10/65 and 10/66 that pressured local authorities to comply with their comprehensive policy. It shows how the Conservative shadow opposition failed to offer a principled opposition to what was occurring. Instead they increased their tendency to carefully make false distinctions between comprehensives that were imposed by central government, which they claimed to oppose, and those proffered by the local education authorities, which were portrayed as simply the prerogative of local democracy. Even following the Party's success in the 1967 local elections, which many within the Conservative Party grassroots saw as a great opportunity to oppose full-scale reorganization, the leadership maintained that secondary education was not to be made into a 'party-political' matter.

No desire to fight

With Harold Wilson's Labour government now wielding power, the situation for existing grammar and secondary modern schools was perilous. A major urban comprehensive scheme was already taking place in Bristol, with the City council proposing to turn all the schools within the area comprehensive. On 27 November 1964 Alan Hopkins, the Conservative Member for Bristol North East, therefore introduced a motion in the House of Commons that sought to protect against the wholesale abolition, 'whether by closure or radical alteration,' of direct grant and maintained grammar schools. Hopkins' position, rather than being intransigent, merely called for a policy of 'co-existence' between selective schools and comprehensives.[1]

Geoffrey Lloyd, whose career had been somewhat obscure since he had been moved from the ministerial post in 1959, now chose to speak up at this point. He reiterated the argument for 'overlap' that had been symbolized by the 1958 White Paper and for allowing 'co-existence' between selective and non-selective schools. Lloyd revealed how an educational trip to America in early 1959 had led to him witnessing the American 'high' school system there. While he had noted the Americans' 'social self-confidence,' he had also been struck by the powerful reaction against the comprehensive idea while there. This had reinforced him in his inclination, as he put it, to 'experiment with circumspection' as minister.² Yet he did not account for why comprehensive schools had in fact grown by a significant degree during his period of office nor acknowledge the perverse impact that his 1958 White Paper had had upon the local education authorities' thinking. These sentiments by Lloyd provoked the inevitable response from Michael Stewart, the new Labour Secretary of State, that if the object of policy under the last Conservative government had been to 'narrow to a minimum' the difference between secondary modern and grammar schools, it was therefore surely futile to separate children in the first place.

In opportunistic spirit, Stewart skilfully drew upon Edward Boyle's own phrase of children needing the opportunity to 'acquire' intelligence as his justification for the Labour government's national policy.³ He pointed out how at the present time, a mere month after the Conservatives had left office, sixty-eight local education authorities responsible for 63 per cent of the secondary school population were now either implementing or examining concrete proposals for comprehensive reorganization. In addition, another twenty-one authorities were also contemplating reorganization while having no definite plans. Claiming that the Labour government were now giving 'a clear lead' by embarking on a national policy, Stewart then delivered the crunch:

> Remarks made by the right hon. Member for Birmingham, Handsworth (Boyle) in 1963 suggest that in coming to that conclusion, the conclusion when I decide that that ought to be done now, *I am only anticipating by perhaps 12 or 18 months what he would have done had he been in a position to do it* (my emphasis). What I say, therefore, is this. In the Government's view we ought now to accept that the reorganisation of secondary education on comprehensive lines should be national policy.⁴

In response to this announcement, Quintin Hogg merely expressed 'regret' that this should be one of the great issues for educational discussion. The real issues in secondary and primary education, according to Hogg, were teacher provision, school building and the curriculum. If the Labour government was to concentrate on those, he almost pleaded, 'we should find that problems of organization would solve themselves in due course.' Not for the first time, Hogg was at pains to forestall any ideological confrontation.

Beyond criticism of the coercive nature of the Government's approach, as opposed to allowing a process of 'slowly evolving' local systems, it was clear early in this Parliament that the Conservatives' opposition was going to lack teeth.⁵ In any case, Hogg had for so long emphasized the importance of the Minister not 'overriding' the local authorities' decisions that he was hardly in an effective position to object to what was now happening.⁶ The Wilson government, through central imposition, was now putting the finishing touches to a situation that the Conservatives had allowed to develop at the local level.

In response to the Government's announcement, a further major debate on secondary education was held in the House of Commons on 21 January 1965. Hogg introduced a Motion that merely proclaimed the Conservative Party opposition to be endorsing the Newsom Report's view that it would be 'premature' to attempt a 'reasoned judgment' of comprehensive and other types of secondary education at this stage. The Government was urged to 'discourage' local authorities from adopting schemes of reorganization at the expense of grammar schools and other schools of proved efficiency and value, and that the Opposition opposed any proposal to impose a comprehensive system upon local authorities.[7] Nevertheless, it was all noticeably tepid in its wording.

Strikingly, Hogg prefaced his opening remarks with an emphasis upon not 'giving undue offence to one another.' In this way, he praised the manner in which Rab Butler, in engineering the passing of the 1944 Act, had supposedly ensured that the educational system had proceeded for many years on a bipartisan and all-party basis. Hogg therefore claimed that he thought, 'despite all evidence to the contrary … that the elements of a bipartisan policy are still present if the right Hon. Gentleman would choose to adopt it.'[8] There was little sign of a desire to attack what the Labour government was doing on any fundamental level.

However, certain lower-ranked Conservative MPs were prepared to fight harder against what the government threatened. Anthony Berry, the Conservative MP for Southgate, keenly pointed out how over 300 secondary modern pupils in his constituency had in fact taken the GCE last year, with 12 pupils being transferred to the grammar school at sixth form level. Nevertheless, this emphasis upon the number of pupils taking the GCE, and thus the secondary modern school being assessed on that basis, tended to advance the argument by Labour that the comprehensive school would ensure that more pupils would have the opportunity to do this in future. In practice, arguments highlighting a greater number of pupils taking academic courses inadvertently played to the objectives of comprehensive campaigners.

Harold Gurden, the Conservative MP for Birmingham Selly Oak, beseeched that they try to extend the grammar schools and build more of them rather than comprehensives, which were so obviously coming at their expense. Joseph Hiley, the MP for Pudsey, claimed that threats amounting to victimization had been made against teachers who had dared to criticize comprehensive schooling. The selective scheme had in fact been killed off, he claimed, by 'mass parental hysteria.' Pointing the finger at Labour members on the opposite side of the House, he claimed that this animosity had been deliberately engineered and that teachers were expressing hostility to the 11 plus because their lives have been made 'almost intolerable.'[9] Yet these perspectives were all falling on deaf ears.

By contrast, the ambiguity on the part of the Conservatives' front bench spokesmen remained. And the Labour side delighted in exploiting their discomfort. Tom Williams, the Labour MP for Warrington, taunted the Conservatives by claiming that, whether in or out of government, the Party had never publicly declared, 'except with the public hypocrisy that it regards as necessary to oil its own wheels back to Parliament,' what real system of education they approved of.[10] In response to this pressure from Williams, Hogg was then forced to admit that he had never believed in the tripartite system as minister. He stated, in spite of his ostensible intention to oppose the government's comprehensive policy, that:

> I simply do not believe and I never have believed and never will believe that children are to be divided into three rigid categories.[11]

In the strictest terms, it was perfectly reasonable. Yet the overall effect of this sentiment was to effectively undermine any position seeking to defend academic selection in the face of a newly elected government determined to destroy all selective schools. All the while, and in a manner markedly similar to that of Boyle, he still would not disclose what kind of secondary system he did in fact believe in.

Boyle, when it came time for his turn to speak, proved to be no less full of ameliorative banalities than Hogg. He claimed to simply believe in rejecting both the idea that all schools should cater for the full range of ability and a 'strict' tripartite system. By picking his way so carefully in response to what the government was proposing, it lacked any real conviction as a form of opposition. And so often, his arguments were interspersed with remarks such as his not wanting in any way, 'to gloss over the defects there are in many of our secondary modern schools.'[12] Inevitably, these sentiments too often appeared to cohere with the prejudices of those on the other side.

He also expressed a revealingly critical view of the grammar schools' role. Amazingly, the Old Etonian Boyle appeared to criticize the grammar schools for snobbery and elitism on their part:

> I have in my time often been critical of some grammar school attitudes. I will be again tonight. I have constantly reminded people on grammar school speech days that it is not only in grammar schools that one finds boys and girls who can do academic work. They must not talk as though they were a tightly knit academic community threatened by barbarian hordes outside.[13]

The critical manner in which Boyle was referring to the grammar schools was marked. It revealed a distinct lack of sympathy for them in spite of their very existence now being threatened.

Given the distinctly circumspect nature of the Conservative opposition's arguments, particularly the manner in which they had effectively echoed Labour's own sentiments over the supposed injustice of selection at 11, the Minister of State Reginald Prentice was thus able to state how 'hardly anyone who has spoken in the debate ... had anything to say in favour of 11 plus selection except for the hon Member for Pudsey' (Hiley). He continued by adding:

> Everyone else was admitting that it was a system which to some extent or other was a bad system, unfair and unjust to large numbers of our children.

Effectively, the Conservative Party had conceded the terms of argument to the pro-comprehensive side by restricting themselves to criticizing unsuitable comprehensive projects in the wrong areas, rather than in fundamental terms. Indeed, Hogg and Boyle remained trapped within a misplaced desire for 'bipartisan' consensus. By contrast, the Labour government had no qualms whatsoever about agitating for what they were seeking in distinctly ideological terms.

The long-held Conservative position of increasing the number of GCE courses in secondary moderns was also dismissed by Prentice. He summed up what of course had been wrong with the Conservatives' position all along by pointing out that if taken to its logical conclusion, they ought to go comprehensive, and anything less than that was 'a failure to go comprehensive.'[14] By the end of the debate, the terms of the Conservatives' original motion had been completely altered by an amendment from the Government. In contrast to the original, it now stated how it was:

> conscious of the need to raise educational standards at all levels, and regretting that the realisation of this is impeded by the separation of children into different types of secondary schools.[15]

It therefore noted 'with approval' the local authority plans for comprehensive schemes. This, it claimed, would 'preserve all that is valuable in grammar school education for those children who now receive it and make it available to more children.' The time was now ripe, it added, for a declaration of national policy.[16] The Labour government's motion was then carried with the help of an abstention of the Liberal Party, who had earlier voted against the Conservatives' resolution. The die was now cast. Furthermore, on the following day of 22 January, Anthony Crosland was appointed the new Secretary of State for Education.

Significantly, Boyle was reappointed by Alec Douglas-Home as Opposition spokesman on education in February. Shortly after this, in a speech to the National Union of Conservative and Unionist Association's Central Council on 6 March, Boyle would only repeat his opposition to the Labour government's 'rapid and universal' imposition of comprehensive schools while also claiming that:

> Nobody should attempt to assert as matter of dogma that whereas socialists are, in principle, in favour of comprehensive schools, Conservatives are equally committed against them.[17]

Boyle was also keen to point out how Rab Butler had apparently told him 'on many occasions' that he had never intended for the 1944 Act to establish a tripartite system of education that should remain 'rigid' for all time. In addition, he stressed that he did not believe that every small market town could expect to maintain its own grammar school.[18]

Instead, the Conservatives' Policy Group on Education and Careers Research, with Boyle as its Chairman, was at this time keenly examining the future of the public schools. It was now trying to ascertain the best response to any further calls for their integration with the maintained schools, which it was felt might lead to their potential abolition. It is striking to consider the extent to which this issue appeared to animate the Conservatives' Policy Group during the spring of 1965, rather than the impending comprehensive 'national policy' for the maintained sector that the Labour government was fixed upon.

The dominant inclination within the Party's Policy Group was again to do as little as possible to highlight the public schools as an issue. Instead, Boyle asked for the Policy Group's views on the suggestion that the schools should simply be left to carry on as they were at present, given that this had been the approach of both Hogg and Eccles. In response, the MP Richard Hornby, who notably would be promoted to chair

Edward Heath's later policy group on education, reinforced Boyle's point by stating that the Conservatives should continue to 'play passive' on the public schools and instead point out how much money was going into the state sector. Boyle was also quick to add that any 'percentage suggestion' of the Fleming Report variety had key difficulties of entailing considerable cost, that it would be difficult to select the appropriate state pupils to the schools and that the expenditure on this section of the community would have to be 'justified' to the general public.[19]

The conclusions of the Policy Group's interim report, published on 21 July, were unsurprising. While acknowledging a growing feeling in the party that the public schools should no longer be the 'exclusive preserve' of those who could afford to pay the fees, they were 'firmly opposed' to the Labour Party's policy to integrate the public schools into the state system. It stated that:

> It would mean, at best, state control of these schools, and, at worst, a fundamental change of character, tantamount to abolition. We should oppose any such policy.[20]

Rather than the public schools' integration, a policy of 'co-operation' was preferred. There was a limited need for boarding education for children currently within the state sector; therefore, they considered that the independent schools could have a part to play in 'supplementing' the current boarding provision by local education authorities. Thus, the whole issue was to be narrowed simply to that of boarding need for children whose family circumstances were difficult or relatively unusual.

Rab Butler, who was perusing the Interim Policy Group reports being submitted at the time, commented on their report. While describing it overall as limited, Butler directed his main attention to the public schools question. According to him, there was in fact no solution. He noted that the Universities of Oxford and Cambridge had gone for entirely free places, 'and almost entirely on entrance or alleged merit.' Nevertheless, he added that, 'if this were tried by the public schools they would lose their identity.' While the model of the leading direct grant Manchester Grammar School was a more open system, 'this would not do for the others.' Instead he underlined, like Boyle, what a small proportion of the total school population attended them. Almost dismissively, Butler suggested that if Eton and some of the others reverted to their old foundation practice of 'letting in a few poor scholars they would do better.' In an echoing of his deft handling of the Fleming proposals twenty years earlier, Butler concluded that 'I recommend not making a political issue out of the public schools question.'[21] The preference to hedge their bets on the public schools and wait for the Labour government's next move continued.

Opposition within the Party

In great contrast, regarding the Labour government's comprehensive policy for the maintained schools, Boyle was throughout the spring of 1965 maintaining that if in government he would essentially continue with their policy. He was quoted by *The Times* on 8 April as saying that he would look forward to having 'many more' comprehensive schools and two-tier systems. Comprehensives were 'much better' in many rural areas than a small grammar school, and therefore he would 'not hesitate' to approve, as he had done when Minister, schemes for developing a market town grammar school into a larger comprehensive. He added that many children had 'a rotten deal' in education at the present time, while including the balancing sentiment that he was firmly against 'this desperate hurry' to get rid of good schools. When asked by *The Times* interviewer what he would do if he were back in Curzon Street he replied that:

> I am sure the trend to comprehensive education would continue. I would support good schemes. But I cannot see a situation developing in which there do not remain grammar schools of integrity.[22]

It was all suitably non-committal. On that same day, *The Times* announced that the County Education Committee in Leicestershire had decided that all children would now transfer from the secondary high schools into grammar or upper schools at the age of 14. The article claimed that this decision had simply been made due to the Labour government's recently announced intention to raise the school leaving age to 16 in 1970.[23] However, the originators of the Leicestershire experiment, as shown earlier, had always carried the ultimate objective of fully comprehensive schools for the area in their minds from the outset. While the plan at present applied to only five areas of the county, the intention was for it to now be extended throughout.

Unsurprisingly, Boyle was having to face increasingly sharp correspondence from Conservative-voting supporters of grammar schools at this time. One particularly astringent correspondent cornered Boyle throughout June that year. Refusing to be satisfied with assurances from Boyle about protecting the public and direct grant schools, the correspondent emphasized how it was of course the fully maintained grammar schools that were fundamentally under a threat of extinction from the comprehensive principle. While a tiny minority might find their way into independent schools, he continued, 'there will be no alternative for the vast majority of our abler pupils but to be condemned to some form of comprehensivism with all the mediocrity that this term implies.' He demanded therefore that the Conservative Party adopt an 'unequivocal attitude' on the subject.[24]

In reply, Boyle offered up the usual sentiments about a comprehensive suiting a market town area better than two smaller selective schools, as well as the standard flannel about conservatives believing in the freedom of local authorities. The correspondent was not to be deterred, however. It was 'irrelevant,' he said, to take into consideration 'mere economic or administrative advantages' in advocating comprehensive schools. Children in small market towns had as much right to the benefits of selection as children living in larger towns. After all, he continued, children had long travelled considerable distances to grammar schools and not resented it, so why should they be condemned to the comprehensive school round the corner? Exactly the same applied to new housing estates. 'Surely,' he added, 'a child's education should not be decided merely on its home address?'[25] Furthermore, he noted that comprehensive schools were as key a part of socialism and communism as nationalization and collectivism.

These were not the sort of fundamental points, of course, that Boyle was used to having to answer from his more expedient-minded Party colleagues.

Events were constantly militating against and undermining the credibility of Boyle's approach. On 12 July, the Labour government published a key circular, named Circular 10/65, on the organization of secondary education. Issued by the Secretary of State, now Anthony Crosland, it 'requested' local education authorities to prepare and submit plans for reorganizing secondary education in their areas on comprehensive lines. It emphasized that the 11–18 model was the Government's ultimate preference for the comprehensive school. However, given that existing buildings were for smaller schools, it would accept two-tier comprehensive arrangements that would fit into the existing pattern for the time being, while leading eventually to an all-through system.

When it came to the direct grant schools, the Secretary of State wanted both local authorities and the governors of these schools to 'consider' changes in their methods, curriculum and the age of entry so that they could 'participate fully' in the local scheme.[26] It was clear that they were intended to be subsumed into the comprehensive system as well.

Local education authorities were required to submit plans within one year of the date of the Circular. In its conclusion, it acknowledged that the complete elimination of selection in secondary education would take time to achieve. Nevertheless, in a nod to the previous Conservative period in government:

> The spontaneous and exciting progress which has been made in this direction by so many authorities in recent years demonstrates that the objective is not only practicable; it is also now widely accepted.[27]

Inevitably, there was now a growing pressure on Boyle from both within the Conservative Party and outside to take a firm and principled opposition towards the threat that had now fully materialized. Yet only days after the Circular was published Boyle was in fact divulging in private correspondence that it was 'too early' to say whether the Conservative Party would formally withdraw the Circular if they were returned to office, 'bearing in mind that it is not couched in terms of compulsion.'[28] Boyle clearly did not want to do anything to oppose it. As a result, he chose to rely on a deliberately naive interpretation of the Government's actions. Meanwhile that summer, Edward Heath was elected to the Conservative Party leadership on 23 July.

Matters came to a head in the weeks leading up to the annual Party Conference in October. The Conservative Teachers' Association was up in arms again. On 4 October, their secretary Barbara Turner wrote to Edward du Cann, the Chairman of the Party, to inform him of the Conservative Teachers' latest meeting only days before. There had been 'tremendously strong' criticism of the Party's public statements on comprehensive education.[29] As a result, the Conservative Teachers' National Advisory Committee had now written to du Cann asking for a clarification of the Party's policy on secondary education. Basing their view of the official policy on Boyle's speech to the Central Council on 6 March, the Conservative Teachers stated that a more positive statement was 'urgently required.' 'Many members of the Party,' they revealed, 'feel that our educational policy is defensive and negative. And thus causes confusion and hesitation among members.'[30]

The CTA also wanted to know whether, if the Labour government took financially coercive policies against local authorities that defended their grammar schools, this would be fought by the Conservative opposition and reversed when they were returned to power. Furthermore, a new Conservative government would need to reverse 'makeshift and doctrinaire' schemes. They added that such a pledge should be publicly made at the Party conference.[31] Boyle and others were being pressed to publicly answer questions that they were doing their utmost to avoid. In further correspondence to Conservative Central Office at this time, Miss Turner revealed that 'the feeling against Sir Edward is quite amazing.' The CTA considered Boyle to have 'sold the pass' with regard to comprehensive schools.[32] Both Walter Higgins and Royston Moore, the Chairman and Vice-Chairman of the CTA, were now anxious to meet du Cann to discuss the matter further.

That same day, du Cann wrote to Boyle informing him of the CTA's feelings, attaching their statement to his letter. He suggested that he and Boyle meet the officers of the CTA at the Party Conference on the Tuesday evening before the debate on education took place. du Cann advised Boyle to deal with the matter in 'general terms,' by offering a clear declaration that they were opposed to all forms of coercion. He continued:

> Where this has occurred at the instance of the Central Government or Local Authority, we would seek to arrest the process if not amend it. Something like this would satisfy everybody without going further, by way of commitment, than necessary.[33]

du Cann considered the CTA's questions in their statement to be 'understandable,' adding that, 'I am anxious, of course, to avoid their being hard-pressed in the first debate on Policy which Ted (Heath) will be answering, or in your own.'[34] Through this kind of stage-managing, they clearly hoped to avoid embarrassing questions at all costs.

As well as this Gilbert Longden, the new Hon Secretary of the CTA, also wrote to Edward Heath on 8 October, informing him how the Association felt the Party had been 'too silent' about the dissolution of the grammar schools, and had appeared to 'acquiesce' in the universal substitution for them of comprehensive schools.[35] He implored Heath to address their concerns in his keynote speech the following week.

But Boyle's conference speech did not answer the CTA's questions at all. Instead, it turned out to be an exercise in avoidance. Most of it was devoted to criticizing the Labour government on the grounds of insufficient spending and expansion, such as their not meeting the Robbins Committees's estimates for the demand for university places. Similar criticisms were made alleging the insufficient expansion of the teacher training colleges. Noticeably, the core issue of the future of the grammar schools was left to the end.

While expressing standard sentiments about not losing 'traditions of excellence,' Boyle stated that some local authorities had reorganization plans that made 'educational sense' for either the whole or part of their areas. The Conservative Party position was that they did not believe in the 'rapid and universal imposition' of the comprehensive principle, and noted the value of established grammar schools in large cities. The Circular was merely criticized as a 'fraud' because, according to Boyle, Crosland had asked local authorities to reorganize on comprehensive lines but had not been in a position to promise them the money 'to do the job properly'. Thus, any criticism of the Government was not based on any fundamental terms, but rather in terms of the manner in which the Labour government was undertaking the policy. As Boyle put it:

> How we react, as a Party, to the Socialist proposals must depend, to some extent, on local circumstances.

To round off his speech he finally proclaimed:

> Let us firmly stand by our ideal of secondary education for all and do not let us ever give the impression that we are interested only in the secondary education of one section.[36]

In spite of the Conservative Teachers' obvious consternation, Boyle was undeterred in reinforcing what he regarded as the 'moderate' response to what the Labour government was doing.

Three months later, when answering questions at the North of England Conference at Harrogate, Boyle let slip that he would not seek to withdraw Circular 10/65 if the Conservatives regained office in the spring general election now looming. Claiming that all schemes should be judged on their merits, in spite of what the Circular was clearly demanding, he stated that it would be 'silly' to withdraw it. If he were in charge, there would simply 'not be the same drive in a comprehensive direction.' Nevertheless, there would be no 'counter-drive in the direction of bipartitism.'[37] This, he continued, would be to reverse not merely Labour policy since 1964 but also the earlier Tory policy to which he was committed.

Speaking secondly at the same conference, the Secretary of State Anthony Crosland made it clear that the Labour government had no interest in heeding Boyle's measured advice. Furthermore, Crosland made it abundantly clear that the direct grant schools were also to be governed by the terms of Circular 10/65 and he did not regard the existing direct grant school regulations requiring them to be academically selective as any barrier to this. If, however, there was any real doubt, he added, 'I shall not hesitate to amend the Regulations in a way which would leave no room for any doubt at all.'[38] The Labour government was effectively intending to plough through. It all showed just what a Secretary of State could do if possessed of sufficient zeal.

Given the furore provoked by his unguarded remarks at Harrogate, Boyle was forced to play down the significance of the Circular in correspondence with grammar school pressure groups at this time. Throughout, he emphasized that it was not a directive and that Crosland had no power to direct local authorities to go comprehensive. The government's Circular was merely a 'request' to know what actions local authorities were willing to take in the short and long term. Furthermore, it was highly unlikely that a future Conservative Secretary of State would send out a counter-circular urging local authorities to, as he put it, 'cut comprehensive ideas out of their heads.'[39]

However, despite Boyle's attempts to dilute the issue, resolutions were now flooding in from Conservative councils criticizing his attitude towards the comprehensive threat. Many were now demanding that schools not originally intended to be comprehensives be restored to their former status when the Party was next in office. In response to this stream of correspondence being sent into him by Clyde Hewlett, the Chairman of the Party's Executive Committee, Boyle claimed that Press reports of his remarks at Harrogate had given a 'distorted' idea of his view. Nevertheless, he continued to flatly refuse their call for all schools not originally intended to become comprehensives to be returned to their former status if the Conservatives regained office. Boyle told Hewlett that this went 'miles' further than their policy had done in the past and 'throws over completely the idea of education as a local service.' A Conservative government, he went on, could not 'force' schools to adopt a particular status irrespective of the wishes of the local inhabitants. (It obviously did not matter that the Labour government was doing precisely this in advancing their pro-comprehensive policy through the issuing of Circular 10/65.)

Yet to Boyle, the pro-grammar schools protestors' views were not based in 'reality,' adding:

> Incidentally there is no clear evidence from what I have been able to see that the electorate as a whole is pining for us to take a more dogmatic attitude on this question.[40]

Those within the Conservative Research Department, which included the future newspaper columnist Simon Jenkins, continued to advise the Conservative opposition to attack the Labour government on their priorities instead. This had resulted, they argued, in the neglect of primary schools and a delay in the necessary increase of the teacher supply. By contrast, the Government's emphasis upon secondary school reorganization was merely to be censured in terms of being 'financially wasteful' and 'irresponsible' in the light of these needs.

The approach that Jenkins advocated was for the Conservative Party to merely discourage local authorities from embarking on major reorganization schemes involving expensive new schools when the secondary schools in the area already carried adequate provision. However, he added:

> In view of the state of flux ... a Conservative government would also discourage authorities from undertaking major building programmes *where schools so built would be incompatible with the possibility of eventual reorganisation on non-selective lines.*[41]

(my emphasis)

In seeking to justify Boyle's stance at Harrogate, Jenkins offered a concern for 'order' as the reason for why a Conservative Secretary of State would continue to request plans drawn up under Labour's Circular 10/65. By doing so, he could then apparently 'take stock' of the national situation.[42] While wanting to be seen to be critical of the Government's policy, they were therefore resolved to not commit themselves to any withdrawal or reversal regarding the Labour government's Circular. Indeed, Jenkins felt that comprehensive and bilateral schools could 'mitigate' some of the consequences of selection and that this was a 'substantial point in their favour.' They were once again playing the part of opposition while not fully committed to it.

And Boyle was following Jenkins' advice to the letter. In the Commons, his opposition remained merely confined to the 'complete and unconditional' abolition of all selective grammar schools. Throughout, Boyle emphasized that 'we on this side are not committed to selection between schools as a principle.'[43] Because of the controversy caused by the government's policy, Boyle claimed, perhaps more revealingly than he intended, that Crosland was having far more disagreements with local authorities than he had ever had as Minister. Indeed, as he put it:

> I do not recall one single occasion during my whole two years when I had a sharp disagreement with a local authority over reorganisation.[44]

It was left to lesser-ranked Conservative MPs such as Harold Gurden to attack comprehensive schools on the more fundamental basis that it represented a form of education that sought to adjust a child's opportunity to the advancement of others who were more limited in capacity.[45] Another notable yet minor Conservative voice, John Astor for Newbury, emphasized that while the Circular may have been presented as a 'request' to local authorities, many of them were now in fact interpreting it as an instruction to produce schemes.

Nevertheless, Boyle continued to express the sentiment that grammar schools 'only make sense morally provided that we extend opportunity in the widest way to all children in the modern schools according to their abilities.'[46] Their moral existence was therefore being held to be contingent on the education of the less able. Grammar schools were thus to be assessed primarily in terms of the needs of the 'Newsom children.'

A second Circular published three days later on 10 March underlined the zeal of the Labour government on the issue. Circular 10/66 was concerned with school building programmes for the next three to four years. It asserted that it would be 'inconsistent' with the government's long-term objectives if future school building programmes included projects fitted for a 'separatist' system of secondary education. Therefore, it proclaimed:

> Accordingly the Secretary of State will not approve any new secondary projects which would be incompatible with the introduction of a non-selective system of secondary education.

In cases where the department did not yet have the necessary information, authorities were asked to describe for each secondary proposal how it would fit into a comprehensive pattern.[47] Proposals were to be submitted not later than 30 April. Therefore, it was clear that the government was in fact embarking upon a form of compulsion, albeit through 'back door' methods. They were tying the Conservatives into a circular's terms just before the forthcoming General Election. Once again, Boyle's evasive position was being increasingly undone by the actual turn of events.

Inevitably, the Conservative Party's 1966 general election manifesto was non-committal on the issue and simply echoed the advice coming from Jenkins and others at the Conservative Research Department. It merely expressed vague sentiments about the need for 'full educational opportunity,' and the need for local education authorities to provide as full a range of courses as possible in all the secondary schools.[48] It was all a model of prevarication.

It was no great national surprise when the Labour Party won a clear and resounding victory in the General Election on 31 March. The issue of Circular 10/65 was now effectively out of Boyle's hands to have to deal with. With the additional publication of Circular 10/66, it was clear that the Labour government was effectively bullying local authorities by withholding money regarding future building plans. The situation was more urgent than ever and demanded that the Conservatives take a resolute approach. Yet Heath chose to keep Boyle on as his education spokesman in the new parliament despite the staunch criticism he had already received within the Party.

The 1966 Franks Report into Oxford University in fact showed the considerable inroads that maintained grammar and direct grant school educated pupils had been making since the 1944 Act in winning places at Oxford University. From a combined percentage of only 32 per cent in 1938–9, compared with 62 per cent from independent schools, their percentage had risen to 45 per cent in 1958–9 compared with 52 per cent for those educated privately. The figures for 1964–5 showed that their climb had been steady but relentless, with grammar and direct grant school pupils, at 34 and 17 per cent, respectively, combining to reach a cumulative total of 51 per cent, outstripping those from independent schools at 45 per cent.[49] Overall, it had been a stunning level of advancement over the past quarter of a century.

Yet throughout the spring of 1966 Boyle continued to advise Conservative MPs to accept comprehensive reorganization plans in their areas, particularly if they cohered with the Conservative opposition's 'moderate' requirements. Ironically, it was in fact the case that many of the building plans that were being enacted at this time had originally been approved by Boyle a few years earlier when Minister. As he admitted to the MP for Ludlow Jasper More in April, the 1966/7 building programme for the Bridgenorth area had been approved by him in April 1964. In terms of another projected plan at Whitchurch involving a three-tier organization, he again approved of these experiments adding, 'as you know, it was I who brought forward legislation enabling experiments to be made with 9–13 (age) schools.'[50] Part of his response inevitably involved rationalizing his own actions undertaken as Minister.

His approach also reflected the caution and political calculation of Heath. In a minute to Boyle on 11 May, Heath described how upon listening to Crosland on television, he had noted that Crosland was no longer stressing the advantages of the comprehensive education system itself, but was instead claiming that the Conservatives wished to maintain 'discrimination' through selection. As Heath then confided to Boyle:

> This appears to me to be a powerful political argument from their point of view and one likely to be very effective with large sections of the electorate, particularly those not tied to either Party.

Heath asked Boyle to give particular consideration to their response to these arguments. He now wanted a 'simple, straightforward statement' made publicly on the Conservative Party's attitude towards selection which could be used by colleagues up and down the country and reproduced in a Party leaflet.[51] In practice, it appears that Heath wanted to pull Boyle even further away from any confrontation with the Government's policy and towards accommodation of the Left's terms of debate.

The closeness in outlook between Heath and Boyle is further evidenced by the fact that Heath also put Boyle in charge of overseeing the Party's policy groups at this time that were set up as part of Heath's overhaul of Conservative Party organization. Boyle was now responsible as Deputy Chairman of the Advisory Committee on Policy for the appointment of members to the various policy groups and for general co-ordination between them and the party committees. As a result, Boyle's view on current educational controversies was going to become even more stamped on the Party. Notably, Heath also appointed Richard Hornby, a renowned 'liberal conservative' favoured by Boyle, as the Chairman for the education policy group in May 1966.[52]

Throughout this time, hostile resolutions continued to pour in from Conservative Party councils to Clyde Hewlett, the Executive Chairman of the National Union. In the case of the Wessex Provincial Area Council, they moved a condemnatory resolution that the Party's policy on education at the last election had been 'totally out of character' with the more realistic approach to the other domestic issues and called upon the policy group concerned to make a fresh appraisal of ideas in relation to secondary education.[53] However, given the make-up of the Party's new policy group, any re-evaluation of the Party's current position was distinctly unlikely.

Inevitably, Boyle took offence at this kind of correspondence. He stoutly defended the Party's policy as it had been outlined in the manifesto and claimed that many party members had in fact criticized the Party's policy for not accepting the comprehensive principle universally. Indeed, he claimed that most of the 'thoughtful' members of the Party 'would by no means welcome a more dogmatic approach' than the one contained within the manifesto.[54]

Despite this, Gilbert Longden, who had been trying to put the best possible spin on the Conservative opposition's comprehensive policy in public, was nevertheless privately anxious, as his correspondence to Boyle at this time shows. While his newsletters to his local association praised the Party's moderate approach in contrast to the Labour Party's radicalism, he was himself perplexed by the Party's policy. And he was of course witnessing first-hand the Conservative Teachers' Association's reaction to what they regarded as Boyle's ineptitude in opposition. A third Labour Government Circular, entitled 13/66, had recently appeared on 23 May that served to further reinforce Circular 10/66. Local education authorities were again required to show for each proposal for their 1968/9 secondary programme that they would be compatible with introducing a non-selective system.

In correspondence with Boyle in May, Longden revealed the CTA 'were, I am afraid, all very hot under the collar and do not think that the Parliamentary Party is pulling its weight.' The Conservative Teachers, Longden reported, felt these government circulars constituted an 'alteration of the law by blackmail.' He informed Boyle how:

> The story repeated time after time by teachers from various parts of the country is that Conservative members of LEAs and Divisional Executives simply do not know what the Party's policy is; and that, if one of them attempts to state what he thinks it is, he is at once countered by some Socialist quoting you.[55]

Longden felt he should raise this matter at the next education committee meeting, while also suggesting that the renewed policy group look again at the whole question.

Boyle's reply, two days later, was indignant. He was at pains to emphasize that 'the Party has _not_ let anyone down over this issue of reorganisation.' He felt he had dealt with the matter sufficiently in two key recent speeches in the House of Commons on 2 March and 25 April. According to Boyle, 'they are the _complete_ _answer_ to any Socialist who uses my words at Harrogate to spread dissension within our own ranks.' Noticeably defensive regarding recent criticism for his stance regarding Circular 10/66, he claimed it would have been wrong to angle his recent Commons speeches more specifically onto it. He stated that many Tories or Tory sympathizers who wished to put up a strong fight, 'as I would' to preserve the identity of first-class existing grammar schools, 'wouldn't wish to see many _new_ grammar schools.' Notably, he included Percy Wilson, the ex-chief inspector of schools and the Conservative MP Angus Maude among those taking this view, adding:

> You'll see that I was highly critical of Crosland for usurping the right of LEAs to initiate proposals, but I was careful _not_ to give the impression that our Party wanted to see a whole lot of _new_ selective schools.

In further explaining his approach to Circular 10/66, he repeated his view that a more 'dogmatic' line on reorganization would 'not be generally appreciated within the Party as a whole.'

However, because of his growing irritation with the Party's National Advisory Committee on Education (formerly the CTA), Boyle suggested to Longden that they both meet so Boyle could advise him on what to tell them.[56] As a result, he felt the Committee would be better informed on Party policy. Revealingly, Boyle praised Longden for doing this 'chore,' and appeared to think that the problem was simply much needed improvement in staff-work between Central Office and the NAC officers so that the latter would better understand the Party's policy. Rounding off, he encouraged Longden to raise the matter at their next meeting, 'but I must say,' with more than a hint of exasperation, 'I shall be very resistant to the idea of yet a _third_ debate on this subject!'[57] It would be better, he maintained, to attack the government over university building and to debate the new White Paper on polytechnics.

None of this satisfied the Party's National Advisory Committee. Over the following month, they sent Hewlett another three resolutions, again calling for secondary reorganisation to be further debated in Parliament. Increasingly impatient,

Boyle again claimed that his two recent speeches in March and April had dealt sufficiently with the issue and complained to Hewlett that:

> I hope you will agree that it is a really rather ludicrous situation for a resolution to be passed by a National Advisory Committee, urging a particular matter to be debated when this has, in fact, been done only a few weeks before.[58]

All the while, the Conservative Research Department was reinforcing his approach. On 5 December it advised that despite many of the current comprehensive schemes being ill-thought through and involving the breakdown of 'recognizably good' grammar and secondary modern schools, nevertheless:

> It is important that, as a Party, we adopt – and are seen to adopt – a positive, not a negative, approach to the changes proposed ... It is very easy to be perceived as adopting a negative, obstructing role – perhaps in part because the press expects us to react in that predictable way to the amalgamation of good with less favoured schools.[59]

It continued:

> However, it is arguable that such an attitude, whether real or imagined, is not appropriate to a Party intent on winning the next election. We should welcome – and be seen to welcome change – provided that what is proposed fulfils certain definite conditions and that it enables positive educational aims to be achieved.[60]

With this type of obfuscation, they therefore sought to rationalize the Conservative Party's acquiescence with the Labour government's policy.

Those Conservative councillors who took the same expedient approach as Boyle and Heath were to be encouraged. The local elections were looming in May that year. In January 1967, the Chairman of the Merton Education Committee Vincent Talbot wrote to Boyle to compliment him on his approach to the comprehensive issue at a meeting of London borough leaders and candidates. This included praising Boyle for his support for the proposed three-tier comprehensive system at Merton. In addition, Talbot expressed his irritation with fellow party members who wanted a tougher line taken against the government and who were critical of Boyle. 'Could you not get across to our people,' he beseeched Boyle, 'that the weakest policy to stand upon is that of "anti"? One must put forward constructive policies.' Talbot reported how at the meeting the Conservative leader of the Inner London Education Authority Seton Forbes-Cockell had referred to Talbot as a 'blackleg' keen to ingratiate himself with 'our socialist masters.' Forbes-Cockell, of course, wanted a tougher line taken against the Labour government. Talbot urged Boyle to continue to use all his influence to get the Tory opposition to the Labour government based on what he termed 'a positive approach.' After all, Talbot continued, only 20 per cent of parents were those of grammar school offspring while 80 per cent were of those within secondary moderns.

Talbot sent Boyle his best wishes and support in his efforts to put 'more realistic' thinking into the Tory views on education.[61]

Much impressed by this missive, Boyle sent a copy to Heath with a note adding that he thought that Talbot would 'dig his toes in effectively' for them on educational matters in the future. Furthermore, he also used Talbot's letter to show Heath that 'the pressures on me do not all come from one side.'[62] Boyle then wrote back to praise Talbot's position at the meeting, and assured him that he was doing all he could to get the opposition to the socialist schemes based upon a 'positive approach.' He reassured Talbot that the Party's policy group chaired by Richard Hornby was of course taking this approach on the subject. As he further put it:

> Incidentally, I very much agree with you that I think a number of Conservatives are wholly unrealistic in their approach to the political implications of this question.[63]

Defending selection was now clearly regarded as politically toxic. A further copy of both Talbot's letter of support and Boyle's reply was sent to Michael Fraser, the Deputy Chairman of the Party, who was now openly supportive of Heath and Boyle's approach. To Fraser, Talbot seemed an 'excellent man,' adding, 'let us hope that there are many more of him up and down the country.' Meanwhile, referring to Talbot's critic on the Inner London Education Authority who was keen to fight the Labour government on the issue, 'we will do our best to continue to contain Forbes Cockell.'[64] They were now determined to stifle pro-grammar school opposition to the government amongst their own ranks.

Yet key educational figures were emphasizing their concerns to the Conservative Party's Education Policy Group at this time. On 26 January, Lord Eric James of Rusholme, a former headmaster of Manchester Grammar School, visited them to express his alarm at the latest developments. To James, the social revolution was going too far. Amidst the constant talk about the underprivileged, it was no longer being acknowledged that the under-representation of the working class was ultimately 'a fact of life.' The solution to the emotive issues of environment that had captured the educational and social zeitgeist lay in the long-term improvement of social conditions, not the destruction of existing institutions. Egalitarianism was putting increasing strain on them, in particular the universities. Furthermore, he detected a growing hatred of intelligence and intellectual excellence in the country. While accepting himself that going back to selection at 11 was 'no good,' he felt nevertheless that they must 'stick fast' on selecting 'at some point' or the 1944 Act would be broken.

James argued that the top 5 to 7 per cent of state pupils had to somehow be salvaged, ideally in direct grant schools and voluntary-aided grammar schools within urban areas. The problem of rural areas was more difficult to resolve. Nevertheless, comprehensive schools would inevitably tend to spread sixth form teaching staff too thinly. Unlike Rab Butler, James was noticeably keen for the public schools to get more involved in trying to limit the damage. Winchester, he suggested, could be used for clever boys at the age of 15 or 16. The new emphasis, he stated to the Policy Group, should be on saving the clever children rather than defending the grammar schools.

In distinctly pessimistic spirit, he pointed to a future decline in the universities' standards in fifteen years' time as a result of going all-comprehensive. In addition, the nation could not afford to expand university education on the scale that was now being done.[65] Clearly James' view, in spite of its pragmatism, was at odds with the approach that the Conservative Party was now resolved upon.

In spite of these warnings by prominent figures such as Lord James, Boyle instead pressed on with cementing the Conservative Party's accommodating response to the Labour government. On 9 February he produced a paper confirming the party's position to the Shadow Cabinet. The Conservative Party's 1958 White Paper's claim that 'borderliners' could be equally well catered for in the higher forms of the secondary modern had, he claimed, been confounded. The issue had not therefore gone away as they had hoped.

Boyle then became more frank. It was about votes. A secondary education leading to a sixth form course was publicly considered the 'indispensable passport' to a university place and 'a good job' in a profession. Far more Tories than they had realized had been 'genuinely worried' about the implications of 11 plus selection for their own children, with the proportion of Tory voters in the electorate more than double the proportion of grammar school places. In addition, it was over ten times the proportion of those who could educate their children in a good fee-paying school. (These sentiments were of course practically identical to those that Talbot had been urging him to adopt.) 'I do not myself,' he added, 'think we are ever likely to see a national swing back to an 11 plus system.' It was interesting, he continued, that even so 'persuasive an elitist' as Lord James had admitted this at the recent policy group meeting. (James had, of course, also said a lot more than this about salvaging the needs of able children.)

With the key local elections to be held in April and May 1967, detailed schemes were now being put before Conservative councillors for acceptance or rejection. Boyle now advised on the broad guidelines to be taken into account when assessing them. There were to be vague assurances that comprehensive schemes should attract first-class teaching staff, that they fit into existing buildings, that there be sufficient consideration of the effect upon the sixth form and whether they were making 'adequate provision' for the brightest children. He then added:

> A vocal – though, I believe, numerically small and declining – section of opinion would like us to go further, and to state categorically that we are opposed <u>on principle</u> to any plan involving the reorganisation of a good existing school.[66]

Boyle stated that there were 'decisive objections' to such a statement. Firstly, it went beyond their practice when they had been in power. Successive Conservative ministers had approved a number of proposals to develop a grammar school into a comprehensive such as at Gillingham and Market Drayton, or had reorganized a secondary modern and a grammar school into a junior and senior high school such as at Felixstowe. Almost all the 'really objectionable schemes,' he claimed, had come from the big cities that were usually Labour-controlled. As a result, 'the tide is now running too strongly for any such statement to make sense.'

Furthermore, Boyle claimed that many 'conspicuously good' authorities such as Hampshire, which were Tory-controlled, were against education being fought out on party lines. They were working hard to achieve a measure of consensus and 'do not want a more dogmatic Tory policy urged on them.' In the future, many grammar schools, he proclaimed, would find their future as senior high schools. Nevertheless, he was also forced to admit that there were other parts of the country where the pattern of school buildings was such as to preclude any completely satisfactory scheme of comprehensive reorganization in the near future.

When it came to the direct grant schools, he noted his approval of the Bristol authority's recently expressed intention to take up places at Bristol Grammar school, while not seeking to 'unscramble' the whole comprehensive scheme. Yet Boyle's inconsistencies nevertheless gave him away. In arguing for the importance to be attached to direct grant schools, he claimed that they provided the answer to the special needs for the 'really high flyer within a comprehensive system.'[67] Yet this of course indirectly conceded that the high flyer was going to be otherwise undermined within it.

Therefore, even if they were successful in the upcoming local elections in May, they were committed to not opposing the basis of the Labour government's policy, no matter how destructive it was. The extent of the pressure on local education authorities by the Government's Circulars was being underplayed and was presented instead as wholly inevitable.

Other influential voices were also advocating going with the chain of events and avoiding confrontation before the May local elections. On 13 April, Sir William Alexander, the Chairman of the Association of Education Committees, emphasized to the Conservatives' Policy Group the importance of 'sufficient agreement' between the two major parties in order that the organization of secondary education would not be altered every five years. Indeed Alexander claimed that the country, having educated the top 15 per cent well, was now doing a 'reasonable' job for the average child with comprehensives. Yet as he also admitted, the comprehensive system was unlikely to do as good a job for the top 5 to 10 per cent of pupils as before, unless there was 'very careful organisation.' He offered the vague hope that a system of 'guided parental choice' at sixth form level might militate in favour of a more specialized sixth form college in an otherwise comprehensive system.[68] Therefore, in spite of the fact that he indirectly acknowledged that it would be detrimental to the more able pupils, Alexander was one of many 'moderate' voices who advocated consensus with the Labour government's policy direction. Clearly, the educational establishment wanted to sit tight and hope for the best.

A hollow victory

The local elections held in April and May 1967 would, ironically, turn out to be a resounding success for the Conservative Party. The Labour Party managed to retain only two counties in England and Wales, as well as only two of the major cities of

Sheffield and Stoke. The vast majority of local education authorities were now in Conservative hands, with many for the first time. Nothing, however, was going to change the resolve of Boyle and Heath on secondary education. They were instead concerned to rationalize the ongoing process of comprehensive reorganization at all costs. Boyle was now advising Conservative councillors that the best system was for three-tier comprehensives, with sixth form work being provided in one or two grammar schools within each local area. Meanwhile, he advocated letting the remainder of secondary schools 'cope' with the whole ability range between the ages of 11 and 15 or 16.

Thus by concentrating sixth form work in a limited number of schools, it was felt this could circumvent the problem for the more able pupils within a comprehensive system. Indeed, Boyle privately remarked at this time that 'I am not sure how much it really matters that bright children in the 11–16 schools will encounter relatively few graduate teachers.' It was felt the system would work as long as those pupils could gain accelerated promotion a year early at 15 to the sixth form college ahead of the other pupils. (This approach had of course been advocated by David Eccles to his officials ten years earlier.) All these suggestions were, he felt, to be preferred to that of 'standing pat' on the existing pattern of organization in defiance of the Secretary of State, 'because I do believe majority opinion does tend to feel today that 11 plus selection cannot really be justified.'[69]

At this point, Edward Heath clearly felt he had to make a public statement on the matter. On 17 June at Overseas House he addressed the Party's National Advisory Committee on Education. While expressing opening remarks about the potential 'erosion' of standards from egalitarianism, at the heart of his speech lay a reinforcement of Boyle's approach. While there had to be selection at some stage, it had 'never been a Conservative principle' that it meant children being 'segregated' in different institutions. Vague support was expressed for local authorities' alternative arrangements such as senior high schools at thirteen or sixth form colleges. Grammar schools, Heath went on, had undergone many changes in the past, and therefore should not be afraid of 'further changes' occurring in their institutional role now. Nevertheless, he expressed support for local authorities keeping open places in direct grant schools, which indirectly conceded the need of able pupils for them in an increasingly non-selective system. Throughout it all, Heath would not spell out what type of secondary system he did in fact advocate. Instead, the local authorities were simply 'free to judge.'

At the same time, potential changes being made to the public schools were criticized. This was in reference to the recently appointed Public Schools Commission Report potentially advocating local authority pupils being allotted a certain percentage of places within them. This was represented as a form of discrimination against the maintained system by 'creaming off' its more able pupils. No notion of change was clearly being advocated for the independent schools. Finishing off his remarks, Heath added that governments had concentrated too much on the 'talented few' and neglected the average, and this was now 'rightly' being corrected.[70]

In reporting Heath's speech, the *Education* journal's editorial noted how the landslide in the local elections had left Conservative local government leaders 'thirsty for guidance.' Yet what they had in fact received had of course been very different. They observed how the speech 'confirmed the often neglected fact that Sir Edward Boyle and Mr Heath are in cahoots: they see eye to eye on education, as on other matters.'[71] Indeed, the head of Heath's private office wrote to Boyle a few weeks later on 13 July emphasizing how he was 'so glad that you feel that Ted's speech was on the right lines. I am sure you are right about not identifying with the 11 plus.'[72]

Other senior figures in the Party also clearly approved of the line that Heath had taken. Quintin Hogg, in correspondence with Jim Prior, simply thought that getting units of the right size would solve many of the problems relating to reorganization. Furthermore, the 'basic fault of the grammar schools at the moment,' he continued to Prior, 'is that they cater for too narrow a segment of educational ability.' If grammar schools were limited to those who were prepared to undertake a five-year course, 'it would more or less do the trick.' The sense of casual complacency was overwhelming. Meanwhile, he shared what he called 'Ted's enthusiasm' for using the independent sector of secondary education as a means of comparison for providing 'a la carte' types of education which parents 'may legitimately desire but which hardly fit into the ordinary system.'[73] The difference in approach by Hogg towards the independent sector compared with the 'ordinary system' was, as ever, striking.

Inevitably, there were further disagreement and confusion existing between local Conservative Associations and Borough Councils for the same area over the direction of Party policy. At this time, the Secretary for the Finchley and Friern Barnet Conservative Association wrote to Heath regarding the comprehensive plan recently approved by the Conservative Group on the Borough Council. The Finchley Association had assumed that Heath would prefer to see the grammar schools remain as they were, while 'adapting themselves' as time went on. By contrast, the Conservative Group on the Council were convinced that Party policy on education was in favour of a fully comprehensive system. Two weeks after its publication, the Group on the Council had now decided by a majority vote to accept a comprehensive plan in which all the grammar schools were to become senior high schools from 14 to 18, with the secondary moderns designated 'junior high schools' from 11 to 14. In addition, a certain number of schools were intended to become 11 to 18 comprehensives.

According to the Finchley Association, the main reason the Conservative Group on the Council had come to their conclusion was that they considered it to be in line with Party policy and had even quoted from Heath's speech. In the view of the Association, if this was so, 'a number of people, certainly in the Finchley constituency, will not vote for our candidates for they will say that we are only propagating socialist policy.' Furthermore:

> This is a matter of great urgency for if this matter becomes public it will show that there is a serious conflict between a Conservative Association and the Conservative Councillors, which is not our desire.[74]

All of these difficulties in communication had of course stemmed from the carefully cultivated opacity of the Conservative leadership.

As a result of this letter, Heath was sufficiently perturbed to ask Boyle for his advice on the draft reply he planned to send to the Conservative leader on the Council. The resulting draft reply from Heath's private office contained the same circumlocutions as in his recent speech. It gave nothing away and would not comment on the particularities of the Finchley case. It was 'too early to say' which schemes were best suited to 'our changing conditions.' Therefore:

> Believing as we do in the importance of local democracy, it would not, therefore, be right for me to advocate a particular pattern or organisation for your area.[75]

Boyle, commenting on the draft reply, approved of these sentiments. But as he then added:

> This is the second occasion that Barnet has 'nibbled' at reorganisation and I do not think there is anything gained politically by prolonged unease and uncertainty which can only affect the schools.[76]

If the majority of the Education Committee could agree on 'a soundly based' scheme of reorganization of the Borough, 'then they can be assured of Mr Heath's backing, and mine.' Equally, if they wanted to go cautiously, they could count on their sympathy. 'It is up to them – it is not for Mr Heath or myself to tell them what to do ...'[77] With this double-speak, Heath and Boyle were thus further extricating themselves from such difficult local cases.

In fact, throughout this period Boyle was even maintaining the view in private correspondence with Heath's private office that the grammar schools had long been 'a cause of class division.' As he added, with unintended irony:

> Personally, as Mr Heath knows, I think there is everything to be said for our Party showing that we are ready to face these difficult issues in a spirit of realism and courage.[78]

Nevertheless, a strong sense of dissatisfaction within the Party came to a head at the Party Conference in Brighton in October. At the debate on education, the initial motion proposed merely criticized 'the hasty and ill-considered imposition' of comprehensives by the Labour Government and its priorities that meant it had neglected teacher supply and primary education.[79] The motion, put forward by Donald Hunt of the Bristol Association, was much criticized. According to Christine Howard of Brighouse and Spenborough, it was a 'non-Motion advocating a non-policy' and was not condemning the Socialist principle itself. Instead, it was 'a pale pink Motion and it recommends pale pink policies.'[80]

Gilbert Longden, in his uniquely difficult position as Hon Secretary of the NACE, notably sought to defend Heath and Boyle to the Conference over selection. (This was in spite of his own privately expressed misgivings to them.) He claimed that Heath and Boyle were aware of the need to select and, 'If there were time, I could quote you chapter and verse from their speeches.'[81] The need to keep on side with the leadership was being maintained at all costs. Predictably, Longden linked the defence of the grammar schools with the particular needs of the public schools. Meanwhile, unsurprisingly, the 'moderates' such as Christopher Chataway, who was now head of the Inner London Education Authority and close to Boyle, backed the original motion.

Others who were lower down the party hierarchy, however, wanted to fight on principle. Mr K.G. Warren, notably from Enfield East, where local electors and parents were now fighting a key battle with the government over comprehensive education without due consultation, opposed the motion unreservedly. The socialist government was committed to the establishment of a completely comprehensive system of education in the country. By contrast, their position as a Party was ill-defined. As he stated somewhat audaciously:

> The statements which have been made, both by Sir Edward Boyle and even in Mr Heath's speech on 17th June, are very carefully worded, but unfortunately they are worded for the few instead of the many.[82]

Were they, he asked, going to fight parents' battles and save the grammar schools or not? He was convinced that not only the majority of Conservative supporters but also the majority of parents of all political persuasions believed it:

> I beg of you, have regard to the consequences if you approve this motion and, in doing so, fail completely to give the urgently needed reassurance to those who are looking to us for help.[83]

This was now the key moment on the issue for the Party. Matters had come to a head. Edward Boyle would be forced to respond to this mood of opposition in his conference speech.

Yet Boyle chose instead to devote the main part of his speech to criticizing the government for the neglect of primary school improvements and for sub-standard school-building in response to the recent Plowden Report's recommendations. Like Chataway, he was merely opposed to the manner in which the government had gone about their comprehensive policy, which in certain cases had led to 'shoddy, ill-thought-out proposals.'[84] Rather than publicly calling for a halt to comprehensive reorganization given the obvious inadequacy of these schemes, Boyle simply maintained the right of local authorities to make up their own minds. Ultimately, it amounted to a slower means of achieving the same result.

A sizeable proportion of the Conference audience knew it. With a vote carried out on the motion, only a small majority was revealed to be in favour. Amid shouts from the audience of 'no!' a ballot was then called. This would turn out to be the Conference's first balloted vote on education in seventeen years. The 'pale pink' motion was then carried by 1,302 votes to 816, a majority of 486.

Nevertheless, *The Daily Telegraph's* editorial termed the vote a 'rebuff' for the Party leadership, noting that the motion that had been carried 'was couched in terms which would have made it possible for anyone not firmly convinced of the inadequacy of the Opposition's education policy to support it.' It was vital, it added, for parents to have the right to have an effective say in the choice of their children's schools, as those in Enfield were now demanding. As the editorial sagely noted, 'This right can be destroyed as effectually by a borough council as by the Department of Education.'[85] To reduce the matter simply to the prerogative of local authority decision-making, as the Conservative leadership was doing, was disingenuous to say the least.[86]

Yet the 1967 Party Conference proved to be a major coup for both Boyle and Heath. Those Conservative party members who wanted to take a tougher line and fight to support local authorities that were holding out against the Government were instead being marginalized and made to look extreme and impractical by the leadership's lawyerly choice of words.

A key survey published later that year by *New Society* magazine contradicted the view of public opinion held by the Party leadership. The largest group, at 46 per cent of respondents, indicated that they would like their child to attend a grammar school, while only 16 per cent favoured a comprehensive school for their own child. A proportion of 52 per cent were broadly 'in favour' of comprehensive education in general. However, 76 per cent supported the retention of grammar schooling.[87] On a question of whether they favoured selection into different types of school specifically at the age of 11, the results in fact revealed a roughly even split, with a slight majority of 46 per cent in favour and 43 per cent against, with 11 per cent 'don't knows'. Whatever level of dissatisfaction was felt about the existing system, it did not show a resounding degree of support for universal comprehensives or hostility towards grammar schools and selection itself, as the sociologist Dennis Marsden, commenting on the survey, admitted.[88]

This contradicts the view of Peter Mandler, whose recent contention is that comprehensive schooling arose out of parental feelings of dissatisfaction with selection and that it ultimately reflected popular aspiration and democratic sentiment.[89] In fact, detailed accounts of schemes such as those in Darlington and Gateshead at this time show an often blatant lack of 'consultative machinery' with parents by pro-comprehensive local councils, with the Ministry of Education consistently taking an approach of laissez faire towards them.[90]

In Enfield, the Labour council there was found to have exceeded its powers three times. The recently appointed Secretary of State for Education Gordon Walker had laid himself open to the charge of acting in a 'thoroughly unreasonable manner in the circumstances' by the Court of Appeal in trying to alter the articles of government of Enfield Grammar School without giving adequate time for objections to be made. Indeed, for eight schools in Enfield, no public notices in accordance with Section 13 had been issued, with the Council claiming that the Minister had advised them that no notices were required. This protracted dispute now forced the issue of local objections to be put under scrutiny.

Nevertheless, those who were influential within the Conservative Party were increasingly urging it to leave the grammar schools behind and seize opportunities to take political credit with the new comprehensive schools. Simon Jenkins, now working for the *Times Educational Supplement* as its news editor, was encouraging the Party to try to take advantage of the situation, particularly given their current powers recently gained in the spring local elections. In his view, incoming Conservative groups needed to win the confidence of education officials as well as teachers and parents if they were to make a 'distinctive impression' on the education service. With a 'sensitive' and 'constructive' approach it could thus turn the victory into a lasting one. In particular, the Party could pick up political capital from the debacle occurring in Enfield between parents and the government at the time. By contrast, the principle of selection, Jenkins emphasized, was 'no longer viable, educationally or electorally.'[91]

An interim injunction was then granted by the Court of Appeal in relation to Bradbury and Enfield Borough Council. It led to a new Education Bill that was given its second reading in the House of Commons on 12 December. The power of Section 13 under the 1944 Act was now to be strengthened. The new Bill was thus seeking to rectify the ambiguity that had long existed about the 'precise ambit' of Section 13 as to when local government electors, parents and others had the opportunity to lodge objections. As seen earlier, it had been the practice under every administration to treat most changes to existing schools as not constituting the setting up of a 'new' school. With this Bill, that became the 1968 Education Act, parents and local electors now had the right to voice objections to any changes in the character of a school by way of alteration of its age range, sex composition or ability range, such as from a selective school to a comprehensive. This was to be the case even if in fact a new school was not being established or an existing one closed. Because of the traditional attitude long in place that had not considered the issuing of public notices in these cases to have been necessary, it was admitted that local authorities, acting in 'good faith,' had in fact been producing invalid schemes for years.

This crucial issue of the strengthening of the case for parental and local electors' notices and thus for Ministerial intervention, which had been so fatefully neglected, was only now being rectified when it was too late. The 'hands-off' approach that had been in operation for so many years under successive Conservative governments, maintained simply because it had been 'ministerial practice,' had enabled too much damage to have already been done.

However, as the Conservative MP Ronald Bell pointed out, these new additions to the grounds on which Section 13 notices could be served could work well only as long as the dominant party at Westminster was not 'doctrinally committed' to destroying all selective schools. Yet since local control and Westminster majorities often coincided, these procedures might in practice be 'quite nugatory.' As he put it, 'A Minister from whom has issued a circular like Circular 10/65 will overrule all objections from parents about selective schools.'[92] What instead was needed, he argued, was a national decision that would not be brushed aside by the swaying fortunes of politics every few years. Ideally, this meant a new clause giving binding to Section 76 of the 1944 Act concerning the freedom of parents and their wishes for their children's education. Nevertheless, in speaking for the Conservative Opposition, Boyle merely continued to emphasize the need for partnership and consultation in regard to education as a local government service.[93] Conflict was to be avoided at all costs.

Confirmation of a non-position

On 16 January 1968, the Labour Government announced their decision to postpone the raising of the school leaving age to 16. It was now to be deferred to 1972. This had been prompted by necessary Government spending economies given the programme of devaluation of sterling at the time. Yet all the plans relating to the reorganization of secondary education had been prepared on the assumption that the school leaving age would be raised to 16 in 1970. Many reorganization schemes could not therefore continue as planned. In regard to the direct grant schools, the government decided to reduce the capitation grant to the schools from £52 to £32 from September 1968. The schools would most likely have to offset their losses in grant by increasing tuition fees. It appeared to be the Government's hope that local authorities would cut the number of places provided in them.

However, by the spring of 1968 Boyle was in an altogether more optimistic mood and according to private correspondence at this time, felt that Conservative Party opinion on secondary school reorganization had been 'considerably more peaceful' in the last few months. He informed Peter Baguley, the new Secretary of the Party's National Advisory Committee on Education, that he was becoming 'a little more forthright' in his support of those local councillors, such as Alderman Hull of Lancashire County Council, who supported his position on secondary reorganization. In spite of the Party's recent success in the local elections, they could not have a 'major upheaval' in schools policy every time there was a change of political control.[94] Amidst this continued approach from Boyle, an even more hard-line pro-comprehensive figure, Edward Short, was appointed the new Labour Secretary of State for Education on 6 April.

It was at this time that a report by the Conservative Party's Education Policy Group was published in July. Entitled *Conservative Education Policy for the Seventies*, it essentially served to justify the party's current position on all the key educational issues of the day. It proved to be a restatement of their current position and did not even undertake any original research. Chaired by Richard Hornby, known to be of decidedly 'liberal' disposition, the Group included Boyle as well as Simon Jenkins, Gareth Jones of the Party's Research Department, Gilbert Longden and Angus Maude, among others.

Now that the vast majority of local education authorities were in Conservative hands since the previous year's local elections, and the future of secondary education was for Conservatives to determine, the report stated how it was 'important that our policy should be clear and unequivocal.' Under a comprehensive system, it was claimed there would be an advantage of the postponement of 'irreversible' choices, as well as a 'flexibility of school organisation' that had proved difficult to achieve under a selective system. While it would mean 'some change' in the character of the grammar schools, a selective entry was not the 'sine qua non' for their success. When it came to the future of the direct grant schools, the Conservatives' report could only limply recommend extending the direct grant system by giving independent schools of high standing the opportunity to join the direct grant school list. There was 'nothing incompatible' about ending 11 plus selection alongside the maintenance of high academic standards.

Yet their attitude towards independent schools was wholly different. The report stated that Conservative policy should rest 'on an absolute commitment to defend the existence of independent schools,' and stressed the 'human right' of parents to send their children to them if they were willing to do so. Using the straightened financial situation at the time as part of their reasoning, it stated how:

> They are at present relieving the state of the duty of educating about 6 per cent of our children and thus lessening the demands upon the classrooms of the State, and upon the public purse at a time when we need every penny to maintain and improve the maintained schools.[95]

The Shadow Cabinet discussed the Policy Group's report in the Leader's room of the House of Commons on 15 July. With Heath in the Chair, all the key figures were present, including Hogg, Boyle, William Whitelaw, Keith Joseph and Margaret Thatcher. Yet according to the minutes, it was only Peter Walker, educated at Latymer Upper School, who voiced concern as to the degree of acceptance by the group of the comprehensive formula, and how he regretted the extent to which 'we were turning our backs on the grammar school.'

The response from the others present was striking. Geoffrey Rippon stated that the public looked upon the secondary modern school as 'a very second rate option.' Boyle then interjected with his oft-repeated sentiment that the 11 plus examination and the secondary modern school were not attractive to the bulk of the population. It was repeated how senior 'high' schools or sixth form colleges could develop brighter pupils instead. While there was considerable attraction in the thought of selection at age 13, this was 'not really viable' given that the school leaving age remained at fifteen. Of course, this idea had never been properly pursued to begin with.

For his part, Quintin Hogg then repeated his view that if the grammar schools had covered a wider range of ability, the problem would not have been so 'acute.' It was of course all being rationalized with the benefit of hindsight. For the most part they clearly wanted, with the exception of the grammar school-educated Walker, to not pursue the matter. Summing up, Heath then stated that it was not proposed to publish the report but that it was intended to form the basis for future policy. As there was 'obviously some criticism' of it in the Leader's Committee, he suggested that members of the Committee who wished to do so should send in written comments on the Report so that the subject could then be reconsidered in the light of them.[96]

Nevertheless, the 1968 Conservative Party Conference proved to be just as divided on the comprehensive issue as the previous year. For the education debate, another deliberately innocuous motion was offered by Marcus Fox of the Shipley Conservative Association that concentrated its ire upon the government's cuts in expenditure. It claimed that since the Conservative gains in local government, the Labour government's comprehensive plans had been thwarted, but also made it clear that purpose-built comprehensives had 'a place in our plans.'[97]

But to Angus Maude, who then got up to speak, this amounted to 'unexceptionable platitudes.' Instead, he called upon the Party to vote to defend Conservative councils trying to save their grammar schools from destruction. They were 'being bullied, bewildered and blackmailed' into feeling that they had no alternative but to destroy their established grammar schools. Instead, he wanted to call the government's bluff. There were no socialist or floating votes to be won by destroying grammar schools, but there were a lot of Conservative and floating voters to be lost. The compliant Conservative authorities had been 'shilly-shallying about' and worrying about having their money cut back and feeling that they had to submit schemes and that the Tories would put it right in the end. 'It can never be right,' he continued, 'to do something you know to be wrong as a result of irresponsible political pressure.'[98] Having revealed to the audience that the Chairman had not seen fit to include his originally proposed amendment, Maude asked them to reject the current motion. Instead, he urged them to appeal to Conservative local authorities who were being blackmailed to honour their promises and save their grammar schools.

It made a huge impact on the Conference audience. As a result of this resounding oratory, he was able to get his amendment accepted as an addendum. It now included a condemnation of the Labour Government's attempt to force schemes of comprehensive reorganization, and called on the Party to give 'clear and unequivocal support' to Conservative local authorities 'which seek in pursuance of their election pledges to resist Government blackmail and preserve their grammar schools from senseless destruction.' It was a fundamental challenge to the leadership's whole perspective. Maude was looking to make trouble.

It turned out that Boyle had not anticipated being asked to speak on the subject. What he had really intended was for his speech to attack the Government over alleged cuts in the school building programme. From his recent correspondence he had thought the comprehensive issue had been put safely behind him. Nevertheless, he was now being forced to address it again. Somewhat irritated, he stated at the outset that they had been debating the issue for the past three years at the Conference, 'and I must admit that I had thought today we might have devoted a larger share of the time to other subjects.' As usual, he described how they remained opposed to legislative compulsion, but would 'really question very much indeed' going as far as Maude and suggesting that Conservative-controlled local authorities could only do 'useless botched up jobs everywhere.'[99] Maude and others were thus effectively painted as running down a number of highly reasonable schemes all over the country.

Summing up, he stated that he had been in politics long enough to have learned that he did not know all the answers, least of all in education, and 'nor,' he added in a noticeably irritated aside to the Conference audience, 'may I say, do any of you.' In addition:

> I will join you willingly and wholeheartedly in the fight against Socialist dogmatism wherever it rears its head, but do not ask me to oppose it with an equal and opposite Conservative dogmatism, because in education it is dogmatism itself which is wrong.[100]

Unsurprisingly, these sentiments did nothing to reassure. In spite of Boyle's attempt at amelioration, Maude's addendum to the motion was added with an overwhelming majority vote, with the reconstituted motion then carried by another huge majority. Maude was now a distinct thorn in the side of both Boyle and Heath.

Also at this time, the responses from the Shadow Cabinet concerning the Education Policy Group's Report were being sent into Central Office. Some of them displayed a marked concern at any possibility of the Report being published. As Joseph Godber, the MP for Grantham, noted in his missive to Michael Fraser, the deputy chairman at Central Office, this had been the only subject on which there had been a level of disquiet at the recent Party Conference. As a result, Godber strongly counselled against the Report being released, fearing it would highlight the degree of division over the issue within the Party. Any document published on the matter, he advised, would be likely to arouse argument. While at times such argument was welcome, 'open divergences of view on this subject within the Party at this time could be a serious embarrassment to many Conservative controlled local authorities, quite apart from the problems that it would pose for us at Westminster.' For Godber, the 'balance of advantage' lay in not publishing the Report at this stage. If the political atmosphere changed nearer the general election, then it might be advisable to put out something later on.[101] Meanwhile, any show of open disagreement that highlighted the comprehensive issue was to be studiously avoided.

By contrast, Peter Walker's attitude was uncompromising. He hated the tone of the Report, particularly what he regarded as its dismissive and fatalistic attitude towards the grammar school and felt they were treating its demise as a foregone conclusion. The grammar school, he emphasized to Fraser, had been instrumental in breaking down social barriers, and if children were not provided with the kind of education best suited to their abilities it would be damaging to the nation. In contrast to the Party leadership, he felt there was a need to encourage authorities to make better provision for the transfer of pupils from secondary modern to grammar schools at the ages of 12 and 13. In addition, much more needed to be done to enable successful pupils from secondary modern schools to join the grammar school sixth form. Instead, the Report's section on secondary education was 'positively encouraging' a theme of eliminating the grammar school as opposed to the comprehensive.

Walker pointed out that if the Conservative Party Report's view of comprehensive education was taken to its logical conclusion, there could logically be no future for the independent schools either. No democracy, he went on, would tolerate a system whereby the great majority were educated at comprehensive schools whilst a 'small wealthy minority' were able to enjoy the benefits of a public school education. If such a system continued, it would 'result in political action against the independent schools within a very short period of time.' Furthermore:

> I am convinced that one of the main reasons for the general toleration of the small section who enjoy the advantages of a public school education has been the availability of a grammar school education to large numbers of pupils who are the children of lower income groups.[102]

Showing his obvious distance on the matter from others in the Shadow Cabinet, Walker advised Fraser to circulate recent publications defending the grammar school to his colleagues that would expose the 'myths' propounded by the comprehensive proponents. Yet Walker's arguments, obvious as they were, were coming too late and in any case were falling on deaf ears. The Conservative Shadow Cabinet wanted to move on.

The Black Papers

Angus Maude had been busy since his intervention at the Party Conference in October. He was now in communication with Professor Brian Cox, a Professor of English Literature at the University of Manchester who was also editor of the *Critical*

Quarterly magazine series, about publishing a pamphlet seeking to publicly argue against the trend towards 'progressivism' and egalitarianism in education. By January 1969 Maude, who formerly had been a journalist, was set to be one of the contributors and was informing Cox of his excitement and commitment to the project that was due for publication in March. Among other contributors were Cox's partner as editor Anthony Dyson, Kingsley Amis and the academic Robert Conquest. For Maude, it was a 'counter-revolution' and was instrumental in organizing publicity for it, with the *Telegraph* newspapers among his contacts.[103] The Black Paper authors' sense of mission was then heightened when the Education Secretary Edward Short announced on 6 February that he intended to issue a forthcoming Bill on comprehensive schools in the near future. A press conference for the pamphlet's publication was therefore set for 12 March. Entitled *Fight for Education*, the pamphlet turned out to be a great success, with both *The Daily Telegraph* and *The Times* covering it the next day amid a blaze of publicity. Soon, the authors were planning to issue a second publication. Maude, always conscious of obtaining the most coverage possible, suggested to Cox that there would be maximum effectiveness in publishing it on 7 October at the beginning of the Conservative Party Conference.[104]

Meanwhile, Boyle's relationship with certain sections of the Party continued to deteriorate. It led to a fiery meeting with Conservative delegates on 21 April. Representatives from Brent, Barnet, Sheffield, Bristol and Liverpool all expressed their dissatisfaction with Boyle and the leadership, particularly after the efforts they had made to get the party elected in the local government elections two years earlier. In particular, they expressed their 'bewilderment' at Tory policy on comprehensive reorganization. To the delegates, Boyle and Heath were simply accepting the trend rather than setting their own.

Those assembled were incredulous. As a result of the last local elections, there were only three counties under Labour control, with the rest now Tory-controlled areas. Yet the vast majority were now implementing socialist education policies. Indeed, as the delegates from Enfield noted, the only thing the Tories tended to do was to 'administer Socialist policies better than the Socialists.' The delegate from Sunderland described how he had been co-opted onto his local education committee following the party's victory in the local elections, having canvassed to preserve the grammar schools there. However, he related how at the second meeting not a single Tory member had backed him up when introducing a plan on secondary education in line with what he had promised voters. Similarly in Bristol, despite the Tory council having gained control from Labour and with 40,000 people having signed a petition to keep four grammar schools selective, the Tories had 'ratted on their promise.' As a result, the number of independent candidates on the right was increasing. All in all, the delegates complained bitterly of the apparent abandonment of academic excellence for 'social' reasons by both Tory politicians and local authorities.

To this, Boyle simply repeated the official mantra of how any authority with a viable comprehensive scheme 'will have my encouragement,' and that the Party was not opposed to a good grammar school being reorganized. He went on to claim that the only way that successive governments could have resisted comprehensive education would have been by establishing GCE courses in every secondary modern school from the beginning. The minutes record how a 'howl of rage' erupted from the delegates upon hearing this. Nevertheless, Boyle maintained that the 'social mix' had been inadequate within the secondary modern school. Alongside the retention of direct grant schools under a future Conservative government, he would merely resist Edward Short's proposed bill to 'compel' local authorities to go comprehensive. Yet given his response to the earlier Labour government circulars, this was hardly likely to make those concerned hopeful for the future. Conservative delegates from Brent and Barnet continued to press Boyle to state that all development plans would be reconsidered in a year or two. Notably, according to the minutes, Boyle gave no reply. The trend of parental opinion, he repeated, was against the 11 plus and he judged this having consulted the 'research department.' Yet when asked by the delegates which research department this was, he simply replied that he paid attention to the Gallup poll.[105]

The Prime Minister Harold Wilson was enjoying Edward Heath's obvious discomfort on the issue in the Commons. Wilson was able to boast of the advances in educational policy that had been carried though 'with the support of the front Bench opposite' and dismissed the arguments of the recently published Black Paper that criticized what he called the 'liberal progress' in education. 'Incidentally,' he markedly added, Boyle and Hogg had 'made their contributions to this.' Wilson claimed to reject totally the Black Paper's perspective, 'which appears to be supported by some backbenchers opposite,' adding, 'whether it is supported by the Front Bench opposite, I suppose we shall never know.'[106] Heath and others did not of course want to be identified with the publication at all.

At this time, Royston Moore, the new Chairman of the Party's National Advisory Committee on Education, was urging Gilbert Longden to communicate to Heath their desperate desire that he publicly support any local education authority that sought to retain its grammar schools upon forming the next government. Moore emphasized to Longden that they did not want the word 'good' to be used to 'section off' some grammar schools from others, but rather to defend as many existing grammar schools as they could.[107] They thus sought to hold Heath's feet to the fire and Longden was the go-between.

Longden dutifully carried out the National Advisory Committee's request.[108] Unsurprisingly, Heath gave Longden nothing. Indeed, he did not even mention the Committee's main request in his reply at all. Instead, Heath merely repeated the statement the Party had made in its recent policy statement *Make Life Better* that the form of reorganization should not be laid down by Whitehall, but decided by local authorities consulting parents and teachers. He would only commit himself to repeating that they would repeal legislation that sought to make comprehensive schools universally compulsory. A Conservative minister would 'not dictate' to local education authorities, even though as Heath put it, 'he might occasionally wish to discuss plans for a particular area with them.'[109] Once again, with this degree of wriggling, there was no assurance that a future Conservative government would do anything to halt what was happening at all. The National Advisory Committee was being stonewalled by the leadership yet again.

Not only was the relationship between Boyle and the National Advisory Committee becoming more tenuous, but now even Longden was experiencing an increased dissatisfaction with the Conservative leadership. He was starting to express open agreement with frustrated party supporters who were bitterly critical of the leadership's approach, including notably inviting a particularly critical grammar school master to associate with the Committee.[110]

Yet Boyle did have his share of support among Conservative councillors. A tempestuous meeting with the National Advisory Committee on 24 September led to Alderman Fred Hutty of Wallasey writing to Boyle to express his sorrow to see Boyle beset by 'immature' opinion that was still trying to hold him to a promise of new grammar schools when next in government. As far as Hutty was concerned, academic selection had gone, and any selection remaining in a few years' time was likely to be regarded as 'a backwards conservatism'.[111] If a Conservative majority was returned, it was claimed that local education programmes that attempted to reverse the present comprehensive trend would affect and even deny majorities to the Party.

Boyle expressed his gratitude for the support, but claimed that his view of grammar schools' political futility was gaining ground in the Party, in spite of the 'pockets of resistance' there had been at the meeting. He very much agreed with Hutty in his assessment of the politics of the situation:

> We are in any event going to have to take a number of most uncomfortable decisions when we are returned to power, and there will be absolutely no political dividends to be gained from any attempt to reverse the present trend in secondary education.

He was relieved that it appeared that Surrey was no longer seeking to reverse plans to go comprehensive in Frimley and Camberley. Boyle therefore assured Hutty that he would keep 'plugging at this question. I will do my best at Brighton.' (Party Conference.)[112] It was now a quest to persuade certain councillors of the folly of their desire to hang onto existing grammar schools in local authority areas stubbornly holding out against the government. The most 'difficult' local authorities were those of Wolverhampton and Gloucester, the first one ironically situated near Boyle's own constituency of Birmingham Handsworth.

In fact it turned out in subsequent correspondence with Douglas Hurd, at that time working in Heath's private office, that Boyle had given a slightly misleading impression at the meeting. Councillor Gill of Wolverhampton had pressed Boyle hard at the meeting over both new grammar schools and replacements. In response, Boyle had not ruled out 'in principle' the replacement of certain grammar schools, as opposed to the creation of new ones under a future Conservative government. He therefore sought to reassure Hurd that he had also added that a future Tory minister would not find it 'easy' to approve any sizeable number of building projects that perpetuated or entrenched selection into different schools at the age of 11 or 12. He thus sought to placate the obviously concerned Private Office that the money for replacements was limited and primary schools were to be the priority in any event. 'The last thing,' Boyle wanted to see, he told Hurd, were press reports that a future Conservative government was likely to replace Wolverhampton Grammar school. Such an announcement, he added, could only prove 'a thorough nuisance' to any Conservative minister in the future.[113] They were clearly at pains not to give solid commitments to local Conservatives that might raise their hopes to any extent.

Meanwhile, the imminent publication of the second Black Paper was encouraging a febrile atmosphere in the lead-up to the party conference in October. The second pamphlet had a greater number of contributors than the previous one, including articles by the educational psychologists Cyril Burt and Hans Eysenck. Other contributors were Tibor Szamuely, a lecturer in politics at the University of Reading, and Rhodes Boyson, the headmaster of Highbury Grove School, a London comprehensive, as well as Kingsley Amis and Robert Conquest.

Cox and Dyson also had the notable support of Enoch Powell, who wrote to Dyson on 7 October, despite their injunction on receiving correspondence, 'because it is encouraging to know that others see the same patterns of danger as I do myself.'[114] (This was in spite of the fact that as we have seen, Powell had been notably pragmatic about the onset of comprehensive schooling some years earlier when he had sat on the Party's parliamentary education committee.) There were by now eight local authorities who had not submitted comprehensive schemes, and Edward Short's proposed bill to enforce comprehensives by law was looming on the horizon.

However, there was little sign of conspiracy on the part of the Black Papers' editor Brian Cox, who appeared to be particularly solicitous not to give offence to Boyle in spite of his concerns. In correspondence with Boyle at this time, he was noticeably anxious to play down his relationship with Angus Maude. 'A great many lies,' he claimed, 'have been published about the first Black Paper, particularly when it has been suggested that we are a closely-knot Angus Maude group who want to oust you.' In this vein, he assured Boyle that most of the contributors had not met each other, adding, 'I've no desire to rock the Conservative boat.' In notably defensive and insecure spirit, Cox was at pains to emphasize that he and Dyson were not extreme right wing, highlighting the extent of their concern about opportunities for the able working-class child.[115] With the intended date for publication set for during the upcoming Conservative Party Conference, he informed Boyle that he would first be sending the proofs of Black Paper Two to him before his speech. Boyle's genial reply was, as usual, good natured albeit with a slight patronizing undertone. He denied that he felt like a victim and stated how he did not think Cox, Dyson and Maude were all right wing extremists, 'though I think you have fed a few extreme right-wing prejudices.' Denying that comprehensive education would lower standards, he assured Cox that he could count on reasoned dissent from him at the Party Conference.[116]

The tone of what would turn out to be Boyle's final conference speech would in fact be notable for its world-weariness. For Boyle, the 'real tragedy' was more that the debate had been high-jacked by extremists 'on both sides,' of which he included the Black Paper authors and Royston Moore. Instead, Boyle cited Quintin Hogg in the value of the belief in 'moderation in all things.' Their position on the whole issue therefore remained, as he somewhat markedly added, 'as I have always tried to explain it to you.' The usual impression was given that he simply wished all would join together in consensus over secondary education and stop making a fuss.

The Black Paper's second pamphlet, while a more 'formidable' document than the first, nevertheless carried a tone that was 'shrill' and 'peevish.' Therefore, the Party should not make the parallel mistake to the one that the socialists were making, of destroying what was left, by themselves 'ossifying' what was left.[117] Boyle's legacy in his final conference speech was essentially the plea for moderation above all else. Yet the result had so often been that this approach had satisfied relatively few.

A few days after this conference speech, Boyle made a surprise announcement that he was stepping down from the role of education spokesman for the Party and from politics altogether. He was due to take up the offer of Vice-Chancellor of the University of Leeds. There is some evidence that by now he felt frustrated at a lack of progress made in achieving his career ambitions. His ideal post had been to become Leader of the House of Commons. Yet clearly he also felt wearied by his battles within his own party. The area of secondary education had surely been the greatest area of difficulty, given the level of dissatisfaction within the Party that had been directed at him over his stance on the issue. Nevertheless, he later confided in interviews with his former Private Secretary Maurice Kogan that he felt the Conservative government and the Department had in fact exhibited too much inhibition rather than promoting comprehensive reorganization 'positively.'[118] Even in private correspondence, he would never admit what the end of selection at the age of 11 had really meant for the grammar schools.

Heath would now appoint the shadow transport spokesman Margaret Thatcher, a far less congenial figure from his perspective, to the role. The MP for Finchley since 1959, her previous positions had included serving in the Shadow Treasury team and as Fuel and Power spokesman. As we shall see, Mrs Thatcher's resulting period in the education post would prove to be her most acrimonious years in political life before becoming Prime Minister a decade later.

The Conservative leadership therefore continued to advocate the long-standing desire for 'bipartisan consensus' on secondary reorganization in spite of the marked lack of respect for this even-handed approach from the Labour government. Following the introduction of Circulars 10/65 and 10/66, the Conservatives' education spokesman Edward Boyle did not oppose them fundamentally or acknowledge their true implications. Indeed, Boyle claimed that requests for local authorities would have continued according to the terms of those Circulars if the Conservatives had regained power. Meanwhile, the future health of the public schools remained a matter of key concern for the Conservative Party leadership, with an associated desire not to highlight them so that they might draw political ire. By contrast, selection within the maintained system was discarded according to the judgement by Heath and Boyle that it was politically unwise to defend. The concerns of the Party's National Advisory Committee on education were marginalized as before. 'Local authority freedom' had thus been effectively used as a tool of displacement throughout this period of Conservative Party opposition.

5

A minister under siege 1969–74

As Secretary of State for education, Margaret Thatcher would view proposals for comprehensive schools on an empirical and pragmatic basis, in response to the intransigence and ideology of the Labour opposition during this period. By vaguely claiming to prioritize 'parental choice' between selective and non-selective schools, it meant there was no clear central strategy on the Conservative government's part. Ultimately, Mrs Thatcher would echo the tendency of her predecessors and increasingly regard secondary school reorganization as a matter for local authorities, rather than one for the Conservative government to stake a position on.

A cautious Thatcher in opposition

Margaret Thatcher's appointment as shadow education spokesman was announced on 21 October 1969. A few days later, the *Birmingham Post* carried a report that showcased her early intentions. She stated that she would fight Edward Short's intended bill to 'impose' comprehensive education on all schools. In addition, she was quoted as saying that she was prepared to try to save a number of grammar schools that had played an important part in their communities. Yet she was also noticeably keen to add that in a newly developed area, a comprehensive might be the best system.[1] This suggested that her approach, even in opposition, was to approach the issue on an individual 'case by case' basis. Nevertheless, given the Conservative Party's belated stance in regard to Short's proposed bill, pro-grammar school supporters were hopeful that a future Conservative government might go further and possibly even extend selective schools.

In the House of Commons in October 1969, with the recent departure of Boyle, the Labour government were gloating that he had left because he could no longer tolerate remaining on the front benches of the Conservative Party. They claimed that it was the supposed intransigence of grammar school supporters within the party that had effectively forced him out. Boyle 'could not stand the heat,' according to William Hamilton the Labour MP for Fife.[2] In similar fashion, other pro-comprehensive Labour MPs such as Arnold Shaw for Ilford South joined him in 'deploring' Boyle's absence from the front ranks.[3] The left was now increasingly turning its ire on those recalcitrant local authorities, such as Wolverhampton and Birmingham along with seven others, who were accused of defying the Government's will by refusing to submit comprehensive schemes.

Labour MPs continued to highlight the ambiguity of the Conservatives' position. Renee Short, the Labour member for Wolverhampton North East, who was virulently critical of her own local council for holding out and sought for the proposed Bill to force their hand, questioned the Conservatives' official claim to oppose selection at 11 plus, while maintaining certain grammar schools. How, she demanded, could they reconcile this position and admit under what arrangements the pupils would continue to be selected?[4] In response, Conservative MPs such as Richard Hornby, who had been given a prominent role by Heath in chairing the party's Parliamentary Education Committee, constantly reiterated that they were not standing up for the 11 plus while keenly emphasizing the number of comprehensive schemes that Tory local authorities had approved.[5] Thus, the majority of Conservative MPs either remained silent or simply maintained a defensive posture in the face of Labour's onslaught. Meanwhile, the 11 plus continued to be presented as the 'bogey-man' of debate.

In her first major encounter on secondary education in the House of Commons as shadow education spokesman, Mrs Thatcher's change of emphasis from that of Boyle was clear. She highlighted the 'great varieties' in comprehensive schools that existed and claimed that there was a significant degree of choice existing between grammar schools, secondary moderns and comprehensives in areas such as her own constituency. What was important to her was 'parental choice', not something that Boyle had ever particularly emphasized within his own approach.[6] While it was not possible in all areas, she stressed that it should be maintained in areas where it could take place. Her approach was therefore piecemeal and circumspect. Such was the nature of so many current secondary school buildings they could not form part of a viable comprehensive system in the near future. Alongside this, she was keen to praise the Conservative Party's overall record on education, drawing comparisons of educational spending between the Conservatives' period in office and the rate of expenditure since 1964 under the Labour government.

Mrs Thatcher was therefore cautious from the outset in her new role. This inevitably affected her degree of personal association with the Black Paper authors. In a letter on 4 November to Anthony Dyson, the co-editor of the Black Papers, she claimed to be unable to meet him due to being overloaded with correspondence and asked him to contact her after Christmas.[7] While this may well have been the case, it nevertheless begs the question as to whether an element of avoidance was involved on her part towards them and whether she sought to not be openly associated with such figures because of a fear of possible stigma by association. By January 1970, one of the contributors to the Black Papers, Richard Pedley of St Dunstan's College in Catford, was still enquiring of Dyson about what had happened to their 'proposed confrontation' with Mrs Thatcher, adding that, 'I hope that we keep the pot boiling with her.'[8] Black Paper activities, he emphasized, needed to be kept up in 1970. Yet she appears to have been somewhat holding back from them even at this stage.

But this was understandable. Any implied agreement with the thinking of the Black Paper authors carried a stigma that was further bolstered by the established Press. Education correspondents for the major newspapers were keen to portray Angus

Maude as occupying an extreme right-wing position within the Party. In a published interview with Mrs Thatcher on 7 November, *The Times* education correspondent Brian MacArthur was eager to point out that she was 'no supporter of the Angus Maude wing of the Tory party,' thus isolating Maude's position.[9] So incensed was Maude by this that he wrote a letter to *The Times* on 15 November to rebut the charge that any such thing as an 'Angus Maude wing' of the party existed, as well as the suggestion that he was at odds with the official Conservative policy. He then called for MacArthur to withdraw, as he put it, 'his little smear by disassociation.' His position, which he claimed to be also that of the Party as a whole, was to support selection, albeit not at 11 plus and with the possibility of reconsideration and transfer. This of course assumed a sizeable selective system remaining. In addition, Maude claimed that while the Party accepted the need for some comprehensives, they were opposed to 'the destruction of good and viable schools.'[10] His approach thus went further than official Tory pronouncements at the time by essentially opposing most of the comprehensive trend. Mrs Thatcher would have been a wary observer of all this. Ultimately, it already seemed that she did not want to be bracketed with Maude.

Nevertheless, she was to some extent active in defending those local authorities that were holding out against the government. Her correspondence in November 1970 with Peter Baguley the new Secretary of the Conservative Party's National Advisory Committee on Education shows that she had clearly authorized him to write to the Chairmen of those authorities who had declined to submit comprehensive schemes, and to give her statements as to the grounds on which they based their position. It is significant that Baguley had also written to the Chairman of Birmingham Education Committee, one of the key rebels, as well as the Conservative members of the County Councils Association Education Committee to ask them to come to London urgently.[11] The proposed Education Bill by Edward Short, which proposed the enforcement of comprehensive schools by law, was soon to be published.

Short's proposed Education Bill ultimately focused on Section 1 of the 1944 Act. According to its terms, the Minister had the power to promote education as well as the 'progressive development of institutions' for that purpose. In its key lines, the Minister was to secure the 'effective execution' by local authorities of the national policy for 'providing a varied and comprehensive educational service in every area.'[12] The Labour government was interpreting this as a duty on all local authorities to plan for a comprehensive system of secondary schools. Because of the Ministerial power to sanction the capital programme, the Secretary of State had almost absolute powers, following discussion with local authorities, over which new schools were to be built in a particular area. However, as Mrs Thatcher pointed out to Short in the debate on the proposed Bill on 12 February 1970, this was quite different from having absolute powers over the pattern of *existing* schools, particularly when seeking to impose a pattern that the local authorities concerned did not want.

As part of her defence of local authority freedom, Mrs Thatcher was once again forced to gloss over the developments in comprehensive schools that had been enacted by past Conservative governments. Schemes such as the Leicestershire Plan of 1957 were described by her in almost glowing terms. The 1950s under the Conservative government were portrayed as a period of 'innovation and experiment,' in which Tory authorities had chosen comprehensive schemes willingly and in a spirit of cooperation, while bearing in mind completely the wishes of local electors.[13] (In fact, as had been previously admitted in the Commons in other exchanges, public notices for these comprehensive proposals had often not even been published for local electors' perusal, amidst an approach by the Ministry of Education that had been decidedly laissez-faire in character.)

Mrs Thatcher then sought to elaborate on her position by arguing that grammar schools and comprehensives could 'co-exist' alongside each other. This was again quite different from the Boyle approach that had tended to be doubtful about the possibilities for comprehensives amidst selective schools and which had accepted the socialist argument by default. Yet using an example from her own area, she described how Dulwich College, a well-known selective independent, and Tulse Hill, a comprehensive, which were both admired schools, were able to operate effectively near to each other. Given that schools in this case could thrive alongside, she stressed that parents have the option for their children to be assessed for well-known grammar schools alongside comprehensives, thus enabling parental choice to be kept open within the maintained system. By contrast, full-scale comprehensive schemes, particularly given cases where the buildings involved were unsuitable, would deprive parents of this.[14]

Mrs Thatcher's view was therefore, in the words of fellow Conservative MP John Boyd-Carpenter, a 'compromise system' to be supposedly concerned with individual needs and circumstances. But what was also apparent was that the Conservative opposition, as the Labour MP Christopher Price taunted, was 'scared stiff' of openly opposing the Labour government's proposed Bill on the comprehensive principle itself.[15] Instead, the official Conservative approach was to merely emphasize freedom for those local authorities that disagreed with the government's plans. And this was despite the fact that the Conservative leadership had not originally sought to back those authorities' defiant stance, either.

It was left to Angus Maude, in his lonely position of seeking to retain selection, to make the key point about the need for flexibility to enable the late developer to transfer from one type of school to another during the early and mid-teenage years. As he noted, this had so often been thwarted due to the lack of spare places in secondary schools. In his constituency of Stratford upon Avon, he had found 'over and over again' grammar or bilateral schools that had wanted to keep some places back for further transfer at the ages of 13 and 15, but had been unable to do so because the pressure of pupils was over-filling them.[16] Inevitably, Maude was regarded on both sides of the House as an extremist on the whole issue.

At this point Edward Boyle made one of his last contributions in the House of Commons. Amongst his usual tepid criticism of Labour policies, he merely continued to express his belief in 'partnership' and 'co-operative relations' between the minister and the local education authority. On certain occasions he had merely invited a local education authority for discussions when he had entertained doubts about a particular proposal. A minister in that case, he continued, might then seek to 'persuade' local authority members to consider a different course of action.

He was opposed to the Labour government policy of centralized compulsion on local authorities to submit proposals that they did not believe in, and expressed the hope that this would not mean the school building programme would be used as a 'principal weapon.'[17] Yet this of course neglected to mention that this was exactly what had been happening for the last four years since the Labour government had issued Circular 10/66, the second of the major circulars that had put major pressure on local authorities to comply. At the time, Boyle had of course been distinctly half-hearted about mounting opposition to these circulars and had even declared that he would not withdraw them when next in office.

Concluding his remarks, Boyle claimed that he did not want to see the end of selective schools altogether, but also did not want to see comprehensive reorganization 'grinding to a halt.'[18] Indeed, he felt that policies of positive discrimination such as banding and zoning might be beneficial for comprehensive schemes in large inner-city areas. His distinctly flaccid admonition to the Labour government was to simply leave the defiant authorities such as Birmingham alone and concentrate on those that wanted to reorganize.

Other Conservative MPs such as Charles Morrison for Devizes and David Lane for Cambridge (in spite of the latter having reservations about the reorganization scheme within his own constituency) affirmed their approval of a gradual move towards a comprehensive future that they felt should not be reversed. To round things off, William van Straubenzee, who would be appointed under-secretary of State by Heath in the next Conservative government, claimed that there was 'not a political controversy' over the principle of comprehensive schooling, and that members of both parties had given 'distinguished service' in its name.[19] Straubenzee's essential criticism merely amounted to the usual charge that the Labour government was imposing the policy without any extra finance for proper reorganization. Throughout the debate, Conservative members therefore fudged their own Party's role in the events that had led to the present predicament where a Labour government was envisaging imposing the comprehensive principle on every maintained secondary school in the country. The Labour Minister of State Alice Bacon therefore had no difficulty in claiming that the Conservative Shadow policy on comprehensive education remained a 'mystery.'

Meanwhile, the Labour Secretary of State Edward Short was zealously determined to see his Bill implemented. In his view, the proposed Bill merely sought to translate the 'request' made to local education authorities five years earlier in Circular 10/65 into a statutory requirement. In personal correspondence on 26 March with Sir William Alexander, the Chairman of the Association of Education Committees, he stated that while the majority of local authorities had co-operated 'excellently,' in regard to the small number that was not complying he was resolute that 'freedom for authorities in the education sector can scarcely include the possibility of frustrating national policy.'

Furthermore, the direct grant schools were also within his sights. Under the Bill, local authorities would have to show in what way and for what purpose they proposed to take up places at direct grant or independent schools. It would be 'implicit' in the proposed Bill, he informed Alexander, that authorities who paid for places within them were to have regard to whether their admission arrangements were based on pupils' ability or aptitude.[20] Any such arrangements would be open to question if they were based on the selection of pupils in this way. Of course, the direct grant schools could no longer exist in their present state on such terms. They were now facing a direct threat of extinction.

In reply Alexander, who epitomized the centrist-minded educational establishment, reduced himself to the level of pleading with Short. He protested that 'extreme' was being countered by 'extreme.' He begged Short to see that the governors of local authorities who were holding out and who were effectively being accused of 'defying the will of the people' were in fact honest people doing their best to look after the interests of the schools as expressed in the Trust Deed. Alexander appeared to simply want all parties to be low-key and civilized in these proceedings, and emphasized the degree of 'sympathetic co-operation' shown in the majority of areas as opposed to the path being taken of enforced compliance. 'Tremendous strides,' he claimed, had been taken by local authorities in broadly meeting the criteria suggested in the Labour government's Circular 10/65. There was nothing to suggest, he added in further wheedling spirit, that acceptance of the comprehensive principle would not in time operate in all local authority areas, including the small number that had not yet made formal proposals. The nominal advantage to be gained from forcing the present Bill through the House would be more than countered by 'the resulting suspicion and bitterness' which would inevitably attend the introduction of new legislation.[21] Along with many others, Alexander had of course thought it best to appease the comprehensive trend even before the Labour government had entered office in 1964. As with Boyle, all the subsequent events had consistently undermined Alexander's approach. His moderate-minded and pragmatic acceptance of the comprehensive principle was effectively blowing up in his face due to the intransigence of the Labour government. Like so many others in the educational establishment, Alexander himself was being hung by his own woolly petard.

Throughout the standing committee stage of the Bill in April and May, the Conservatives made the case for the direct grant schools' continuation through a series of suggested compromises, including taking free places at 16 and widening the ability range regarding entry. In the words of Boyle, who attended the meetings, the leading direct grant schools should be retained because of their particular quality, while of course simultaneously accepting the general comprehensive trend for the fully local authority-maintained schools. In his usual vein, he felt that 'somehow or other, the sensible line seems to me a series of compromises which enable both those things to happen.' Mrs Thatcher, by contrast, continued to cannily emphasize parental choice and the retention of flexibility in the system. She was particularly keen to expose those Labour MPs such as Christopher Price regarding their own choices for their children's education that was often in leading independent and direct grant schools. Characteristically, she criticized the Labour opposition for approaching the issue on a 'theoretical political basis' rather than relating it to their own choices as parents.[22] Nevertheless, the Conservative shadow position still amounted to an unconvincing mixture of retaining a small number of highly selective direct grant schools on the grounds of quality while essentially accepting the comprehensive trend for the vast majority of those that were fully maintained by local education authorities. The Tories teetered uneasily along these lines throughout. By contrast, the Labour position always carried the advantage of its sheer simplicity.

Nevertheless, Mrs Thatcher scored a notable victory during committee on 14 April, when the Bill was being deliberated regarding the clauses for selection arrangements for sixth form colleges. On this crucial occasion, two Labour members absented themselves from a crucial vote and the Bill's progression was thrown into disarray as a result. On 22 May, Harold Wilson then announced that he was going to the country, and the standing committee meetings for the proposed Bill were wound up. Consequently, Short's Bill ended up being aborted due to the intervention of the 1970 general election.

The Conservative Party's general election manifesto *A Better Tomorrow* was characteristically cagey. Amidst a general tone of accusing the Labour government of gimmicks and short-term thinking, it sought to present Heath as a man of principle. Within its section on education, Labour's attempt to insist on compulsory comprehensive reorganization on 'rigid lines' was described as contrary to local democracy and to pupils' best interests. Nevertheless, while professing that Conservative local authorities would maintain the existing rights of local education authorities to decide what was best for their areas, it added that:

> They will take into account the general acceptance that in most cases the age of eleven is too early to make final decisions which might affect a child's whole future.

The manifesto was also noticeably keen to add that many of the most imaginative new schemes abolishing the eleven plus had been introduced by Conservative councils. They were therefore anxious to portray themselves as being essentially unopposed to the general comprehensive trend for the vast majority of the fully maintained schools. Nevertheless, their defence of the direct grant schools involved claiming that they provided opportunities 'which may not otherwise be available for children of academic ability regardless of their parents' income.'[23] This again indirectly conceded the deficiencies of the otherwise fully comprehensive system, particularly for the able child. In the same vein, they typically underlined the freedom of parents to send their children to independent schools if they wished.

Against all expectations, the Conservatives gained a clear majority in the 1970 general election, with Heath the new Prime Minister. Heath's 'man of principle' stance appeared to have paid off with the public. This would prove ironic given his subsequent 'u' terms in office, as well as the Party's already incoherent stance on education which would be continued by Mrs Thatcher throughout this period.

A flexible minister

Upon her appointment as Secretary of State in the new Heath government on Saturday 20 June 1970, Mrs Thatcher began her new role the following Monday, and took the immediate action of withdrawing Circulars 10/65 and 10/66. She was then accused by Short, now her shadow in opposition, of announcing her decision to withdraw Circular 10/65 at a press conference in Curzon Street before informing the House.

Furthermore, she was accused of circumventing standard procedure by neglecting to issue another circular in its place. She was already squarely in the firing line.

She responded to this latter accusation by producing a short circular entitled Circular 10/70, which claimed to restore the local authorities' freedom to their level before the Labour government's circulars had been issued. As the new circular put it, secondary reorganization plans were now to be based on 'educational considerations' rather than on the comprehensive principle. The new Conservative government, it added, believed it was wrong to impose a 'uniform pattern' of secondary education on local authorities by legislation or other means. Circular 10/65 was therefore being withdrawn, along with any restrictions on building projects related to it. Adding that the 'rapid' recent changes to secondary provision had imposed 'considerable strains' within the education system, it emphasized that:

> Where a particular pattern of organisation is working well and commands general support the Secretary of State does not wish to cause further change without good reason.[24]

This was as far as she was prepared to go. The onus was to be shifted onto the local authorities once again.

However, she also faced further accusation from her critics that Circular 10/70 had been sent out without any consultation of teachers and local authority associations and that it amounted to an invitation for authorities to change their reorganization plans. The Labour opposition now launched a motion of censure against the new Conservative government, with the education debate set to take place on 8 July following the Queen's speech. Those who were ranged against Mrs Thatcher were trying to bully her right from the start.

In the Commons, she replied to the Opposition's charge by stating that she had merely been implementing the promises made in the Conservatives' manifesto concerning the maintenance of the local education authorities' right to decide their secondary school arrangements for themselves. Those who had submitted plans but not had them approved were merely being invited to indicate if they wanted them considered or instead wished to withdraw them. She had therefore had 'no alternative' but to withdraw Circulars 10/65 and 10/66. Explaining her lack of readiness to issue a new circular, she stated that she was 'enlarging' the rights of local authorities and not 'circumscribing' them.[25]

Yet part of Mrs Thatcher's justification, however, involved describing how local authorities had been moving towards comprehensive reorganization long before Circular 10/65 had been issued, including under successive Conservative governments. Indeed, she pointed out how two-thirds of local authorities had been moving this way by November 1964, the same statistic that Boyle had often liked to use. Defending the 1944 Act's opacity in which it had not sought to lay down the type of school considered ideal, she argued that without this feature the comprehensive system could 'never have developed as it has from the early 1950s.' The clear intention on the Conservative government's part was to portray themselves as being sufficiently 'on side' historically with the comprehensive trend when justifying present actions.

She explained how the Secretary of State, having received local authorities' submissions for comprehensive schemes under Section 13 of the 1944 Act, acted in a 'semi-judicial capacity'. As she admitted, it in fact gave a 'wide discretion' to the minister. Indeed, she told the Commons how her predecessor Edward Boyle had regarded them merely as reserve powers to turn down any proposal thought to be 'educationally damaging.' This admission of course unintentionally gave great insight into just how much depended on the individual bent of the minister as to how he chose to interpret his powers of intervention in local authorities' schemes. In contrast to Boyle, Mrs Thatcher's approach was to be more all-encompassing. She would stick to the wording of the Act and take all educational factors into account, including plans for other schools in the area as well as objections from parents and representations made by educational bodies.[26] In short, Mrs Thatcher was going to go much further in her role as minister and take each case's particular circumstances into account under her powers of intervention contained within Section 13.

Nevertheless, she reiterated that the government's view was that the age of 11 was 'too early' to make final decisions on pupils' futures.[27] Yet to grant this kind of concession to the pro-comprehensive opposition was inevitably going to put the Conservative government on difficult ground in terms of formulating its own stance. She repeated her earlier view that in many cases it was possible to have a mixed system of both comprehensive and grammar schools existing alongside each other, particularly within urban catchment areas. Furthermore, she repeated the Circular's words that where a particular pattern was 'working well,' she did 'not wish to cause further change.'[28] Clearly, she had no desire to state which form of secondary education she herself preferred. The main purpose of the Circular, she emphasized, was merely to resist compulsion on democratically elected authorities. As ever, Angus Maude was one of the notable exceptions to the rule on the Conservative side by continuing to underline the long-standing shortage of grammar school places and the resulting lack of flexibility that had not enabled the selective system to work fully. On this crucial point, he told Mrs Thatcher that it was in fact the case that more grammar school places were needed.

But Maude was increasingly a lone voice in the wilderness amongst his colleagues. Despite their recent general election victory, other Conservative MPs were clearly signalling their acceptance of matters proceeding even further in the comprehensive direction. Charles Morrison, the MP for Devizes, continued to claim that under a Conservative government they would go forward albeit, 'with rather more care and greater common sense.'[29] Indeed Morrison, an Old Etonian, described himself as a 'strong protagonist' for comprehensive education, and recounted how he had been Chairman of a Conservative-controlled education authority in Wiltshire that had decided to reorganize on comprehensive lines in 1963. He revealed that by September 1969, 46 per cent of children transferring to secondary schools in Wiltshire were being admitted to comprehensive schools, and there had been 'nothing hurried' in how it had come about.

It was at this moment that a fellow Conservative MP, John Jennings, the Member for Burton who was a known defender of grammar schools, asked whether all the grammar schools had been destroyed in the case that Morrison had just described. In reply Morrison, claiming he did not understand what Jennings meant by 'destroyed,' said that some grammar schools had been joined together or merged with other schools to form the comprehensive system. To this, Jennings retorted that it had in fact been a 'hodge-podge.' Morrison simply replied that there were plans for the process to continue and while expressing support for the demise of Short's Bill and the withdrawal of Circular 10/65, claimed that under a Conservative government the comprehensive system could nevertheless continue to 'evolve.'[30] The whole issue continued to be loftily spun in this way, particularly from the grander sections of the Conservative benches.

Kenneth Marks, the Labour MP for Manchester Gorton, noting this awkward gulf between Morrison and Jennings, sought to exploit its significance. Questioned further regarding his intervention in Morrison's speech, Jennings admitted that he was 'taking my hon. Friend to task' because a Tory council had 'departed from Tory principles' and 'literally destroyed grammar schools in the sacred name of comprehensivisation.' It had involved, he went on, the destruction of the grammar school, and its substitution by 'a hodge-podge of three different schools combined together as a comprehensive school.'[31] Marks exulted at this rare show of open disagreement on the Tory side. The veneer of unity on the issue was in fact decidedly flimsy in places.

It was also increasingly clear how hard the Labour opposition was determined to fight now that a Conservative Secretary of State was heading the Department of Education. The Labour MP Renee Short vowed that 'we shall do everything that we can, in the House and in the country, to let people understand clearly what the consequences of the right hon. Lady's policies are.'[32] There was clearly going to be a war of propaganda to undermine anything that Mrs Thatcher sought to do that they felt opposed the comprehensive advance.

It then came the turn of Mrs Thatcher's under-secretary William van Straubenzee, a friend of Edward Heath, to speak. Yet like so many others in the Conservative Party, his sentiments largely appeared to seek to placate the Labour opposition. He was at pains to emphasize that a system that he described as 'rigid selection' at age 11 that he claimed had permitted no moving across for the late developer was too early and was 'no longer a debating matter.' In answer to Shirley Wiliams' lofty-minded hope that selection would no longer be a matter of political contention, Straubenzee claimed that there was 'no valid argument' to be based on selection at the age of 11.[33] Seeking to further reassure Mrs Williams, he emphasized that Circular 10/70's notion of the minister not seeking to effect change where a particular pattern was working applied just as much to those seeking to 'unscramble' the comprehensive system as it did the other way round.[34] Continuing the flow of empty banalities, he claimed to believe that a well-run comprehensive school with a full range of courses would be freely chosen in preference to a selective school by most parents in the future.

Meanwhile, Mrs Thatcher already had problems within her own constituency. The Barnet Borough education authority, which covered her own area of Finchley, had earlier that year accepted a comprehensive scheme for the area entitled 'Plan C.' The Chairman of Barnet Education Committee, Victor Ussher, a friend of Mrs Thatcher, had approved it. Yet on 26 June, during the first week of Mrs Thatcher's tenure as Secretary of State, the *Finchley Times* reported that approximately one-third of Barnet's councillors opposed it and had asked Mrs Thatcher to review the proposed scheme.

The *Finchley Press* further reported that Councillors Jimmy Sapsted and Frank Gibson were planning to visit the Department as representatives of nineteen Tory councillors openly rebelling against it. They claimed that its withdrawal would have the welcome result that unsuitable school linkages could be delayed until suitable buildings and equipment became available. Gibson was also reported as saying that he thought Barnet Council would think again about the plan, 'now that they no longer have a pistol held to their heads,' which, he added, 'was one of the main reasons they fell in with the Labour government's demand.'[35]

By contrast, Victor Ussher claimed that he had decided to accept Plan C because he had felt the rest of the Council were in favour. The scheme was planned for September 1971, and therefore needed to be settled by the end of 1970 at the latest. Notices of closure for those affected by the scheme had already been put up in local schools. It was also revealed that Mrs Thatcher planned to receive a deputation of officers from Barnet Parents' Council who were also opposed to the plan. Clearly, those with an inclination to rebel against the comprehensive scheme had been emboldened not only by the general election result, but also by Mrs Thatcher's appointment. She was therefore caught in the middle of an educational cross-fire in her own backyard.

Meanwhile, Angus Maude was reaffirming his commitment to the Black Paper series, informing Brian Cox that he was 'delighted' that there was a third Black Paper in the offing and that he 'would be delighted to give you any help I can.'[36] Maude was still setting out to make waves as a man of principle on selection. By contrast Mrs Thatcher, who was also in correspondence with Cox, while thanking him for his 'kind letter' of support following the Commons debate in July, remarked warily in response to Cox's emphasis upon his moderate credentials that:

> I also regard myself as a 'moderate' but anyone who believes as we do in excellence in education is liable to be called a 'right wing extremist.'[37]

Understandably, she did not want to be tagged with this label at all. Ultimately, she was already set upon careful manoeuvring around the whole issue.

Throughout the summer of 1970, the Conservative Party's Research Department kept up their long-standing and tenuous balancing act between being critical of the previous Labour government's comprehensive policy and emphasizing that they were not opposed to comprehensive schemes. They continued with their usual line that a great deal depended on 'local circumstances,' and it was therefore 'sensible to allow more freedom to local education authorities to decide these matters for themselves.' In similar obfuscatory terms, it was claimed that local authorities would prepare better schemes, 'if they do so voluntarily rather than under duress.' Indeed, the Research Department quoted Mrs Thatcher from the recent Debate on the Address as stating that:

> It is fair, in regard to any general plan submitted by a local education authority, to start by presuming that the responsible local authority, being a democratically elected body with statutory duties, has submitted sound proposals.[38]

Nevertheless, the Conservative Party's National Advisory Committee was still hopeful in 1970. Peter Baguley, their secretary, wrote to Mrs Thatcher in August to inform her that the Committee had overwhelmingly approved a recent resolution praising her actions in scrapping the 'infamous' directive of the last government. As a result of her decision, the object of policy would be equality of opportunity, rather than equality itself, and pupils would now be more likely to receive secondary education 'suitable to their needs.'[39] There was a clear sense of hope in the air. The resolution was then forwarded to her through the normal channels of the National Union.

But Mrs Thatcher, having been informed of the resolution, nevertheless maintained the standard rhetoric about Circular 10/70 simply leaving local education authorities 'freer.' It was wrong to impose a 'uniform pattern' and it had been important to remove the 'restrictive influence' of Circular 10/65. To cap off the slight air of rehearsed banality, Mrs Thatcher was careful to remind the National Advisory Committee that:

> I do not wish to prevent sensible progress and development which produce better opportunities for children but where existing arrangements are working well and have general support, I hope that they will continue undisturbed.[40]

She was thus being notably circumspect with the National Advisory Committee too.

The Black Papers' editor Brian Cox, who was still optimistic, sought to keep up correspondence with Mrs Thatcher that autumn. On 14 September he sent her the current issue of *Critical Quarterly* highlighting an article on 'Threats to Academic Freedom' by Edmund Ions. This suggests that he was seeking to influence her and keep her in a chain of communications as an ally. Yet it appears that Mrs Thatcher was increasingly keeping her distance from him, as well as being noticeably reluctant regarding what she was prepared to commit herself to in terms of positive action.

In her first Party Conference speech as Secretary of State in Blackpool on 7 October, she was noticeably keener to draw attention to the priority the government attached to primary education as well as a planned enquiry into teacher training. In the same way, she claimed, that Boyle had announced over six years ago the 'biggest schools improvement programme that we have ever seen' for secondary schools, she was going to concentrate similarly on the primary sector.

Regarding secondary education, she would only commit herself to saying that she was 'suspicious of panaceas.' Inevitably, because of the money available for secondary schools, there would be a mixed system comprising all kinds of school for many years yet. Using further vague rhetoric, she emphasized how she would rather keep the secondary school system 'flexible' and added that she was concerned to see that 'some variety of choice should be retained in the system.' She would allow herself to go no further than that. Indeed, it amounted to uncharacteristic flannel.

However, she appeared to stake a position in one area. In regard to the existing direct grant schools, particularly those within the Inner London Education Authority area that were being threatened, she professed that she would do everything she could to 'encourage' them. Regarding them as a bridge between the completely independent schools and the state sector, she felt they offered opportunities to pupils regardless of their parents' income or background and therefore was particularly concerned that those opportunities should remain open. She informed the Conference audience that if local education authorities chose not to keep open opportunities in London and elsewhere for pupils to enter direct grant schools, she would attempt, by arrangement with them, to enable pupils from that area to apply directly to the direct grant school itself. In this way, she would keep open choice for parents 'who would otherwise have none.' As she then added, 'We cannot do it for everyone, but let that not stop us from at least doing it for some, regardless of the income or background of the child.'[41]

Throughout this time, she was getting little support from Edward Heath, whose attitude towards her appeared to be little short of contempt. For some months after becoming education secretary she had sought a meeting with him to discuss the 'principles of education.' Yet Heath kept putting it off and indeed appears to have been avoiding her. In an office minute to Heath at this time, his private secretary suggested meeting Mrs Thatcher for dinner along with her permanent secretary or three or four senior officials. In withering terms, his private secretary added:

> I doubt if it would be practicable to exclude her from the discussion, but you might perhaps like to bring in a number of non-officials to liven things up.

The suggestion met with Heath's scribbled response that 'I certainly can't spare a weekend,' and that he thought it 'more business-like' to meet her round the Cabinet table, adding that he would not be able to do so for a few weeks.[42] In short, Heath appeared somewhat anxious to avoid any discussion on educational fundamentals, particularly with Mrs Thatcher.

Yet despite her earlier sentiments at the Party Conference, in an interview with Stephen Jessel of *The Times* on 12 November, she revealed that she had no plans to reopen the direct grant school list. She was merely in consultation with the direct grant committee about arrangements for the existing schools, 'and I would rather get that sorted out before really closely considering the other question.' When it came to the future of non-selective education generally, she was treading carefully:

> I think it is coming with increasing speed.

And yet she added:

> I do not accept that it will stop there: that is to say that non-selective education is not the last word in education. I believe that in many areas it is a stage we shall only go through: some will stop there, some will go on to something different. I fully accept that there will be a system of some selective schools again ... and this is one reason why I am absolutely determined not to impose one system and none other.[43]

Mrs Thatcher was trying, albeit tactfully, to keep all options open for the foreseeable future for as long as possible without openly declaring herself.

Nevertheless, her approach was in fact encouraging trends that in practice undermined the remaining selective system further. She had of course pledged to raise the school leaving age to 16 in 1972. As she noted in conversations with Heath, there was bound to be truancy in bad areas and yet, 'at any rate initially a blind eye would have to be turned.'[44] Furthermore, Mrs Thatcher was instituting the transfer of mentally handicapped children into the education service, as well as a general emphasis on 'slow learners' within comprehensive schools. The strains posed by the all-ability system were becoming more and more apparent.

At this time, the *Birmingham Evening Mail* reported how in her speech to the pro-grammar school Conservative group on Birmingham City Council she made only an 'oblique' reference to Birmingham's successful 'Keep the grammar schools campaign.' Instead, she preferred to direct her remarks towards the future possibility of greater nursery education provision.[45] Likewise, the following month she was particularly keen in her speech to the National Union of Teachers in Scarborough to tell of her proposed urban programme to expand nursery education in socially deprived areas. Over 15,000 places had been approved at a capital cost of approximately £4 million, three-quarters of which was to come directly from the Exchequer. She also highlighted the 1972–3 school building programme (the first that she was responsible for) which included over 400 projects for the replacement or improvement of old primary schools at a cost of £385 million (more than twice the cost, she keenly added, of the previous year).[46] An overwhelming impression of high spending and commitment to the further development of the welfare state was being conveyed by her.

Nevertheless, her manoeuvrings were wholly understandable. Already, those such as Edward Short were prophesizing for Mrs Thatcher that she was likely to become the 'apotheosis' of Florence Horsbrugh.[47] The parallels between the way that she was being treated and that of her predecessor nearly twenty years earlier would have been all too apparent to her. During this period, above all else, she was a woman desperate to hang onto her job at all costs.

By early 1971, she was fully in the midst of surveying the deluge of local authority comprehensive schemes being sent to her under Section 13. In the House of Commons on 21 April, she was at pains to emphasize that because of current confusion surrounding the acceptance of local authority schemes, the department would no longer issue approval of plans (as had been the standard practice) but instead merely say that they had 'taken note' of them. As a result, she hoped the full Section 13 process, which was of course the statutory procedure laid down by Parliament, would be 'restored to its full significance in the public view.'[48]

In spite of this, the overall situation suggested that comprehensives were well on the march to becoming the majority form of secondary schooling. Of the 163 local education authorities, it was now the case that 131 had had plans for either the whole or part of their areas approved in principle, with 40 having completed reorganization of their secondary school provision under the Section 13 procedure. Nevertheless, it was still the case that the majority of the 131 had yet to submit Section 13 proposals indicating that they wished to take their plans further. Meanwhile, this left thirty-eight local education authorities who had submitted no Section 13 proposals to change the character of their schools.

Angus Maude was still trying to keep up the pressure on Mrs Thatcher by reminding her in Commons debates at this time of the risk to the direct grant schools' future and that therefore, as he put it, it was greatly necessary for her to 'do a little more than simply protect.' Given how the direct grant schools had been actively penalized under the previous Labour government, which meant they had been forced to raise their fees due to the withdrawal of the state's help, they needed 'reassurance' as well as financial assistance.[49] He therefore wanted urgent attention to be brought to the question of opening the direct grant school list to include independent and voluntary schools as well as maintained selective schools that might apply for direct grant status. Yet Mrs Thatcher continued to maintain that she had no plans to do this.

There was now grim satisfaction felt within the Labour ranks at the chain of events since Circular 10/70 had been issued the previous year. Jack Dormand, the Labour member for Easington and a committed protagonist for comprehensives, gleefully noted that every plan submitted by January 1971 had contained proposals for comprehensive schools within them. By the end of March 1971, only two local education authorities had told Mrs Thatcher that they were reconsidering their reorganization proposals. As Dormand scornfully put it, 'the Tory mountain of Circular 10/70 has produced a mouse of just two local education authorities.' Furthermore, he was confident enough to assert that 'we have moved to the next phase, which is to ask how comprehensive education is working.'[50] Yet extraordinarily, in spite of the fact that Mrs Thatcher was clearly approving the vast majority of reorganization proposals sent to her, the Conservative government continued to be relentlessly accused by the opposition of 'perpetuating privilege' as well as the social disadvantages of a divided nation.

Simultaneously, Mrs Thatcher was having to cope with the intransigence of local authorities who were hell-bent on gaining acceptance for their comprehensive schemes and were pressuring her to quickly approve them. Throughout, they constantly accused her and the department of deliberately seeking to hold up their proposals and thus creating 'chaos' for the coming school year.[51] As they had for so many years, the most intransigent local authorities appeared to regard the Secretary of State's role to be a mere rubber-stamp for their schemes.

At the time of the Party Conference in October 1971, Mrs Thatcher was also embroiled in an infamous furore over the withdrawal of local authorities' duty to provide school milk to children under seven years old. This was in spite of the fact that this policy had originated under the previous Labour government. It was therefore significant how at this point, in addition to the planned primary school improvements and the much highlighted extra sum of £170 million over four years for 'educational priority areas,' she now announced that she wanted to extend nursery education. This was in spite of what she had stated earlier about its expense. She was clearly desperate to offset the terrible publicity that she was getting.

In addition, there was the commitment to the raising of the school leaving age planned for 1972. She herself was part of the educational consensus that emphasized the importance of a greater proportion of young people gaining academic qualifications at the age of 16. As part of the justification for this major change, she emphasized in her Party Conference speech how it would be easier for pupils to enter the industrial training system as well as further education and get a better job with an employer as a result of gaining academic qualifications. Of those who left school at 15, she emphasized how 91 per cent had no 'O' level or 'CSE' passes at all, compared with only 7 per cent of those staying on the extra year. Academic qualifications under Mrs Thatcher were therefore being viewed in increasingly utilitarian terms as well. Indeed, her intrinsic justification for raising the school leaving age involved the supposed benefit to children of average or less than average ability who were to be the 'great priority.'

Regarding the local authorities that were demanding approval for their schemes without delay, she admitted that she and her Parliamentary Under-Secretary Lord Belstead were very much aware that Section 13 was not designed for circumstances such as these in which they were getting massive numbers of applications to change the nature of secondary schools. By this time, it was clear the comprehensive trend was simply going to continue, with Mrs Thatcher vaguely suggesting that a number of the problems regarding reorganization would go if those who were tackling reorganization and wished to get rid of selection before the age of 16 would 'look at the possibility of smaller comprehensive schools.'[52] It was clear by now that she had effectively given in regarding local authority maintained grammar schools.

By the time of the debate on the Address in the House of Commons on 5 November 1971, Mrs Thatcher was at her lowest ebb. She informed the House of her marked decision to concentrate on primary schools in the 1972–3 and 1973–4 building programmes to the exclusion of the improvement of old secondary schools. Alongside this announcement she also informed the House of her intention for the capitation grants to direct grant schools to be increased. The combination of these two measures turned out to be explosive.

Her actions regarding the direct grant schools were part of fulfilling the Conservatives' manifesto pledge to 'encourage' them. The capitation grant payable for each pupil in the schools was now to be increased from £32 to £62 per annum, thus restoring the cut of £20 imposed by the previous Labour government, as well as making a contribution to the increases in cost since then. Inevitably, higher government grants were being paid to the direct grant schools. This, she argued, would make it easier for parents of modest means to benefit from the much-esteemed education these schools could offer their children.[53]

Unsurprisingly, Edward Short attacked her with relish. He claimed that her direct grant schools policy was being enacted at the expense of poor children, with the expense involved coming out of the £9 million saved from cutting primary school milk. According to Short, she was subsidizing education for those who were better off at the expense of the poor.[54] Furthermore, he accused her of deliberately going over the heads of local authorities who were likely to become Labour controlled in May 1972 by asking taxpayers to subsidize a minority, while out-of-date primary and secondary schools were being neglected.

And then came what was clearly Short's key concern. He claimed that the 'running down' of the secondary school replacement programme would have a detrimental effect upon the reorganization plans of any local education authority planning to go comprehensive, and that this was all part of her furtherance of Circular 10/70. This claim was made in spite of the huge number of comprehensive schemes that she was now approving. Indeed, Short's rhetoric verged at times on paranoia:

> Authority after authority, including, to their credit, some Tory authorities, including even the right hon. Lady's own authority, have defied her and her Circular 10/70 and gone ahead with their secondary reorganisation. This is one of the right hon. Lady's methods of stopping them.[55]

Local authorities, 'much to her annoyance,' had continued to submit 'sensible, viable schemes' for approval in spite of the obstacles she had supposedly set for them. Authorities such as Barnet in her own constituency had been expected to withdraw their schemes altogether, but instead 'did no such thing.'[56] She replied by pointing out that between 1 July 1970 and 30 September 1971, a total of 2,802 statutory proposals had in fact received her approval. In all, only twenty-seven proposals had so far been rejected by her.

Inevitably, many Labour MPs such as Samuel Silkin for Dulwich echoed Short's accusation that the slowing down of expenditure on secondary school replacements meant that Mrs Thatcher was deliberately trying to halt the comprehensive advance. Similarly, Nigel Spearing, the Member for Acton, accused the government of 'authoritarian decision-making' as well as maintaining and extending 'privilege' as a result of the direct grant policy.[57] Thomas Cox, the Labour MP for Wandsworth Central, claimed that she was giving direct grant schools priority over nursery schools provision and therefore handing over £2 million 'to an already privileged section of society.'[58] This was in spite of Mrs Thatcher's reasoning that the increase in capitation fees went across the board and would in fact make free places cheaper for local authorities as well as fee-paying parents.

The abuse then became crudely personal. William Hamilton the Labour member for Fife West voiced descriptions of Mrs Thatcher as 'Mrs Scrooge with the painted face,' 'a reactionary cavewoman' and 'a desiccated calculating machine with a head full of figures ... but no bloody vision.' Amazingly, the Speaker did not interrupt his vulgar and misogynistic tirade. According to Hamilton, Edward Boyle had been 'driven out' because in his approach to educational matters, 'he was far too liberal for the Tory party.'[59] In reference to the milk policy that in fact had begun during the previous Labour government, he nevertheless claimed that Short had not done it 'with the obvious glee and deliberation' with which the present Government supposedly acted.[60]

Yet despite being in the midst of her political woes, Mrs Thatcher finally succeeded in securing a meeting with Heath to discuss education in more fundamental terms on 12 January 1972 at Chequers. Alongside her was her private secretary Sir William Pile. The minutes of the meeting show that Mrs Thatcher emphasized to Heath the intractable nature of the controversy that had arisen over the disappearance of renowned grammar schools in a number of areas, including Marylebone, Chislehurst and Kidderminster as well as Heath's own area of Bexley. She described how in some cases the number of local objections to the comprehensive schemes had been very large, and that the decision of the local authority had often not been arrived at by a majority of elected councillors but had in fact turned on aldermanic votes. The minutes also show that she admitted how in the past 'only a few' comprehensive schemes had been turned down, mainly on the grounds of the buildings simply being unsuitable. More fundamental objections had rarely been raised. This of course revealed the way that comprehensive schemes had long been viewed for decades by officials in her department.

At last, it now seems that Heath was beginning to take more of an interest in the comprehensive issue, given the actual results of what had transpired in the last seven years, including within his own area. Indeed, the record of the meeting shows that he asked Mrs Thatcher whether certain comprehensive schemes could be turned down on 'educational grounds.' Mrs Thatcher's reply was revealing. She disclosed that it might be possible for the Secretary of State to argue that a comprehensive scheme would involve the loss of a uniquely good grammar school and that the local authority had not, as she put it, 'discharged the onus of proof.' Nevertheless, she informed Heath that in practice it was difficult to establish that a child would suffer from the introduction of a comprehensive scheme, 'as educational opinion, rightly or wrongly' was still 'strongly in support of comprehensive schools.' Clearly, Mrs Thatcher did not want any fundamental row with the ranks of highly influential educationists who were pro-comprehensive.

Indeed, the minutes further show that those present at the meeting now agreed that secondary school reorganization 'was a matter for local government rather than Westminster.' Thus, Mrs Thatcher was attaching herself to the traditional line that Boyle and others in the Conservative Party had long taken of disclaiming central government responsibility from what was happening in secondary education. The issue was to be effectively palmed off onto the local authorities as before. The long-standing tendency of cynical political calculation was now emanating from Mrs Thatcher herself. The minutes show how those present felt that:

> If the procedure of local objections was allowed to influence policy, as opposed to being simply a means of allowing the difficulties of individuals to be taken into account, the Government might get the worst of both worlds.[61]

Notes written by Mrs Thatcher in an aide-memoire to Heath in January 1972 further display her dilemma about how to strike a balance between defending existing grammar schools and leaving local education authorities free to make their own decisions. Entitled 'The Situation in Education,' it noted how educational issues had 'become much more sensitive, politically, than they were even five years ago. There are many articulate and well organised pressure groups which get a ready hearing from the press and the media.' Vast numbers of proposals requiring her statutory approval had been submitted which involved the loss of an existing grammar school, usually through a merger with another school to form a comprehensive. She added:

> Some Government supporters, in Parliament and outside, are uneasy about this. But many of our own local councils are running with the comprehensive tide.[62]

It was clear that Mrs Thatcher was now taking the same line of least resistance as so many of her predecessors.

By now, Mrs Thatcher was particularly keen to highlight the expansion of provision for higher and further education instead. Following on the Robbins Committee's original recommendations, she disclosed that there would in fact be 238,000 students in the universities within the academic year of 1971–2, with a doubling of that number by 1981. It would inevitably result in a massive expansion of national resources for educational purposes. According to Mrs Thatcher, it was 'a far more vigorous programme than ever achieved previously.'[63]

In a speech to the pro-comprehensive National Union of Teachers (NUT) on 4 April, Mrs Thatcher was noticeably conciliatory towards her assembled audience. She was keen to emphasize the huge number of comprehensive schemes that she had approved in the past year, stating that the figures reduced 'to proper proportions' those local controversies 'which receive such a large share of national publicity.' Furthermore, she claimed to have been 'strongly impressed' by teachers' contribution both in the preparation of schemes and in their implementation. While noting the number of comprehensive schemes that had been introduced in existing buildings that were not designed for the full ability range, she was nevertheless quick to claim that it was to the credit of the teaching profession, as well as to local education authorities, 'that they have been able to achieve so much in physical conditions so far from ideal.'[64] She was noticeably keen not to antagonize the NUT. This was an altogether different figure from the combative Prime Minister and her famous confrontation with the trade unions ten years later.

Those on the right were now starting to realize that relatively little was being intended by the government to further their position. Rhodes Boyson, writing in *The Daily Telegraph* on 21 January, advocated a voucher system in order for parents to exercise choice in the primary and state systems in order to counter the worst tendencies of comprehensive schooling. What was required from the government was 'a return to belief in educational standards and in real parental choice,' he wrote, 'not huge building programmes and a competition with the Labour Party as to which can spend most State money.'[65] Disillusionment with what had been a self-proclaimed radical Conservative government was growing.

As a result of the local elections in May 1972, many towns and cities changed hands to Labour, including the Inner London Education Authority. Parallel to this change came a key intervention from Edward Boyle. Writing in the *Journal of Educational Administration and History*, he offered a historical overview of his version of events regarding secondary reorganization over the past twenty-five years. True to his usual tendency, he essentially sought to rationalize the development of comprehensive education in terms of growing parental aspiration. He also added his thoughts about the Secretary of State's present policy.

While he felt it right that the Secretary of State should retain the powers under Section 13 to reject 'clearly undesirable' proposals on educational grounds, he nevertheless added that 'one or two recent exercises of this power, as in the case of Surrey, may have seemed puzzling.' In addition, he 'very much' questioned her Section 68 powers preventing the actions of 'unreasonable' local authorities being used in this context. His preferred approach was to be altogether more emollient than Mrs Thatcher, who he implied was at times enforcing her personal views. The minister's powers, he added, had hitherto only been used in cases where 'any reasonable man' in his position would have felt the local authority was acting perversely, as opposed to an approach embodying personal conviction on the matter:

> There is, surely, a significant difference between these two approaches; and whilst I have never believed that education should, or could, be 'taken out of politics,' it has always seemed to me inherent in the 1944 Act that the Secretary of State has certain 'quasi-judicial' functions to perform as well as a political function.

The clear suggestion was that she was being overly political rather than acting more in concert with the local authorities in the traditional consensual manner. It was now 'reasonable' to predict that by 1974/5, a non-selective transfer would become the norm, 'and what may then surprise us, looking back, is not that this change took place, but that its implementation waited so long.'[66] All this of course amounted to a kind of pressure, albeit subtly exercised, on Mrs Thatcher towards further accommodation to the comprehensive principle in spite of the concessions she was already making.

For her part, Mrs Thatcher claimed all the while to be attempting to conserve 'parental choice' within the system. Her use of Section 68, she maintained, had been due to local authorities attempting to apply a rigid zoning system as part of their reorganization plans. This had sometimes meant being forced to act by using these powers and thus directing the local authority, as in a recent case in Surrey.[67]

In an interview with the *Spectator* in July 1972, she was by now claiming that the issue of secondary reorganization had become an 'artificial question.' What mattered more, she maintained, was what went on within the schools, and she was more interested in getting the kind of education suitable for a child rather than focusing upon school arrangement or organization. Apparently, a 'red herring' of a debate about educational systems had been pursued, rather than an emphasis on 'quality.' In short, she was now fudging the issue about selection and distancing herself from it. Furthermore, she claimed, in spite of her own recently commissioned report on reading standards, that the general standard in school education was rising, given that 'the numbers getting some certificate of education are increasing.'[68]

In her speech to the Conservative Party Conference on 12 October she simply urged local authorities to give parents as wide a choice as possible. She revealed that she had by now upheld ninety-two objections, usually in favour of famous or well-known grammar schools. In fact, such statements only served to highlight the vast majority of schemes that she had approved over the last two years. In remarks to the conference audience that showed her awareness of their feelings on the issue, Mrs Thatcher then added:

> I can only express the hope that those who believe intensely in the future of grammar schools and what they have to offer will be as vocal in their own areas and outside this conference hall as they are today.[69]

Yet of course, she and the others at the Chequers meeting had in fact already stated privately that they did not want local objections to influence policy.

For the direct grant schools, she announced that if local authorities decided not to take up places, as was the case in Bradford where the local education authority had recently decided to do away with free places at the local direct grant school, parents could apply directly to the direct grant school for a free or income-assisted place, and would not have to go through the local education authority. Nevertheless, she reiterated that she was still not intending to re-open the direct grant school list.[70]

Other local authorities at this time, most notably in Birmingham, were instructing their chief education officers to make no arrangements for junior school leaving examinations at 11 that were set for the next year. This was despite the fact that the period for objections to Birmingham's comprehensive proposals did not expire until 13 January 1973. Clearly, Birmingham City Council was already trying to abolish the 11 plus examinations for the following spring, and was being fully supported in this by both the National Union of Teachers and the National Association of Schoolmasters.[71]

A politics of distraction

Yet ever the consummate politician, in late 1972 Mrs Thatcher was focusing strategically on other matters. On 9 October she sent a minute to Heath concerning proposals for a new Education White Paper for the coming decade. The key proposal was that nursery education should be expanded over a period of ten years to provide places for up to 90 per cent of 4-year-olds as well as 50 per cent of those aged 3. This decision was partly based on her certainty that their primary school improvement programme had not only made both economic and educational sense, but had been attractive to voters. 'Politically,' she informed Heath, a new statement of government policy in education was required, adding pointedly that 'the educational world and informed opinion is expecting one.'[72]

She urged that they take the opportunity of the forthcoming Queen's speech to announce their broad intentions and accompany them as soon as possible with a White Paper. She also proposed to announce their intentions for nursery education at the forthcoming Party Conference later that month. In this way, she was looking to turn the corner with a raft of new measures. In spite of the known problems that the constant expansion of all educational sectors at this time of economic turbulence would bring, the Conservatives were anxious to not be seen to be in any way opposed to them.

The Chancellor of the Exchequer Anthony Barber was therefore proud to announce that educational spending was expected to exceed 14 per cent by 1976–7, which Mrs Thatcher keenly reiterated at her speech opening the North of England Conference in January 1973. 'Expansion' was thus being urged on all fronts. The proposed White Paper, entitled *Education: A Framework for Expansion*, was set to be published on 6 December. The Cabinet were now especially keen to consider how the strategy could most effectively be presented to the public and to the Party, as well as the correct approach for the Press briefing and publicity required.

As for the huge number of comprehensive schemes that she and her officials were still adjudicating, Mrs Thatcher was now resolved to not allow local objections to have too much weight in the decision process. Ultimately, she was not prepared to break with standard practice and strengthen anti-comprehensive objectors' position when in disagreement with the local authority concerned. She informed the pro-grammar school pressure group the National Education Association in December 1972 that the local education authority's comments would be passed onto the objectors only with the permission of the authority concerned and when such a course was considered 'essential for a proper understanding' of the submitted proposals. She added, pointedly, 'I do not consider that it would be desirable, or indeed practicable, to alter the normal practice.'[73] Instead, the local education authorities were to remain essentially unaccountable to local feeling and continue to carry the upper hand in the whole process.

At this time, the Education Correspondent for *The Times* Ronald Butt noted perceptively in his weekly column how it was clear by now that the Conservative government did not want to challenge the 'progressive' educationists and their ideology, in spite of the increasing voices of protest from pressure groups and organizations bodies springing up at this time such as the National Council for Educational Standards. Butt felt that Mrs Thatcher had awoken to the issue, unlike her senior colleagues, but 'there is a limit to what she can do on her own.' Instead, Butt noted, the Conservative government tended to be 'bored or embarrassed' by arguments about educational doctrine. While noting how they sent their own children privately to schools that maintained high educational standards, nevertheless they paid 'convenient obeisance to the views of the so-called progressive educational establishment so far as the nation's schools are concerned.'[74]

But Margaret Thatcher was not the embattled loner, swimming against the social democratic tide both outside and within her party, that Butt implied at all. Instead, she appeared to be embodying the very spirit of Lady Bridget Plowden with her impetus for nursery education to be targeted at areas of disadvantage and homes that were 'culturally and economically deprived.'[75] Over 13,000 extra nursery places had already been approved under the Urban Aid Programme for poorer areas. Significantly, the Government's White Paper was at this time being welcomed by the educational world, the Press and by the Association of Education Committees for its 'firm and progressive structure.'[76] The government was clearly more anxious to receive plaudits from the educationists.

She had by now approved approximately 2,650 statutory proposals and rejected only 115, a rate of a mere 4 per cent. And yet in spite of the massive number of comprehensive proposals she had already approved, in February 1973 the Labour opposition moved a motion of censure upon her. In proposing the motion, Roy Hattersley the Labour member for Birmingham, Sparkbrook condemned her 'arbitrary and capricious' use of powers and claimed that she was playing 'ministerial roulette' with the education service.[77] Furthermore, he tried to undermine the number of local objections in particular cases by questioning the figures that had been produced. Attacking her in a notably similar manner to that of Short over Circular 10/70, Hattersley accused Mrs Thatcher of stimulating local campaigns against comprehensive schemes, including helping to institute 'Save our School' campaigns in Woking involving the local Conservative MP Cranley Onslow. The parallels with the way Florence Horsbrugh had been targeted over Kidbrooke nearly twenty years earlier were eerily similar.

Hattersley cited both Boyle in his recently published journal article and the approach taken by Hailsham over a case of Aylesbury grammar school in 1957 in his arguments against Mrs Thatcher's recent actions. By way of making negative comparisons with her, he recounted how Hailsham had not regarded it as appropriate to override a local authority unless he was convinced that it was not merely wrong, but 'prejudiced'.[78] The high bar that both Hailsham and Boyle had set for when it was to be considered appropriate for the Minister to intervene against comprehensive schemes was still being dangled over her head.

In response, Mrs Thatcher merely protested that she was concerned with the rights of local electors under Section 13. As she put it, a proposal did not amount to a decision, 'and the precise machinery for objection is not mere decoration, although the hon. Member (Hattersely) would have it that way.' In similarly defensive fashion, she emphasized how in the last two and a half years, her vast number of approvals were leading to a wide range of comprehensive schemes. Referring to recent controversial cases in London, she informed the House that she had turned down proposals for Tulse Hill because it had involved the enlargement of an 11 to a 13 form entry comprehensive. In relation to the Strand grammar school that was also involved, the parents had taken the school to court with Mrs Thatcher upholding the objections. Any Secretary of State, she continued, who was concerned solely with patterns of organization and not with parental choice in specific cases would be 'betraying his office'.[79] These were all of course small-scale interventions.

The current Under-Secretary of State Norman St John-Stevas then claimed that by mentioning Boyle's recent pronouncements, Hattersley had tried to 'to drive a wedge' between the views of Boyle and Mrs Thatcher. Indeed, Stevas disingenuously claimed that Boyle's policy and principles were 'exactly the same' as her own. However, the Labour MP Kenneth Marks then reminded him of the uncomfortable fact that in 1966 Boyle, when asked if he would withdraw Circular 10/65, had of course said that he would not do so. At this awkward moment, Stevas simply replied that he would not enter into an 'exegesis' of that nature.[80] He naturally did not want to be drawn on this key area of division within the Party.

Instead, Stevas merely expressed the standard blandishments that 'we accept comprehension,' and that he felt it would eventually become the dominant part of the secondary system. What they as a Conservative government rejected was universal compulsory reorganization imposed without any consideration of local educational needs or parental wishes. It could all have come straight out of the mouth of Boyle himself. Referring to the relentless attacks mounted by the Labour opposition upon Mrs Thatcher, Stevas added, 'If anyone is entitled to criticize her it is my hon. Friend the Member for Stratford on Avon (Maude) because she has approved too much comprehension rather than too little.'[81]

It was a justified criticism to make. In a further interview in April with Ronald Butt of the *Sunday Times*, it was again clear that Mrs Thatcher was increasingly confining herself to only opposing the worst extremes of comprehensive reorganization, and instead centring on the somewhat vague notion of 'parental choice'. Local councils such as the Inner London Education Authority were increasingly embarking upon policies of 'banding' and 'bussing' in which children were banded into ability ranges and sent by bus to different local schools in order to preserve an equal spread of ability. By contrast, she claimed that she wanted to support parents in having the right to choose for their children the kind of school that they, rather than the educational establishment, deemed best. Yet this supposed choice that she was defending was to occur within a system that was rapidly becoming completely all-ability in nature. In the interview, her opposition was therefore simply directed at those who thought all children should attend one type of school in a local area, and was now claiming that this was where the real point of division existed. She had thus shifted the goal-posts of contention.

Yet such was the inadequate nature of some urban comprehensive schemes they simply could not be accepted in their present state. In June 1973, Mrs Thatcher gave her judgement on the proposals for Birmingham's secondary education scheme intended for implementation the following September. The proposals related to 112 schools, and involved a non-selective scheme of consortium for all parts of the city, that included schools being sited on split premises. Of the 112 schools in total due to be affected, she approved 52 of them, while rejecting 60. The proposals also potentially affected thirty selective schools of grammar, technical or bilateral kinds. Of these, twelve were approved and eighteen were rejected. The reason for the high rate of rejection was due to the inadequate period of preparation for such a substantial and complicated organizational pattern. Equally inadequate comprehensive schemes were also submitted for Nottingham at this time that affected the notable Clifton and Mundella grammar schools.

Throughout 1973 pro-comprehensive organizations such as the Confederation for the Advancement of State Education (CASE) continued to put pressure on Mrs Thatcher to approve reorganization proposals instantly. On a notable occasion, Rolf Drefner of CASE led a deputation of local officials, MPs as well as a clergyman to try to persuade Mrs Thatcher to make all schools in Sutton in Surrey go comprehensive. Once again, a recourse to misogyny from men on the left was apparent, with Drefner later describing his unsuccessful talks with her to the *Wallington and Carshalton Times* as 'more like an argument with an awkward wife than with a Secretary of State'.[82] The 80,000 local objections that had been issued there were routinely dismissed by his organization, with Drefner claiming that it was simply the same parents making objections to each school in their area. Mrs Thatcher was accused throughout of deliberate hindrance and delay, and thus abusing her powers. The arrogance and, indeed, ruthlessness of the pro-comprehensive left were always evident.

Nevertheless, Mrs Thatcher continued to receive praise from within the Conservative Party for her efforts, particularly from those on the right of the party spectrum that included the notable Monday Club. According to their newsletter, in contrast to most 'if not all' of her predecessors, 'who invariably stood aloof from the public and whispered sweet nothings into the ears of a few left wing vice-chancellors, in the hope that they would vote Tory,' she had always been prepared to listen and talk to those concerned with education, particularly parents. Furthermore, it added, 'she has stood up to left wing militants like a swan defending its cygnets; above all she has made every possible effort to be scrupulously fair and unbiased, especially in making difficult decisions on comprehensive proposals.'[83]

However, private notes circulating within her department at this time suggest Mrs Thatcher and her officials continued to be more anxious to retain good relations with the education correspondents in the national press. A series of meetings from 2 to 3 October had indeed been planned by them for this purpose.[84] This was partly due of course to the more recent increase in rejected proposals in areas such as Birmingham. As a result, the anxious purpose of these two meetings was 'to re-establish friendly contact' with the education correspondents. The educational press and their influence were always to be respected and, indeed, feared.

In addition to Birmingham, recent rejections of urban reorganization schemes occurred in Leicester, Dudley, Sunderland, Liverpool and Bristol. In these cases, Mrs Thatcher explained her decisions on the grounds that a uniform type of education was being imposed without adequate planning or consultation leaving those areas bereft of parental choice, particularly where existing schools were successful and well-liked. In the case of Birmingham, for instance, over forty appeals had been lodged by parents alleging that the local authority was acting unreasonably in refusing to admit children to the school of their choice. Yet by now, over 3,200 comprehensive school proposals had been approved nationally while 325 had been rejected. This amounted to a rate of rejection of a mere 9 per cent.

In November 1973, the National Education Association's Chairman Edward Maynard Potts complained bitterly in private correspondence with Gilbert Longden how, despite the Conservatives having been in power for three and a half years, it was in fact Labour's education policies that were being imposed on the nation. Potts, who travelled the country helping parents to object to comprehensive proposals, reported that they were aware that Labour would 'ruthlessly carry out all that they threaten.' By contrast, they felt that 'Conservatives rarely fight for education.' Indeed, Potts went on, if a Labour minister had been given the whole-hearted support that Mrs Thatcher had received at the party conference in Blackpool the previous month, they would have been far more ambitious in government.

Potts noted that there was no suggestion in the recent Queen's speech of government legislation counteracting Roy Hattersley's recently announced policy of the immediate destruction of the direct grant schools if the Labour Party was re-elected, in addition to what they claimed would be the planned elimination of the 3,000 schools in the private sector. No effort was being made by the Conservative government to stop this future policy of 'compulsory uniformity.' The Conservatives continued to sit passively, while the momentum lay entirely with the left.

Potts urged Longden to consider voucher schemes as well as enabling voluntary-aided and controlled schools, which held varying degrees of autonomy from local authorities, to become direct grant. He further warned, 'The object of my letter is to tell you that potential Conservative voters are abstaining and that failure to counteract Labour's education proposals could lose the Conservatives half a million votes.'[85] There was still hope, nevertheless, that the Conservatives might save schools of quality in spite of Labour's intransigence. Action in this Parliament, he added, would encourage an optimism that would prove beneficial to the Party and grow into an electoral asset. Longden's simple reply on 5 December merely stated that 'I am afraid that I can only agree with what you say.'[86] Longden had of course always been far more opinionated about the failings of the Conservative Party in private correspondence than he ever was to the leadership's face.

Economic reality bites

By May 1973, it was clear that the economy was overheating and inflation rising. As a result of the Yom Kippur war in October 1973, the Arabs set an embargo on oil that sent prices soaring. This meant that the current levels of planned public expenditure simply could not be sustained. In late 1973, Mrs Thatcher therefore agreed with Patrick Jenkin, the new Chief Secretary of the Treasury, that there would have to be reductions in the education budget. Furthermore in December, Anthony Barber implemented an emergency budget with sharp cuts in capital spending.

On 29 January 1974 in the House of Commons, Timothy Raison, who had recently been appointed under-secretary at the department, was forced to confirm cuts on educational building in order to save fuel and energy. Mrs Thatcher inevitably had to suspend the programme for the replacement of out-of-date schools for both the primary and secondary stages. This was also to be the case for the nursery school expansion programme, as well as a reduction in the rate of expansion of student numbers. In all, the reduction in the Department of Education and Science (DES) budget for 1974/5 was £182 million, out of £1,200 million total cuts in public spending.

Union militancy was now rife within the teaching profession, with teachers in inner London taking industrial action at this time for a larger London allowance. There were also the inevitable calls for greater student grants. This of course was set against a national backdrop of uncontrolled union activism involving the National Union of Miners and the Trade Union Congress over pay 'relativities.' With the increased demands for greater subsidization and state spending, the economic situation was dire. Labour members such as Ernest Armstrong cynically took this opportunity to call for direct grant schools to receive cuts amid the restrictions that had had to be made elsewhere in the service. These 'already privileged' schools, the Labour opposition claimed, were not having to make their share of sacrifices.[87] Given the straightened economic circumstances, it was inevitable that the direct grant schools would be vulnerable. Their future was now distinctly uncertain. Amidst this air of polarization and emergency, Heath called the general election for 28 February 1974.

During the election campaign, Mrs Thatcher approved a written statement of Conservative education policy prepared by Central Office that focused upon the future of the education service and the priorities of her successor if the Conservative government was not re-elected. It named the main priority for the next Secretary of State to be to control the expansion of demand within the education service that would always be out of proportion to the resources available. The statement, printed in the *Times Educational Supplement* on 22 February in the week before the general election, was emphatic that 'education policy cannot be discussed in an ivory tower, bolted against general economic exigencies.' Yet the Conservative government, including Mrs Thatcher herself, had of course been instrumental in implementing high spending and expansionary policies throughout a period of economic uncertainty themselves. Indeed, the scale of demand on the building industry was one of the key established measures of inflationary pressure. Yet this was something that Mrs Thatcher had herself helped to stimulate.

Once again, the Conservative Party claimed in a form of double speak that the education debate apparently needed to be shifted from what it termed the 'sterile' issue concerning the kind of school to the 'more fruitful one' of the kind of education that was needed. The test to be applied in future was simply whether the education offered promoted 'the fullest development of the whole personality of the child.'[88]

In spite of the Conservatives securing 38 per cent of the vote to Labour's share of 37 per cent, the Labour Party was ultimately victorious with 301 seats to the Tories' 297. Following a futile attempt at collaboration with the Liberal leader Jeremy Thorpe, stemming from a deluded belief that the result simply indicated the country's desire for 'National Government' based on a coalition, Heath was forced to resign as Prime Minister. The so-called 'peasants' revolt' for the leadership of the Conservative Party would still be a long time coming. Most of the top ranks of the Conservative Party favoured a non-confrontational approach to the trade unions and supported Heath's continued leadership of the Party.

For her part, Mrs Thatcher claimed in a note to Professor John Vaizey on 7 March that, 'in spite of all the problems,' she had 'thoroughly enjoyed' her three and a half years at the Department of Education and Science and felt her successor, the moderate Labourite Reginald Prentice, would work 'very well' with its officials.[89] Thus came to an end a period of her career that perhaps caused her the most regret and embarrassment. She had been the key vehicle for what amounted to a leftist agenda and policies that she naturally disliked. She had demonstrated her own form of appeasement paralleling her Conservative government's submission to union militancy and their introduction of statutory prices and incomes policies.

Mrs Thatcher's later criticisms of Heath's actions as those of an unprincipled technocrat with no strategic coherence had in fact been echoed by her own stance at this time, with its broad utilitarianism and focus upon economics. She would of course later claim in her memoirs that 'we had all of us' been too interested in the 'inputs' of new buildings, expensive equipment and more teachers, rather than the 'outputs' of quality of teaching, levels of achievement and standards of behaviour.[90] Yet all this was said with the comfort of hindsight. By March 1974, Britain was now on the road towards an almost completely comprehensive education system at secondary level.

In summary, Mrs Thatcher withdrew Circular 10/65 and was more exacting and far-reaching in her use of Section 13 powers in investigating each local authority proposal than her predecessors. She also pursued a pragmatic policy of 'co-existence' between selective and non-selective schools. Nevertheless, she was noticeably careful to detach herself from the positions of those such as Angus Maude who clearly espoused later selection amongst his proposals for improving an endangered system. By contrast, her own position amounted to an ambiguous one of supporting direct grant schools for a minority of pupils while increasingly accepting the comprehensive principle for the vast majority. More fundamentally, she would align herself with the conventional mantra of supporting the freedom of local education authorities' decision-making, a position very different from that contained in her later approach as Prime Minister, when she would attempt to circumscribe their powers from the centre.

The invidious distinction that had long been made in High Tory circles between central and local government's responsibility for comprehensive schemes was ultimately maintained by her as well. While Mrs Thatcher did give financial assistance to the direct grant schools, no action was taken in terms of opening the direct grant school list to enable more schools, including maintained grammars, to be included. Nor, given what was known about the Labour Party's intentions, was there any attempt at implementing legislation to protect the direct grant schools' status and thus ensure their survival. Furthermore, she had actively promoted policies of increased public expenditure and expansion that she would later keenly disown. It was, in all, a supreme irony. From now on, the vast bulk of Britain's secondary education system would be cast in a comprehensive mould that there would be no turning back from.

6

Opposition from 1974–9

The chapter examines the subsequent years of Tory opposition during the Labour governments led by Harold Wilson and James Callaghan. The Conservatives' expediency over selection continued, as evidenced by their wariness of openly supporting the few brave authorities, most notably Tameside, that stood out against the Labour government. Throughout this period, there was clear division existing between the opposition spokesman Norman St John-Stevas, who was resigned to the comprehensive trend, and his second in command Rhodes Boyson, who wanted the Party to support a policy of education vouchers and offer encouragement to selection within urban areas when they were returned to office.

Resigned to comprehensives

Having achieved its narrow general election victory, the Labour government was determined to finish what it had started during its previous period in office. It hurriedly issued Circular 4/74 that once again sought to impose a universal comprehensive system on the country. In future, local authority expenditure was to be forced to contribute to reorganization. The second Wilson government also wanted to ensure that the comprehensive principle was spread to polytechnics, and by association to all levels of maintained education. Indeed, polytechnics were now being described as the tertiary equivalent of the secondary modern school. The new Labour government was now openly admitting their intention of seizing further powers in order to achieve their objectives.

Edward Heath's initial choice of opposition spokesman on education for his remaining period as Conservative Party leader was William van Straubenzee, whose criticisms of Labour's imminent circular were as tepid as expected. However, a new voice for the Conservative Opposition was represented by Dr Rhodes Boyson, who had been elected as Conservative member for Brent North in the recent February general election. A renowned headmaster of a successful comprehensive, Highbury Grove, and now a co-editor of the Black Papers, he had quickly become a prominent figure on the Party's National Advisory Committee on Education, as well as a distinctive voice in Commons debates on the subject.

Boyson was a direct obstacle to van Straubenzee, and in notably populist spirit constantly emphasized the disadvantage to the able working-class child posed by the imposition of universal neighbourhood schools within urban areas. Yet in doing so, he inevitably described his own Party as never having had a proper policy regarding comprehensive schools.[1] In addition, Boyson sought more parental involvement on school governing boards as well as the introduction of education vouchers, which he wanted to be a cornerstone of future Conservative education policy when they were returned to office.[2]

In contrast, as Opposition spokesman, William van Straubenzee felt it important that the Party should not give the impression of being opposed to the comprehensive system. He thought it would be impossible for them to unravel a system that had of course made a considerable advance during their own period in office. Importantly for Straubenzee, he felt that large numbers of Conservative voters were 'devoted adherents' of these schools.[3] Furthermore, he felt it important that the Party should not greatly associate itself with direct grant and independent schools either. Indeed, he claimed at this time that he wanted to 'help' the Labour government in its education programme, was 'sick and tired' of education being part of a game of political football and was glad it had not been an issue at the last general election.[4] By early June 1974, Straubenzee was merely recommending a position of 'co-existence' of selective and non-selective schools, along with the preservation of diversity and parental choice.

However, by this time van Straubenzee was locked in a power struggle with Norman St John-Stevas to hang onto his role as opposition spokesman. Stevas had been an Under-Secretary at the Department of Education and Science and later Minister of State for the Arts during the Heath government. Since the general election, he had been appointed Vice-Chairman of the Parliamentary Education Committee and was continuing as opposition spokesman on the Arts. The outcome of the battle was victory for Stevas, who was appointed opposition spokesman for education at the end of the month.

Yet having gained the position, Stevas did not in fact espouse a position that differed greatly from that of Straubenzee. He stressed that when next in office a Conservative government would withdraw Circular 4/74, but emphasized that their alternative would not be the restoration of the 11 plus. In a slight play on words, he was keen to underline choice between different types of comprehensive school rather than between comprehensives and selective schools. For too long, he claimed, the Tories had been on the defensive by merely 'reacting' to the dogmatic views and opinions of left-wing educationists. Nevertheless, he was noticeably quick to add that they did not favour the 'arbitrariness' of the eleven plus examination 'with its rigid categorization of children.' Instead, selection, where circumstances required it, was to be made by flexible means of assessment allowing for transfer at different ages.[5] There was therefore nothing very specific on selection that he was prepared to countenance.

He also maintained a vague invocation of 'parents' rights.' By July he was advocating that a statutory obligation be imposed on school boards that half of all governors and managers should be drawn from the parents of children currently at the school, to be directly elected by all parents at an annual meeting or by postal ballot. He was also calling for greater parental involvement through parents' representatives on local authority education committees.[6] Other proposals from Stevas included a pledge to reopen the direct grant schools list. Nevertheless, little was being directly said about the vast majority of maintained schools that were by now comprehensive. Stevas' emphasis on 'parent power' essentially amounted to a means of simply managing the comprehensive system better. Apart from vague remarks about increasing choice within the maintained sector, there was a distinct sense that Stevas felt that nothing of great consequence could now be done.

However there were those within the Conservative Party who were emboldened by Stevas' appointment and wanted to fight Circular 4/74 harder. In June 1974 Stuart Sexton, a Conservative councillor in Middlesex, was urging Stevas to put 'more Conservative guts and determination' into Conservative local education authorities in regard to fighting the Circular.[7] The perennial cry, of course, was that there needed to be stronger links between the Parliamentary Party and the Conservative-run local authorities. According to Sexton, these local authorities still did not understand the importance of education both nationally and locally. But this renewed pressure was coming too late.

Instead, following another general election held in October 1974, comprehensive reorganization proceeded rapidly under Harold Wilson's second Labour government. By January 1975, 68 per cent of secondary pupils in England and Wales were now in comprehensive schools and only one local authority – Kingston upon Thames – had none at all. A mere seven local authorities had declared their intention of retaining some measure of selection in principle.

Against the odds, Margaret Thatcher was elected the new leader of the Conservative Party in February 1975, deposing Heath. One of her key appointments was to make Angus Maude Chairman of the Conservative Research Department. But this made no difference to the educational situation. Only a year later, the Labour government was embarking on a new education bill to extinguish any remaining local authority opposition to its comprehensive policy. The 1976 Education Act was a new version of the aborted 1969 Education Bill, and sought to give the Labour Secretary of State Fred Mulley sufficient powers to require local education authorities to submit proposals within a specified period and call for 'further progress' if he considered developments to be insufficient. The Act involved amendments being made to Section 13 of the 1944 Act, with clauses 3 and 4 of the Bill together placing a duty upon local education authorities and governors of voluntary schools to submit reorganization proposals at the Secretary of State's request. In addition, it included a section within clause 5 that limited the powers of local education authorities to pay for places in independent schools. The intention was of course to destroy the remaining direct grant schools. According to Mulley, the clause prevented a local authority from 'seeking to circumvent' the Bill by using the take-up of independent or direct grant school places as a means of avoiding establishing a fully comprehensive system within its area.[8] The degree of centralization intended for the education service was thus being taken to an unprecedented level.

Yet Stevas' opposition to the Labour government's proposed Bill merely amounted to impotent sentiments such as that the government should have focussed on how to improve the existing schools, instead of forcing the educational discussion back to what he described as the 'sterile conflict' between grammar and comprehensive schools.[9] In practical terms, the Conservative opposition merely sought to introduce an amendment designed to strengthen parents' rights under Section 76 of the 1944 Act that affirmed parental wishes in education. Nevertheless, Stevas ultimately claimed to want to 'improve' the Government's Bill, emphasizing that 'we want a dialogue in education, not a punch up.'[10]

The long-held tendency for limp and half-hearted criticism from the Conservative side thus continued. William van Straubenzee, now on the opposition's back benches since his demotion, merely argued that the administration of the education service should be 'bipartisan,' and that there was not the additional money in real terms for 'meaningful' secondary reorganization. Nevertheless, he emphasized that Conservative opposition be towards compulsion rather than 'the comprehensive system as such.' Addressing his fellow MP Rhodes Boyson, who had been chosen to close the education debate for the Opposition, Straubenzee pointedly asked, 'Will he make it clear that the next Tory government, as part of their responsibilities, will want to sustain and particularly to understand the problems of comprehensive and other schools in difficult areas?'[11] Implicitly, Straubenzee was advocating that they do nothing to turn back the tide when next in office.

In fact, Boyson himself stated that the next Conservative government did not want to 'unscramble' the comprehensive schools that currently existed, but merely that comprehensives should not be planted all over the country until an assessment had been made that they were academically and socially more desirable. Nevertheless, he was keen to add that 'in many areas we are removing selection by examination and replacing it with selection by the purse.'[12] He argued that the Government's policy involved the destruction of opportunity for the able working-class child and promised that the Opposition would fight the Bill in committee. If it went through, they would repeal it when next in office.

Throughout this period, Margaret Thatcher's Conservative opposition continued to worm itself uneasily around local controversies within key areas. In the summer of 1976, a dispute raged over intended secondary reorganization in the Conservative-run area of Tameside, Greater Manchester, with Fred Mulley announcing that he intended to give an order directing the local authority to comply with the comprehensive plan he had approved in November 1975. As a result, the Conservative-run council would be forced to abandon their intention, upon which they had won the recent local election, to retain their existing grammar schools.

Because of the nature of the controversy, Boyson asked for a debate on the Tameside situation under an issued standing order in the House of Commons. In order for the debate to take place, he needed forty of his fellow Conservative MPs to support him. Yet it appeared that on the day in question there were not forty Tories in the House and only a desultory thirty-five stood up. The Speaker was thus obliged to put the question to the House and Boyson was beaten by Labour votes. This was in spite of the Conservative whips' office having been fully aware of Boyson's application to the Speakers office which they had themselves put through. Yet nothing had been done to ensure that a sufficient number of Conservative MPs were present to deliberate on a local issue of national significance.[13]

At the very least, it appeared to indicate a lack of interest within the higher reaches of the party to fight on the issue. Reporting on the matter, Ronald Butt of *The Times* deduced that 'it is often hard for many leading figures in the Tory party really to share the depth of feeling that their followers have on this kind of issue.' Indeed, he noted that many at the top of the party appeared to consider the Tameside councillors' fight to be 'a little embarrassing' and to 'prefer compromises.'[14]

During this period, records show that in its weekly meetings the Shadow Cabinet stated that it intended to support Tameside Council's stand. Nevertheless, it was also keen that Stevas discourage them from embarking upon an 11 plus method of selection, and preferred what they termed 'alternative means of selection' instead.[15] However, upon then hearing that the Tameside councillors wanted to go further and challenge Mulley in the courts on the grounds that he was acting unreasonably, the Shadow Cabinet felt it could not advise them whether to proceed or not due to the legal considerations. Instead, they would simply support the councillors' appeal if they chose to pursue it.[16] (Significantly, this was the same week as Boyson's attempted debate in the Commons.) The Tameside councillors would in fact turn out to be successful in their legal action. Yet no Tory-run local authority wanted to follow Tameside's lead. In addition by the end of 1976, due to government regulations for the cessation of grant, the direct grant schools were no longer in existence. Of the 174 direct grant schools, 46 were absorbed into the maintained sector, while the remainder became independent as their grant was phased out.

An unlikely duo

Well-publicized scandals involving stories of inadequate state schools, such as the notorious junior school William Tyndale with its indiscipline and poor standards, raged during this period.[17] By the time of the Prime Minister James Callaghan's speech on education at Ruskin College in October 1976, public concern was growing over educational standards. In his speech, Callaghan called for greater central control over the school curriculum due to consternation at educational standards and schools' ability to prepare pupils for working life.

In seemingly direct response to Callaghan's speech, Mrs Thatcher promoted Boyson by offering him the number two slot in education for the opposition in November 1976. Clearly, she wanted to take back the initiative on educational matters and appear robust. Meanwhile, Stevas remained in position as the main spokesman. Yet it soon became apparent that Stevas and Boyson were an unlikely duo. While committed to his new role, Boyson continued to agitate alongside in *Black Paper 1977* for the comparative results of comprehensives to be compared with selective schools and published nationally.[18] If comprehensive schools in certain areas proved ineffective, he argued that local authorities should 'diversify' their provision by reintroducing selective schools of varying types. In addition, Boyson advocated an 'early leaving scheme' for pupils at age 15 involving suitable leaving tests with jobs to go to. This of course sat at odds with what Mrs Thatcher had implemented as education secretary with the raising of the school leaving age in 1972. Clearly, Boyson was advancing beyond the Party's stated policy and holding out for more radical policy change in the future.

Stevas and Boyson were soon at odds. While Stevas was arguing that the present Secretary of State Shirley Williams and the Labour government accepted the need for higher standards in education as a result of what he claimed was the effectiveness of the Tory opposition's arguments, Boyson by contrast wanted an all-out attack upon the government. In February 1977 he stated that the Labour government's recent public sentiments about standards were bogus, citing their continued comprehensive policy which had resulted during this time in the closure of two successful grammar schools, namely Marylebone Grammar and Mary Datchelor. Boyson was therefore intent on popularizing his own idiosyncratic standpoint within the party on altogether separate lines from that of Stevas, who desired a more ameliorative stance towards the government. Indeed, Stevas even claimed in February 1977 in the Commons that it was 'fruitless' to get into a discussion of whether standards had fallen and that 'we cannot in the nature of things establish that matter.'[19] Naturally, the Labour government delighted in the schism between Stevas and Boyson.

By March 1978, Stevas was still being noticeably circumspect on the issue of academic selection. He proclaimed that when next in office they would retain existing grammar schools of proven worth and 'consider sympathetically' proposals for new selective schools. Nevertheless, it appeared that he was mainly concerned to tweak the comprehensive system for improvements rather than embark on any fundamental changes in the secondary schools' organization if returned to office. Although he acknowledged that they were likely to return to power before many local authorities had completed their reorganization schemes, he added that 'it is likely that most will wish to continue along that path even when compulsion is removed.' Such merely practical measures as reducing comprehensives' size and moving towards streaming and setting would, he claimed, ensure that comprehensives would work for children of all abilities. Alongside this, Stevas was keen to add his desire to improve relations with the teaching unions, including platitudes such as that 'we should take every opportunity of showing our support for the teaching profession and our concern and sympathy for their problems.'[20] This was hardly the voice of a radical restorer of selection.[21]

In an interview with *The Times* education correspondent Ronald Butt that also took place at this time, Stevas was forced to be more candid. While continuing to mouth vague intentions about 'continuous selection' and 'a varied choice at several ages' to help the gifted but disadvantaged child, when pressed as to what the next Conservative government would actually do regarding local authority areas dominated by inadequate comprehensives, he admitted that 'we are not proposing to take powers to order local authorities around.' To Butt's further pressing he replied, 'then there would be nothing you could do except start an assisted-places scheme in that area.' Unlike the Labour government, Stevas was not prepared to use ministerial powers to effect any fundamental change upon local authorities when next in office.

In response to Butt's questioning as to what a Conservative government would do if local authorities did not even adopt the methods he was recommending to improve their schools, Stevas was fatalistic:

What do you do when you've inherited a system which isn't working well and which is operating in this way? You can't go back to the selective system: that would create a real state of war. So we're left with saving what remains of the old grammar schools, and helping to establish a new direct grant system – and then concentrating all the efforts we can on improving the comprehensive system itself.[22]

In spite of his approach being, as Butt described it, 'persuasive' rather than compulsory, Stevas nevertheless claimed throughout the interview that a future Conservative government could alter the educational climate.

Butt's questions were also put to Rhodes Boyson. In contrast to Stevas, he thought that given that they were already accepting the principle of selection by planning to have an assisted places scheme when returned to office, selection could be reintroduced in the long term. In answer to the key question about what the Conservatives would actually do about comprehensives in view of their belief that the present system did not work well as a whole, Boyson repeated his intention of a 'thorough inquiry' into the state of the schools. This would include collating comprehensives' relative performance in public exams, literacy, staying on rates and other key measures. When they had the figures, he told Butt, they could then say what they would 'advise' the local authorities to do with their new-found freedom. He then added:

> But again, my personal belief is that school selection will certainly have to come back in the interests of the abler children in inner-city areas. Gifted children from deprived homes are the ones who have been worst affected by the switch to comprehensive schools.[23]

Furthermore, he even claimed to Butt that existing large comprehensive schools could be split up, with each floor occupying a different school, akin to how the London board schools of the past had sometimes been run. Comprehensives could also develop 'specialities' with popular, well-subscribed schools selecting pupils for their particular subject or area of interest.[24] Boyson was going out on a limb.

Boyson was now giving off a distinct sense of impatience with the pace of the Conservative Party's impetus for educational reform. Throughout 1978, he was giving speeches, most notably to the Conservative North West Advisory Committee on Education in April, which called for the national publication of school examination results that involved comparing selective and non-selective schools, as well as particular schools before and after reorganization. In spite of Boyson's ostensible role in supporting Stevas, he appeared to be propagating the position of the right of centre pressure group the National Council for Educational Standards (NCES). This was not party policy.

The tension existing between Stevas and Boyson culminated at a conference held for the NCES at the Pembroke Hotel in September 1978. At Brian Cox's suggestion, Boyson released the A level results for Manchester's schools to the press. In doing so, it inevitably highlighted the gulf between Manchester's Labour-controlled county comprehensives and those of Trafford that had managed to retain a selective bipartite system and whose results were markedly superior. It thus directly reflected on what the Labour government had recently been attempting to do in Tameside. Boyson's obvious intention was to highlight the deficiencies of city comprehensives and, it appeared, set in train any potential momentum towards a return to selection within urban areas.

Boyson was of course attacked by the teacher unions and Labour leaders of local education committees. He was also censured by John Howell, the Conservative Chairman of the Association of County Council Education Committees, and by

Malcolm Thornton, the Conservative Chairman of the Association of Metropolitan Authorities Education Committee. Nevertheless, local Manchester Conservatives came to his defence. In response, Stevas publicly rejected any idea of publishing league tables of school exam results. On 22 September, in a speech at Chelmsford, he stated that while he expected individual schools to publish exam results within their prospectuses, national league tables were not official Conservative policy. Noticeably, he did not refer to Boyson in his speech. The following day, the Party's notorious Monday Club came to Boyson's defence and opposed Stevas' publicly expressed view that schools' exam results instead be seen within their 'social context.' Summing up these events, the *Financial Times*, on 25 September, called it 'another embarrassing split on education.'[25]

As a result, there came another opposition reshuffle in November 1978. Mrs Thatcher appointed a known 'moderate,' Mark Carlisle, to be the new education spokesman for the opposition, thus replacing Stevas who was appointed the opposition Leader of the House of Commons. Boyson, who was notably disappointed at not being promoted, was kept on as second in command. There was a distinct sense within the Party that he needed to be contained. His agitations over school examination results, as well as his public promotion of education vouchers, were regarded as political dynamite.

Meanwhile in March 1979, on the eve of what would turn out to be Margaret Thatcher's historic general election victory, Boyson's co-author Brian Cox was still publicly noting how, in spite of his claim that the Black Paper series had led partly to a return to formal methods of instruction, 'the battle which the Black Papers have yet to win is over comprehensive schools.' He went on to add that 'the Black Paper authors have consistently argued that no comprehensive system of schooling will ever work.' In urban districts, he emphasized that comprehensive schooling would have to end at 13 or 14, and bright children enabled to move over to those schools with 'proper academic resources.'[26] Thus Cox was advocating that the next Conservative government ought to be pressured to disband the comprehensive system given its professed commitment to what he termed 'traditional standards.'[27] However, given that Mrs Thatcher had chosen the left-leaning Mark Carlisle to be the new education spokesman, the signs did not augur well for these aims.

We have seen how the Wilson and Callaghan Labour governments carried out the rest of their original mission with the reorganization of the vast majority of remaining local authority maintained grammar schools bar a very few areas. In addition, all the direct grant schools were phased out by 1976 through the cessation of their grants. The Conservative opposition trod a tenuous path between expressing a defence of parental rights and choice, and at the same time accepting that the vast majority of local authorities had gone comprehensive and that it was unlikely that the situation would change in the near future. Unsurprisingly, there was no clear future policy regarding secondary education during this period, and philosophical points of contention were avoided. Voices such as those of Rhodes Boyson, who sought to publish the comparative results of selective and non-selective schools in opposition to Party policy, were sidelined by the more circumspect Norman St John-Stevas, who wanted to avoid controversy regarding this long-standing issue.

7

Thatcherism in education 1979–90

Grammar schools continued to close during the first years of Margaret Thatcher's premiership and the government did not stake an overall position on them. However, the notion of parental choice gained greater substance in policy terms during the Thatcher era. Policies such as open enrolment that allowed successful and popular schools to expand their capacity, and most notably grant maintained schools in which the government sought to establish schools independent of the local education authorities, were enacted. Strikingly, the Thatcher government was turning against the pro-local authority conventions of the past. This culminated in the 1988 Education Reform Act.

Early dilemmas

Upon regaining office, the new Conservative government under Margaret Thatcher moved swiftly on the educational front. A new Education Bill was one of the first priorities in their legislative programme. The 1979 Education Act set out to do what the Conservative Party had long promised by removing the compulsion enshrined within Labour's 1976 Education Act upon local authorities to reorganize on comprehensive lines. Those comprehensive proposals approved under the 1976 Act but which had not been finalized could now be withdrawn if the local authority in question chose to approach Mark Carlisle. The new Secretary of State emphasized to Norman St John-Stevas in correspondence that given the publicity attached to the Act, it would be 'extremely embarrassing' if the new government was to lose the political initiative that would be gained by its early introduction. It therefore needed to gain Royal Assent in time for local authorities to be relieved of their statutory duty by the beginning of the school year in September 1979.[1]

The Bill was thus represented as restoring local freedom once again. Individual local authorities were now 'free to choose' what kind of education they wanted for their particular area. Of course in practice, in spite of Mark Carlisle and Rhodes Boyson's grandiose claims, approximately 83 per cent of secondary schools were now comprehensive and the vast majority of local authorities were looking distinctly unwilling to change. Inevitably, the 1979 Act represented a symbolic gesture rather than anything of far-reaching consequence.

As a result of the government's action, there were immediate difficulties that presented themselves. The Labour opposition could justifiably ask just what particular system the new Conservative government favoured as it appeared to be advocating a multiplicity of local systems, and it was claimed by the Labour opposition that this would result in educational chaos. Furthermore, Rhodes Boyson's own expressed views eleven years earlier in the second Black Paper that selection by ability beyond a limited percentage of pupils would harm neighbouring non-selective schools, as well as a speech by Norman St John Stevas at the 1977 Party Conference that had emphasized no return to the 11 plus, could constantly be used as ammunition against the new Conservative government.[2] Even the Conservative MP James Pawsey, who had served on the Warwickshire County Council education committee and was now influential on the Party's education policy group, was keen to underline that the 1979 Bill should not be interpreted as an attack upon the comprehensive principle. The notion of local authorities having the 'right to choose' once again meant little in practice.[3]

Early the following year, the 1980 Education Act was issued. It introduced the Parents' Charter that affirmed that parents be given key information about schools, including examination results, and exercise the right to choose a school outside the area of the local education authority. In addition, it outlined clearer admissions criteria and strengthened the local appeals procedure, as well as enabling parents and teachers to serve on the governing boards of maintained schools. The notion of 'parental choice' was accentuated as a statutory duty upon local authorities.

The 1980 Act also introduced the Assisted Places Scheme, thus honouring the pledge to restore the direct grant system in what the government claimed was an improved form. The previous Labour government's statutory restriction upon local authorities' freedom to submit pupils for independent school places was therefore removed. Parents would be assisted with fees depending on a means test, with the prospective pupils required to pass the necessary independent school entrance examinations. The proposed plan was set to start in 1981 beginning at a cost of £3 million to provide for the admission of approximately 6,000 pupils a year.

Such a policy highlighted awkward questions about the government's position on the vast majority of maintained schools that were now comprehensive. It could easily be claimed that the scheme amounted to a 'Poor Law complex,' in the words of the Labour MP Nigel Spearing, to enable a deserving minority of maintained pupils to flee the state sector.[4] Another predictable but effective accusation from Labour's new education spokesman Neil Kinnock was that the government was undermining the vast majority of maintained schools by using public money to boost the independent sector amidst a period of financial stringency. Even some Conservative MPs such as Robert Hicks and Gordon Miscampbell considered the assisted places policy politically bad due to this emphasis upon the independent sector, rather than the government concentrating resources upon maintained schools.

In reply, Carlisle emphasized that the policy was about the needs of the individual child. According to the new Secretary of State, 113 out of the 118 ex-direct grant schools that had become independent had indicated their interest in being involved in the assisted places scheme. He denied that the opportunities provided by the scheme would harm those available in the state sector.[5] Meanwhile, Carlisle ominously announced in February 1980 that the government was in favour of a 'common exam' at 16 plus.[6]

Carlisle therefore had to face pressing decisions regarding secondary education in those vital first months of the Thatcher government. The first major proposal came from the Bexley local authority, which had long campaigned against the Labour government's comprehensive policy, to split the Erith comprehensive school currently on split sites of some distance into a secondary modern and a grammar school. To illustrate Carlisle's state of mind, he initially accepted the proposal but changed his position a week later. He claimed to Mrs Thatcher that there had been vast local support to keep the school as it was. He also stated that the comprehensive framework allowed pupils of lower ability to transfer to academic courses more easily and that the secondary modern envisaged would have poorer facilities. Politically, Carlisle felt that the current situation, even in this particular case, could not be altered. Records show that the swift nature of this 'turn around' clearly irritated Mrs Thatcher, but she accepted his decision.[7]

There were other tough cases lying on Carlisle's desk. A notable one involved Highbury Grove, Rhodes Boyson's old school, in which the Inner London Education Authority intended to substantially decrease its size. In addition, there was a proposal affecting Tameside for it to be granted, after all the protracted battles, a wholly comprehensive system now that Labour was in local charge again. If approved, the proposal would therefore overturn the legal decision upholding the Conservative councillors in 1977. This was in spite of over 67,000 local people having signed a petition to retain the grammar schools there. A third key case for Carlisle to consider involved a proposal to turn the comprehensive Sutton Coldfield girls' school into a grammar school thus giving girls the same opportunities as boys for grammar school education within the area.[8]

Carlisle's intention was to accept the Sutton Coldfield proposal and announce his decision on 23 April, well before the upcoming local elections which were set for 1 May. But this was a risk, given that Birmingham was likely to return to Labour control after the local election. Meanwhile, he planned to announce his decision to turn down the Highbury Grove proposal the following week (which was hardly surprising given its proximity to Boyson) and announce his acceptance of Tameside's comprehensive proposals elections on 6 May.[9] Everything, of course, was about appropriate timing.

The degree of consternation that Carlisle's decision caused is shown by the correspondence at the time between Mrs Thatcher and Nicholas Sanders, her private secretary. Sanders strongly cautioned the Prime Minister against approving Carlisle's choice of timing for these announcements. He felt it would be far better to announce the positive news for Highbury Grove first before the local elections and leave the announcements regarding Tameside and Sutton Coldfield until after the local results had come through. For Sanders, there was a good chance that the Birmingham authority, once Labour were returned after the election as they were likely to, would seek to overturn Carlisle's decision for Sutton Coldfield. Ultimately, he felt the Labour authority would end up fighting Carlisle in the courts. Given that they would be democratically elected, the Birmingham local authority was likely to win any legal judgement against a minister seeking to impose central direction upon them. As usual, ultra-caution was being urged on a Conservative Secretary of State considering the restoration of selection.

Sanders urged that Carlisle defer any decision for Sutton Coldfield until after the local elections. If pressed, Carlisle 'could with a straight face say that he was not going to play politics' by announcing Section 13 decisions before a local election. By doing so, if Labour took over Birmingham, the government could then easily withdraw the proposal, assuming that no decision had been publicly announced, and therefore according to Sanders, 'there would be no great publicity about it.' As Sanders then added in his correspondence with the Prime Minister:

> It is equally important that the very first example of such a change should be one where there is every prospect of a smooth transition, and not one where there is a chance – and perhaps a very significant chance – of the enterprise ending in humiliation.[10]

Those surrounding the Prime Minister were therefore keen for the government to be prepared to kick the issue into the long grass again if necessary.

However, the records show that Mrs Thatcher agreed to Carlisle's original decision about the timing for his announcements. When justifying his decision for Tameside to have full-scale comprehensives, Carlisle pleaded for 'a period of stability' among local authorities choosing school systems. He further expressed the hope that in local areas where the party in power changed regularly, there should be agreement to a system of education that neither party attempted to change at each local election.[11] But as Ronald Butt of *The Times* noted, there was never any sign of compromise on the pro-comprehensive Labour side. In practice, the price of 'stability' always meant movement in one direction only. As before, a Tory minister would not support a victorious Conservative authority that wanted to restore selection, as had been the case with the Erith school at Bexley. In Butt's words:

> In practice the price of stability is acceptance by Conservatives of a movement along a one-way route towards a wholly comprehensive system to which those who disagree are allowed no resistance, even when they are in a majority.[12]

It hardly added conviction to the government's own proposal for a tiny element of assisted places at selected independent schools if they allowed the extinction of all selection, even when there was local demand for it, in the state sector. It was now clear to Butt that there was to be no plan for reversal under Mrs Thatcher's new government. Further secondary reorganization on comprehensive lines occurred in Bolton, Cornwall and Cumbria at this time. Events were continuing to move towards a complete comprehensive monopoly of all publicly maintained secondary education under a newly elected Conservative government.

However, this did not stop Rhodes Boyson, now Under-Secretary of State, writing in notably hopeful spirit to Mrs Thatcher in late 1980 and early 1981 detailing the examination success of Northern Ireland under its selective system in recent years compared with comprehensive England and Wales. In particular, he outlined the latter countries' relative decline in 'A' level results over the past twenty years. Mrs Thatcher appears to have been grateful for the correspondence, thanking him effusively for the information and asking for more statistics to be sent to her. Boyson clearly hoped he could still influence Mrs Thatcher.[13]

The Joseph period 1981–6

Ultimately, Mark Carlisle was judged to be a less than successful education minister and was removed halfway through Mrs Thatcher's first term of office amidst her purging of those deemed politically uncongenial within her cabinet. Carlisle was replaced on 14 September 1981 by Mrs Thatcher's great ally and inspiration Keith Joseph. However, Joseph's solutions to the deficiencies of the education system were to be essentially based upon coordinated planning and micromanagement by central government. The Secretary of State intended to acquire 'an ability to foster developments to which he attaches particular importance' through direct financial support for 'specific purposes.'[14] Joseph thus sought to centrally control the school curriculum in order to emphasize scientific and practical-based subjects. He also sought to institute a major reform of teacher training and to prune higher education courses to focus on science and information technology. With supreme irony, this Conservative government was intent upon planning initiatives from the centre.

The aim of achieving further parental choice was initially explored through the potential development of a voucher system. Nevertheless, Joseph had always been cautious, and stressed in November 1982 that pilot projects would have to be the first step. In response, the Financial Secretary Nicholas Ridley, in a minute to the Chancellor of the Exchequer Geoffrey Howe, thought Joseph was being 'too timid.' Ridley saw little point in waiting for the results of pilot schemes which he felt would only be fought from the outset by teachers' unions and education pressure groups. He therefore felt it would be better to 'press on' with a full scheme.[15] Indeed, vouchers were viewed by Ridley as a means of transferring educational expenditure from local to central government and thus reining in profligate local authorities. For Ridley, the remainder of local authority expenditure would ideally be completely funded on reformed rates and, possibly, a poll tax.

Yet as 1982 drew to a close, no such idea had been accepted, despite the hopes of those such as Rhodes Boyson. In March 1983 the Party's education policy group that significantly included figures such as William van Straubenzee and Malcolm Thornton (who had been so opposed to Boyson's actions in 1978) and Brian Cox (who was now critical of Conservative Party policy in spite of his initial high hopes) rejected the proposal that local authorities experiment with vouchers. So the policy was sidelined, with the noticeably ambivalent Joseph declaring the voucher 'dead' in June 1983.

Meanwhile, a full-scale exercise had been moved between the government, the examining boards and the teachers' organizations regarding reform of the 'O' level and CSE exams in order to 'improve and standardize' the exam syllabuses. The government claimed that there was too much choice between them and therefore sought to reduce the 'excessive' number of examining boards. For the time being, the government still maintained that it was too early to say whether this would mean a future amalgamation of the two exams or whether they would continue in parallel but in 'greater harmony'.[16] Nevertheless, under Keith Joseph the government was moving towards a 16 plus examination for all.

And despite the landslide general election victory for the government on 9 June 1983, Joseph simply kept up a standard reply in answer to questions about the possible reintroduction of new grammar schools in the future. It was, he claimed, simply a matter for local education authorities if they wanted to submit proposals to him. He studiously refused to depart from this reply.[17]

In December 1983, Boyson's replacement as Under-Secretary of State Robert Dunn confirmed in the House of Commons that the government had no intention of using education support grants in setting up new grammar schools. This was in response to a Labour motion that public money should not be used to assist selective schools in any way. In addition, Dunn revealed that since 1979 the government had in fact approved twenty-two sets of proposals to end selection and five to amalgamate grammar schools, with only one proposal having been approved to establish a new grammar school. In terms of rejected proposals, while they had rejected six seeking to end selection and one intending an amalgamation, they had also rejected two proposals for new selective schools.[18] Despite being securely in power and now holding a landslide majority, Margaret Thatcher's government was very much maintaining the educational status quo when it came to the comprehensive principle.

In addition, concern was increasingly being felt among Brian Cox, Stuart Sexton and others that the impetus for the new common examination at 16 was growing. Yet despite their protests, Keith Joseph appeared to be showing every sign of wanting to press on with it in spite of his ostensible commitment to raising standards. His 1984 speech to the North of England Education Conference and the White Paper *Better Schools* published in 1985 confirmed his intentions in this area.[19]

Joseph wanted an examination with a non-selective nature that would ensure a higher pass rate for approximately 80 per cent of pupils, particularly for those who currently failed at 'O' level. By early 1986, Joseph was set upon the new GCSE exam being introduced at the beginning of the next school year in September. Yet records of correspondence between Joseph and Mrs Thatcher in March 1986 show her consternation at the proposed exam. In defending the GCSE, Joseph claimed it would be a 'differentiated' exam system with standardized benchmarks of achievement defined for different ability groups. Alongside this, he claimed that the O level had undervalued too many pupils by simply ordering them on merit while not sufficiently emphasizing 'practical skills' and adequate 'understanding' of subjects. Indeed, Joseph even claimed that in future under the GCSE, 80–90 per cent of pupils would reach the level currently achieved by average candidates under the present system. To this, Mrs Thatcher wrote that he was misrepresenting the O level exam. Yet Joseph was determined to press on, dismissively informing her that she was 'misleading' herself with her concerns.[20]

Simultaneously, Mrs Thatcher was receiving parallel advice from Brian Griffiths, the head of her policy unit, that confirmed her view that the proposed GCSE would lower standards with its refusal to acknowledge the necessary distinction between O level and the CSE. They had never of course been intended to be the same type of exam. Both Mrs Thatcher and Griffiths felt that the GCSE, with its greater breath and inordinate emphasis upon coursework, embodied a 'can't fail mentality' that would encourage teacher bias and even potential indoctrination. Griffiths therefore advised her to tell Joseph to postpone the new examination until more work was done to improve its rigour before teachers started to implement it.[21]

In spite of Mrs Thatcher then holding successive meetings where she informed Joseph of her concerns about the GCSE, Joseph remained dismissive. He was convinced that it was a step forwards with its emphasis on practical skills and problem-solving and, revealingly, its move away from the 'academic bias' of the existing system. He claimed it would offer opportunities to a much wider range of schoolchildren and involve far fewer syllabuses and examining boards than at the present time.[22] Indeed, much of the case for the new exam appeared to be about standardization for the sake of administrative convenience. In response, Mrs Thatcher urged Joseph to ask Her Majesty's Inspectorate for their opinion before going ahead with the new exam in the autumn. Once again, educational events were spinning out of her control.

Secondary school reform

Joseph also wanted radical change in how maintained secondary schools were run. His answer was to set up a number of schools outside local education authority control and micro-manage the rest of the system from the centre. Joseph was convinced, along with Oliver Letwin the head of Mrs Thatcher's policy unit, of the need to bypass inner-city local education authorities and rescue working-class families from their clutches. The proposed schools would receive grant from central government and follow the national school curriculum that the government was planning for them. The actual running of the schools, Joseph was keen to emphasize, would not be carried out by the DES, but by local businesses, trusts and groups of parents. It was therefore hoped that the policy would build up a potential voter base for schools outside local authority control. It would thus be a reformulation of the old direct grant system under the new name of Grant Maintained or 'GM' schools.

By contrast, Joseph was now firmly against the idea of introducing vouchers or credits. Under this system, money would have followed the pupil through 'per capita' funding, which Joseph thought was both practically and politically unworkable, citing the extent of legislation and monitoring that would be needed to manage such a system. However, he was also frightened at the potential degree of opposition from Tory local authorities themselves, and feared it would split the party. The records show Mrs Thatcher's annoyance at his continued reluctance regarding vouchers, scrawling 'nonsense' in the margin of his explanation to her.[23] Instead, Joseph wanted to press on with the creation of GM schools that were to be implemented in London and the industrial city areas. Meanwhile, the Assisted Places system was to be continued, although not radically extended, for fear that it would take in pupils who would instead be using the proposed GM schools. In so doing, they thus sought to open up a 'middle way' through GM schools between the public and private sectors of education.

Yet this still left the vast majority of maintained schools remaining under local authority control for the foreseeable future. This was particularly so in Labour-run areas that would inevitably be hostile towards GM schools. But Joseph was determined to try to gain control of the local education authorities. He wanted central government, through the grant it gave local authorities, to be able to exercise 'leverage' over them. The proposal that Joseph hit on was for the funding to be restructured as a block grant but with a sufficient amount of specific grant mixed into it in order to get the local authorities to fulfil the government's specific requirements regarding curriculum and teacher appraisal. Along with an increased use of performance indicators to measure 'value-added' results, he thought the Conservative government could exercise real change in the way the vast majority of maintained schools were run.[24]

The opposition to Joseph came from different sides. Mrs Thatcher's advisor Brian Griffiths thought it would simply mean transferring local government to central government and therefore handing more powers to the Department of Education and Science. He also thought the proposed GM schools would not in fact be like the old direct grant schools at all, and that any independence they would have would be ephemeral. While in favour of the essential idea, Griffiths thought the GM schools would simply end up being controlled by the DES.[25]

In meetings held with Mrs Thatcher, Nigel Lawson and Norman Tebbit along with Douglas Hurd and William Whitelaw, it was clear that some of those assembled had cold feet. The prospect of a potential clash with local education authorities and the teacher unions over GM schools along with the attempt to gain greater 'leverage' over the local authorities perturbed them. While Tebbit was keen, and proposed his own version of Joseph's suggestion that involved formulating contracts with the local authorities, others in the group tended to sound notes of caution against radical change. Furthermore, any reintroduction of direct grant schools, they counselled, would create division and reduce the morale of the state sector. Such points against the scheme kept undermining any obvious conclusion. Nevertheless, Mrs Thatcher continued to emphasize the need for both per capita funding and open enrolment for popular schools to expand to their full capacity, and that the proposed GM schools would ideally be run by foundations and charities with the DES in a merely supervisory role.[26]

The GM schools policy was therefore a major plank of the Conservatives' 1987 General Election Campaign. However, the subject of secondary education turned out to form the basis of one of the major 'gaffes' of the campaign for Mrs Thatcher. When answering a question at a press conference regarding the policy, her reply gave the impression that grant-maintained schools would have the freedom to 'top up' grants received from the State and have control over their admissions policies to include potentially selecting pupils by ability.[27] In spite of her private feelings, she was therefore forced to give assurances to the contrary and stage a public climb-down on the issue.

Nevertheless, the twin features of 'per capita' funding and 'open enrolment' to allow schools of renowned quality to be filled to their full capacity were key features of the education policies pursued during the remainder of Mrs Thatcher's period in government. Grant-maintained schools were eventually introduced under the 1988 Education Reform Act with Kenneth Baker as Secretary of State and would attract a moderate number of proposals. By May 1990, thirty-seven proposals for GM schools had been approved, with a reasonable level of support indicated by parental ballots. In addition, a limited number of City Technology Colleges (CTCs) were established that were also independent of local authorities and sought private sponsorship. However, the percentage of secondary school pupils in local authority maintained grammar schools had by 1989 declined from 4.2 per cent ten years earlier to 3.3 per cent.[28]

Mrs Thatcher would soon become embroiled in chaos regarding another part of the centralizing policy that Kenneth Baker was implementing. She would always claim that the National Curriculum, which also formed part of the 1988 Act, had merely been intended to establish key benchmarks for pupil knowledge. Yet the whole enterprise mushroomed and was captured by Her Majesty's Inspectorate and the DES along with progressive educational theorists. With Baker at the helm, the working group curriculum reports for the core subjects of English, Maths, Science and History were examined throughout 1987 to 1989. The proposals for the assessment of the various subjects were considerably influenced by the practitioners of educational ideology who had in fact been consulted by Baker. The 'progressive' interests in education had staged a rear-guard fight back over the national curriculum and sought to subvert it for their own agenda.

By 1990, Mrs Thatcher had appointed a new Secretary of State John MacGregor in the hope that he would ensure the government's intentions for the National Curriculum were followed. Nevertheless, she felt he did not put them across effectively. By the time of her forced resignation from office in November, several intentions, including the attempt to reform teacher training to result in 'licensed' and 'articled' teachers instead of those produced by teacher training colleges, lay unfulfilled. The policy of grant maintained schools funded by central government had represented a major attempt in the latter years of the Thatcher government to wrest control of the education service away form the local authorities and the educational establishment. Yet in spite of a moderate advance on GM schools and an extension of the assisted places scheme that meant approximately 27,000 pupils were being given places by 1990, the general lack of progress made in reducing the left's essential control of maintained education over these eleven years would prove one of her biggest regrets upon leaving office.

8

The Major years 1990–7

The Major government promoted greater opportunities for maintained schools to opt out of local authority control and attain grant maintained status. A new statutory body, the Funding Agency, was set up to distribute grant to GM schools and was given planning responsibilities for them. The government's policy also emphasised local management of schools and greater scope for them to specialise in areas such as science, technology and music. However, successive government ministers were reluctant to emphasise academic selection, which became subsumed under the general heading of 'choice and diversity'. Amidst media accusations that it was centralizing the education service, the government produced a White Paper and subsequent Bill proposing greater selective powers for schools in 1996. However, the Bill would become derailed by the advent of the 1997 General Election.

Selective statements

Under Margaret Thatcher's successor John Major, the grant-maintained schools policy was continued, along with the further development of the national curriculum and national systems of testing. Major's first Secretary of State for Education was Kenneth Clarke, who had been appointed by Margaret Thatcher shortly before her political demise. However, the long-standing ambiguities over selection would emanate from Clarke, also. In the weeks leading up to the 1992 general election, Clarke refused to give concrete assurances about the potential for new grant-maintained schools to turn themselves selective and adopt grammar school status. Instead, Clarke claimed vaguely that it ought to be a matter left to parents, while stating that he had 'no problem' with a number of one in ten GM schools becoming selective as long as there were not too many.[1] Any answer based on general principle was avoided. In response, *The Times* newspaper, under the editorship of Simon Jenkins, claimed that by giving hope to grammar school supporters in this way, Clarke was risking the Conservative government's chances of re-election.

Also at this time, John Major expressed critical sentiments on comprehensive education in public correspondence with Fred Jarvis, the former general secretary of the National Union of Teachers. Yet following the Conservatives' surprise general election victory in April 1992, Major noticeably appeared to back down. By June,

Major was at pains to claim that Jarvis' questions 'were based on the false premise that I was critical of comprehensive schools.' Major now claimed to have been criticizing the 'ideas' within the state comprehensive system, and stressed 'freedom of choice' rather than selection.[2] For his part, Jarvis noted exultantly that Major had indeed backtracked from his earlier position, and would not answer the question of whether he intended formally to bring back selection or would 'allow it to re-emerge via the back-door.'[3]

By now, successive Conservative governments had in fact closed more grammar schools since 1970 than their Labour opponents. Of the 890 to close since that period, 469 had disappeared under Conservative governments, with 106 since 1979. Stuart Maclure, the former editor of the *Times Educational Supplement*, pointed out that the government's GM schools policy was being used as a means of 'avoiding a discussion of principles.'[4] Leaving the initiative with each individual school to become grant maintained appeared to be a way of keeping the possibility of local selection open while taking it off the agenda of national politics.

And like so many of his predecessors, Clarke's actions were at odds with his public utterances. By this time, he had approved proposals by the County Council in the Salisbury diocesan Board of Education to close Foster's and Lord Digby's grammar schools along with St Adhelm's secondary modern, with their replacement by a £5.5 million Church of England voluntary-controlled school. Parents of pupils at the two grammar schools affected asked the judge to quash Clarke's original decision and order him to reconsider GM status for the schools involved. In March, *The Times* reported how a High Court judge refused to allow the affected Dorset grammar schools to opt out of local authority control and become grant maintained in order to avoid closure. Following the verdict against them, the parents accused Clarke of failing to follow the government's own policy of giving priority to parental choice.[5] The government was not necessarily practising what it preached.

Choice and diversity

Nevertheless, following the 1992 election victory the Major government, with a new Secretary of State John Patten, was anxious to further the Thatcherite grant-maintained schools policy of freedom for parents and schools from local authority control. A new White Paper was released, entitled *Choice and Diversity*. It emphasized local management and greater delegation of powers to schools from local education authorities as well as measures for the easier transition of schools to GM status. A new statutory body, the Funding Agency, was to be given responsibility for distributing grant to GM schools and financial monitoring, as well as wider planning responsibilities as the number of the schools increased. The issue of selection, however, was downplayed. Instead, it preferred to focus on 'specialization' for schools in certain subjects such as science, music or technology. For schools applying to become selective it stated it was not the Government's intention 'either to encourage or discourage such applications.'[6] In November 1992, Patten was giving marked reassurances that the Labour opposition would only be able to look 'in vain' for evidence in the government's forthcoming Education Bill that their proposals for increasing 'diversity' in fact meant 'selection by the back door.'[7] Grant-maintained schools, Patten continued, would not be allowed to 'discriminate' among applicants on grounds of ability unless they were already selective schools, and would not be able to change their admissions arrangements without coming to him first.[8] Therefore, when it came to enabling GM schools to go even partially selective, the Major government was dragging its feet.

In spite of this, Patten was constantly being forced to give assurances in response to attacks coming from both Labour authorities and sections of the media that the government's policy was not a mere camouflage for a return to selection at 11 with less favoured schools becoming secondary moderns. The chairman of the GM Schools Foundation Robert Balchin was also constantly forced onto the defensive. He emphasized that no great shift in the balance between selective and non-selective education was imminent. Only one GM school, the Queen Elizabeth school in Penrith, had opted for full selection by ability, and the number of pupils in selective schools had not altered since 1979. No GM school, he protested in *The Times*, could 'choose pupils at will,' and they could only do so in accordance with their issuing a published policy. He was further forced to deny that the Funding Agency for the schools had the power to refuse non-selective schools wanting to come under its wing.[9]

Amidst this pressure coming from the state educational and media establishment, which included organized boycotts over testing, Patten's health suffered. Major replaced him in July 1994 with Gillian Shephard, who was commonly regarded as an altogether more conciliatory figure. Major's timing for this choice would turn out to be striking and deliberate.

Grammar school supporters had hoped that Patten's efforts, which had included encouraging community groups and commercial sponsors to set up schools, would result in a number of new grammar schools alongside other schools specializing in subject areas such as technology and languages. An earlier ministerial approval for the Queen Elizabeth's boys' school in Barnet to be able to select pupils on academic and musical ability had been expected to lead to a series of further applications. Yet by September 1994, this particular decision was now considered to be the last likely case of a GM school taking the grammar school route. The number of schools seeking GM status started to plateau at this point. Tellingly, the decision to approve Queen Elizabeth's change of character had been taken before Shephard's appointment.

The signs that Gillian Shephard was resolved against upsetting the status quo came in the first week of her official duties. On her first school visit as Secretary of State she was quoted as assuring teachers at Northgate Primary School in Nottingham that the government's national curriculum tests would not pave the way for a return to selection by ability in national policy. *The Times* reported that she also gave the same assurance to union leaders. Shephard was also heard to remark at the meeting that, speaking as a former teacher and education advisor at Norfolk County Council, she viewed a system of grammar school selection to be 'wasteful of talent.' She would instead be seeking to foster academic excellence through an emphasis on streaming by ability within comprehensive schools, along with a discouragement of mixed ability classes.[10] Therefore, Major's decision to appoint Shepherd in the place of the more combative Patten was looking more calculated by the day. It appeared that the main intention was for Shephard to take the role of managing the educational establishment's prejudices.

In the spring of 1995, a number of independent schools that had held direct grant status in the past, including notably Manchester Grammar School, indicated a willingness to rejoin the state sector. Their condition was that they be able to retain the freedom to select their pupils by ability, while more affluent parents would continue to pay fees. The Conservative MP George Walden was particularly supportive of this development, asking the government to support the former direct grant schools' desire to close what he termed was now an educational 'apartheid' between the independent and state sectors. In contrast, Walden was notably dismissive of the government's assisted places scheme, describing it as 'Dickensian' in its desire to rescue lucky pupils from the state system so that they could be given places in independent schools. (In fact, all but one of the former direct grant schools that had gone independent had joined the assisted places scheme, and catered for nearly two-thirds of the pupils within it.)[11]

Ultimately, Walden wanted to bring the two systems together. Yet as Robin Squire the Parliamentary Under-Secretary of State pointed out to Walden in the Commons debate, if the former direct grant schools came into the state sector, the cost would be in the region of £3.5 million at the least. Increased public expenditure of that order, he added, would be 'difficult to justify'. For Squire, the 'best answer' was merely to encourage a system which gave the choice of independent education to as many as possible regardless of income, and to target finite resources as effectively as possible.[12] Unsurprisingly, the response from the more idealistic Walden was to claim that Squire and his fellow Conservative MPs were advocating 'inaction' and, 'in real life, shutting the door to any significant movement across the frontier between state and private.'[13] As a result, any possibility of the ex-direct grant schools re-entering the maintained system quickly passed away due to an evident lack of interest on both sides of the House.

Meanwhile, the Major government's grant-maintained schools policy continued to be attacked. The criticisms were flowing not only from the Labour opposition and the teachers' unions, but from key sections of the media. The charge was that 'opted out' schools were using covert academic selection, with Simon Jenkins claiming that Major's policy was driven by 'a visceral hatred of local government.' The government also faced the charge that the policy amounted to the outright centralization of schools through the Funding Agency, alongside the lofty accusation that an education service that had once been 'the pride and joy' of Britain's local councils was being systematically eroded.[14]

Of more immediate damage was the claim that the Prime Minister's Policy Unit was at odds with Shephard's Education Department. In November 1995 it was reported that Major was putting increasing pressure on Shephard to encourage more maintained schools to select by ability. It was also claimed that Major wanted to go further with the GM schools policy and move towards removing all secondary schools from local authority control. Shephard was now issuing concrete proposals for a 50 per cent increase in the proportion of pupils that GM schools were allowed to select without applying to Whitehall for a change of character. By now, grant-maintained or 'opted out' schools were showing markedly superior GCSE results compared with those run by local authorities.[15]

Selection rears again

In January 1996 it was announced that the government planned to enable fully local authority-run comprehensives the freedom to select up to 15 per cent of their pupil intake at their own discretion. The cries from those such as Simon Jenkins were all too predictable. It was claimed to be no more than a precursor to the re-establishment of the formal apparatus of selection at 11. The policy, Jenkins claimed, was 'blatantly unfair,' and was simply a means of enabling already popular schools to make themselves yet more desirable, and would involve giving middle-class parents a chance of getting their children into schools from which comprehensive criteria would have excluded them. The problems of comprehensives were merely susceptible to better teaching, according to Jenkins, and had nothing to do with structure. The 15 per cent policy merely conjured the secondary modern 'reject' schools 'back to life.'[16] Pointing to the future, he urged David Blunkett, the Labour opposition education spokesman, to pledge to force selective schools to take a broad-based local intake and not be allowed to 'vacuum up' bright pupils from other boroughs when next in office.[17]

Yet despite this avalanche of opposition, Major appeared to be trying to press matters further. In March 1996 it was reported that Major's advisors had hit on the idea that where a clear demand existed, parents could join together and set up a board of governors to take over an empty school and reopen it as a grammar. Alternatively, if no suitable building was available, groups of parents should be free to apply to build a new school, with the capital costs met by the private sector with the governors paying the lease from government grants.

According to reports, some Cabinet ministers were impatient with Gillian Shephard's seeming reluctance to endorse these proposals. Insiders claimed that Shephard had been taken aback by Major's advisors briefing the press about a new wave of grammar schools and wanted to row back. Indeed, it was claimed by *The Times'* education editor John O' Leary that she resented attempts to 'bounce' her into accepting a widespread return of grammar schools.[18] While promising further moves to boost selective schooling, Shephard sought to distance herself from the idea of grammar schools being launched with private funding. On 11 March she told a conference of head teachers and governors in Birmingham that the disclosures leaked the previous weekend had taken her by surprise, and emphasized that any such new projects would have to satisfy the existing criteria of government approval.[19] Meanwhile, an application from Buckinghamshire County Council to build a new grammar school alongside the existing comprehensives in Milton Keynes had not received an answer from Shephard for several months.

Shephard appeared to be caught in the crossfire between the Prime Minister's Policy Unit on one side and the hostility of the Department of Education and Employment and the teachers' unions on the other. Unsurprisingly, she was notably circumspect in her public statements, couching her support for selection only in terms of the extension of parental choice alongside other types of school as part of the mantra of 'choice and diversity.' Selective schools were therefore categorized by Shephard and the Minister of State Cheryl Gillan as merely having 'an important part to play' in diversity alongside grant-maintained and local authority schools, the fifteen City Technology Colleges and specialist colleges in technology and languages.[20]

Furthermore, both David Blunkett and Stephen Byers of the Labour opposition could readily quote the comments Shephard had previously made about selection being 'wasteful' and reiterate that she did not favour a widespread return to grammar schools. Indeed, on 20 March she was asked by Byers how, given the comments she had supposedly made, she could reconcile her position with Major's enthusiasm for a rapid expansion of selective schools. In typically circumspect fashion, Shephard would only reply that she and the Prime Minister were 'absolutely at one' in their desire to see 'a diversity of provision' within the school sector, 'because we both believe that it drives up standards.'[21] Behind this public flannel, it appeared that there was some divergence between Shephard and Major that she was doing her best to conceal.

By June 1996, only two comprehensives had returned to being fully selective having left local authority control and attaining GM status, while only one other had applied to follow suit. However, there were more GM schools that had opted to become partially selective, with five having opted to choose half their pupils on academic ability and another thirty-two schools introducing a selective stream into their otherwise comprehensive intakes. A new White Paper, entitled *Self-Government for Schools*, was now published that focused upon permitting existing schools greater freedom to select. The Funding Agency would have additional powers to put forward proposals to set up new schools in areas of shortage, including, potentially, GM grammar schools. Furthermore, if a non-GM school's governing body wished for it to become a grammar school, the Secretary of State would look to the LEA to respond 'constructively.'[22] Nevertheless, it was keen to assert throughout how this patented 'diversity' would go well beyond the 'outmoded division' between grammars and secondary moderns.[23]

Despite this, Margaret Dewar, the chairman of the National Grammar Schools Association, told her annual conference at this time of her 'great scepticism' that the Prime Minister's intentions for selective education would ever come to fruition.[24] After all, Buckinghamshire County Council was still awaiting a decision regarding the proposed grammar school for Milton Keynes that had been sitting on Shephard's desk since May 1995. It was particularly pressing given that the area needed two new secondary schools to cater for rising numbers of pupils. If agreed to, it would represent the first purpose-built grammar school for thirty years. Significantly, Dewar claimed that Shephard's approval of the Milton Keynes proposal would be a sure sign of the government's commitment.

As if this was not enough, the plans to allow greater academic selection were even being opposed by Conservative local authorities. A report by Westminster City Council claimed that the government's policy risked disrupting the education system and alienating parents, and that change on this scale should not be undertaken 'lightly or in haste.' The consequence of the policy of giving schools greater freedom to select pupils, it added, would diminish parents' rights to select schools and result in 'fewer rather than more satisfied parents.'[25] As before, it was Conservative-run local authorities that formed part of the obstacle to any fundamental change.

Nevertheless, in the dying months of the Major government, a new Education Bill was launched in October 1996. It was introduced under a general banner of greater freedom for schools to introduce or extend selection and specialization. There would be more grammar schools if that was what parents wanted, while at the same time Shephard keenly professed to welcome 'all types of school,' as long as they provided 'a good education' for their pupils.[26] The Bill thus set further thresholds for the percentages of pupils that school admission authorities could select by ability or aptitude without having to seek central government approval. Grant-maintained secondary schools could now select up to 50 per cent of their pupils, while local education authority-run specialist schools were free to select 30 per cent of their intake within their specialist subjects without having to seek statutory approval. For local authority-run schools that were non-specialist, the percentage was to be raised to 20 per cent. Furthermore, the Bill required the governing bodies of secondary schools to annually review whether to introduce or extend selection as part of their plans for raising standards and improving service to local parents. While no school was obliged to introduce selection, they were nevertheless to consider it and regularly report their conclusions to parents.

The Bill was certainly intended to sound ambitious. It gave governors of local authority schools that wished to become fully selective the right to publish their own proposals for central approval if they had already been blocked by their local authority. In addition, LEA technology and language colleges, and in future sports and arts colleges, would also have a right of appeal against a hostile local authority. The scope of the assisted places scheme was to be extended to cover independent primary schools. Therefore, in its last year of office, the Major government was clearly trying to strengthen the hand of individual maintained schools and drive a further wedge between them and the local authorities. Yet as the Labour MP Peter Kilfoyle was able to point out, only 41 of the 1,100 GM schools that had been created had sought an element of selection in their admissions criteria, with a mere three schools having sought full grammar school status. The intransigence of Labour local education authorities along with the threat from a future Labour government had caused a slowdown in the rate of schools becoming grant maintained in the last few years.

The response from the Labour opposition to the government's proposals was unsurprising. It was claimed that the policy would be to the further detriment of less favoured schools in the local areas concerned. It also argued that the further powers in the Bill for GM schools to create nursery classes and sixth forms would 'disrupt' the planning of further education colleges in the local neighbourhoods concerned. Ultimately, it was claimed that the policy to allow a greater scope for selection would return to what the Labour opposition described as the 'education apartheid' of the past.[27]

On 27 January 1997 the government suffered defeat over its reforms regarding GM schools' ability to increase their capacity by more than half. The Tories had apparently not expected Labour MPs to turn out in force for the vote. As a result, a main plank of the proposed Bill to increase individual schools' freedom and reduce the control of local authorities was lost. This inevitably carried dire implications for other parts of the Bill.

Therefore, despite its proposals the Bill that became the 1997 Education Act would prove ineffectual. There was no essential change of direction during the rest of the Conservatives' period in government. This surely begs the question of just what motive lay behind this last ditch attempt by the Major government to highlight selective schooling again as an issue in their last eighteen months of office. As it happened, the clauses relating to selection by ability were in fact dropped from the version of the Bill that received Royal Assent shortly before the 1997 general election.

During the 1997 general election campaign, Labour was noticeably opaque about its intentions towards grammar schools if they were to gain office. Their education spokesman David Blunkett would not confirm whether they intended for parental ballots to be held in local authority areas to decide existing grammar schools' future. In particular, Blunkett would not specify how many signatures would be necessary in those cases. Nevertheless, there remained fears that Labour activists would try to trigger ballots to close remaining grammar schools under a future Labour government. Meanwhile, Labour policy towards grant-maintained schools was clear: the intention was to abolish them and return them to 'foundation' or local authority status. During the campaign, Tony Blair called the Tory schools policy 'a policy of rejection' and that it meant a 'dangerous' return to the 11 plus. Instead, he spoke vaguely about selection within schools, with more setting to take place inside comprehensives.[28]

The crushing, and inevitable, victory by the Labour Party on 1 May thus put an end to eighteen years of Conservative government. Those reforms in the education service that had been made, in particular the grant-maintained schools policy, were now set to be swept away. Both Margaret Thatcher and John Major had attempted to diffuse selection by ability within general notions of parental choice and greater school autonomy without clearly stating whether selection would be an ideal policy for maintained schools to aim for or not. It amounted to an attempted 'backdoor' approach.

A further ambiguity characterized the Major period. This was symbolized by his government's ending of the 'binary line' between universities and the polytechnics and colleges enacted by the Further and Higher Education Act of 1992. Major was noticeably keen to emphasize that the traditional divide had represented 'an increasingly artificial distinction' that had maintained old prejudices against vocational education and qualifications.[29] The potential for the former polytechnics, in ironic fashion, to in fact lose their distinctively vocational studies in favour of a more academic direction was brushed aside amid lofty government assurances that funding incentives as well as student demand would prevent this occurring. In addition, by 1996 Major was trumpeting the fact that one in three young people were entering higher education compared with a figure of one in eight in 1979.[30] The long-term trends that had militated against acknowledging differences of individual suitability for academic versus vocational education thus continued under successive Conservative governments within all stages of the education system.

Thus, Major appeared to use selection more as a vehicle to promote his populist and meritocratic credentials, rather than to embark on anything substantial. And in spite of the grant maintained schools policy, successive education secretaries extricated themselves from directly supporting selection, with Gillian Shephard notably unenthusiastic herself. Selection was thus obscured under 'choice and diversity' which meant an inevitable avoidance of principles. The GM policy had been, at most, an indirect method of enabling selection without the government having to state what it actually favoured.

9

New Labour 1997–2010

The Blair government's introduction of parental ballots within selective local authority areas potentially threatened the remaining grammar schools' existence. However, certain aspects of the previous government's GM policy were continued under the academies and foundation schools programme. Nevertheless, safeguards were set in place to ensure that schools could not opt for selection by ability. Under the Conservative opposition leadership of David Cameron, grammar schools were again the victim of political expediency in higher Tory circles.

Ballots and new restrictions

With the new Labour government led by Tony Blair elected by a landslide majority, the future for existing grammar schools looked perilous. Despite promises having been made during the election campaign by both Blair and David Blunkett the new Secretary of State that the government posed no threat to any type of school, the legislation issued in the first years of the Blair government suggested a marked intransigence on their part. The School Standards and Framework Act 1998 forbade the creation of any new grammar schools and introduced ballots in those local authority areas that still contained them.[1] Once a petition had been started, it needed to reach a 20 per cent threshold of signatures to trigger a ballot. This suggested that in order to appease their backbench MPs and Labour activists, Blair and Blunkett were not only seeking to prevent the creation of new selective schools but also prepared to allow all existing grammars to be abolished under the guise of local parents' choice while keeping their hands clean. Alternatively, if the threshold for triggering a ballot proved too high and no ballots therefore took place, the issue could be kicked into the long grass and submerged. Thus the Education (Grammar School Ballots) Regulations came into effect on 3 December 1998.

Those local authority areas that carried a majority selective system were directly in the firing line. One of those areas was Trafford in the Greater Manchester area, whose MP the Conservative Graham Brady was particularly vociferous within Tory ranks in withstanding attacks on the selective system operating within his constituency. As he pointed out in House of Commons debates at the time, the Labour government's ballot question itself was rigged by asking whether the parent was in favour of the local area moving to an admissions system encompassing children of all abilities, rather than there being any mention of the loss or destruction of grammar schools contained within it. Alarmingly, in areas with 'stand-alone' grammar schools in feeder areas (as opposed to a majority selective system) parents whose pupils were currently at the grammar school in question would not be eligible to vote. Furthermore, there was evidence that Labour Party workers, including trade unions affiliated to the Labour Party, were using public money to fund and promote local campaigns against existing grammar schools.[2]

In fact, a ballot was only triggered once. This was in the case of Ripon grammar school in North Yorkshire. In March 2000 it voted 2:1 to retain the grammar schools in its area and continue selection.[3] Inevitably, this provoked howls of protest from Labour members, most notably Stephen Ladyman the MP for Thanet South, as well as triggering demands that the threshold be lowered so that a mere 1 per cent of signatures could trigger a ballot rather than the 20 per cent that was needed. Nevertheless, the government's legislation enabled petitions to be started up again within a four-year period. Even a grammar school that had been reprieved could not rest easy in the knowledge that its long-term future would be assured.[4]

Nevertheless, the Blair government's approach to selection was ambiguous. While pledging not to introduce any new grammar schools and dismantling the assisted places scheme, it was still keen to follow in Tory footsteps by echoing the mantra of 'choice and diversity'. While grant-maintained status was abolished, with the former GM schools now becoming 'foundation' schools, the Labour government encouraged comprehensive schools to specialize in the areas of sport, modern foreign languages, and performing and visual arts. Furthermore, these 'specialist schools' were to be free to select 10 per cent of their pupils by aptitude (as opposed to ability) if the governing body decided that the school had a speciality area.

However, New Labour's most striking new type of secondary school was to be the 'city academy'. The brainchild of Andrew Adonis, a former education advisor who would later be appointed a minister, these schools were to be established in partnership between the government and local businesses and civic organizations, and were to be allowed much greater freedom and independence, including over their admissions policies. Although the government was committed to them being 'inclusive' by remaining comprehensive in terms of pupil entry, their freedom regarding their admissions policies was enough to provoke left-wing critics, both inside and outside the government, to fulminate against the risk of them engaging in the 'covert' selection of pupils.

Though it was clear that the New Labour government was borrowing the clothing of the opposition in emphasizing 'choice and diversity', in practice there was little substance behind the rhetoric. Academies were to have freedom in terms of tailoring their curriculum to different pupils' requirements, as the Minister for School Standards David Miliband obliquely presented it, as well as to have greater autonomy regarding the make-up of their governing bodies. Yet Miliband repeatedly affirmed that city academies would have no more ability to select than local authority-run comprehensive or 'community' schools.[5]

Similarly, the new concept of 'specialist' school did not constitute anything significant, either. Those schools that had attained specialist status had achieved slightly improved GCSE results. This was now being used as a pretext for encouraging as many secondary schools to attain specialist status as possible. Yet, as Graham Brady and others argued, amidst this supposed respect for diversity of provision the government was staunchly opposed to grammar schools, which of course 'specialized' in academic excellence.[6]

Alongside the Labour government's rhetoric of getting away from the 'one-size-fits-all' comprehensive, it was forced to reveal through the school standards minister Stephen Timms that by 2002 it had spent a total of £436,000 on petitions and ballots for deciding the remaining grammar schools' future, with only one ballot in fact having taken place.[7] Also, the government still maintained that in feeder school ballots grammar school parents would remain ineligible to decide on their children's schools' future. In addition, there was no intention either to prolong the period before which another petition could be brought in order to give the grammar school more of a sense of security as Graham Brady and others desired.[8]

In fact, the Blair government was being pushed and pulled in different directions all at once in this period due to pressure from the educational left. The 2005 White Paper *Higher Standards, Better Schools For All* called for the development of self-governing 'trust' schools intended to have greater independence from local authorities to the consternation of those claiming 'backdoor selection'.[9] Yet while espousing the language of freedom and autonomy for schools along with parental choice, the government was simultaneously advocating policies that neutralized this. The 2006 Education and Inspections Act reaffirmed a general restriction on selection by ability. It also included a strengthened admissions code designed to ban the use of so-called 'backdoor selection' thought to result from schools having greater control over their admissions.[10] While successful schools were to be allowed to expand, the Education Secretary Ruth Kelly keenly emphasized that there were to be new safeguards against selection.[11]

The sheer irony of the situation was symbolized by the fact that the Labour Cabinet in May 2006 contained only 5 individuals who were products of a state comprehensive school, with the other 18 members being products of either selective private or grammar schools. Furthermore, *The Times* newspaper uncovered the fact that of the five, three of them in the case of David Miliband, Hilary Armstrong and Hilary Benn came from extraordinary families. Only two, John Prescott and Jacqui Smith, could be said to be the products of 'bog standard,' non-selective state education. Furthermore, a quarter of the government had attended fee-paying schools compared with only 16 per cent of Labour backbenchers. Yet with supreme irony, Labour MPs were now voting on a bill to stamp out selection 'by the back door' in order to reinforce the comprehensive ideal, with the new education bill's admission code seeking to ban all interviews and give extra powers to local education authorities to investigate allegations of selection.[12]

A new Conservative direction

Meanwhile the Conservative Party had, by late 2005, suffered three consecutive general election losses. Having experienced electoral disaster under the leaderships of William Hague and Iain Duncan-Smith, the latest defeat in the 2005 general election under Michael Howard indicated that the Conservatives had closed the gap somewhat. Nevertheless, they still faced a steep climb in order to gain outright electoral success and Howard resigned as leader citing his age.[13]

The new leader elected in October 2005, David Cameron, was clearly determined from the outset to 'modernize' the party at all costs in order for it to become electorally successful again. Yet part of this modernizing agenda involved a rejection of viewpoints regarded as 'right wing' and therefore politically toxic. Those advising the new leader were now urging that the Conservative Party separate itself from any attachment to grammar schools in order to overhaul the party's image in the public eye. In January 2006, Bob Balchin, the former education advisor to the Major government on school autonomy, was publicly advocating that Cameron not allow the party to continue what he termed its 'obsession' with grammar schools. In a *Times* newspaper article, Balchin reasoned that the Party could not advocate more grammar schools since most children, however bright, could not go to them. To Balchin, there were 'vastly more urgent educational tasks' that the Party, when next in government, should concentrate on.[14]

In his first Party Conference speech as leader in October 2006, Cameron duly delivered. The Party's history told him, he intoned, that their success lay on the 'centre ground.' This was where, he added, the dreams and aspirations of most people were. In a skilful re-definition of what was to now be considered acceptable territory and that which was to be discarded as politically irrelevant, he portrayed the Conservative Party as having been concerned with matters that did not relate to the public's real concerns. Using markedly populist rhetoric, he described parents as being concerned with mundane practical matters such as childcare, 'getting the kids to school,' and 'balancing work and family life.' While these so-called 'ordinary parents' were concerned about standards in thousands of secondary schools, he claimed, 'we obsessed about a handful more grammar schools.'[15] Amazingly, the furtherance of standards in state education and the desire to protect and increase grammar schools were depicted as being at odds with each other. Indeed, grammar schools appeared to be being portrayed as lying in opposition to the education of most people. Clearly, grammar schools were part of the 'right wing' baggage that Cameron wanted to junk.

Nor did it appear to deter Cameron that his former headmaster at Eton College Eric Anderson, who had also taught Tony Blair at Fettes College, gave a speech that week to the Headmasters' and Headmistresses' Conference for leading independent schools calling for a modern system of selection for state pupils at age 11. In Anderson's view, it ought to be based on primary school results as well as teachers' advice and parental wishes. This was the only way, he argued, that Britain could compete in the global economy. At the same time, Brian Wills-Pope of the National Grammar Schools Association cited a recent poll by ICM that suggested, in direct contrast to Cameron's sentiments about parents' aspirations, that 70 per cent of parents supported selection.[16]

Yet on 16 May 2007, Cameron's shadow education spokesman David Willetts went one step further. In a speech to the Confederation of British Industry Willetts, in pledging support for Labour's academy programme, claimed that grammar schools entrenched advantage amongst middle-class children. He cited as evidence that only 2 per cent of children within them were on free school meals. Willetts added:

> We must break free from the belief that academic selection is any longer the way to transform the life chances of poor bright kids. We have to recognise that there is overwhelming evidence that such academic selection entrenches advantage, it does not spread it.[17]

Willetts was effectively killing off the possibility of the Conservatives embarking on a future policy of increasing the number of grammar schools and revoking the Labour government's legislation should they be returned to office. It appeared that Cameron and Willetts had thrown down a gauntlet to their backbench MPs, with grammar schools used as a political football as part of the Party's modernizing agenda.

The reaction within the Conservative Party was instant. Inevitably, such sentiments from Willetts undermined the morale of existing grammar schools within Tory constituencies. Graham Brady broke ranks to publicly defend grammar schools by arguing that an increased number of them, particularly in inner cities, would have a major impact on the number of bright pupils from poor backgrounds entering university.[18] In response, the Cameron team leapt into action. Brady was forced to issue a quick climb-down, telling *The Times* newspaper later the same day that he supported the policy of more City Academies and that 'I fully accept the Party policy.' Furthermore, while existing grammar schools would continue, he was forced to state that 'there will be no return to the eleven plus under a future Conservative government.'[19]

Nevertheless, it led to what *The Times* reported as a 'stormy' meeting of the backbench 1922 Committee, at which senior Conservatives lined up to criticize Willetts. Notable Party figures including David Davis, Liam Fox and even Michael Howard were reportedly angry at this public disavowal of grammar schools. Roger Gale, the MP for Thanet North, went as far as to publicly state that he hoped every member of the Shadow Cabinet who supported Willetts would give a 'clear undertaking' that their own children and grandchildren were not receiving their education in independent schools, given that the Labour government's abolition of the assisted places scheme had meant poorer children could no longer attend them.

Meanwhile, David Cameron continued to dismiss the issue, stating that 'a pointless debate about creating a handful of extra grammar schools is not going to get us anywhere.'[20] Yet he now thought it politic to make clear that there was absolutely no intention to abolish the remaining grammar schools. Only days later in a salvaging exercise, Willetts offered an olive branch to backbench MPs by informing them that he would 'consider' a pledge to repeal the current laws that allowed parents to vote to scrap existing grammar schools. This action on Willetts' part was obviously designed to appease the Party's grassroots. Nevertheless, Nadine Dorries the MP for Mid Bedfordshire claimed that the leadership's public rejection of more grammar schools had effectively pre-empted the conclusions of the party's group that was formulating policy on public services.[21]

The key issue to consider is the extent of Cameron's role in formulating Willetts' CBI speech that seemed to actively target the minority of remaining selective state schools. All the while, Cameron's allies denied that Willetts' speech had been intended to provoke a 'Clause Four' moment for the Conservative Party, and claimed they were surprised at its reception. Apparently, Willetts had carried out focus group research to test his message first, and therefore he and Cameron had been taken aback by the reaction. The essential question, however, remains as to whether the speech had been motivated by ruthless calculation on the part of Willetts and Cameron in order to provoke backbench opposition, or simply arose out of an arrogant complacency that did not heed the potential reaction.

All the while, Cameron and Willetts continued to use rhetoric about the prioritizing of 'raising standards' in the 3,000 secondary schools across the country that was to be set against the whole subject of grammar schools. The two issues, therefore, continued to be portrayed as being unconnected and at odds. By now, Cameron was trying to manoeuvre the terms of discussion onto school discipline regarding head-teachers having greater freedom to expel unruly pupils. A populist sweetener was thus being cynically offered in order to appease the 'law and order' elements of the party and prove the leadership's small 'c' conservative credentials.[22]

Defending his policy regarding grammar schools in an article for *The Times* on 22 May, Cameron described an instinctive conservative belief in 'rigour, parental choice and competition' as the best way of raising standards, but did not of course include selection by ability. Yet again, he informed readers that he wanted to move on from a 'sterile debate' about building 'a few more grammar schools,' and claimed that international studies showed that academic selection did not work as well as pupils choosing schools rather than schools choosing pupils.[23] He reaffirmed his intention when next in government of accelerating the academies programme by making it easier to enable 'federations' of schools rather than a separate contract having to be negotiated for each one. Essentially, the shadow education team was set to echo the policy of the Blair government with a few extras on top.

At the same time, Willetts continued to issue mollifying sentiments for Tory backbenchers incensed by his speech. He now stated that in office he would make it easier for specialist schools to select their allowed proportion of 10 per cent of pupils by aptitude in certain subjects. Willetts was therefore practising more manoeuvring on the issue. Although 80 per cent of state secondary schools had achieved specialist status by May 2007, a mere 6 per cent had taken advantage of selecting pupils. Willetts said he wanted to extend the number of subjects they could select in, which would involve getting rid of the government's distinction between aptitude and ability 'to make more sense of their ability to select'. However, he keenly denied that this represented a wholesale move towards selection by ability as it would continue to involve only 10 per cent of places: 'Ninety per cent of places would not be affected,' he emphasized.[24] Thus, contradictory and opaque sentiments abounded within the Conservative opposition's public statements.

Meanwhile, Cameron wanted to move the debate onto discipline in schools. The Party's spin machine was therefore in motion to shift the focus of attention. At the same time, reports were starting to circulate that Graham Brady would face the sack from his position as the Party's Europe spokesman in next month's shadow cabinet reshuffle. Cameron clearly wanted the grammar schools issue to be quickly put to bed.

Yet in spite of the recent furore, in an interview with *The Times*' Alice Miles and Helen Rumbelow, Willetts nevertheless continued the tenor of his CBI speech by appearing to criticize middle-class parents. Part of the challenge for the 'baby boomers,' he claimed, 'is that we may be better parents than we are citizens.' Selection at 11 was unfair, he continued, because the middle classes entrenched their advantages at a much younger age, with less able rich toddlers overtaking poor, bright ones at 5 years old. Willetts was thus employing an analysis more commonly used by the practitioners of egalitarian social engineering.

Willetts spoke as if grammar schools had been a major part of Tory education policy in recent years. In oblique and circumlocutory style, Willetts claimed that one of the great strengths of conservatism was a 'wariness for a new set of fancy ideas.' Furthermore, 'every generation of Conservatives has to remake its policies to take account of the way the world has changed.'[25] Yet when questioned further, Willetts, who had himself been educated at the highly selective direct grant school King Edward's School in Birmingham in the late 1960s, was forced to admit that he sent his own children to highly selective independent schools. He explained that 'I did what I thought was best for those children. I don't condemn any parent for trying to do that.' Willetts was thus saying two things at once. As Miles and Rumbelow then put it to him, his own enthusiasm for a non-selective system appeared to have 'blossomed' only once his children were safely shielded from it. Nevertheless, Willetts backed the government's academy programme with his own additions, emphasizing that he hoped they would achieve 'a social mix where children from a variety of backgrounds come in.' 'New academies' were clearly to remain very much as comprehensives according to his educational vision, too.

Willetts' opacity continued throughout the interview. To the question of whether he thought parents should sacrifice their child's best interests for the good of others, he would not at first answer. Eventually he ended up by saying that every parent was entitled to do the best they could for their child, 'rather than use their child for the pursuit of some political agenda.'[26] He finally proposed that parents ought to campaign for new and better local schools for other people. Willetts, amidst his flexible-minded evasion, did not appear to know what he really meant. By now, Cameron was deliberately highlighting academic setting within non-selective schools as well as talking about 'a grammar stream in every school,' in order to defuse the issue.[27]

On Sunday 27 May Cameron declared the row to be over, while nevertheless calling critics of his approach 'inverse class warriors.' But the following day, Graham Brady released data to the Press that showed that areas with full and partially selective systems outperformed areas with totally non-selective ones in their GCSE results. His statistics showed that within areas with no selective education, 42.6 per cent of pupils were awarded at least 5 GCSEs at A* to C, partially selective ones at 46 per cent, with fully selective areas coming out on top with 49.8 per cent.[28] The research therefore appeared to show that grammar school education could improve the results of entire neighbourhoods and areas, contrary to what their enemies often claimed, particularly among ethnic minority children. It effectively demolished Willetts' argument. Drawing from these conclusions, Brady now called for an increase in grammar schools within inner city areas.

According to a Tory source, Cameron 'hit the roof' over Brady's comments. He and his Chief of Staff Ed Llewellyn instructed Patrick McLoughlin, the Chief Whip, to deal with Brady before Cameron flew off on holiday for the half-term break. Brady was then 'severely reprimanded' by the Chief Whip and told to stick to his brief. In addition, the Tory high command publicly disputed the validity of the research that Brady had used, claiming that the results for selective and non-selective areas could not be compared because of what they claimed were children's differing social backgrounds between them. In this, they cited research from Professor Paul Gregg of Bristol University that asserted that selection 'had little or no impact on attainment'.[29] It was claimed that a clever child from a poor background was significantly less likely to pass the eleven plus compared with a more affluent high-ability child. This was despite the researchers also having acknowledged the impressive performance of poorer pupils once they had attained places in grammar schools. The Tories were now deriving left-wing conclusions from academic research as part of their internal battle with Brady.

On 29 May, Brady jumped before he was pushed. He announced he was stepping down as Europe spokesman after learning from newspaper reports that he was likely to be dismissed in next month's shadow cabinet reshuffle. Apparently, Brady had been kept in a state of limbo amid reports that he would be sacked going unchallenged. In his resignation letter to Cameron, Brady claimed that the Conservative leader's position was undermining the four grammar schools in his constituency.[30] This was particularly pertinent given that Gordon Brown was likely to succeed Tony Blair as Prime Minister the following month as well as the distinctly uncertain result of the next general election. If the Labour Party under Brown's leadership was returned to power, both main parties would effectively be opposed to selective state education. Potentially, grammar schools were being thrown to the wind.

Yet even with Brady out of the way, the controversy would not die down. Later that week, the Shadow Attorney Dominic Grieve undermined the Party's position further when emphasizing to his local newspaper the *Buckinghamshire Examiner* that there would be no question of changing the selective system operating in his constituency of Beaconsfield. He then added that 'We must also ensure that if further grammar or secondary schools are needed they can be supplied within the county.' As a result, the Conservative high command was forced to admit that their general future policy might include more grammar schools if the demographics required it.[31] Labour was thus able to accuse them of performing a 'U' turn on the issue. The Conservative Party of course denied this, claiming that it had decided eighteen months ago that more grammar schools could be built if rises in population demanded it, but the position had not been mentioned in any press release because it had been deemed 'not important enough.'[32] It was therefore claimed, unconvincingly, that Grieve's sentiments had not in fact opposed the status quo.

However, there were claims circulating that Cameron had ordered a small change in policy to avoid having to sack Grieve, a valuable ally, so soon after the departure of Graham Brady. An unnamed member of Cameron's front bench told the press, 'We seemed to have arrived at a good policy. The real question was could they afford to lose Dominic Grieve, and clearly they could not.'[33] Clearly, Brady had been considered dispensable, but this had not been the case with Grieve. It appeared that Greg Clark, the MP for Tunbridge Wells, had also received an assurance that one or more new grammar schools could open in his area. Tory MPs with grammar school constituencies were anxious to reassure and protect their areas. Despite the efforts of the Party hierarchy, Willetts' bald statements of a few weeks earlier were continuing to backfire on them.

Many appeared to feel that it had been Willetts' original presentational inadequacy that had let matters deteriorate to this point. The episode had made Willetts and Cameron look incompetent when it came to party management. And now, the recently sacked Graham Brady was keen to stick his oar in, telling Sky News at this time that

'These are things that don't lend themselves to easy solutions that can be thought up behind closed doors by one or two people having a eureka moment.'[34] Brady was clearly a somewhat alienated figure by now. Luckily for the Tory leader, results from the Conservative home website showed that Tory grassroots members largely blamed Willetts for the debacle rather than Cameron.[35] It was not a surprise when Cameron moved Willetts to the higher education brief the following month and replaced him with Michael Gove. Cameron was obviously anxious to close this awkward chapter as quickly as possible.

A worsening divide

Meanwhile, the latest figures showed that independent schools were continuing to tighten their grip on the leading universities. Findings by the Sutton Trust in 2007 showed that a mere 3 per cent of leading independent schools accounted for a third of admissions to Oxford and Cambridge universities in the past five years, with the proportion from the leading thirty independent schools double that of the top thirty grammar schools. At the best thirty comprehensives, only one third of their expected pupils gained admission, even with three 'A' grades having been achieved. Research also showed that Westminster sent nearly half of its leavers to Oxbridge along with St Paul's Girls, with Winchester, Wycombe Abbey, St Paul's boys and Eton College sending approximately a third of their leaving sixth form. Of the state schools, the Royal Grammar School High Wycombe sent 27 per cent, while the only 'comprehensive' school in the list was the London Oratory (the school to which Tony Blair sent his son) with 20.6 per cent.[36] In reaction to this, the Sutton Trust clamoured for day independent schools and grammar schools to do more to admit disadvantaged pupils, amidst other short-term solutions being offered.[37]

Nevertheless, the academic left continued to inveigh against selection within maintained schools. It was claimed by Professor David Jesson of the University of York that parents within grammar school areas were either having their pupils coached for the 11 plus exam or disproportionately had their children educated in private 'prep' schools beforehand. Using the same terms of reference as the Conservative opposition, such academic research attacked grammar schools for not enrolling a sufficiently large percentage of pupils on free school meals compared with the proportion in their local areas.[38]

Even the Blair policy for 'specialist' schools that involved the limited freedom to select a small proportion of pupils by aptitude was increasingly attacked by researchers. A government-backed report by Sheffield Hallam University and the National Centre for Social Research claimed that the policy entrenched advantage among middle-class parents who were more likely to invest time and money in developing their children's aptitudes. Instead, the authors suggested yet more devices for ending 'backdoor selection,' such as further use of banding to ensure equal proportions of pupils of different ability, subsidized transport and even lottery systems to ensure sufficient 'social representation.'[39] Other researchers at the London School of Economics proposed that faith schools and academies be stripped of their power to choose pupils, with the role to be handed over to supposedly 'independent' bodies to ensure greater 'fairness'. This included, of course, local education authorities. By way of justification, Anne West of the Education Research Group at the LSE claimed that the proportion of secondary schools selecting by aptitude had increased from 3 to 5 per cent between 2001 and 2008.[40]

With Gordon Brown now Prime Minister, the Schools Secretary Ed Balls was revealing an underlying hostility towards grammar schools. Balls claimed that secondary modern schools within selective areas were underperforming, and that therefore grammar schools damaged educational standards in their communities. In June 2008 he was putting pressure on grammar schools to merge or 'work closely' with under performing schools where fewer than 30 per cent of pupils achieved five good GCSEs.[41] Thus, the remaining grammar schools were being pressured to jump through hoops to prove their public virtue by assisting inadequate schools in order to justify their existence. It was also notable that in October 2008 Andrew Adonis, the Blairite architect of city academies, was moved from education to the Department of Transport. The climate against grammar schools under Gordon Brown and Ed Balls was becoming even more hostile. And given the Conservative leadership's recent pronouncements, the official opposition was hardly likely to combat it.

Indeed, there was some evidence that the vacuum in the Tory opposition's policy was leaving the existing grammar schools open to attack. It was claimed in September 2008 that two Conservative-controlled authorities, namely Kent County Council and Lincolnshire, were now planning to cut grammar school places by merging single-sex schools into coeducational ones, with their joint admissions numbers being cut substantially in the process. Robert McCartney, the Chairman of the National Grammar Schools Association, also alleged that the Balls policy meant that successful grammar schools were being federated or merged or having their budgets and pupil intakes reduced. In other cases, tax payers' money was being used to 'poach' grammar school head teachers to other, less academically selective schools.[42] The Cameron opposition's position was therefore having a demoralizing effect on the remaining grammar schools' ability to defend themselves while facing the Labour government's overt hostility.

Simultaneously, notable figures within the independent school sector such as the headmaster and educational commentator Anthony Seldon increasingly argued that academies were a panacea for a state system noticeably falling behind the private sector. In Seldon's view every independent school, such as his own Wellington College, should be involved in setting up a new academy. Furthermore, it was advocated that independent schools form 'partnerships' with struggling state schools in order to assist them.[43] Politically expedient 'half-way house' solutions were therefore being advocated with independent schools being morally pressured to support the state comprehensive sector.

In August 2009, the Conservatives' Shadow Children, Schools and Families Secretary Michael Gove conceded that many of his current policies were in fact derived from the Blair educational programme.[44] Predictably, Gove was opposed to new grammar schools and in favour of improving an essentially comprehensive system through an increase in city academies. This included having academies take over neighbouring schools deemed to be failing. He was silent about selection by ability but instead advocated the establishment of Swedish-style 'free schools' that were independent schools run by parents and charities but paid for by the state, and claimed it would work effectively in the UK. Nevertheless, they would be bound by the Admissions Code and would have no powers to select beyond those available to existing maintained schools.[45] Gove had reportedly been receiving advice from John McIntosh, the former head of the London Oratory School and an advisor to the Conservatives. Like Willetts, Gove sought to play the populist card as part of the attempted overhaul of the Tories' image, with his emphasis upon giving children from dysfunctional backgrounds a 'level-playing field' with those from homes that were more affluent.

However, Gove's approach to Conservative Party education policy at this time contained important omissions. In his speech to the Centre for Policy Studies on 6 November 2009, while making important points about the need to boost the calibre of the teaching profession by requiring a higher level of qualifications as well as outlining plans for the reform of Ofsted, he put the responsibility for the relative deficiency of state schools onto 'bureaucracy' and an 'over-centralised system'.[46] The corresponding success of leading independent schools was put down to their relative lack of this. The fact that these schools selected by ability (normally through the Common Entrance exam at 13) was never mentioned. Policies of diverting resources to poorer pupils through such schemes as the Pupil Premium were being advanced instead.

Competition for the remaining grammar schools was growing ever fiercer at this time due in part to the financial recession of November 2008. More parents were apparently schooling their children privately in 'prep' schools in order to prepare them for selective grammars at 11. The cost of independent schools was rocketing, with it being estimated that top 'public' schools at secondary level were charging fees often in the region of £18,000, compared with £7,500 for day pupils in prep schools. Meanwhile in 2009 in Kent, 11,873 children registered to take the 11 plus, a figure up 7 per cent from the previous year, with thousands of those believed to come from outside the county in areas without grammar schools.[47] Inevitably, such findings boosted the contention that grammar schools were dominated by the affluent middle class, rather than the more obvious conclusion being reached that grammar schools were popular with parents and that therefore more needed to be built in other areas. Indeed, figures released from the Department for Children Schools and Families at this time revealed there were now 156,798 pupils registered as attending grammar schools in 2007 compared with 128,712 in 1997. This represented an increase of 22 per cent since Tony Blair had taken office.[48]

The Brown government then produced a revised version of the School Admissions Code, which was published in December 2008. It sought to bar maintained schools from holding interviews or asking parents to make financial contributions or offer practical support.[49] Balls thus sought to reassure the left that changes he had implemented in the governance and curriculum requirements as well as the sponsorship regime of academies would remove left-wing concerns that they were selective and outside the local authority structure.

A year later, in November 2009 the government barred state schools from offering Cambridge University exam board's new elite International GCSE in core subjects. Inevitably, this raised fears that the divide in standards between state and private schools would grow all the more.[50] At the same time, independent schools were increasingly opting for the International Baccalaureate and Cambridge University's Pre-U, while in terms of vocational education, the Brown government merely offered 'diplomas' in construction, media, engineering, IT and society and health and development.

In an ironic twist for the Conservative Party, it was looking increasing likely as the 2010 General Election approached that Graham Brady would become the next chairman of the backbench Tory 1922 Committee. The other candidates, Nicholas Soames and Richard Ottaway, were regarded as being too close to David Cameron and unlikely to stand up to him. Brady, who noticeably did not mention Cameron in his local campaign literature, thus symbolized the division existing in the Party over the direction in which it was being taken by the leadership in key areas.[51]

The 2010 General Election was held on 6 May. After the uncertain result, with no party able to gain an absolute majority and following a week of fevered negotiation, Gordon Brown resigned as Prime Minister on 11 May. David Cameron then formed a coalition government with the Liberal Democrats. Cameron's 'modernizing,' centrist project was now to be finally put into practice in government with many issues of contention within the Conservative Party remaining unresolved.

This chapter has shown how David Cameron portrayed grammar schools as a symbol of Tory traditionalism that he wanted to renounce as part of his modernizing strategy. Selective state education remained a point of controversy and division within the Party, with an obvious gulf in sympathy between the leadership and the pro-grammar elements within the Party's grassroots. The existing grammar schools were particularly undermined by the Cameron approach at a time of great vulnerability, given the incoming Brown government's hostility towards them. The long-standing trends noted throughout this book therefore continued under the Cameron leadership.

10

A door half opened under Cameron and May 2010–present

In 2010 there were signs of a significant degree of public support for grammar schools and the Conservative education secretary Michael Gove initially made positive noises about them. Yet the Conservative-led coalition would not overturn the Blair government's 1998 legislation forbidding the creation of new selective schools. The position was reduced to that of allowing existing grammar schools the freedom to expand their numbers. Nevertheless, the eventual introduction of a grammar school 'annexe' in Kent showed a degree of pragmatic acceptance by the Conservative-led coalition amidst much opposition from educational vested interests. Following Cameron's resignation, the chapter examines Theresa May's seemingly pro-grammar school policy intentions before her premiership was undermined by her disastrous 2017 general election result. Finally it sums up the situation as it stands today, with inevitably dire effects upon schooling caused by policies enacted during the Coronavirus pandemic. However, grammar schools have continued to be used as a symbol of meritocratic aspiration by certain ministers as part of the Johnson government's 'levelling up' agenda.

Positive signals

In terms of the evidence regarding public attitudes, the signs were auspicious for grammar schools in 2010. A survey conducted by ICM in February that year had shown that more than three quarters of adults believed that more academically selective schools should be opened, particularly in inner cities with poor educational standards. Furthermore, 85 per cent of people aged 18–24 backed the idea of introducing new grammars in areas without academic selection. In addition, nearly three quarters of those questioned also supported the retention of the UK's remaining grammar schools as 'self-governing' authorities run independently of local councils.[1] Yet as Robert McCartney the Chairman of the National Grammar Schools Association noted, none of the three largest political parties 'seriously' supported existing selective schools or opening new ones.[2]

There had in fact been a small increase in the number of grammar school pupils since the Thatcher period in government. In 1983, there had been 117,147 pupils, or 3.1 per cent of the population, attending them. By 2010, the figure had risen slightly to 158,120 at 4.86 per cent, reflecting an increase in competition among parents to send their children to them as well as the schools expanding their sixth forms due to increased demand.[3] The few remaining grammar schools were being hotly competed for in those local areas that retained them.

By October 2010, it seemed that there was a new mood afoot in the recently assembled Conservative-led coalition with the Liberal Democrats. Michael Gove, who had kept his position at education, reportedly told a packed reception at the House of Commons held by the Friends of Grammar Schools group that existing grammars would be allowed to create more places. Crucially, they could also be given permission to build new premises and start 'satellite' schools. Michael Fallon, the MP for Sevenoaks, one of the areas likely to demand such changes, attended the meeting as well as Lord Ashcroft. Also present was the Labour MP Frank Field who was conducting a 'social justice' review for David Cameron. Gove was giving grammar school campaigners the boost they needed.

Circumspect as ever, Gove told the assembled gathering that his foot was 'hovering over the pedal' of allowing parents more access to selective schooling. Graham Brady, who was by now the Chairman of the 1922 committee of Tory backbenchers, questioned Gove and urged him to go further. He made the vital, if obvious, point that a policy of selective schools where parents wanted it was surely the next logical step for a government that claimed to believe in localism. After all, legislation allowing parents, charities and businesses to set up new free schools had been passed that summer, with sixteen schools set to open by September 2011. By way of response, Gove replied that he would have to see what his 'co-driver' Nick Clegg had to say on the matter.[4] The question therefore remained of whether this was simply a case of 'smoke and mirrors' from the wily Gove, who had previously advocated a policy of free schools and academies that would remain non-selective in nature.

Further positive signals for selective education appeared in June 2011. Nick Gibb, the Schools Minister, announced that new rules would enable state grammars alongside academies and free schools to admit extra pupils without having to seek the permission of local authorities. Changes to the Schools Admissions Code would make it easier for popular schools to expand, thus scrapping the existing rules requiring schools to consult the local community on admissions rules every five years. Gibb also advocated that more grammars convert into independent academies which would enable them to possess more freedoms over the curriculum and staff pay. Unlike his predecessors, Gibb was prepared to acknowledge how well disadvantaged pupils could perform in selective schools in relation to their more affluent peers.[5]

However, the Coalition continued to cynically hedge their bets. While the freedom of existing grammar schools to expand appeared to be being strengthened, there was still no intention to increase their number. This encouraged certain heads of grammar schools such as Shaun Fenton of the Grammar School Heads' Association (GSHA), who was also the head of Pate's grammar school in Cheltenham, to increase their claims that new-style freedoms should be used by grammar schools to give preference in admissions to poorer pupils rather than middle-class ones in order to 'enable social mobility'.[6] The Conservative-led coalition's reluctance to increase their number was therefore giving effect to misguided priorities among those such as the GSHA who perversely claimed to champion grammar schools' meritocratic interests. A policy of social engineering for existing selective schools was being advocated in certain quarters rather than the obvious answer of increasing grammar school numbers in less affluent areas.

Nevertheless, Gibb's promises came to fruition in December of that year. It was confirmed that grammar schools would now be able to expand and take on extra pupils and local authorities would no longer have control over their expansion. Also under the new plans, complaints from local parents who were opposed to the expansion of grammars would no longer be referred to the Chief Schools Adjudicator. It also blocked objections to schools that wished to opt-out of local authority control. In addition, over-subscribed schools were being given greater freedom to expand. Nevertheless, in a nod to the egalitarian tendency, Gibb also advocated that academies and grammar schools strike up partnerships with local comprehensives to assist with the teaching of tougher academic subjects. Inevitably, comprehensive school campaigners such as Margaret Tulloch of Comprehensive Future claimed these new freedoms would be to the detriment of non-selective schools, with the usual argument made that the newly liberated schools would 'cream off' the more able pupils.[7]

A proposed expansion

Such policies started off other initiatives. In January 2012 it was reported that in Sevenoaks, 1,500 of the town's residents had signed a petition backing a campaign for their own grammar school. All the other local authority areas of Kent were already catered for in this respect. At the time, parents in Sevenoaks could only choose between the comprehensive Knole Academy, which had been formed a year before out of the merger of two struggling comprehensives, and Sevenoaks school, a leading independent which in 2012 was charging £18,000 a year for day pupils alongside £28,000 for boarders. The petition called for a satellite campus in the town catering for 120 pupils a year and was intended to open in 2016. It was also reported that a grammar school in Torquay, Devon, was considering proposals to take over a private school in Newton Abbot, about 10 miles from its base, and turn it into an annexe. Unsurprisingly, the head teacher of Knole Academy Mary Boyle was dead set against the Sevenoaks proposals, while the Conservative government, who were of course now in coalition with the anti-grammar school Liberal Democrats, remained ambiguous.[8] They had long promoted the academies programme of all-ability 'independent' state schools. The key question therefore remained as to how academically selective schools fitted into their existing position. They were certainly not taking 'localism' to anything like its logical extent.

On 28 March Kent County Council, having considered the report recommending the proposed satellite for Sevenoaks, now approved it at a full council meeting. The decision was made on the grounds of the sheer numbers of current applications for each place in Kent's grammar schools. At the time, they were oversubscribed to the extent of five applicants for every place. The proposed extra provision would encompass two 'satellites', each with sixty places, run by existing grammars in other towns and would therefore have two sets of management.[9] Yet it still amounted to half-measures. The 'annexe' had effectively reflected a compromise by Kent County Council. And in spite of the recent signals he had been sending out, Gove was still maintaining the existing ban on new grammar schools stemming from the Blair government's 1998 legislation.

These events were taking place within a relentless climate of media hostility towards existing grammar schools. Constant emphasis was put upon pupils being 'coached' for the 11 plus, as well as the fact that prospective pupils had to gain nearly perfect scores in admissions tests due to the sheer number of applications.[10] The key point, that more grammars would mean less fevered competition for places at the limited number of existing schools, was rarely made.

More attacks came from the academic left. Professor David Jesson of the University of York, associate director of the Schools Network (formerly the Specialist Schools and Academies Trust) that had been funded by the Labour government to drive its academies programme, claimed that at twenty-five grammar schools at least 30 per cent of places went to privately educated pupils. In this vein, Jesson asserted that success in the 11 plus assessment reflected 'coaching' stemming from family wealth.[11] Under pressure, Kent County Council was now thinking of withdrawing its 11 plus exams in favour of teachers' assessment of prospective pupils. It was also being advocated that 'disadvantaged' pupils with 'potential' should be picked out in advance, in what could only be a subjective and politicized process. Objective assessment was thus being undermined by grammar school enemies. Other research by the BBC's Chris Cook as well as the Sutton Trust claimed that grammar schools entrenched inequalities between local areas producing an unequal society.[12] The head of Ofsted Michael Wilshaw himself claimed at this time that grammar schools were 'stuffed full of middle class children.'[13] And of course, the Tories' earlier sentiments in 2007 had helped to add fuel to this long-held view by the educational establishment.

In 2013 five leading grammar schools in Birmingham that formed part of the King Edward VI charity foundation revealed that they were planning, through the use of the Coalition government's 'Pupil Premium' and their greater freedoms regarding admissions, to purposefully seek out pupils from poorer homes using the criteria of free school meals. Schools were already receiving 'Pupil Premium funding' at a sum of £900 for every disadvantaged pupil admitted. Pupils qualified for it if their parents were on benefits or earning less than £16,000 a year. The Conservative Party leadership had in fact been advocating academies and other maintained schools being 'incentivised' to seek out pupils from 'more challenging' backgrounds since 2007.[14] James Turner, the lead researcher of the Sutton Trust, regarded the policy as 'an important step forwards.'[15] Thus the Conservative-led coalition government was clearly promoting a policy of social engineering. The Department of Education of course denied that this new move, backed by the 'progressive' oriented Grammar School Heads Association, discriminated against the middle classes. A year later, ninety grammar schools were planning to follow suit.

The target the Birmingham schools had set themselves was for 1 in 5 pupils admitted to be in receipt of free school meals. The reasoning was based on the statistic, assiduously promoted by the Sutton Trust, that grammar schools enrolled an average of 3 per cent of pupils on free meals compared with 18 per cent of those in their surrounding areas. Furthermore, the schools involved were also running 'outreach programmes' as well as 11 plus 'familiarisation' sessions for poorer candidates.[16] With supreme irony, they were therefore engaging in the very type of 'coaching' that they were accusing middle-class families of doing privately. The avalanche of criticism directed at grammar school admissions tests as well as the left-wing approach of adopting social engineering to achieve egalitarian aims had thus been absorbed by many of those running grammar schools themselves.

It appeared that it was the Liberal Democrat Schools Minister David Laws who was the motor behind the free school meals admissions policy as well as the designing of 'fairer' tests that were resistant to coaching. Indeed, Laws, educated at the independent St George's College Weybridge, wanted all selective schools to aim for the same proportion of children on free school meals in their schools as in their local area. In the case of potential local objections to the Pupil Premium policy, Laws emphasized that as long as the technical details in the school's funding agreement with the Education Secretary reflected this, 'then there is no case for schools to answer'.[17] The impact of the Liberal Democrats within the coalition government was therefore being particularly felt in the area of education, with grammar schools being morally pressured to comply with 'progressive' socio-political objectives.

Nevertheless, in June 2014 following a complaint from a parent the Birmingham grammar schools' policy was found to be contravening the funding agreement rule signed by the Education Secretary. The complaint was that schools should not give priority to children according to the financial and educational status of the parents applying and that it was therefore 'unreasonable' for two children with the same experience and scores to be treated differently based on parental income. However, the objection was merely upheld on a technicality rather than in any fundamental terms. The Office of the Schools Adjudicator (OSA) ruled that one of the Birmingham schools had simply not yet made necessary changes to their funding agreement with the Education Secretary to implement the changes for the 2015 academic year.[18] The OSA nevertheless maintained that the rules now gave schools the right to discriminate in favour of poorer pupils. The school leaders remained confident that they could make the admissions change from 2016.

Further revisions made to the School Admissions Code reinforced the right of schools to discriminate using the Pupil Premium with changes that came into force in December 2014.[19] Nine months later, it was revealed that Birmingham's five state grammar schools had doubled their admission of 'disadvantaged' pupils in a single year by setting a lower qualifying score in their 11 plus test by 7 per cent for Pupil Premium pupils compared with those considered more affluent.[20]

The ambiguity of Michael Gove and the Department of Education became further heightened when in December 2013 it was revealed that the annexe proposal for Sevenoaks had been turned down by the Department of Education's Funding Agency. It was claimed that it did not fulfil the legislative criteria laid down in New Labour's 1998 Act, and that it thus constituted an attempt to open a new selective school. Paul Carter, the leader of Kent County Council, was understandably furious at the decision. Such a conclusion at this time was extraordinary, given that the government had recently approved a considerable number of new 'free' schools, which were state-funded but independent of local authorities, of different sizes and religious denominations.

It therefore appeared the Conservative-led coalition had no intention of reversing Labour's 1998 legislation due to fears of a rift with the Liberal Democrats who they felt would not accept this. However, Carter claimed that at a recent meeting with Gove the Education Secretary had assured him that he would be open to accepting fresh proposals. As Carter said, given their massive expansion of the 'free' schools policy, this was 'an uncomfortable position' for a Conservative-led government to be in.[21]

In July 2014 David Cameron suddenly moved Gove from his position in a cabinet reshuffle. Gove had proved a divisive and disliked figure from the standpoint of the teaching unions and educational establishment, not least for his attempts to introduce more rigour into the national primary and secondary curriculums and reform the GCSE exam. He was replaced by Nicky Morgan, who had been Financial Secretary to the Treasury and had little experience in education. But in December 2014, there was some suggestion that she too might be prepared to accept new annexe proposals for the Sevenoaks area.[22]

Still, in early 2015 with a general election looming that summer, Cameron was hedging his bets. He was simply confining himself to stating that 'good schools' should be able to expand in response to parental demand.[23] There was now speculation that the decision over whether to approve Britain's first 'new' grammar school was being deliberately shelved until after the general election. At the same time, plans were being unveiled to open 500 new 'free' schools with an extra 270,000 places as part of Gove's reforms.[24] The situation thus epitomized the opaque machinations of the Cameron-led coalition. Nothing was quite what it appeared.

A small victory for selection

Following the Conservative Party's unexpected victory with a small majority in the general election in May 2015, there appeared to be greater conviction on their part in regard to the Sevenoaks annexe. On 14 October, it was announced that Morgan, who had retained her post at education, was expected to accept the latest annexe proposal from Kent County Council.[25] It would form part of the Weald of Kent girls' grammar school and would enrol 450 girls starting in September 2017. Of course, Morgan wished to emphasize that this in no way represented an actual increase in the number of grammar schools nor a change in the government's position on selection.[26] It would not, as she put it, 'open the floodgates,' and any new proposals for grammar schools would have to go through the existing legislation that included Labour's 1998 Act.[27]

Nevertheless, pro-comprehensive pressure groups such as Comprehensive Future claimed that the government had circumvented the law in allowing this process to occur. They also complained that they were not in a position to mount a judicial review to the annexe as the government had delayed their opportunity to examine the plans detailing how it would function.[28] In fact, the pro-comprehensive campaigners were strictly correct in that the annexe proposal by Kent County Council did represent their taking advantage of a legal loophole. This had had to be the case because the Conservative government still did not have the political courage to scrap the 1998 legislation.

Under the new Cameron government, Morgan would faithfully continue the academies and free schools policy, and showed every inclination to back the educational status quo. Indeed, she defended conventional GCSE exams and urged independent schools not to take the International or 'IGCSE' exams which many preferred, with Morgan claiming that they were not sufficiently rigorous when in fact the evidence was to the contrary. Her argument was that the Government's reforms to the GCSE had restored rigour to the exam.[29] She also aroused controversy as a result of unveiling the latest stage in the Cameron education policy by telling a NASUWT Conference in March 2016 that every secondary school was set to become an academy by 2022 and invited the unions to help shape the reforms. This aroused great opposition, including among Tory backbenchers, who claimed that it would force small rural schools to close.[30] The policy was in fact soon dropped and became intended only for underperforming local authorities.

Moreover, following the political convulsions set in train by the European Union referendum in June 2016 and the victory for the Leave campaign that triggered Cameron's resignation from office, the new Prime Minister Theresa May sacked Morgan from education and replaced her with the former Secretary for International Development Justine Greening.

Selective schools to work for 'everyone'

The recently anointed Theresa May, riding on a tide of popularity as the woman who would manage the UK safely through leaving the European Union, was bullish. Strikingly, in September 2016 she announced that secondary schools would be given the opportunity to become academically selective if they chose, thus hinting at a considerable number of new grammar schools being created for the first time in over fifty years. As a result, May proclaimed in deliberately populist rhetoric, Britain would be 'a country that works for everyone,' rather than for 'the privileged few.'[31] The Autumn Statement of 2016 confirmed that there would be £50 million per year of new funding to expand existing grammar schools.

Of course, the May government knew there would be considerable opposition to the plans, particularly coming from the House of Lords that was disproportionately made up of Labour and Liberal Democrat peers, as well as from within the Conservative Party itself. The government's consultation *Schools that Work for Everyone* thus contained a whole set of terms that the new or expanding selective schools would have to adopt. Predictably, they would have to take a substantial quota of youngsters from disadvantaged backgrounds. If they did not, the schools would have to fulfil other government requirements in order to receive funding. These included sponsoring an under-achieving non-selective academy or alternatively setting up a primary 'feeder' school in areas with a high proportion of low-income families and to engage in 'outreach' programmes. Thus, a plethora of social engineering requirements were to be imposed on new or expanding grammar schools in order to prove their commitment to 'social mobility.' Selective schools were to be held 'to account' for their partnered non-selective schools' success with sanctions for future funding streams and even their ability to select by ability in future potentially threatened.³² Universities and independent schools were to have similar obligations involving 'fair access,' the sponsorship of non-selective state schools and partnership schemes imposed on them. These were tied to their being able to charge higher fees and to retain their charitable status, respectively.³³ No doubt the May government considered this the only way to get the policy approved, given the hostile make-up of the House of Lords. Yet it also showed that the Conservative government, whether out of conviction, calculation or a mixture of the two, had again absorbed the arguments of the academic left regarding grammar schools. In practice, it appeared to be conceding that without egalitarian social requirements foisted on them, grammar schools adversely affected 'social mobility.'

The March 2017 budget earmarked £320 million for 140 new free schools that the new selective schools would be part of. The Chancellor of the Exchequer Philip Hammond was also promising that free school transport would be made available for up to 15 miles for poorer pupils attending a grammar school.³⁴ Strikingly, Theresa May's chief advisor Nick Timothy was an alumni of the King Edward VI grammar school in Birmingham that was part of the foundation that had spearheaded the Pupil Premium idea, and was himself a key architect behind the policy. This was clearly a government that believed in tinkering from the centre in educational politics.

As noted earlier, the previous Cameron-led coalition government had already funded state schools according to their proportions of 'Pupil Premium' pupils. There were lower proportions of grammar school pupils eligible for free school meals, a key aspect of the Pupil Premium qualification, at 2.5 per cent in 2016 compared with the national average across all secondary schools of 13.2 per cent.³⁵ Grammar schools were therefore already being financially penalised compared with the non-selective majority. By now enforcing Pupil Premium quotas requirements further, along with a raft of social obligations involving partnership and outreach, the tentacles of the May government were going to be all over any new selective schools that materialized.

Yet despite these caveats, there was concerted opposition to the policy nevertheless. This included from the former Education Secretary Nicky Morgan, who joined forces with Nick Clegg of the Liberal Democrats and Lucy Powell of the Labour Party as a triumvirate to openly oppose it. The trio then published an article in *The Observer* newspaper claiming that grammar schools damaged social mobility and that the government's approach would reverse positive changes that had occurred due to Coalition policies.³⁶ Similarly, academics such as Anna Vignoles of Cambridge University and the Conservative MP Neil Carmichael who headed the all-party Education Select Committee claimed that grammar schools adversely affected non-selective schools in their areas and damaged social mobility for the poorest pupils in spite of the actual evidence for this being thin. In addition, they claimed that there were not enough 'gains' for pupils in non-selective schools in grammar school areas. Noticeably, the academics Rebecca Allen and David Jesson in their contributions to the Select Committee gave grammar schools no credit for developing academic pupils' performance and claimed that they were 'wrongly rewarded' due to their pupils being at the higher end of the attainment profile and for progress they had already made before the age of 11.³⁷ The whole issue was being viewed through the lens of closing the attainment gap in favour of the most disadvantaged, as opposed to any other section of society. Grammar schools' existence was thus held to be contingent on the achievement of pupils in non-selective schools and those held to be 'disadvantaged.' Ultimately, the most negative interpretation possible of the government's policy was made by Carmichael in the committee's conclusions.[38] Meanwhile, pressure groups such as the Sutton Trust were continually making pin-pricks against grammar schools for their social class composition amid their calls for 'contextual admissions' for selective schools and universities and other social engineering requirements.[39]

And then disaster struck the May government. Having called a surprise general election in June 2017, it suffered a humiliating result by falling eight seats short of an overall majority. May was only able to then form a majority government with the Democratic Unionist Party of Northern Ireland. As a result, there was no Education Bill contained within the Queen's Speech in June. Despite optimistic noises coming from Graham Brady in the immediate aftermath about modest pilot schemes in inner-city areas, there was now little prospect for any major future developments in selective schooling.[40] Yet at the end of 2017 Theresa May was still sounding vague sentiments about continuing the policy of allowing existing grammar schools to expand on their sites with Nick Gibb the Schools Minister justifying the government's position, albeit in distinctly egalitarian terms, by continuing to claim that the 'attainment gap' between richer and poorer pupils was reduced more in grammar schools than in their non-selective counterparts.[41]

In spite of the fact that the ban on new selective schools would be retained, the government's response to the *Schools that Work for Everyone* consultation announced a new £50 million selective school expansion fund for 2018–19. A Memorandum of Understanding was also issued between the Department for Education and the Grammar School Heads Association, whose members now included the vast majority of grammar schools. 'Fair access,' partnership and outreach schemes involving local primary schools for disadvantaged and Pupil Premium pupils were inevitably reinforced.[42] A joint understanding was also issued between the Department and the Independent Schools Council with similar terms involving teacher and facilities sharing and minority subject support expected. In spite of this, the education secretary Damian Hinds was at pains to underline what a small percentage of funding grammar schools were receiving from the overall capital budget compared with the comprehensive majority. Hinds emphasized in response to repeated Labour opposition attacks that 'there is no extra revenue funding for grammar schools' and that they would in fact receive less money per pupil compared with non-selective schools.[43]

There were sixteen grammar schools that were ultimately successful in their bids for expansion in December 2018. Most of them, according to reports, had committed to lowering their pass mark requirements for those receiving the Pupil Premium as part of 'fair access' requirements.[44] Anna Vignoles of Cambridge University argued that to rely on actual pass results, including even the use of Pupil-Premium favouring 'tie-breakers' to decide between two pupils with the same scores, would mean richer children would inevitably gain the vast majority of places. Quotas and lower passmarks continued to be advocated.[45] Ironically, Vignoles's fellow witness to the 2016 education select committee, the director of Education Data Lab Rebecca Allen has, albeit unintentionally, pointed out the problems of favouring poorer pupils in this way. She has described how those grammar schools that encounter difficulties meeting these requirements will potentially have to 'dip so far down' in their ability intake that those pupils are likely be conspicuously different from their classmates. It would therefore mean entry requirements being 'loosened' to such an extent that the relevant schools would no longer be regarded as selective.[46] Yet there is now major financial pressure from government on the limited number of existing selective schools to comply in this manner.

In March 2019 it was announced that two more Kent schools, Queen Elizabeth Grammar School in Faversham and Barton Court Grammar School in Canterbury, were hoping to build satellite campuses if granted government funds.[47] Following the repeated failure of Theresa May's Brexit negotiations, she resigned as Prime Minister in May 2019, with her successor Boris Johnson ultimately gaining a resounding majority of eighty in the general election of December 2019.

A summation

The previous nine years represented huge opportunities missed. The coalition's decision to relax restrictions and allow expansion showed that they were willing to extend a degree of latitude to selective schools. However, the presence of the Liberal Democrats provided a cover for the Cameron-led coalition to embark on socially progressive goals for them. In spite of the 2015 general election victory, there is little indication that Cameron would have overturned the ban on new grammar schools originating from the 1998 School Standards and Framework Act, given his position taken in 2006–7.

Theresa May had gone further by committing to the funding of new selective schools upon attaining office in 2016. Yet she displayed the modern Conservative Party tendency to try to square the two opposing circles of a supposed Tory belief in educational rigour with egalitarian angst about the unequal underperformance of poorer pupils relative to others within the state education system. The degree of social engineering targets that were to be imposed on any new selective schools that emerged meant they would have been effectively subservient to government and not free to run their admissions in their own particular interests. The lack of commitment to opposing the educational vested interests on principle thus remained, alongside the apparent desire to gain the acceptance of contemporary educational opinion. Any major developments regarding the number of selective state schools now look distinctly unlikely. This is due not least to the impact of 'lockdown' policies implemented during the Coronavirus pandemic of 2020 which, amongst other consequences, destabilized the education system.

Yet regardless of these unprecedented events, Boris Johnson has long shown ambiguous signals on selective state education. While appearing in 2014 to lament grammar schools' disappearance in previous decades as a 'a real tragedy for this country' and creditably admitting that he himself is both the beneficiary and user of selection within an independent sector that runs 'absolutely ruthless' selection, he has nevertheless painted the selection process of the past as 'brutal.'[48] Indeed, in carefully roundabout fashion he ultimately defended David Willetts's attack on selection in 2007, noticeably describing the past in similarly derogatory terms to that of David Cameron as a 'shaming sheep and goats' separation of children.[49] While the 2019 Conservative Party manifesto emphasized choice for parents and the £50 million selective school expansion fund was kept, reports suggested the Department for Education had no plans for major legislative change in this area. The Education Secretary Gavin Williamson was more concerned about 415 'stuck schools' in the Midlands and North of England and to vaguely 'raising standards' in existing ones.[50]

In March 2022, Williamson's successor Nadhim Zahawi signalled the protection of grammar schools' status if they joined multi-academy trusts. This led to hopes of potential funding for selective schools and sixth form colleges in the northern 'Red Wall' seats that were instrumental in Boris Johnson's general election victory in 2019. It was felt by some Conservative backbench MPs that this could be a key aspect of the government's otherwise opaque 'levelling up' agenda. However, a Department for Education spokesman hastily confirmed that there were no plans to permit the opening of new grammar schools.[51]

At the time of writing, since Johnson's resignation as Prime Minister, the Conservative Party leadership candidates Liz Truss and Rishi Sunak have both made noises about supporting grammar schools and potentially increasing their numbers. Indeed, Truss went out on a limb, and suggested that she would end the existing ban on the establishment of new selective schools. By contrast, Sunak was noticeably careful to add that there was, 'a lot we can do with the school system as we have it.'[52] It was later clarified by his team that he meant merely the possible expansion of existing grammars. It will be fascinating to see if anything materialises in this vein. Nevertheless, given the long-standing tendencies noted throughout this book, those in 2022 hoping fervently for the restoration of grammar schools any time soon would be well advised not to hold their breath.

11

A need for honesty

The development of comprehensive schools in Britain cannot simply be portrayed as a 'bottom-up' phenomenon. It involved Conservative ministers of education giving their approval both directly and indirectly through signals of encouragement emanating from the top. Successive Conservative governments' calculated ambivalence at key moments, such as the 1958 White Paper *Secondary Education for All*, which was contained within the approach of ministers such as David Eccles, Geoffrey Lloyd and Edward Boyle, greatly contributed to its steady development by local authorities during this period.

According to Anthony Quinton, while morality is a matter of universal principles, politics 'is a matter of the expedient pursuit of the public advantage,' and an emphasis on 'expediency, convenience and public advantage' is a necessary condition for the long-term survival of the Conservative Party.[1] This will mean a great deal of flexibility in relation to practical policy and include, in the words of W. H. Greenleaf, 'piecemeal concession.'[2] Iain Gilmour, a renowned 'wet' who reflected this highly influential tendency within the Party, felt this meant 'removing grievances before they fester,' leading to 'greater moderation' by Labour governments.[3] This book has noted these recurring tendencies within Conservative governments' education policies over several decades.

The long-term consequences of the British political establishment's group-think regarding state schooling have been profound. In 2021, the subject of secondary education is now dominated by egalitarian-oriented social engineering to try to advance state comprehensive school pupils and those from 'disadvantaged' backgrounds in comparison with those considered more affluent and who are educated within the often highly selective independent sector. Impositions have been imposed on universities involving quotas, offers of lower grades as well as special 'foundation' years for students from lower socio-economic backgrounds.[4] Both Oxford and Cambridge colleges as well as the other Russell Group universities are actively involved in these schemes. It is noticeable that this accelerated during both the Cameron Coalition and May governments. Ever-increasing pressures from the Office for Fair Access are placed on leading universities and employers' organizations, and have continued under the pragmatic Boris Johnson.

By measuring the British state education system in terms of pupils' performance in the GCSE examination at the age of 16, there is inevitably no questioning of whether there should instead be different 'tracks' by this age, with separate but flexible academic, technical and vocational training and apprenticeship routes. This has long been the case in Germany, Austria and Switzerland with different pathways established for pupils by the age of 10 or 11. This is a somewhat premature stage for pupil sorting, but there is evidence to suggest that the system has become more flexible in recent decades. Furthermore, in Germany there are advanced technical and vocational training schools for 15- to 16-year-olds named *Berufsschule,* that both the federal government and industrial groups and trade unions financially support and supervise, as well as technical universities termed *Technische Hochschulen* that exist as alternatives to the academic route. Both the Czech Republic and Poland have different tracks for pupils by the age of 15, based on a tripartite structure that offers vocational and technical routes alongside the academic. In addition, the Czech Republic enables gradated stages of selection at the ages of 11, 13 and at 15 to the academic *gymnazium.* Italy, with a similar population size and land mass to that of England, introduces the more academic high school *liceo* involving classical, scientific and fine arts strands at the age of 14, while different types of teacher training, artistic, technical and professional *instituto* are provided for pupils seeking vocational training. This process involves all pupils undergoing the same state-mandated academic curriculum in the first two years with specialized courses termed *indirizzi* beginning in the third year of what is normally a five-year course.

Even those of a pro-comprehensive and social democratic mindset, such as the education historian Susanne Wiborg, have acknowledged, albeit indirectly, the almost innate difficulty England has had in incorporating comprehensive education due to its particular historical and political development. This is highlighted by comparison with the Scandinavian countries of Denmark, Sweden and Norway. These societies established social-democratic mainstream political norms in the late nineteenth century with alliances made between rural interests and white-collar professionals in favour of notions of liberty that favoured equality and what Wiborg terms 'social integration.'[5] This naturally led to egalitarian education systems in all three countries which, revealingly, sought to avoid the 'enhancement' of academic standards at the expense of 'social cohesion.'[6] By contrast England, with its political culture grounded to a far greater degree in classical liberalism amid a stratified social structure that militated inevitably in favour of parallel and differentiated school arrangements, could not do this without the upheaval of existing institutions of renowned quality.

Today, discussion of the existing selective grammar and independent schools in England is characterised by attacks from highly influential organizations such as the Sutton Trust for the socio-economic backgrounds of their pupils, with their abilities often disparaged. Policies of social engineering favouring those considered disadvantaged are therefore advocated for these schools' admissions.[7] By contrast, the state comprehensive system has rationalizations routinely made for it because the underlying problem, namely the destruction of rigour associated with selection by ability, is too painful for political and media elites to admit. The supreme irony is that over the last forty years comprehensive schooling alongside cultural egalitarianism has led to the dominance of the independent schools as well as the very widening of the gulf between them and the state sector that the progressive-minded claim to abhor.

Principled individuals must fight for the preservation of objective quality and truth against the politics of envy and identity, which includes the 'doctoring' of results and admissions to suit socio-political requirements. Historically, the British Conservative Party has not fought these battles unequivocally. Instead of the cynical retreat that this book has documented, those who object to this must turn and fight.

Notes

Introduction

1 S. Harris, '"Grammars just fuel privilege," claims Archbishop Welby as he attacks proposals to expand selective schools,' *Daily Mail*, 9 December 2017.

Chapter 1

1 *Report of the Consultative Committee on The Education of the Adolescent* (HMSO, 1926), para.87.
2 Ibid, para.88.
3 See paras.87–9.
4 Ibid, para.88.
5 Ibid, para.94.
6 Ibid, p.xxi.
7 Ibid, para.177.
8 Ibid, para.170.
9 Ibid, para.81.
10 Ibid, para.93.
11 Ibid, para.90.
12 P. Gordon, R. Aldrich & D. Dean, *Education and Policy in the Twentieth Century* (The Woburn Press, 1991), p.178.
13 *Report of the Consultative Committee on Secondary Education with Special Reference to Grammar Schools and Technical High Schools* (HMSO, 1938), p.307.
14 Ibid, p.106.
15 Ibid, p.296.
16 Ibid, p.291.
17 Ibid, p.292.
18 Ibid, p.319.
19 Ibid, p.339.
20 Ibid, p.340.
21 Ibid.
22 *Report of the Committee of the Secondary Schools Examinations Council on Curriculum and Examinations in Secondary Schools* (HMSO, 1943), p.2.
23 Ibid.
24 Ibid, p.3.
25 Ibid.
26 Ibid, p.4.
27 Ibid, p.5.
28 Ibid, p.15.

29 Ibid, p.16.
30 Ibid, p.15.
31 Ibid, p.18.
32 Ibid, p.70.
33 R.A. Butler, *The Art of the Possible* (Penguin, 1973), p.88.
34 The 1936 Education Act had originally sought to raise the school leaving age to 15, but the Second World War intervened and delayed its implementation.
35 Butler, *Art of the Possible*, p.92.
36 Ibid.
37 Ibid, pp.92–3.
38 Ibid, p.93.
39 W.S. Churchill to R.A. Butler, 13 September 1941, Butler Papers, Trinity College, Cambridge, G13.
40 Butler, *Art of the Possible*, p.96.
41 A. Howard, *Rab: The Life of R.A. Butler* (Jonathan Cape, 1987), pp.118–19.
42 Ibid, p.120.
43 Ibid.
44 Butler, *Art of the Possible*, p.121.
45 Ibid, p.121.
46 Howard, *Life of Butler*, p.122.
47 Ibid, p.123.
48 R.A. Butler to A. Dunglass, 18 October 1941, Butler Papers, G13. See also K. Jefferys, 'R.A. Butler, The Board of Education and the 1944 Education Act,' *History*, vol 69, no 227 (1984), pp.426–8.
49 Board of Education, *Educational Reconstruction* (HMSO, 1943), para.1.
50 Ibid, para.17.
51 Ibid, para.18.
52 Ibid, para.27.
53 Ibid, p.31.
54 Ibid, para.28.
55 Ibid, para.29.
56 Ibid, para.31.
57 Butler, *Art of the Possible*, p.125. In his ambiguous way, Butler would go onto bemoan the way that the grammar schools had since been turned into a 'political football' through the 'obsessive insistence of the Labour Party on a doctrinal rather than an empirical approach to composite or comprehensive schemes of secondary organisation.' p.125. In this vein, he proposed, writing in 1971 at the height of comprehensive reorganization, simply 'to take another look at the wide variety of secondary experiments so that knowledgeable advice and not dictation can be given to education authorities.' Butler was always one for the oblique statement.
58 Education Act, 1944, 7 & 8 GEO. 6. CH.31, Section 68, p.51.
59 Butler, *Art of the Possible*, p.124.
60 Ibid.
61 Central Committee on Post-war problems education sub-committee, file no 7, 'The School Leaving Age and Continued Education,' Butler Papers, Trinity College, Cambridge, H70, p.261.
62 Ibid.
63 Ibid.
64 Ibid, p.262.

65 Ibid.
66 Ibid.
67 Ibid, p.263.
68 N. Middleton & S. Weitzman, *A Place for Everyone*, Appendix: The Green Book, 'Education After the War,' June 1941 (Victor Gollancz Ltd, 1976), p.398.
69 Central Committee, 'Chairman's Tentative Suggestions for Discussion,' 30 March 1944, Butler Papers, H70, p.45.
70 Ibid.
71 G. Faber to Sir D. Maxwell Fyfe, 5 March 1945, Butler Papers, H70, p.196.
72 Central Committee, 'The School Leaving Age and Continued Education,' Butler Papers, H70, p.263.
73 Ministry of Education, *The Nation's Schools: Their Plan and Purpose* (HMSO, 1945), p.21
74 Ibid, p.23.
75 Ibid, p.24.
76 Ibid, p.26.
77 Ministry of Education, *The New Secondary Education* (HMSO, 1947), pp.22–3.
78 Ibid, p.55.
79 Ibid, p.56.
80 Ibid, p.57.
81 See R. McKibbin, *Classes and Cultures* (Oxford University Press, 1998), pp.226–7.
82 Conservative Party Education Committee, (49) 2, 1st July 1949, 'A Note on Education for the Supply Day on Tuesday, 5 July 1949,' p.1.
83 H. Linstead, *What do you think? ... About Education* (Conservative Political Centre, 1949), p.6.
84 Ibid, p.5.
85 See R. Law, *Return from Utopia* (Faber and Faber, 1950), pp.179–200 for an example of these concerns.
86 Conservative and Unionist Party, *The Right Road for Britain* (Conservative and Unionist Central Office, 1949), p.7.
87 Ibid, p.8.
88 Ibid, p.43.
89 Ibid.
90 Ibid, p.44.
91 Hansard, 24 July 1951, vol 491, col.328.
92 Ibid, col.324.
93 R. Barker, *Education and Politics, 1900–1951: A Study of the Labour Party* (Oxford University Press, 1972), p.83.
94 The Labour Party, *A Policy for Secondary Education* (The Labour Party, 1951), pp.8–12.
95 Hansard, 24 July 1951, vol 491, cols.250, 265.
96 Ibid, col.265.

Chapter 2

1 R.A. Butler to F. Horsbrugh, 4 October 1952, ED 136/892.
2 Horsbrugh to Butler, 17 October 1952, ED 136/892.
3 Ministry of Education, 'Major Policy Changes,' 13 October 1952, ED 136/892.

4   Memorandum by the Chancellor of the Exchequer on supply expenditure, 30 January 1953, CAB/129/58.
5   See meeting of the Cabinet, 28 July 1953, CAB 128/26.
6   See Butler to Horsbrugh, 7 October 1953, ED 136/890 and Horsbrugh to Butler, 27 October 1953, ED 136/890.
7   The Labour Party, *Challenge to Britain* (Labour Party, 1953), p.21.
8   Ibid, p.22.
9   'No Rigid Pattern: Miss Horsbrugh on the Comprehensive Schools,' *The Manchester Guardian*, 20 February 1953.
10 Ibid.
11 'Miss Horsbrugh's Faith in the "Modern" School,' *The Manchester Guardian*, 3 July 1953.
12 See *Report of the 52nd Annual Conference of the Labour Party*, pp.166–77 for account of the Party conference on the issue.
13 Ibid, p.168.
14 See *Education*, Journal of Association of Education Committees, 16 October 1953, pp.535–6.
15 B. Simon, *Education and the Social Order 1940–1990* (Lawrence & Wishart, 1991), pp.172, 203.
16 K. Jones, *Education in Britain: 1944 to the Present* (Polity Press, 2016), pp.48,51,103.
17 R. Lowe, *Education in the Post-War Years: A Social History* (Routledge, 1988), pp.120,133,140.
18 G. McCulloch, *Failing the Ordinary Child? The Theory and Practice of Working-Class Secondary Education* (Open University Press, 1998), pp.91–109, M. Sanderson, *The Missing Stratum: Technical School Education in England 1900–1990s* (Bloomsbury Academic, 2015), pp.129–53.
19 *Official Report of the 73rd Annual Conference of the National Union of Conservative and Unionist Associations, 1953*, pp.38–42.
20 See Hansard, 4 June 1954, vol 528, cols.1603–4 & 1627–8.
21 Ibid, col.1625.
22 Ibid, cols.1635–8.
23 *Education*, Journal of Association of Education Committees, 4 December 1953, p.826.
24 Educational correspondent, 'The Liberal Policy for Education,' *Observer*, 12 September 1954.
25 The Conservative and Unionist Teachers' Association was one of the National Advisory Committees created on the recommendation of the Maxwell-Fyfe Committee on Party Organisation in 1947. It was intended to facilitate better communication between the National Union and Conservative Central Office on educational matters. It was serviced by an educational department along with a secretary based within Central Office.
26 Conservative and Unionist Teachers' Association, 'Report on Secondary Education,' 27 February 1954, p.2, ED 147/206.
27 Ibid, p.2.
28 Ibid, p.8.
29 Ibid, p.10.
30 Ibid, p.11.
31 Ibid, p.13.
32 Lord Swinton to Horsbrugh, 14 April 1954, ED 136/896.

33　There were, ironically, parallels between Horsbrugh's position here and Margaret Thatcher's difficulties with school milk twenty years later.
34　Hansard, 15 July 1954, vol 530, col.682.
35　Cabinet memorandum by the Minister of Education, 'Education Policy,' 12 November 1954, CAB 129/71.
36　Ibid.
37　Internal memorandum in Ministry of Education, 3 January 1955, ED 147/207.
38　D. Eccles to secretary, 'Our meeting on secondary education,' 22 February 1955, ED 147/206.
39　Ibid.
40　Minutes of meeting on secondary education, 23 February 1955, ED 147/206, p.1.
41　Ibid, p.3.
42　Ibid, p.4.
43　Ibid, p.6.
44　Ibid, p.8.
45　Ibid, p.11.
46　Ibid, p.12.
47　Ibid.
48　Ibid, p.13.
49　Minister's meeting, Secondary Education (Examinations) 9 March 1955, ED 147/206, p.2.
50　Ibid, p.3.
51　Ibid, p.4.
52　David Eccles speech to the National Union of Teachers Conference, Scarborough, 13 April 1955, ED 147/209, p.2.
53　Ibid, p.3.
54　Ibid, p.4.
55　Ibid.
56　Memorandum for the Cabinet by the Minister of Education, 'Secondary Education,' 20 April 1955, CAB 129/75, p.1.
57　Ibid, p.2.
58　Ibid.
59　Hansard, 26 April 1955, vol 540, col.823.
60　Ibid, col.813.
61　Ibid, col.791.
62　Ibid, col.851-2.
63　Joint Committee of the Four Secondary Associations to Sir Anthony Eden, 11 May 1955, ED 147/209.
64　Sir Anthony Eden to Joint Committee of the Four Secondary Associations, 20 May 1955, ED 147/209.
65　Ibid.
66　Eccles to Sir Anthony Eden, 'Education Policy,' 6 June 1955, PREM 11/1785.
67　Eccles to Butler, 10 August 1955, ED 136/894.
68　Butler to Eccles, 2 November 1955, ED 136/894.
69　Eccles to Butler, 3 November 1955, ED 136/894.
70　Hansard, 24 January 1957, vol 563, col.373.
71　Ibid, col.1301.
72　Ibid, cols.374-5.
73　Hansard, 14 March 1957, vol 566, col.1282.

74　J. E. Floud (ed.), *Social Class and Educational Opportunity* (Greenwood Press, 1973), pp.146-9.
75　Ibid, pp.57-8.
76　Ibid, pp.148-9.
77　R. Pedley, *Comprehensive Education: A New Approach* (Victor Gollancz Ltd, 1956), pp.164-79, 195-203.
78　Hansard, 5 April 1957, vol 568, col.731.
79　Ibid, col.759.
80　Ibid, col.760.
81　Ibid, col.762.
82　Ibid.
83　Ibid, cols.762-3.
84　'Education Policy', Conservative Research Department, 6 May 1957, ACP/57/55, p.3.
85　R. Birley to Lord Hailsham, 14 January 1957, Hailsham Papers 2/3/7.
86　Hailsham to Birley, 17 January 1957, Hailsham Papers 2/3/7.
87　'Education Policy', Conservative Research Department, ACP/57/55, pp.3-4.
88　Ibid, p.5.
89　Ministry of Education, 'Interview Memorandum', 29 March 1957, ED 147/624.
90　Ibid, pp.4-5.
91　Cabinet Home Affairs Committee meeting, 19 July 1957, CAB 134/1968.
92　'Educational: Capital Expenditure', Memorandum by the Minister of Education, 11 October 1957, CAB 129/89.
93　Meeting of the Cabinet, 15 October 1957, CAB 128/31.
94　*Official Report of the 77th Annual Conference of National Union of Conservative and Unionist Associations, 1957*, p.112.
95　Ibid, p.114.
96　Minutes of meeting of the Conservative Parliamentary Education Committee, 23 June 1958, p.5, CRD 2/33/6.
97　The Labour Party, *Learning to Live: A Policy for Education from Nursery School to University* (Labour Party, 1958), p.33.
98　Ibid, p.60.
99　Minutes of meeting of the Conservative Parliamentary Education committee, 7 July 1958, pp.1-2, CRD 2/33/6.
100　Ibid, p.2.
101　Ibid, p.3.
102　Ibid, p.4.
103　Ibid.
104　Minutes of meeting of the Conservative Parliamentary Education Committee, 14 July 1958, p.3, CRD 2/33/6.
105　Ibid.
106　Ibid, p.7.
107　Ibid, p.8.
108　Ibid, p.9.
109　Memorandum by the Minister of Education, 'A Drive in Education', 14 July 1958, p.1, CAB/129/93.
110　Ibid, p.3.
111　Ibid.
112　Ibid, p.4.
113　Meeting of the Cabinet, 24 July 1958, CAB/128/32.

114 G. Lloyd to Lord Hailsham, 6 October 1958, CCO 4/8/75.
115 Hansard, 31 July 1958, vol 592, cols.1571–2.
116 Ibid, col.1573.
117 This potential problem had been forewarned in Ministry of Education, *Early Leaving: A Report of the Central Advisory Council for Education (England)* (HMSO, 1954), paras.54–5. The Report emphasized the importance of greater grammar school provision as part of its key recommendations. Eccles found this overall message most unwelcome and counter to his own approach, as he put it in the foreword to the report.
118 Hansard, 31 July 1958, vol 592, col.1578.
119 Conservative and Unionist Party, *Onward in Freedom* (Conservative and Unionist Central Office, 1958), p.24.
120 *Education*, 3 October 1958, pp.551–2.
121 *Official Report of the 78th Annual Conference of the National Union of Conservative and Unionist Associations, 1958*, pp.67–8.
122 Ibid, p.68.
123 Ibid.
124 Ibid, p.69.
125 Ibid, p.70.
126 *Education*, 17 October 1958, pp.633–4.
127 *Official Report of 78th Annual Conference*, pp.71–3.
128 Ibid, pp.73–4.
129 *Education*, 10 October 1958, p.604.
130 H. C. Dent, *Secondary Modern Schools: An Interim Report* (London: Routledge & Kegan Paul, 1958), p.v.
131 Ibid, p.185.
132 Ibid, p.176.
133 *Secondary Education for All: A New Drive* (HMSO, 1958), para.10, ED 136/942.
134 Ibid, para.15.
135 Ibid, para.19.
136 Ibid, para.20.
137 Ibid, para.20.
138 Ibid, para.21.
139 Ibid, para.36.
140 Meeting of the Cabinet, 25 November 1958, CAB/128/32.
141 M. Eckstein, 'Britain's White Paper on Education and Its Implications,' *Comparative Education Review*, vol 3 (June 1959), p.20.
142 G. Lloyd to H.Macmillan, 30 December 1958, PREM 11/2643.

Chapter 3

1 Minutes of meeting of Conservative Parliamentary Education Committee, 8 December 1958, CRD 2/33/6, p.4.
2 Ibid, p.7.
3 H. Macmillan speech, 19 January 1959, from 'Education Under the Conservatives,' CCO 4/8/75, p.11.
4 D.H. Morrell to J.E.R. Wyndham, 6 January 1959, PREM 11/2643, p.22.
5 E. Boyle, 'Comprehensive schools in rural areas,' CCO 4/8/75, p.4.

6   Colonel R. Glyn to G. Lloyd, 21 January 1959, ED 147/637.
7   Boyle to Glyn, 10 February 1959, ED 147/637.
8   H. Lee to W.H.L. Urton, 31 January 1959, CCO 4/8/75.
9   Ibid.
10 R.M. Fraser to W.H.L. Urton, 5 February 1959, CCO 4/8/75.
11 H. Lee to W.H.L. Urton, 14 February 1959, CCO 4/8/75.
12 'Backbench Criticism of Schools Policy,' *Daily Telegraph*, 2 March 1959.
13 H. Macmillan to G. Lloyd, 8 March 1959, PREM 11/2644.
14 G. Lloyd to H. Macmillan, 23 March 1959, PREM 11/2644.
15 Ministry of Education minute sheet, 'Building Programme Submissions: Comprehensive Schools,' 26 March 1959, ED 147/640.
16 G. N. Flemming to Lloyd & Boyle, 1 April 1959, ED 147/640.
17 Boyle to Flemming, 7 April 1959, ED 147/640.
18 T.R. Weaver to Mr Jameson, Ministry of Education, 20 April 1959, ED 147/640.
19 See Memorandum by the Chancellor of the Exchequer, 'The Crowther Report,' 15 March 1960, CAB 129/101.
20 Ministry of Education brief, L. R. Fletcher to Mr Weaver, 29 March 1960, ED 147/641.
21 Ibid, p.2.
22 Ibid, p.3.
23 Ministry of Education, 'Notes on Various Forms of Secondary School Organisation,' 10 December 1960, p.7, ED 147/641.
24 Ibid, p.8.
25 M. Smieton to D. Eccles, 9 March 1961, ED 147/641.
26 Boyle to K. Thompson, April 1961, ED 147/641.
27 Thompson to Boyle, undated, ED 147/641.
28 House of Commons Debates, 5 July 1961, vol 643, cols.130–1W.
29 House of Commons Debates, 13 July 1961, vol 644, col.553.
30 Conservative and Unionist Teachers' Association, 'The State of Secondary Schools (including comprehensive) with Special Reference to Organisation, Examinations and Curricula,' 28 October 1961 (Interim Report), ED 147/641.
31 D. Eccles to Miss B. Turner, Secretary of Conservative and Unionist Teachers' Association, 14 December 1961, ED 147/641.
32 Ibid.
33 Memorandum by the Chief Secretary to the Treasury and Paymaster-General, 'Educational Expenditure,' 8 December 1961, CAB 129/107.
34 Memorandum by the Minister of Education, 'Education Policy,' 4 January 1962, CAB 129/108.
35 J.F. Snowden to I. Macleod, 7 June 1962, CCO 4/9/137.
36 Private correspondent to I. Macleod, 19 June 1962, CCO 4/9/137.
37 K. Thompson, 9 July 1962, CCO 4/9/137.
38 Minutes of a meeting of the Conservative Parliamentary Education Committee, 26 November 1962, CRD 2/33/6.
39 Conservative and Unionist Teachers' Association, 'The State of Secondary Schools (including comprehensive) with Special Reference to Organisation, Examinations and Curricula,' 2nd Interim Report, 8 December 1962, ED 147/641.
40 Ministry of Education minute sheet, Miss W.H. Harte, 16 January 1963, ED 147/641.
41 E. Boyle to Miss B. Turner, 30 January 1963, ED 147/641.
42 Conservative and Unionist Party, *Conservative Care for Education* (Conservative and Unionist Central Office, 1963), p.3.

43 Ibid.
44 *Report of the Committee Appointed by the Prime Minister under the Chairmanship of Lord Robbins 1961-63* (HMSO, October 1963), pp.151-2, 159-61.
45 Conservative and Unionist Party, *Educational Opportunity* (Conservative and Unionist Central Office, 1963), pp.3-4.
46 Conservative and Unionist Party, *This is Conservative Policy for Education* (Conservative and Unionist Central Office, 1963), pp.7-9.
47 House of Commons Debates, 11 July 1963, vol 680, cols.1400-1.
48 *Half Our Future: A Report of the Central Advisory Council for Education (England)* (HMSO, 1963), foreword, p.iv.
49 Ibid, p.xvi.
50 Ibid.
51 Ibid, paras.15-21.
52 Ibid, para.277.
53 Ibid, para.288.
54 Ibid, para.292.
55 Ibid, para.330.
56 E. Boyle to G. Woodcock, 10 December 1963, ED 147/642.
57 Minutes of the meeting of the Conservative Parliamentary Education Committee, 17 February 1964, p.2, CRD 2/33/6.
58 Ibid, p.3.
59 Minutes of the meeting of the Conservative Parliamentary Education Committee, 16 March 1964, p.3, CRD 2/33/6.
60 Ibid, p.4.
61 Hansard, 21 April 1964, vol 693 col.1104.
62 Ibid, col.1105.
63 Ibid, col.1106.
64 Minutes of the meeting of the Conservative Parliamentary Education Committee, 29 June 1964, p.1, CRD 2/33/6.
65 Ibid, p.4.
66 Conservative and Unionist Party, *Strategy for Schools* (Conservative Political Centre, 1964), p.47.
67 Ibid, p.68.
68 Ibid, p.62.
69 Hansard, 9th April 1964, vol 257, col.261.
70 Hansard, 1 July 1964, vol. 697, col.1419.
71 Ibid, col.1429.
72 Ibid, col.1452.
73 Ibid, col.1466-8.
74 Ibid, col.1474-5.
75 See Hansard, 14 May 1964, vol 695, cols.577-8.
76 Hansard, 1 July 1964, vol 697, col.1482.
77 Ibid, col.1484.
78 Ibid, col.1491.
79 B. Simon, *Education and the Social Order 1940-1990* (Lawrence& Wishart, 1991), p.172.
80 I. G. K. Fenwick, *The Comprehensive School 1944-1970* (Methuen, 1976), pp.64, 72-3.
81 Ibid, p.107.
82 Ibid, p.148.
83 B. Simon, 'The Tory Government and Education, 1951-60: Background to Breakout,' *History of Education*, vol 14, no 4 (1985), p.295.

84 Ibid, pp.293–4.
85 R. Lowe, *Education in the Post-War Years: A Social History* (Routledge, 1988), pp.148–9.
86 Ibid, p.144.
87 G. McCulloch, *Failing the Ordinary Child? The Theory and Practice of Working Class Secondary Education* (Open University Press, 1998), p.91.
88 Ibid, p.96.
89 D. Eccles, memo, 'Secondary education,' 18 September 1956, ED 147/636.
90 R.H. Heaton, memo, 'Secondary education,' 2 October 1956, ED 147/636.
91 Ibid.
92 McCulloch, *Failing the Ordinary Child*, p.96.
93 Interview memo, Dr R. Pedley with Minister of Education, 16 October 1956, ED 147/636.
94 McCulloch, *Failing the Ordinary Child*, p.94.
95 P. Mandler, *The Crisis of the Meritocracy: Britain's Transition to Mass Education Since The Second World War* (Oxford University Press, 2020), p.62.
96 Ibid, pp.50–5, pp.62–6.
97 D. Dean, 'Preservation or Renovation? The Dilemmas of Conservative Educational Policy 1955–1960,' *Twentieth Century British History*, vol 3, no 1 (1992), p.22.
98 Ibid, pp.7–8, 17–18, 21–2.
99 Ibid, p.22.
100 Ibid, p.30.
101 Ibid, p.30.
102 According to Peter Gosden, the middle school system 'was adopted on a pragmatic basis in many areas as the best means by which to adopt the comprehensive system within the strict limitations of the existing building provision.' See P. Gosden, *The Education System Since 1944* (Martin Robertson, 1983), p.35.

Chapter 4

1   Hansard, 27 November 1964, vol 702, col.1705.
2   Ibid, col.1763.
3   Ibid, col.1783.
4   Ibid, col.1785.
5   Ibid, col.1800.
6   See 'Backbench Criticism of Schools Policy,' *Daily Telegraph*, 2 March 1959.
7   Hansard, 21 January 1965, vol 705, col.413.
8   Ibid, col.418.
9   Ibid, col.483.
10 Ibid, col.493.
11 Ibid, col.494.
12 Ibid, col.512.
13 Ibid, col.518.
14 Ibid, col.524.
15 Ibid, col.541.
16 Ibid.
17 E. Boyle, speech to the National Union of the Conservative and Unionist Association's Central Council, 6 March 1965, Boyle Papers MS 660/22929.

18 Ibid.
19 Minutes of the meeting of the Policy Group on Education and Careers Research, 7 March 1965, CRD 3/8/4, p.4.
20 Interim Reports of the Education and Careers Research Policy Group, Conservative Research Department, 'Independent, Direct Grant and Aided Schools,' 21 July 1965, ACP 3/13 (65) 16, para.4.
21 R.A. Butler, 'Policy Group Reports – Education,' Butler Papers, Trinity College, Cambridge, G44, pp.157–8.
22 'Need for Research in Britain: Swedes Lead the Way,' *The Times*, 8 April 1965.
23 'Changed scheme for "comprehensives,"' *The Times*, 8 April 1965.
24 R.B. Ward to E. Boyle, 29 June, Boyle Papers, MS 660/25454.
25 Ward to Boyle, 9 July 1965, Boyle Papers MS 660/25458.
26 Department of Education and Science, 'The Organisation of Secondary Education,' *Circular 10/65*, (HMSO, 1965), para.39.
27 Ibid, para. 46.
28 E. Boyle to correspondent, 26 July 1965, Boyle Papers MS660/25466.
29 B. Turner to E. du Cann, 4 October 1965, CCO 4/9/19.
30 Request by National Advisory Committee of Conservative and Unionist Teachers' Association for clarification of policy on organization of secondary education, 2 October 1965, CCO 4/9/119.
31 Ibid.
32 B. Turner to Mr Craig, 5 October 1965, CCO 4/9/119.
33 E. du Cann to E. Boyle, 5 October 1965, CCO 4/9/119.
34 Ibid.
35 G. Longden to E. Heath, 8 October 1965, Longden Papers 9/12.
36 E. Boyle, speech to Conservative Party Conference, 14 October 1965, Boyle Papers MS 660/22934.
37 *Education*, 127, 14 January 1966, p.80.
38 Ibid, p.72.
39 E. Boyle to D. Lavington, 11 January 1966, Boyle Papers MS 660/25537.
40 E. Boyle to C. Hewlett, 31 January 1966, Boyle Papers MS 660/22843.
41 S. Jenkins, 'Secondary Reorganisation and Educational Priorities,' Education and Careers Research Policy Group, 25 February 1966, Conservative Party Archives, CRD 3/8/4.
42 Ibid.
43 Hansard, 2 March 1966, vol 725, col.1389–94.
44 Ibid, col.1402.
45 Ibid, col.1405.
46 Ibid, col.1410.
47 'School Building Programmes,' *Circular 10/66*, 10 March 1966, Department of Education and Science (HMSO), para.5.
48 *Action Not Words: The New Conservative Programme* (Conservative and Unionist Central Office, 1966) www.conservativemanifesto.com/1966/1966-conservative-manifesto.shtml.
49 University of Oxford, *Report of Commission of Inquiry* (Oxford University Press, 1966), vol ii, statistical appendix, p.47, table 31.
50 E. Boyle to J. More, 27 April 1966, Boyle Papers, MS 660/25643.
51 E. Heath to E. Boyle, 11 May 1966, Boyle Papers MS 660/25654.
52 See minutes of Leader's Consultative Committee meeting, 16 May 1966, Conservative Party Archives LCC 1/2/6.

53 C. Hewlett to E. Boyle, 24 May 1966, Boyle Papers, MS 660/22853.
54 E. Boyle to C. Hewlett, 8 June 1966, Boyle Papers, MS 660/22855.
55 G. Longden to E. Boyle, 25 May 1966, Longden Papers, 9/12.
56 In 1966, the Conservative and Unionist Teachers' Association changed its name to the Conservative National Advisory Committee on Education.
57 E. Boyle to G. Longden, 25 May 1966, Longden Papers 9/12.
58 E. Boyle to C. Hewlett, 14 June 1966, Conservative Party Archives, CCO 505/3/12.
59 G. Jones, 'An Approach to Secondary School Reorganisation,' 5 December 1966, Conservative Party Archives, CRD 3/8/4.
60 Ibid.
61 V. Talbot to E. Boyle, 17 January 1967, Boyle Papers, MS 660/25744.
62 E. Boyle to E. Heath, 18 January 1967, Boyle Papers, MS 660/25746.
63 E. Boyle to Alderman V. Talbot, 18 January 1967, Boyle Papers, MS 660/25745.
64 R.M. Fraser to E. Boyle, 20 January 1967, Boyle Papers, MS 660/25753.
65 Minutes of the fifth meeting of the Policy Group on Education, 26 January 1967, Conservative Party Archives, LCC 1/2/8.
66 E. Boyle, 'Secondary School Reorganisation,' 9 February 1967, Conservative Party Archives, LCC 1/2/8, LCC (67) 127.
67 Ibid.
68 Minutes of the eighth meeting of the Policy group on Education, 13 April 1967, Conservative Party Archives, CRD 3/8/4.
69 E. Boyle to W.H. Crossman, 8 June 1967, Boyle Papers, MS 660/25812.
70 E. Heath, speech to National Advisory Committee on Education, 17 June 1967, circulated by Conservative Central Office News Service, Gilbert Longden Papers 9/12.
71 S. Maclure, 'Mr Heath's Cautious Lead,' *Education*, 23 June 1967, p.1165. See also D. Crook, 'Edward Boyle: Conservative Champion of Comprehensives?' *History of Education*, vol 22, no 1 (March 1993), pp.49–62.
72 J. MacGregor to E. Boyle, 13 July 1967, Boyle Papers, MS 660/ 25832.
73 Q. Hogg to J.M.L. Prior, 22 June 1967, Boyle Papers, MS 660/25822.
74 R. Langstone to E. Heath, 3 October 1967, Boyle Papers, MS 660/25864.
75 E. Heath to A. Fletcher draft letter, 12 October 1967, Boyle Papers MS660/25864.
76 E. Boyle to J. Stevens, 13 October 1967, Boyle Papers MS 660/25865.
77 Ibid.
78 E. Boyle to A. Tillard, 18 October 1967, Boyle Papers, MS 660/25867.
79 *Official Report of the 85th Annual Conference of the National Union of Conservative and Unionist Associations,* 1967, p.55.
80 Ibid, p.58.
81 Ibid, p.59.
82 Ibid, p.60.
83 Ibid, p.61.
84 Ibid, p.62.
85 'Boyle rebuffed,' *Daily Telegraph*, 20 October 1967.
86 By contrast, the Guardian Newspaper claimed that Boyle had saved the Conservative Party 'from its wildest reactionaries' on educational policy. 'Saved from reactionaries,' *The Guardian*, 20 October 1967.
87 D. V. Donnison, 'Education and Opinion,' *New Society*, vol 10, no 265 (26th October 1967), pp.583–7.

88 D. Marsden, 'Politicians, Equality and Comprehensives,' in R. Bell, G. Fowler & K. Little, *Education in Great Britain and Ireland* (Routledge & Kegan Paul, 1973), pp.123–8.
89 P. Mandler, *The Crisis of the Meritocracy: Britain's Transition to Mass Education Since the Second World War* (Oxford University Press, 2020), pp.39–49, pp.50–71.
90 See R. Batley, *Going Comprehensive: Educational Policy-Making in Two County Boroughs* (Routledge & Kegan Paul, 1970), pp.39–40, pp.89–93.
91 S. Jenkins, *Conservatives and Comprehensives* (Conservative Political Centre, 1967), pp.7–9.
92 Hansard, 12 December 1967, vol 756, col.281.
93 Ibid, col.235–41.
94 E. Boyle to P. Baguley, 9 April 1968, Conservative Party Archives CCO 505/3/9.
95 'Conservative Education Policy for the Seventies,' a report by the Education Policy Group, (Conservative Central Office, 1968), paras.33–50, Conservative Party Archives, CRD 3/8/4.
96 Minutes of the Leader's Consultative Committee, 15 July 1968, Conservative Party Archive, LCC 1/2/13.
97 *Official Report of the 86th Annual Conference of the National Union of Conservative and Unionist Associations*, 1968, p.41.
98 Ibid, p.42.
99 Ibid, pp.45–6.
100 Ibid.
101 J. Godber to R.M. Fraser, 24 October 1968, Conservative Party Archives, CRD 3/8/5.
102 P. Walker to R.M. Fraser, 13 November 1968, Conservative Party Archives, CRD 3/8/5.
103 A. Maude to C.B. Cox, 22 January 1969, Cox Papers 1/2/1/171.
104 See A. Maude to C.B. Cox, 16 June 1969, Cox Papers 1/2/1/156.
105 Minutes of meeting of Conservative delegates with Sir Edward Boyle, 21 April 1969, Boyle Papers, MS 660/26063.
106 Hansard, 6 May 1969, vol 783, cols.259–62.
107 J. Roysten Moore to G. Longden, undated May/June 1969, CCO 5/3/26.
108 G. Longden to E. Heath, 19 June 1969, Longden Papers 9/12.
109 E. Heath to G. Longden, 26 June 1969, Longden Papers 9/12.
110 See G. Longden to R.B. Ward, 10 July 1969, Conservative Party Archives, CCO 505/3/26.
111 F.H. Hutty to E. Boyle, 25 September 1969, Conservative Party Archives, CCO 505/3/9.
112 E. Boyle to F.H. Hutty, 29 September 1969, Conservative Party Archives, CCO 505/3/9.
113 E. Boyle to D. Hurd, 30 September 1969, Boyle Papers, MS 660/26123.
114 J.E. Powell to A.E. Dyson, 7 October 1969, Cox Papers 1/2/1/201.
115 C.B. Cox to E. Boyle, 12 September 1969, Cox Papers, 1/1/1/73.
116 E. Boyle to C.B. Cox, 30 September 1969, Cox Papers 1/1/1/72.
117 *Conservative Party Annual Conference Report 1969*, pp.42–4, Boyle Papers, MS 660/22942.
118 M. Kogan, *The Politics of Education* (Penguin Books, 1971), p.115.

Chapter 5

1. 'Comprehensives may be best for new areas – Shadow Minister,' *Birmingham Post*, 23rd October 1969, www.margaretthatcher.org/document/101305.
2. Hansard, 31 October 1969, vol 790, col.539.
3. Ibid, col.563.
4. Ibid, col.555.
5. Ibid, col.568.
6. Ibid, col.594–5.
7. M. Thatcher to A.E. Dyson, 4 November 1969, Cox Papers 1/2/1/226.
8. R.R. Pedley to A.E. Dyson, 19 January 1970, Cox Papers 1/2/1/186.
9. M. Thatcher interview with B. MacArthur, *The Times*, 7 November 1969, The Times Digital Archive.
10. A. Maude, 'Tory Education Policy.' *The Times*, 15 November 1969, The Times Digital Archive.
11. See Margaret Thatcher correspondence with National Advisory Committee on Education, 13 November 1969, Conservative Party Archives, CCO 505/3/44.
12. Education Act 1944, 7 & 8 GEO. 6. CH.31, Section 1(1), p.1.
13. Hansard, 12 February 1970, vol 795, col.1476.
14. Ibid, col.1482.
15. Ibid, col.1509.
16. Ibid, col.1523.
17. Ibid, col.1529.
18. Ibid, col.1534.
19. Ibid, col.1566.
20. E. Short to W. Alexander, 26 March 1970, National Archives ED 207/151/2.
21. W. Alexander to E. Short, 28 April 1970, National Archives ED 207/151/2.
22. House of Commons Standing Committee [Education (recommitted) Bill], 5 May 1970, www.margaretthatcher.org/document/101744.
23. Conservative and Unionist Party, *Conservative 1970 Manifesto: A Better Tomorrow* (Conservative and Unionist Party, 1970), p.20, Conservative Party Archives, PUB 156/1.
24. Department of Education and Science, 'The Organisation of Secondary Education,' *Circular 10/70* (HMSO, 1970), paras.1–3.
25. Hansard, 8 July 1970, vol 803, col.678.
26. Ibid, cols.681–2.
27. Ibid, col.683.
28. Ibid, col.687.
29. Ibid, col.758.
30. Ibid, cols.761–2.
31. Ibid, col.764.
32. Ibid, col.776.
33. Ibid, cols.791–2.
34. Ibid, col.794.
35. M. Thatcher, Interview for *Finchley Press*, 26th June 1970, www.margaretthatcher.org/document/101777. See also M. Thatcher, Interview for *Finchley Times*, 26 June 1970, www.margaretthatcher.org/document/101766
36. A. Maude to C.B. Cox, 29 July 1970, Cox Papers 1/2/1/150.

37 M. Thatcher to C.B. Cox, 3 August 1970, Cox Papers 1/2/1/224.
38 Conservative Research Department, 'Notes on Current Politics,' 3 August 1970, No 11, pp.266–9.
39 P. Baguley to M. Thatcher, 12 August 1970, Conservative Party Archives CCO 505/3/44.
40 M. Thatcher to C. Hewlett, 1 September 1970, Conservative Party Archives CCO 505/3/44.
41 M. Thatcher, speech to Conservative Party Conference, 7 October 1970, www.margaretthatcher.org./document/101783
42 Private Office minute to E. Heath, 13 October 1970, PREM 15/823, www.margaretthatcher.org/document/109467
43 S. Jessel, 'Government against student loan scheme,' *The Times*, 12 November 1970.
44 Minute of Chequers meeting with E. Heath, 31 December 1970, PREM 15/864, www.margaretthatcher.org/document/109460
45 M. Thatcher, speech to Birmingham City Council Conservative Group, 12 March 1971, www.margaretthatcher.org/document/102095
46 See M. Thatcher, speech to National Union of Teachers Conference, 13 April 1971, www.margaretthatcher.org/document/102102
47 Hansard, 21 April 1971, vol 815, col.1199.
48 Ibid, col.1212.
49 Ibid, col.1237.
50 Ibid, cols.1289–90.
51 Chairman, County Borough of Derby Education Committee to M. Thatcher, 16 June 1971, CCO 505/3/46.
52 M. Thatcher, speech to Conservative Party Conference, 14 October 1971, www.margaretthatcher.org/document/102141
53 Hansard, 5 November 1971, vol 825, col.506.
54 Ibid, col.513.
55 Ibid, cols.516–17.
56 Ibid, col.519.
57 Ibid, cols.544–5.
58 Ibid, col.557.
59 Ibid, cols.563–4.
60 Ibid, col.565.
61 Department of Education and Science, minute of Chequers meeting with E. Heath, 12 January 1972, PREM 15/863, www.margaretthatcher.org/document/109464
62 Department of Education and Science, 'The Situation in Education,' Aide-Memoire by Secretary of State for Education, 11 January 1972, PREM 15/863, www.margaretthatcher.org/document/109464
63 Hansard, 5 November 1971, vol 825, col.510.
64 M.Thatcher, speech to National Union of Teachers, 4 April 1972, www.margaretthatcher.org/document/101949
65 R. Boyson, 'Turn of the tide in education?', *Daily Telegraph*, 21 January 1972. See also R. Boyson, *Battle Lines for Education* (Conservative Political Centre, 1973).
66 E. Boyle, 'The Politics of Secondary School Reorganisation: Some Reflections,' *Journal of Educational Administration and History*, vol 4, no 2 (June 1972), pp.37–8.
67 For a highly critical analysis of Mrs Thatcher's use of her ministerial powers, see R. Woods, 'Margaret Thatcher and Secondary Reorganisation, 1970–74,' *Journal Of Educational Administration and History*, vol. 13, no. 2, 1981, pp.51–61.

68 M. Thatcher, Interview for *Spectator*, 8 July 1972, www.margaretthatcher.org/document/101821
69 M. Thatcher, speech to Conservative Party Conference, 12 October 1972, www.margaretthatcher.org/document/102222
70 See Hansard, 19 October 1972, vol 843, cols.433–5.
71 See Hansard, 23 November 1972, vol 846, cols.1495–7.
72 M. Thatcher-G. Campbell minute to E. Heath reg. Education White Papers, 9 October 1972, PREM 15/931, www.margaretthatcher.org/document/109465
73 M.Thatcher to R. Bradbury, 6 December 1972, Thatcher Papers, Churchill Archives Centre, 1/6/1.
74 R. Butt, 'Tories who go too willingly to school,' *The Times*, 11 January 1973.
75 See M. Thatcher, Speech opening North of England Education Conference, 2 January 1973, www.margaretthatcher.org/document/102240
76 Conservative Research Department, *Notes on Current Politics – Education*, 29 January 1973, No 2, p.20.
77 Hansard, 1 February 1973, vol 849, cols.1639–43.
78 Ibid, col.1650.
79 Ibid, col.1668.
80 Ibid, cols.1743–4.
81 Ibid, col.1746.
82 '11 plus battle – Minister who hears but won't listen,' *Wallington & Carshalton Times*, 20 September 1973, Conservative Party Archives CCO 505/3/47.
83 'Tories "could win 1m votes" with fight against all-in schools,' *Daily Telegraph*, 6 August 1973.
84 Brief for the Secretary of State for Education and Science, 'Meetings with Education Correspondents 2 and 3 October,' Thatcher Papers, Churchill Archives Centre, 1/6/3.
85 E.W. Maynard Potts to G. Longden, November 1973, Gilbert Longden Papers 9/12.
86 G. Longden to E. W. Maynard Potts, 5 December 1973, Gilbert Longden Papers 9/12.
87 Hansard, 29 January 1974, vol 868, cc.238.
88 Conservative Central Office, Written Statement on education policy, originally published in *Times Educational Supplement,* 22 February 1974, www.margaretthatcher.org/document/102345
89 M. Thatcher to Prof J. Vaizey, 7 March 1974, www.margaretthatcher.org/document/110892.
90 M. Thatcher, *The Path to Power* (HarperCollins, 1995), p.184.

Chapter 6

1 Hansard, 1 May 1974, vol 872, col.1211.
2 See R. Boyson, *Parental Choice* (Conservative Political Centre, 1975).
3 W. van Straubenzee, Education paper for Conservative Research Department, 5 June 1974, Conservative Party Archives ACP 3/21A (74) 6.
4 'Opposition will help ministers on education,' *The Times*, 15 April 1974.
5 N. St John-Stevas, 'Schools: A return to quality,' *The Times*, 1 August 1974.
6 N. St. John-Stevas, Education paper for Conservative Research Department, 10 July 1974, Conservative Party Archives 3/21A (74) 6a.

7   S. Sexton to N. St. John-Stevas, 23 June 1974, Gilbert Longden Papers 9/12.
8   Hansard, 4 February 1976, vol 904, col.1228.
9   Ibid, col.1235.
10 'Mrs Williams says Opposition doing all they can to water down comprehensive principle,' *The Times*, 10 November 1976, The Times Digital Archive.
11 Hansard, 4 February 1976, cols.1284–5.
12 Ibid, cols.1318–19.
13 See Hansard, 14 June 1976, vol 913, col.35.
14 R. Butt, 'Five absent Tories who struck despair in Tameside,' *The Times*, 17 June 1976.
15 Leader's Consultative Committee 111th meeting, 19 May 1976, www.margaretthatcher.org/documents/110053
16 See Leader's Consultative Committee 115th meeting, 14 June 1976, www.margaretthatcher.org/documents/110061
17 'Freedom that led to chaos in school,' *The Glasgow Herald*, 17 July 1976, p.3. See also M. Jackson & J. Gretton, *William Tyndale: Collapse of a School – or a System?* (George Allen & Unwin, 1976).
18 See R. Boyson & C. B. Cox (eds), 'Letter to Members of Parliament,' in *Black Paper 1977* (Maurice Temple Smith, 1977), pp.5–10.
19 Hansard, 17 February 1977, vol 926, col.726.
20 N. St-John-Stevas, 'Conservative Policy on Education and the Arts,' 8 March 1978, www.margaretthatcher.org/document/109856.
21 See also N. St-John-Stevas, *Better Schools for All: A Conservative Approach to the Problems of the Comprehensive School* (Conservative Political Centre No. 617, 1977).
22 R. Butt, 'Cutting the monster schools to size,' *The Times*, 23 March 1978.
23 Ibid.
24 See also S. Sexton, 'Evolution by Choice,' in C.B. Cox & R. Boyson (eds), *Black Paper 1977* (Maurice Temple Smith, 1977), pp.86–9.
25 'Bid to Damp Down Stevas-Boyson School Examinations Row,' *Financial Times*, 25 September 1978.
26 C. B. Cox, 'We are all (or nearly all) Black Paper-ers now,' *The Times*, 2 March 1979.
27 C. B. Cox, 'Tories must restore faith in education,' *The Times*, 20 April 1979.

Chapter 7

1   M. Carlisle to N. St John Stevas, 18 May 1979, PREM 19/732, f229, www.margaretthatcher.org/document/137796
2   See R. Boyson, 'The Essential Conditions for the Success of a Comprehensive School,' in C. B. Cox & A. E. Dyson (eds), *Black Paper Two* (Critical Quarterly Society, 1969), p.60. See also N. St John-Stevas, speech to Conservative Party Conference, 11th October 1977, Oxford, Bodleian Libraries, NUA 2/1/81.
3   See Hansard, 16 July 1979, vol 970, cols.1097–160.
4   Hansard, 12 February 1980, vol 978, col.1456.
5   Ibid, cols.1433–76.
6   Hansard, 19 February 1980, vol 979, cols.99–100W.
7   See M. Pattison minute to M. Thatcher, 29 February 1980, PREM 19/201 f10, www.margaretthatcher.org/document/118659

8   M. Carlisle to M. Thatcher, 21 April 1980, PREM 19/732, f 166, www.margaretthatcher.org/document/137794
9   Ibid.
10 N. Sanders to M. Thatcher, 21 April 1980, PREM 19/732, f 163-4, www.margaretthatcher.org/document/137794
11 Hansard, 6 May 1980, vol 984, cols.6-9.
12 R. Butt, 'Give the schools back to the people,' *The Times*, 8 May 1980.
13 See R. Boyson to M. Thatcher, 16 December 1980, THCR 1/6/8 (3), www.margaretthatcher.org/document/119214
14 K. Joseph, 'Five Year Forward Look,' [Department of Education and Science plans for the next five years] 22 December 1982, THCR 1/15/10, f 176, www.margaretthatcher.org/document/123016
15 N. Ridley minute to G. Howe, 25 January 1983, www.margaretthatcher.org/document/136574
16 *Conservative Campaign Guide 1983*, 1 April 1983, p.201, www.margaretthatcher.org/document/110800
17 See Hansard, 22 November 1983, vol 49, cols.104-5, cols.152-4.
18 See Hansard, 6 December 1983, vol 50, col.190.
19 See K. Joseph, speech to North of England Education Conference, Sheffield, 6 January 1984, *Oxford Review of Education*, vol 10, no 2, pp.137-46 and Department of Education and Science, *Better Schools* (HMSO, 1985), pp. 29-32.
20 K. Joseph to M. Thatcher, 6 March 1986, PREM19/1722, f 252-4.
21 B. Griffiths to M. Thatcher, 7 March 1986, PREM 19/1722, f 249-50.
22 M. Addison to M. Smith, [record of PM discussion reg. GCSE examination] 20 March 1986, PREM 19/1722, f 226-7.
23 K. Joseph to M. Thatcher, 'How to Get Better Schools,' 26 March 1986, PREM 19/1722, f 131.
24 See K. Joseph minute to M. Thatcher, 'How to Get Better Schools,' 26 March 1986, PREM 19/1722, f 124-41.
25 See B. Griffiths to M. Thatcher, 3 April 1986, PREM 19/1722, f 76-82 & 14 April 1986, PREM 19/1722, f 49-54.
26 See D. Norgrove to R. Smith, [account of PM discussions on 'How to Get Better Schools,'] PREM 19/1722, 29 April 1986, f 6-8 & PREM 19/1723, 15 May 1986, f 280-2.
27 See General Election Press Conference, 22 May 1987, www.margaretthatcher.org/document/106828
28 Hansard, 17th October 1989, vol 158, cols. 12-3.

Chapter 8

1   J. O'Leary, 'Grammar schools plague Tory ministers,' *The Times*, 4 February 1992, The Times Digital Archive.
2   J. O'Leary, 'Major rules out return to selective education,' *The Times*, 29 June 1992. See also F. Jarvis, *Education and Mr Major* (The Tufnell Press, 1993), pp.25-6, 33-4.
3   Jarvis, *Education*, p.35.
4   S. MacLure, 'Back to the 11 plus?' *The Times*, 2 May 1992.
5   J. O'Leary, 'Grammar schools rescue fails,' *The Times*, 5 March 1992, The Times Digital Archive.

6   Department for Education, *Choice and Diversity: A New Framework for Schools* (HMSO, 1992) p.10.
7   Hansard, 9 November 1992, vol 213, col.636.
8   Ibid, col.653.
9   R. Balchin, 'No return to selection in grant-maintained schools,' *The Times*, 4 July 1994.
10 J. O'Leary, 'Shephard dashes hopes of reviving grammar schools,' *The Times*, 12 September 1994.
11 Hansard, 26 April 1995, vol 258, cols.812–15.
12 Ibid, col.818.
13 Ibid, col.817.
14 S. Jenkins, 'School for control freaks,' *The Times*, 25 October 1995.
15 See J. O'Leary, 'Shephard promises more selection,' *The Times*, 24 November 1995. See also Department for Education and Employment, *Self-Government for Schools* (HMSO, 1996), pp 23–4.
16 S. Jenkins, 'A selective memory,' *The Times*, 10 January 1996. Jenkins never acknowledged the inconsistencies within his own worldview. Indeed, he keenly defended the Labour MP Harriet Harman against the charge of hypocrisy for having sent her son to the selective St Olave's school in Orpington, stating that he was 'on her side.' According to Jenkins, there was 'no incompatibility in seeking to reform a public service and yet continuing to use it in its pre-reformed state.' In addition, if an individual did not like part of the welfare state he was free to opt out and go private, provided that he paid taxes 'to benefit the rest.' By contrast, the question of how best to organize the public sector of education was 'a different matter. It involves public money and should be based on equity.'
17 S. Jenkins, 'Tough on hypocrisy,' *The Times*, 24 January 1996.
18 P. Webster & J. O'Leary, 'Major goes into battle over schools,' *The Times*, 20 March 1996.
19 J. O'Leary, 'Shephard cool on new grammar era,' *The Times*, 12 March 1996.
20 G. Shephard, Interview for *On the Record*, 28 April 1996, BBC Online.
21 Hansard, 20 March 1996, vol 274, cols.367–70.
22 Department for Education and Employment, *Self-Government for Schools* (HMSO, 1996), p.44.
23 Ibid, p.37.
24 D. Charter, 'Grammar school chief doubts Major pledge,' *The Times*, 26 April 1996.
25 P. Webster & D. Clarke, 'Tory council criticises more pupil selection,' *The Times*, 10 October 1996.
26 Hansard, 11 November 1996, vol 285, col.41.
27 Ibid, col.106.
28 J. Sherman, 'Blair selects grammars for attack,' *The Times*, 28 April 1997.
29 Department for Education, *Higher Education: A New Framework* (HMSO, 1991), p.2.
30 See J. Major, Speech on Opportunity, 19 March 1996, https://johnmajorarchive.org.uk/1996/03/19/mr-majors-speech-on-opportunity-19-march-1996

Chapter 9

1   School Standards and Framework Act 1998, sections 99 (2) & 104.
2   See Hansard, 20 October 1999, vol 336, cols.361–83.

3   R. Smithers & M. Wainwright, 'Parents vote to retain Ripon grammar school,' *The Guardian*, 11 March 2000.
4   See Hansard, 27 June 2000, vol 352, cols.758–84.
5   See Hansard, 15 July 2002, vol 389, cols.117–26.
6   See Hansard, 30 October 2003, vol 412, cols.425–7.
7   See Hansard, 10 April 2002, vol 383, col.195–6W.
8   See Hansard, 6 February 2002, vol 379, cols.972–82.
9   Department for Education and Skills, *Higher Standards, Better Schools for All* (HMSO, 2005), pp.25–8.
10 Education and Inspections Act 2006, sections 39 & 40.
11 Press Association, 'Kelly renews pledge on schools admissions,' *The Guardian*, 9 February 2006, P. Webster & D. Charter, 'Read my lips: no schools that select will be allowed to grow,' *The Times*, 16 March 2006.
12 See R. Bennett, 'Selection is good for us, not for you,' *The Times*, 24 May 2006.
13 T. Happold, 'Howard to stand down as Tory leader,' *The Guardian*, 6 May 2005.
14 B. Balchin, 'See me after school please, Mr Cameron,' *The Times,* 9 January 2006.
15 D. Cameron, speech to Conservative Party Conference, 1 October 2006, https://conservative-speeches.sayit.mysociety.org/speech/599995
16 A. Frean, 'Blair's teacher argues for selection in state schools,' *The Times*, 4 October 2006. See also National Grammar Schools Association, 'Seventy per cent want more grammar schools,' ngsa.org.uk/nlet-may2006.php
17 D. Willetts, speech to CBI Conference on Public Service Reform, 16 May 2007, https://conservativehome.blogs.com/torydiary/files/better_schools.pdf
18 See G. Brady, 'Brady's stance on Grammar schools,' *New Statesman*, 16 May 2007, https://www.newstatesman.com/uk-politics/2007/05/grammar-schools-brady-children
19 F. Elliott & A. Frean, 'Cameron faces a revolt over his grammar schools policy,' *The Times*, 17 May 2007.
20 Ibid.
21 See F. Elliott, 'Senior Tory retreats after grammar schools attack,' *The Times*, 18 May 2007.
22 See F. Elliott & G. Hurst, 'Cameron attacks "deluded" grammar school defenders,' *The Times*, 22 May 2007.
23 D. Cameron, 'This sterile fixation with grammar schools is a dead end,' *The Times*, 22 May 2007.
24 A. Frean and G. Hurst, 'Tories want to increase right of selection by secondary schools,' *The Times*, 22 May 2007.
25 A. Miles & H. Rumbelow, 'Grammar-school boy risks a caning for telling Tories state academies are the way to go,' *The Times*, 26 May 2007.
26 Ibid.
27 H. Mulholland, 'Cameron promises "grammar streaming" in schools,' *The Guardian*, 18 June 2007.
28 S. Coates, 'Tory faces sack after defying Cameron on grammar schools,' *The Times*, 29 May 2007.
29 A. Atkinson, P. Gregg & B. McConnell, *The Result of 11 plus Selection: An Investigation into Opportunities and Outcomes for Pupils in Selective LEAs* (The Centre for Market and Public Organisation 06/150, University of Bristol, 2006), p.27.
30 R. Ryan, 'Tory frontbencher resigns over grammar schools,' *The Guardian*, 29 May 2007.

31 T. Branigan, 'Tories in confusion as Willetts seeks to reassure rebels over grammar schools,' *The Guardian*, 1 June 2007. P. Webster, 'Cameron faces U-turn taunts after another MP mangles his grammar,' *The Times*, 1 June 2007.
32 S. Coates, 'That's life, shrugs Cameron after 18 days of grammar school chaos,' *The Times*, 2 June 2007.
33 Ibid.
34 G. Hurst, 'Cameron, back after half-term, vows to end grammars row,' *The Times*, 4 June 2007.
35 ConservativeHome's Tory Diary, 'Grassroots members send a protest message to leadership Conservative Home poll,' 3 June 2007, https://conservativehome.blogs.com/torydiary/2007/06/grassroots_memb.html
36 The Sutton Trust, *University Admissions by Individual Schools* (The Sutton Trust, 2007), p.32, https://image.guardian.co.uk/sys-files/Education/documents/2007/09/20/Strust.pdf
37 See N. Woolcock, 'Handful of independent schools seize a third of Oxbridge places,' *The Times*, 20 September 2007.
38 See A. Frean, 'Grammar schools accused of creating "ghettos for the advantaged,"' *The Times*, 21 November 2007.
39 J. Coldron, E. Tanner, E. Finch, S. Shipton, L. Wolstenholme, & C. Willis, *Secondary School Admissions* (DCSF Research Report RR020, 2008), pp.192–200.
40 A. West, E. Barham, & A. Hind, *Secondary School Admissions in England: Policy and Practice* (Research and Information on State Education Trust, 2009), pp.3–5. See also A. Frean, 'Schools face curbs on backdoor selection,' *The Times*, 3 March 2009.
41 N. Woolcock, 'Balls attacks grammar school elitism for making less academic pupils feel a failure,' *The Times*, 20 June 2008.
42 G. Paton, 'David Cameron warned over grammar schools policy,' *Daily Telegraph*, 24 September 2008. See also National Grammar Schools Association, 'Letter to David Cameron,' 21 September 2008, https://ngsa.org.uk/com-009.php
43 See A. Seldon, 'How to bridge the great classroom class chasm,' *The Times*, 19 May 2008.
44 See S. Jagger, 'Blair inspired my education policies, top Tory says,' *The Times*, 24 August 2009.
45 The Conservative Party, *Raising the Bar, Closing the Gap*, Policy Green Paper No. 1 (Conservative Party, 2007), pp.43–4.
46 M. Gove, speech to Centre for Policy Studies, 6 November 2009, https://conservative-speeches.sayit.mysociety.org/speech/601248
47 J. Sugden & R. Taylor, 'Parents paying for top prep schools to secure places in best grammars,' *The Times*, 3 October 2009.
48 L. Clark, 'Grammar schools growing – despite Labour laws designed to stop selective schooling,' *Daily Mail*, 26 June 2008.
49 A. Lipsett, 'School admissions code tightened up,' *The Guardian*, 4 December 2008.
50 P. Curtis, 'Government bars state schools from offering International GCSE,' *The Guardian*, 4 November 2009.
51 See F. Elliot, 'Awkward squaddie refuses to march to Cameron's drum,' *The Times*, 1 May 2010.

Chapter 10

1. Grammar Schools Survey CATI Fieldwork: February 5–72010, Prepared on behalf of the National Grammar Schools Association by ICM Research, https://www.ngsa.org.uk/downloads/ICM_Grammar_Schools_Poll_Feb7_2010.pdf
2. G. Paton, 'Grammar schools "should be expanded"', *Daily Telegraph*, 9 February 2010.
3. G. Paton, 'More pupils turning to grammar schools,' *Daily Telegraph*, 14 May 2010.
4. M. Kite, 'Grammar schools will be allowed to expand,' *Daily Telegraph*, 30 October 2010.
5. See G. Paton, 'Grammar schools "should be allowed to expand," says Gibb', *Daily Telegraph*, 23 June 2011.
6. D. Marley, 'Call to help the poor access grammars,' *Tes News*, 3 July 2009.
7. D. Gardham, 'Grammar schools get go-ahead to expand,' *Daily Telegraph*, 11 December 2011.
8. G. Paton, 'A green light for more grammar schools?' *Daily Telegraph*, 10 January 2012.
9. See P. Stanford, 'Parents triumph in the battle to expand grammar school places,' *Daily Telegraph*, 29 March 2012.
10. See G. Paton, 'Grammar school entry threshold "inflated by coaching,"' *Daily Telegraph*, 16 March 2012.
11. J. Henry, 'Grammar school tests to be made "tutor-proof,"' *Daily Telegraph*, 4 November 2012. See also D. Jesson, 'Grammar schools in the 21st century and "social mobility,"' 17 January 2010, http://www.davidjesson.com/2010/01/grammar-schools-in-the-21st-century-and-social-mobility/
12. C. Cook, 'Grammar school myths,' *Financial Times*, 28 January 2013. See also J. Cribbs, Professor D. Jesson, L. Sibiela, A. Skipp & Professor A. Vignoles, *Poor Grammar: Entry into Grammar Schools for Disadvantaged Pupils in England* (Sutton Trust, November 2013).
13. D. Boffey, 'Ofsted chief declares war on grammar schools,' *The Guardian*, 14 December 2013.
14. See The Conservative Party, *Raising the Bar, Closing the Gap*, Policy Green Paper No. 1, (Conservative Party, 2007), pp.41–2.
15. G. Paton, 'Grammar schools "distorted in favour of middle-classes,"' *Daily Telegraph*, 30 November 2013.
16. G. Paton, 'Grammar schools "to favour poor pupils in admissions,"' *Daily Telegraph*, 1 May 2014.
17. D. Laws, speech to Grammar School Heads Association, 19 June 2014, https://www.gov.uk/government/speeches/david-laws-speech-on-grammar-schools
18. G. Paton, 'Grammar schools "barred from giving priority to the poor,"' *Daily Telegraph*, 12 June 2014.
19. See Department for Education, *School Admissions Code*, December 2014, paras.1.9(f), 1.39A–1.39B.
20. R. Garner, 'Grammar schools set lower pass mark for poorer children,' *Independent*, 25 March 2015.
21. G. Paton, 'Plan for new grammar school blocked by Michael Gove,' *Daily Telegraph*, 13 December 2013.
22. R. Tingle, 'Calls to open a large number of grammar schools,' *Daily Telegraph*, 22 December 2014.

23 R. Mason, 'David Cameron backs new grammar schools after pressure from Tory right,' *The Guardian*, 17 February 2015.
24 C. Hope, 'Grammar schools can expand, says David Cameron,' *Daily Telegraph*, 9 March 2015.
25 N. Harley, 'First grammar school in 50 years to be approved,' *Daily Telegraph*, 14 October 2015.
26 House of Commons Written Statement 242, 15 October 2015, vol 600, cols. 25–6WS.
27 S. Coughlan, 'First "new" grammar school in 50 years,' 15 October 2015, https://www.bbc.co.uk/news/education-34535778
28 J. Gurney-Read, 'Grammar school expansion legal challenge dropped,' *Daily Telegraph*, 11 January 2016.
29 E. Malnick, 'Private schools should drop "less challenging" IGCSEs, says Education Secretary,' *Daily Telegraph*, 29 January 2015.
30 S. Coughlan, 'Teachers' union votes for strike ballot over academies,' 26 March 2016, https://www.bbc.co.uk/news/education-35905064
31 T. May, 'Britain, the great meritocracy,' 9 September 2016, https://www.gov.uk/government/speeches/britain-the-great-meritocracy-prime-ministers-speech See also P. Dominiczak, 'All schools get chance to become grammars,' *Daily Telegraph*, 9 September 2016.
32 Department for Education, *Schools that Work for Everyone: Government Consultation* (Crown copyright, 2016), p.26.
33 Ibid, pp.14–16 & pp.18–20.
34 H. M. Treasury (ed.), *Spring Budget 2017* (Crown copyright, 2017), p.42. See G. Rayner, 'Theresa May unveils plans for new generation of grammar schools,' *Daily Telegraph*, 7 March 2017.
35 Department for Education 2016, 'Schools, Pupils and their Characteristics' and Education Policy Institute analysis of underlying data, September 2016.
36 N. Morgan, L. Powell & N. Clegg, 'On this we can all agree. Selection is bad for our schools,' *Observer*, 19 March 2017.
37 House of Commons Education Committee, *Evidence check: Grammar schools*, Fourth Report of Session 2016–17, p.11.
38 'Government must show new grammar schools close attainment gap,' 13 February 2017, https://committees.parliament.uk/203/education-committee/news/102531/government-must-show-new-grammars-close-attainment-gap/
39 C. Cullinane, *Gaps in Grammar*, Sutton Trust Research Brief, Edition 15, December 2016.
40 See B. Kentish, 'Grammar schools: Flagship Tory education plan "likely to be derailed by election failure,"' *The Independent*, 11 June 2017 & R. Pells, 'Queens's speech: Theresa May's grammar school expansion plans scrapped,' *The Independent*, 21 June 2017.
41 See E. Harding, 'We've not given up on grammars, says May: PM backs expansion of selective schools for first time since election,' *Daily Mail*, 17 October 2017.
42 Department for Education, *Schools that Work for Everyone: Government Consultation Response* (Crown copyright, 2018), pp.11–13.
43 Hansard, 14 May 2018, vol 641, col.46.
44 K. Sellgren, 'The 16 grammars that have won funds to expand,' *BBC News*, 3 December 2018.
45 B. Jeffreys, 'Grammar schools: Thousands of new places created,' *BBC News*, 1 August 2018.

46 See House of Commons Education Committee, *Evidence Check: Grammar Schools*, p.19 & Education Data Lab, *Research Briefing: Grammar Schools*, September 2016.
47 C. Turner, 'First new grammar school could open under the Theresa May expansion plan,' *Daily Telegraph*, 21 March 2019.
48 S. Weale, 'Boris Johnson gives backing to grammar schools,' *The Guardian*, 11 November 2014.
49 B. Johnson, 'Grammar schools are not a magic bullet,' *Daily Telegraph*, 17 May 2007.
50 W. Hazell, 'Government rules out more grammar schools and bids to focus resources on raising standards,' *inews*, 18 January 2020.
51 See C. Turner, 'Grammar schools to be protected in shake-up of education system,' *Daily Telegraph*, 25th March 2022.
52 H. Stewart, 'Ben Wallace endorses Liz Truss as Sunak backs new grammar schools,' *The Guardian*, 29th July 2022.

Chapter 11

1 A. Quinton, *The Politics of Imperfection* (Faber and Faber, 1978), p.11.
2 W. H. Greenleaf, *The British Political Tradition: The Ideological Heritage, Volume 2* (Methuen, 1983), p.212.
3 I. Gilmour, *Inside Right* (Hutchinson, 1977), p.129.
4 See C. Turner, 'Cambridge to admit students who fail to make the A grade,' *Daily Telegraph*, 13 January 2021.
5 See S. Wiborg, 'The Enduring Nature of Egalitarian Education in Scandinavia: An English perspective,' *Forum*, vol 51, no 2 (2009), pp.117–30.
6 Ibid, p.122.
7 J. Cribb, Professor D. Jesson, L. Sibiela, A. Skipp & Professor A. Vignoles, *Poor Grammar: Entry into Grammar Schools for Disadvantaged Pupils in England* (Sutton Trust, November 2013), pp.7–8, 20–1.

Bibliography

Place of publication is London, unless otherwise shown.

Manuscript sources

Boyle Papers, Brotherton Library, Leeds
Butler Papers, Trinity College, Cambridge
Churchill Papers, Churchill College, Cambridge
Conservative Party Archive, Bodleian Library, Oxford
Cox Papers, John Rylands Library, Manchester
Hailsham Papers, Churchill College, Cambridge
Horsbrugh Papers, Churchill College, Cambridge
Longden Papers, London School of Economics and Social Science Archives
National Archives, London: (specific references to i) Cabinet papers and minutes, ii)
    Ministry and Department of Education (and Science) archives are provided in the notes.)
Thatcher Archives, Churchill College, Cambridge

Official publications

Report of the Consultative Committee on the Education of the Adolescent (Sir Henry Hadow) 1926
Report of the Consultative Committee on Secondary Education with Special Reference to Grammar Schools and Technical High Schools (Sir Will Spens) 1938
Curriculum and Examinations in Secondary Schools. Report of the Committee of the Secondary Schools Examinations Council (Sir Cyril Norwood) 1943
Educational Reconstruction (Cmnd. 6458) 1943
Education Act 1944 7 & 8 Geo. 6. Ch.31, 1944
The Nation's Schools, Their Plan and Purpose, Ministry of Education pamphlet no.1 (1945)
The New Secondary Education, Ministry of Education pamphlet no.9 (1947)
Hansard, House of Commons Debates, 1951 - present
Early Leaving: A Report of the Central Advisory Council for Education (HMSO, 1954)
Secondary Education for All: A New Drive, 136/942 (1958 White Paper)
Fifteen to Eighteen [The Crowther Report] (HMSO, 1959)
Half Our Future [The Newsom Report] (HMSO, 1963)
Children and Their Primary Schools [The Plowden Report] (HMSO, 1967)
Educational Priority, EPA Problems and Policies, vol. 1 (HMSO, 1972)
Education: A Framework for Expansion (Cmnd.5174) (1972 White Paper)
Better Schools (HMSO, 1985)

Higher Education: A New Framework (HMSO, 1991)
Choice and Diversity: A New Framework for Schools (HMSO, 1992)
Self-Government for Schools (HMSO, 1996)
School Standards and Framework Act, 1998
Higher Standards, Better Schools for All (HMSO, 2005)
Education and Inspections Act, 2006
Schools Admissions Code, December 2014
Schools That Work for Everyone: Government Consultation (2016)

Conservative Party publications

The Right Road for Britain (Conservative and Unionist Central Office, 1949)
What Do You Think? ... About Education (Conservative Political Centre, 1949)
One Nation: A Tory Approach to Social Problems (Conservative Political Centre, 1950)
Tory Democrat: Two Famous Disraeli Speeches (Conservative Political Centre, 1950)
Conservatism 1945–1950 (Conservative Political Centre, 1950)
Britain: Strong and Free (Conservative and Unionist Central Office, 1951)
Tradition and Change (Conservative Political Centre, 1954)
Change Is Our Ally (Conservative Political Centre, 1954)
The New Conservatism (Conservative Political Centre, 1955)
The Public Schools (Conservative Political Centre, 1957)
Onward in Freedom (Conservative and Unionist Central Office, 1958)
Conservative Care for Education (Conservative and Unionist Central Office, 1963)
Educational Opportunity (Conservative and Unionist Central Office, 1963)
This Is Conservative Policy: For Education (Conservative and Unionist Central Office, 1963)
Strategy for Schools (Bow Group, 1964)
Action Not Words (Conservative Party Election Manifesto, 1966)
Conservatism Today (Conservative Political Centre, 1966)
Conservatives and Comprehensives (Conservative Political Centre, 1967)
Education: Quality and Equality, (Conservative Political Centre, 1968)
Make Life Better (Conservative Party Policy Document, 1968)
Re-think on Education (Conservative Political Centre, 1969)
A Better Tomorrow (Conservative Party Election Manifesto 1970)
Campaign Guide (Conservative Central Office, 1970)
Battle Lines for Education (Conservative Political Centre, 1973)
Parental Choice (Conservative Political Centre, 1975)
How to Save Your Schools (Conservative Political Centre, 1975)
Better Schools for All (Conservative Political Centre, 1977)
Raising the Bar, Closing the Gap (Conservative Party, 2007)

Labour Party Publications

A Policy for Secondary Education (Labour Party, 1951)
Challenge to Britain (Labour Party, 1953)
Learning to Live: A Policy for Education for Nursery School to University (Labour Party, 1958)

Newspapers & Periodicals

The Conservative Teacher
The Daily Mail
The Daily Telegraph
Education
The Financial Times
Finchley Press
Finchley Times
The Guardian
New Society
New Statesman
The Observer
The Schoolmaster
Spectator
The Times
Times Educational Supplement

Books

Addison, P. *The Road to 1945: British Politics and the Second World War* (Cape, 1975)
Aldrich, R (ed.) *A Century of Education* (RoutledgeFalmer, 2002)
Ball, S. & Holliday, I. *Mass Conservatism* (Frank Kass, 2002)
Ball, S. & Seldon, A. *The Conservative Century* (Oxford University Press, 1994)
Ball, S. & Seldon, A. *The Heath Government 1970-74* (Longman, 1996)
Ball, S. & Seldon, A. *Recovering Power* (Palgrave Macmillan, 2005)
Ball, S. J. *The Education Debate* (Polity Press, 2017)
Bantock, G. H. *Education in an Industrial Society* (Faber, 1963)
Barker, R. *Education and Politics: A Study of the Labour Party 1900-1951* (Oxford University Press, 1972)
Batley, R. *Going Comprehensive* (Routledge & Kegan Paul, 1970)
Beer, S. H. *Modern British Politics* (Faber & Faber, 1969)
Behrens, R. *Conservative Party from Heath to Thatcher* (Saxon House, 1980)
Bell, R. (ed.) *Education in Great Britain and Ireland* (Open University Press, 1973)
Benewick, R. (ed.) *Knowledge and Belief in Politics: The Problem of Ideology* (Allen and Unwin, 1973)
Bentley, M. *Lord Salisbury's World: Conservative Environments in Late-Victorian Britain* (Cambridge University Press, 2001)
Blake, R. *Conservative Party from Peel to Thatcher* (Methuen, 1985)
Blake, R. & Patten, J. *The Conservative Opportunity* (Macmillan, 1976)
Boyson, R. *The Crisis in Education* (Woburn, 1975)
Boyson, R. *Centre Forward* (Temple Smith, 1978)
Boyson, R. *Speaking My Mind* (Peter Owen, 1995)
Burke, E. & Mitchell, L. G. *Reflections on the Revolution in France* (Oxford University Press, 1999)
Butler, R. A. *The Art of the Possible* (Penguin, 1973)
Butt, R. *The Unfinished Task* (Centre for Policy Studies, 1986)
Callaghan, D. *Conservative Party Education Policies 1976-1997* (Sussex Academic Press, 2006)

Campbell, J. *Margaret Thatcher* (Pimlico, 2001)
Cecil, H. *Conservatism* (Butterworth, 1912)
Centre for Contemporary Studies (Education Group), *Unpopular Education: Schooling and Social Democracy in England since 1944* (Hutchinson, 1981)
Chitty, C. *Education Policy in Britain* (Palgrave Macmillan, 2014)
Clarke, J. C. D. *Ideas and Politics in Modern Britain* (Macmillan, 1990)
Clarke, F. *Education and Social Change* (Macmillan, 1940)
Cowling, M. *Conservative Essays* (Cassell, 1978)
Cox, B. & Dyson, A. E. (eds) *Black Paper 1, Fight for Education* (Critical Quarterly Society, 1969)
Cox, B. & Dyson, A. E. (eds) *Black Paper 2, The Crisis in Education* (Critical Quarterly Society, 1969)
Cox, C. B. & Dyson, A.E. (eds) *Black Paper 3, Goodbye Mr Short* (Critical Quarterly Society, 1970)
Cox, C.B. & Boyson, R. (eds) *Black Paper 1975* (J.M. Dent & Sons, 1975)
Cox, C. B. & Boyson, R. (eds) *Black Paper 1977* (Temple Smith, 1977)
Crosland, C. A. R. *The Future of Socialism* (Cape, 1956)
Dent, H. *A New Order in English Education* (University of London Press,1942)
Dent, H. *Secondary Modern Schools – An Interim Report* (Routledge and Kegan Paul, 1958)
Eccles, D. *Life and Politics* (Longmans, 1967)
Eccleshall, R. *Political Ideologies* (Routledge, 1984)
Eliot, T. S. *Notes Towards the Definition of Culture* (Faber, 1948)
Evans, B. & Taylor, A. *From Salisbury to Major: Continuity and Change in British Politics* (Manchester University Press, 1996)
Fenwick, I.G.K. *The Comprehensive School, 1944–1970: The Politics of Secondary School Reorganisation* (Methuen, 1976)
Floud, J. (ed.) *Social Class and Educational Opportunity* (William Heinemann Ltd, 1957)
Francis, M. & Bagielowska, I. *The Conservatives and British Society* (University of Wales Press, 1996)
Freeden, M. *Ideologies and Political Theory: A Conceptual Approach* (Oxford University Press, 1996)
Gamble, A. *The Conservative Nation* (Routledge and Kegan Paul, 1974)
Garnett, M. *The Conservatives in Crisis* (Manchester University Press, 2003)
Gilmour, I. *Inside Right* (Hutchinson, 1977)
Glass, D. V. *Social Mobility in Britain* (Routledge and Paul, 1954)
Gold, A. *Edward Boyle: His Life by His Friends* (Macmillan, 1991)
Gordon, P., Aldrich, R. & Dean, D. *Education and Policy in the Twentieth Century* (The Woburn Press, 1991)
Gosden, P. *The Education System since 1944* (Martin Robertson, 1983)
Green, E. *Crisis of Conservatism* (Routledge, 1995)
Green, E. *Ideologies of Conservatism* (Oxford University Press, 2002)
Greenleaf, W. H. *The British Political Tradition: The Ideological Heritage, Volume 2* (Methuen, 1983)
Harris, R. *The Conservatives: A History* (Bantam Press, 2011)
Hayek, F. *The Constitution of Liberty* (Routledge Kegan Paul, 1960)
Heffner, R. *Alexis de Tocqueville, Democracy in America* (Mentor, 1956)
Hickson, K. *Political Thought of the Conservative Party* (Palgrave Macmillan, 2005)
Hogg, Q. *The Case for Conservatism* (Penguin,1947)
Howard, A. *Rab: The Life of R.A. Butler* (Jonathan Cape, 1987)

Howarth, T. *Prospect and Reality* (Collins, 1985)
Jackson, M. & Gretton, W. *William Tyndale: Collapse of a School – or a System?* (George Allen & Unwin, 1976)
James, E. *Education and Leadership* (George G. Harrop, 1951)
Jarvis, F. *Education and Mr Major* (Tufnell Press, 1993)
Jones, K. *Education in Britain: From 1944 to the Present* (Cambridge Polity Press, 2016)
Joseph, K. *Stranded on the Middle Ground* (Centre for Policy Studies, 1976)
Joseph, K. & Sumption, J. *Equality* (John Murray, 1979)
Judge, H. *A Generation of Schooling* (Oxford University Press, 1984)
Kelly, C. *Conservative Party Conferences* (Manchester University Press, 1989)
Knight, C. *The Making of Tory Education Policy in Post-War Britain 1950–1986* (Falmer, 1990)
Kogan, M. *The Politics of Education* (Hammondsworth, Penguin, 1971)
Kogan, M. *The Politics of Educational Change* (Fontana, 1978)
Law, R. *Return from Utopia* (Faber and Faber, 1950)
Lawton, D. *The Tory Mind on Education 1979–94* (Falmer Press, 1994)
Layton-Henry, Z. *Conservative Party Politics* (Macmillan, 1980)
Lewis, R. *Margaret Thatcher* (Routledge and Kegan Paul, 1975)
Lowe, R. *Education in the Post-War Years: A Social History* (Routledge, 1988)
Lowe, R. *Schooling and Social Change 1964–1990* (Routledge, 1997)
Maclure, S. *Education Development and School Building: Aspects of Public Policy*, 1945–73 (Harlow, 1984)
Maclure, S. *Education Documents*, (Methuen, 1986)
Mandler, P. *The Crisis of the Meritocracy* (Oxford University Press, 2020)
Maude, A. *The Common Problem* (Constable, 1969)
McCulloch, G. *Educational Reconstruction: The 1944 Education Act and the Twenty-First Century* (The Woburn Press, 1994)
McCulloch, G. *Failing the Ordinary Child? The Theory and Practice of Working-Class Secondary Education* (Open University Press, 1998)
McKibbin, R. *Classes and Cultures* (Oxford University Press, 1998)
Middleton, N & Weitzman, S. *A Place for Everyone* (Victor Gollancz, 1976)
Norton, P. & Aughey, A. *Conservatives and Conservatism* (Maurice Temple Smith Ltd, 1981)
Oakeshott, M. *Rationalism in Politics and Other Essays* (Methuen, 1947)
O'Hear, A. *Education, Society and Human Nature: An Introduction to the Philosophy of Education* (Routledge and Kegan Paul, 1981)
O'Sullivan, N. *Conservatism* (Dent, 1976)
Pedley, R. *Comprehensive Education: A New Approach* (Victor Gollancz, 1956)
Quinton, A. *The Politics of Imperfection* (Faber and Faber, 1978)
Ramsden, J. *The Making of Conservative Party Policy: The Conservative Research Department since 1929* (Longman, 1980)
Ramsden, J. *The Age of Churchill and Eden 1940–57* (Longman, 1995)
Ramsden, J. *Winds of Change* (Longman, 1996)
Ribbins, P. & Sherratt, B. *Radical Educational Policies and Conservative Secretaries of State* (Cassell, 1997)
Rubinstein, D. & Stoneman, C. *Education for Democracy* (Penguin, 1970)
Sanderson, M. *Educational Opportunity and Social Change in Britain* (Faber and Faber, 1987)
Sanderson, M. *The Missing Stratum* (Bloomsbury Academic, 2015)
Santayana, G. *The Life of Reason* (Constable, 1905)
Scruton, R. *The Meaning of Conservatism* (Palgrave, 2001)

Seldon, A. *Churchill's Indian Summer: The Conservative Government 1951-1955* (Hodder & Stoughton, 1981)
Simon, B. *Intelligence Testing and the Comprehensive School* (Lawrence and Wishart, 1953)
Simon, B. *The Politics of Educational Reform 1920-1940* (Lawrence and Wishart, 1974)
Simon, B. *Education and the Social Order 1940-1990* (Lawrence and Wishart, 1990)
Tawney, R. H. *Secondary Education for All: A Policy for Labour* (The Labour Party, 1922)
Thatcher, M. *The Path to Power* (HarperCollins, 1995)
University of Oxford. *Report of Commission of Inquiry* (Oxford University Press, 1966)
Vaizey, J. *The Costs of Education* (Allen & Unwin, 1958)
Wheatcroft, G. *The Strange Death of Tory England* (Penguin, 2005)
Williams, R. *Culture and Society* (Columbia University Press, 1958)
Wilson, P. *Views and Prospects from Curzon Street* (Basil Blackwell, 1961)
Worthstone, P. *The Socialist Myth* (Cassell, 1971)
Young, M. *The Rise of the Meritocracy* (Thames & Hudson, 1958)

Essays & Articles

Bantock, G. H. 'The Cultural Implications of Planning and Popularisation', *Scrutiny: A Quarterly Review*, vol. 14, no. 3, 1947, pp.171-84
Bilski, R. 'Ideology and the Comprehensive School', *Political Quarterly*, vol. 44, no. 2, 1973, pp.197-211
Bogdanor, V. 'Book Review: The Politics of Comprehensive Education', *Oxford Review of Education*, vol. 3, no. 2, 1977, pp.185-93
Boyle, E. 'The Politics of Secondary School Reorganisation, Some Reflections', *Journal of Educational Administration & History*, vol. 4, no. 2, June 1972, pp.28-38.
Bulpitt, J. 'The Discipline of the New Democracy: Mrs Thatcher's Domestic Statecraft', *Political Studies*, vol. 34, no. 1, 1986, pp.19-39
Clarke, D. 'The Conservative Faith in a Modern Age', in R.A. Butler (ed.) *Conservatism 1945-1950* (Conservative Political Centre, 1950), pp.7-42
Cretney, S. 'Hogg, Quintin McGarel, second Viscount Hailsham and Baron Hailsham of St Marylebone (1907-2001)', in *Oxford Dictionary of National Biography* (Oxford University Press, January 2005; online edn, October 2008)
Crook, D. 'Edward Boyle: Conservative Champion of Comprehensives?' *History of Education*, vol. 22, no. 1, March 1993, pp.49-62
Crook, D. 'Local Authorities and Comprehensivisation in England and Wales, 1944-74', *Oxford Review of Education*, vol. 28, nos. 2 & 3, 2002, pp.247-60
Dean, D. W. 'The Difficulties of a Labour Educational Policy: The Failure of the Trevelyan Bill, 1929-1931', *British Journal of Educational Studies* 17, vol. 17, no. 3, 1969, pp.286-300
Dean, D. W. 'Problems of the Conservative Sub-Committee on Education, 1941-45', *Journal of Educational Administration and History*, vol. 3, no. 1, December 1970, pp.26-37
Dean, D. W. 'Consensus or Conflict? The Churchill Government and Educational Policy 1951-55', *History of Education*, vol. 21, no. 1,1992, pp.15-35
Dean, D. W. 'Preservation or Renovation? The Dilemmas of Conservative Education Policy 1955-1960'. *Twentieth Century British History*, vol. 3, no. 1, 1992, pp.3-31

Donnison, D. V. 'Education and Opinion', *New Society*, vol. 10, no. 265, 26th October 1967, pp.583-7

Eccleshall, R. 'English Conservatism as Ideology', *Political Studies*, vol. 25, no. 1, 1977, pp.62-83

Eckstein, M. 'Britain's White Paper and Its Implications', *Comparative Education Review*, vol. 13, no. 1, June, 1959, pp.14-20

Fair, J. D. & Hutcheson, J. A. 'British Conservatism in the Twentieth Century: An Emerging Ideological Tradition', *Albion*, vol. 19, no. 4, 1987, pp.549-78

Fielding, S. 'What Did 'the people' want? The Meaning of the 1945 General Election', *The Historical Journal*, vol. 35, no. 3, 1992, pp.623-39

Francis, M. 'Economics and Ethics: The Nature of Labour's Socialism, 1945-51', *Twentieth Century British History*, vol. 6, no. 2, 1995, pp.235-9

Francis, M. 'Mr Gaitskell's Ganymede? Re-assessing Crosland's The Future of Socialism', *Contemporary British History*, vol. 11, no. 2, 1997, pp.50-64

Garnett, M. 'Maude, Angus Edmund Upton, Baron Maude of Stratford upon Avon (1912-1993)', in *Oxford Dictionary of National Biography* (Oxford University Press, September 2004; online edn, May 2007

Gosden, P. 'The Educational System of England and Wales since 1952', *British Journal of Educational Studies*, vol. 30, no. 1, 1982, pp.108-21

Grant, M. 'Historians, the Penguin Specials and the State of the Nation' Literature, 1958-64', *Contemporary British History*, vol. 17, no. 3, 2003, pp.29-54

Greenleaf, W. H. 'The Character of Modern British Conservatism', in Benewick, R., Berki, R.N. & Parekh, B. (eds) *Knowledge and Belief in Politics: The Problem of Ideology* (London: George Allen and Unwin, 1973), pp.177-212

Jefferys, K. 'R.A. Butler, the Board of Education and the 1944 Education Act', *History*, vol. 69, 1984, pp.415-31

Jefferys, K. 'British Politics and Social Policy during the Second World War', *Historical Journal*, vol. 30, no.1, 1987, pp.123-44

Jones, H. 'New Conservatism? The Industrial Charter, Modernity and the Reconstruction of British Conservatism after the War', in Conekin, B., Mort, F. & Waters, C. (eds) *Moments of Modernity* (Rivers Oram Press, 1999), pp.177-88

Joseph, K. speech to North of England Education Conference, Sheffield, 6th January 1984, *Oxford Review of Education*, vol. 10, no. 2, 1984, pp.137-46

Lowe, R. 'The Second World War, Consensus, and the Foundation of the Welfare State', *Twentieth Century British History*, vol. 1, no. 2, 1990, pp.163-4

Pinto-Duschinsky, M. 'Central Office and "Power" in the Conservative Party', *Political Studies*, vol. 20, no. 1, 1972, pp.1-16

Powell, J. E. 'Conservatives and Social Services', *Political Quarterly*, vol. 24, no. 2, 1953, pp.156-66

Pugh, M. 'Eccles, David McAdam, First Viscount Eccles (1904-1999)', in *Oxford Dictionary of National Biography* (Oxford University Press, September 2004)

Ramsden, J. 'Boyle, Edward, Charles Gurney, Baron Boyle of Handsworth (1923-1981)', in *Oxford Dictionary of National Biography* (Oxford University Press, September 2004; online edn, January 2009)

Rao, N. 'Labour and Education: Secondary Reorganisation and the Neighbourhood School', *Contemporary British History*, vol. 16, no. 2, Summer 2002, pp.99-120

Seyd, P. 'Factionalism within the Conservative Party: The Monday Club', *Government and Opposition*, vol. 7, no. 4, November 1972, pp.464-87

Simon, B. 'The Tory Government and Education, 1951–60: Background to Breakout', *History of Education*, vol. 14, no. 4, 1985, pp.283–97

Tomlinson, J. 'Comprehensive Education in England and Wales, 1944–1991', *European Journal of Education*, vol. 26, no. 2, 1991, pp.103–17

Walsha, R. 'The One Nation Group: A Tory Approach to Backbench Politics & Organisation, 1950–55', *Twentieth Century British History*, vol. 11, no. 2, 2000, pp.183–214

Wiborg, S, 'The Enduring Nature of Egalitarian Education in Scandinavia: An English Perspective', *Forum*, vol. 51, no. 2, 2009, pp.117–30

Woods, R. 'Margaret Thatcher and Secondary Reorganisation, 1970–4', *Journal of Educational Administration and History*, vol. 13, no. 2, 1981, pp.51–61

Reports

Andrews, J., Hutchinson, J. & Johnes, R. *Grammar Schools and Social Mobility*, Education Policy Institute, September 2016

Atkinson, A., Gregg, P. & McConnell, B. *The Result of 11 Plus Selection: An Investigation into Opportunities and Outcomes for Pupils in Selective LEAs*, The Centre for Market and Public Organisation 06/150, University of Bristol, 2006

Coldron, J., Tanner, E., Finch, E., Shipton, S., Wolstenholme, L. & Willis, C. *Secondary School Admissions*, DCSF Research Report RR020, 2008

Cribb, J., Jesson, D., Sibiela, L., Skipp, A. & Vignoles, A. *Poor Grammar: Entry into Grammar Schools for Disadvantaged Pupils in England*, Sutton Trust, November 2013

Cullinane, C. *Gaps in Grammar*, Sutton Trust Research Brief, Edition 15, December 2016

Education Data Lab *Research Briefing: Grammar Schools*, September 2016

House of Commons Education Committee. *Evidence Check: Grammar Schools*, Fourth Report of Session, 2016–17

Sutton Trust. *University Admissions by Individual Schools*, The Sutton Trust, 2007

West, A., Barham, E. & Hind, A. *Secondary School Admissions in England: Policy and Practice*, Research and Information on State Education Trust, 2009

Web sources

Margaret Thatcher Foundation www.margaretthatcher.org
National Grammar Schools Association www.ngsa.org.uk
SayIt – Conservative Party Speeches www.conservative-speeches.sayit.mysociety.org

Conservative home www.conservativehome.com

Index

Locators followed by "n." indicate endnotes

Abrams, Mark 84
Adonis, Andrew 174, 182
Adoption of Children (Regulation) Act (1939) 28
Alexander, William 54, 103, 123–4.
    See also centrist-minded educational establishment
all-ability system 132, 142, 152, 173, 187
Allen, Rebecca 192
Amis, Kingsley 114, 117
Anderson, Eric 176
Armstrong, Ernest 144
Armstrong, Hilary 175
Ashcroft, Lord 186
assisted places scheme 50, 152–3, 156–8, 162–3, 167, 171, 174, 177
Association of Education Committees 72
Astor, John 96
attainment gap 192–3, 222 n.38
Attlee, Clement 21–2, 25
Autumn Statement (2016) 191
Aylesbury grammar school 141

Bacon, Alice 25, 41–2, 123
Baguley, Peter 110, 121, 130
Baker, Kenneth 163
Balchin, Robert 167, 176
Baldwin, Stanley 46
Balfour, Arthur 6
Balls, Ed 182–3
Barber, Anthony 139, 144
Barker, Rodney 25
Barnet Council 129
Barton Court Grammar School (Canterbury) 194
Beamish, Tufton 77
Bell, Ronald 109
Belstead, Lord 134
Benn, Hilary 175
Berry, Anthony 87

Berufsschule 198
Beveridge Report (1942) 41
bilateral arrangements/schools 14, 22–3, 26, 36, 47–8, 55, 61–3, 76, 81, 96, 122, 142
bipartite system 32, 68, 72, 79, 82–3, 94, 153
Birch, Nigel 77
Birley, Robert 44–5, 49–50, 52
Birmingham Evening Mail (newspaper) 132
Black Papers 113–18, 120, 129–30, 147, 151, 154, 156
Blair, Tony 172–6, 178, 180, 183
    educational programme 182
    legislation (1998) 185, 188
    parental ballots 173
    policy for specialist schools 181
Blunkett, David 169, 171–3
Board of Education 166
    Consultative Committee 7
    education, types 6
    free places 9
    Green Book (1941) 20
    Secondary School Regulations (1905–6) 6
Bow Group 78
Boyd-Carpenter, John 122
Boyle, Edward 2, 41, 45, 48–9, 51–2, 60–1, 63, 66–7, 69–73, 75, 77–80, 86, 88–101, 103–20, 124, 126–7, 135–7, 141, 197, 209 n.17, 211 n.87
    banding and zoning 123
    defeatism 84
    developments under 41–4
    partnership and co-operative relations 122
    'segregation' 76
Boyle, Mary 187

Boyson, Rhodes 117, 148, 150–4, 155–7, 159–60
　early leaving scheme 151
　voucher system 137, 147
Brady, Graham 173–5, 177–81, 184, 186, 193
Bristol Grammar school 103
Brooke, Henry 68
Brown, Gordon 180, 182
　diplomas 184
　School Admissions Code (2008) 183
Bryce Report (1895) 5
Buckinghamshire County Council 169–70
Buckinghamshire Examiner (newspaper) 180
Burt, Cyril 117
Butler, Richard Austen 'Rab' 12–15, 17–18, 27–8, 33–4, 40, 46, 51, 87, 89, 101, 201 n.57. *See also* war-time developments (Butler)
　Interim Policy Group reports (1965) 90
Butt, Ronald 140, 142, 150, 152–3, 158
Byers, Stephen 169

Callaghan, James 147, 151, 154
Cambridge University 90, 97, 181, 197
Cameron, David 173, 176–82, 184, 191, 195
　coalition government 2, 184, 190, 192, 194, 197
　resignation 185
　social justice review 186
　socially progressive goals 194
Carlisle, Mark 154–5, 157–9
Carmichael, Neil 192–3
Carter, Paul 189–90
Central Advisory Council for Education (England) 63, 67, 73
Central Committee on Post-War Problems 18–20, 33, 201 n.61
centralization, educational 5–7, 149, 168
centrist-minded educational establishment 124
Certificate of Secondary Education (CSE) 67
Charity Commission 6
Chataway, Christopher 106

Churchill, Winston 14, 21, 27–8, 34
Circulars (Labour government) 92, 94, 96, 99, 103
　Circular 10/65 85, 92, 94–5, 97, 109, 118, 123–6, 128, 130, 141, 145
　Circular 10/66 85, 96–9, 118, 123, 125–6
　Circular 13/66 98
　Circular 10/70 126, 128, 130, 133–5, 141
　Circular 4/74 147–9
City Technology Colleges (CTCs) 163, 169
Clark, Greg 180
Clarke, Kenneth 165–6
Clegg, Alec 73
Clegg, Nick 186, 192
Clifton Hall Girls' Grammar School (Nottingham) 142
co-existence policy 85, 145, 148
Cole, John 45–6
common curriculum 78
Comprehensive Future 187, 190
comprehensive reorganization 69, 79, 81, 84, 86, 97, 103–4, 107, 112, 118, 123, 125–6, 142, 149, 201 n.57
comprehensive schemes 2, 29, 47, 51, 55–6, 59, 62, 64–5, 76, 78, 100, 102–3, 114, 120–1, 127–9, 132–3, 135–7, 140–1, 146, 201 n.57
　full-scale 122
　urban 85, 142
comprehensive schools/education 2, 22, 24–5, 33, 39, 41, 48, 53, 56, 60–2, 70, 74, 78–9, 81, 83, 87, 89, 103, 107–8, 123, 127–8, 133–4, 143, 148, 153, 166, 174–5, 181, 209 n.102
　backdoor methods 76
　degree of choice 120
　development 2–3, 27, 31, 36, 38, 41, 67, 121, 197
　and egalitarianism 2, 83, 198
　full-scale 65
　Labour opposition on 52
　London School Plan 30
　proposals for changes 64
　rural 43, 62

slow learners 132
  in the United States 47
compulsory full-time education 63
compulsory uniformity, policy 143
Confederation for the Advancement of State Education (CASE) 142
Conquest, Robert 114, 117
Conservative-led coalition 185–6, 188, 190
Conservative North West Advisory Committee on Education 153
Conservative Opposition 109, 147, 149–50, 154, 181
Conservative Party 1–2, 26, 40, 44, 53, 63, 85, 119, 145, 149, 176, 184, 197–8
  Conference 30, 47, 111, 114, 117, 138
  deliberations within 18–21
  early controversies 27–34
  Education Policy Group 89–90, 101, 103, 110
  hierarchy 23, 107, 180
  Parliamentary Education Committee 47–8, 70, 75–6, 120
  progressive reform 12
  public statements on education 71–2
Conservative Research Department 23, 44–5, 100, 129
Conservative Teachers' Association (CTA) 30, 32–3, 68, 70–1, 76–7, 81, 92–4, 98–9, 203 n.25, 207 n.30, 207 n.39
Cook, Chris 188
Cook, Josephine 47
Cooke, Robert 80
Coronavirus pandemic 194
Cox, Brian 113–14, 117, 129–30, 153–4, 159–60
Cox, Thomas 135
Crosland, Anthony 77, 89, 92, 94, 96–7, 99
Crowther, Geoffrey 63
Crowther Report (1959) 63

Daily Telegraph (newspaper) 72, 107, 114, 137
Davis, David 177
Dean, Dennis 83
Dent, Harold 55–6
Department of Education and Science (DES) 144, 161–3

Dewar, Margaret 170
Digby, Lord 166
direct grant schools 6, 17–18, 67, 85, 90–2, 94, 97, 101, 103–4, 109–10, 115, 123–5, 130–1, 139, 143, 148–9, 151–2, 156, 162, 167–8
  future of 110, 133–5
diversity 9, 11, 16, 83, 169–70
  and parental choice 148, 166–8, 172, 174
  of secondary schools 71
Dormand, Jack 133
Dorries, Nadine 177
Dorset grammar schools 166
Douglas-Home, Alec 77, 89
Drefner, Rolf 142
du Cann, Edward 92–3
Dulwich College 122
Duncan-Smith, Iain 175
Dunn, Robert 160
Dyson, Anthony 114, 117, 120

Eccles, David 2, 28, 30, 34, 40, 51, 58, 63–9, 71, 83, 89, 197, 204 n.52, 206 n.117
  Colleges of Advanced Technology (CATs) 83
  11 plus selection 82
  opposed wholesale transfers 35, 42
  overlapping, idea 34–40
  secondary modern schools, development 36–7, 55
Eckstein, Max 57
Ede, James Chuter 12, 43
Eden, Anthony 39–40
Education Act (1870) 5
Education Act (1899) 5
Education Act (1902) 6
Education Act (1918) 7
Education Act (1936) 201 n.34
Education Act (1944) 2, 5, 24–5, 38, 61–2, 64–5, 77–9, 84, 87, 97, 101, 109, 121, 126–7, 138, 149
  basis for 15–18
Education Act (1968) 109
Education Act (1976) 149, 155
Education Act (1979) 155–6
Education Act (1980) 156
Education Act (1997) 171

Education and Inspections Act (2006) 175
Education (Grammar School Ballots) Regulations 173
Education (journal) 54, 104
Education Reform Act (1988) 155, 163
egalitarianism 2, 58, 70–2, 83–4, 101, 104, 114, 193, 197–8
11 plus examination 35, 38–9, 43, 48, 51, 53, 65, 72, 77–8, 102, 111, 139, 181, 188
  arbitrariness 148
  battle 215 n.81
  familiarisation 189
  selection 82–3, 88, 102, 104, 110, 120, 151
Eltham Hill (girls' grammar school) 30–1
Enfield Grammar School 108
England
  education system 164
  grammar schools, free places 9
  paying fees 9
  secondary education system 146
  secondary pupils in 149
  self-governing authorities, grammar schools as 185
Erith comprehensive school 157
European Union referendum (2016) 191
ex-direct grant schools 157, 168
expenditure, school 27–8, 34, 47, 50, 68, 72, 90, 120, 135, 143, 147, 159, 168
Eysenck, Hans 117

Faber, Geoffrey 20
fair access 192–3
Fallon, Michael 186
federations of schools 178
Fenton, Shaun 186
Fenwick, Ian 81
Field, Frank 186
Financial Times (newspaper) 154
Finchley Association 105–6
Finchley Press (newspaper) 129
Finchley Times (newspaper) 128
Fisher Act (1918) 7
Fisher, H. A. L. 7
Fleming, David Pinkerton 14
Fleming Plan/Report (1944) 14, 18, 46, 48, 90
  public schools, policy 45

Fletcher, Ralph 64–6
Fletcher-Cooke, Charles 42
Floud, Jean 42
Forbes-Cockell, Seton 100–1
Forster, W. E. 5
Fox, Liam 177
Fox, Marcus 111
Franks Report (1966) 97
Fraser, Richard Michael 61–2, 101, 112–13
free school(s) 183, 186, 190–2
  expansion, policy 190
  Swedish-style 183
Friends of Grammar Schools group 186
Fulford, R. J. 30
full-time education 23, 63, 74
Funding Agency 165–8, 170, 189
Further and Higher Education Act (1992) 172

Gale, Roger 177
GCSE exam/results 160, 168, 174, 179, 182, 190–1, 197
General Certificate of Education (GCE) 33, 37, 42, 67, 87–8, 114
  examinations 56
  and non-GCE 55
  'O' and 'A' level 35, 37, 54–6, 78
General Election (1945, 1951, 1997 & 2010) 45–6, 81, 97, 165, 184
Gibb, Nick 186–7, 193
Gibson, Frank 129
Gillan, Cheryl 169
Gillingham grammar school 60–1, 102
Gilmour, Iain 197
Gladstone, William 5
Glyn, Richard 52, 60
Godber, Joseph 112–13
Gosden, Peter 209 n.102
Gove, Michael 181–3, 185–6, 188–90
Governing Bodies Association 14, 50
Gower, Raymond 76–7, 84
Grammar School Heads Association (GSHA) 186, 188, 193
grammar schools 5, 7, 9–13, 19–20, 22, 33, 37, 40, 44, 50–1, 63, 65, 67, 83, 85, 96–7, 108, 119, 155, 185, 191–2, 194–5, 201 n.57. *See also* technical schools
  annexe 185, 188

authority-maintained 17
degree of choice 120
dissolution 93
facilities 6
funding 193
future 80, 177
and junior technical schools 6–7, 9
media hostility 188
merging 60
objective assessment 188
'Open Sesame' 53
places/free places 9, 32, 35–6, 41, 48, 52
provision 25, 35, 37, 41, 43, 53, 59, 68, 206 n.117
selection of children 73
selective places for 66
selective system 51
for snobbery and elitism, criticism 88
and tripartite system 30, 83
unsatisfied demand 25
Grant Maintained (GM) schools 2, 161–8, 170–2, 174, 184
Green Book (1941) 13, 20
Greenleaf, W. H. 197
Gregg, Paul 179
Grieve, Dominic 180
Griffiths, Brian 161–2
Gurden, Harold 87, 96

Hadow Committee 8–9
Hadow Report (1926) 7–9, 12, 16
Hadow, Henry 7
Hague, William 175
Hamilton, William 119, 135
Hammond, Philip 192
Hampshire 103
Harman, Harriet 218 n.16
Harte, Wilma 70–1
Hattersley, Roy 140–1, 143
Heathcoat Amory, Derick 63
Heath, Edward 2, 41, 89–90, 92–3, 97–8, 100–1, 104–7, 111–12, 114–16, 118, 120, 123, 128, 135–6, 139, 144–5, 147–9
principles of education 131
Henry, Martin 53
Hewlett, Clyde 95, 98–100
Hickman, R. G. K. 47

Hicks, Robert 156
Higgins, Walter 93
Highbury Grove School 147, 157
high school system 29, 59–60, 72, 85, 198
Hiley, Joseph 87
Hinds, Damian 193
Hogg, Quintin (Lord Hailsham) 2, 30, 41–2, 44–6, 51, 60, 62, 65, 77–80, 82–3, 86–9, 105, 111, 115, 117, 141
defeatism 84
'educationally viable' scheme 80
Hopkins, Alan 85
Hornby, Richard 48, 89, 98, 101, 110, 120
Horsbrugh, Florence 2, 27–31, 33–4, 40, 83, 132, 141, 204 n.33
Howard, Anthony 14–15
Howard, Michael 175, 177
Howe, Geoffrey 159
Howell, John 153
Hull, Alderman 110
Hunt, Donald 106
Hurd, Douglas 116, 162
Hutty, Fred 116

independent schools 5, 78, 82, 90–1, 97, 104, 110, 122–5, 133, 148–9, 155–6, 158, 163, 181–4, 187, 191–2, 198
dominance 1
fee paying and 14, 19, 44–5, 52
highly selective 179
maintained/state sector and 1, 6, 13, 18, 45, 130, 168
partnerships 182
public schools 5, 25, 27, 29
Inner London Education Authority (ILEA) 101, 130, 137, 142, 157
Interim Policy Group 90
International GCSE 184
Ions, Edmund 130
Iremonger, Tom 48
Irving, Sydney 41

James, Eric 101–2
Jarvis, Fred 165–6
Jenkin, Patrick 144
Jenkins, Simon 95–7, 108, 110, 165, 168–9, 218 n.16

Jennings, John 76, 80, 127–8
Jessel, Stephen 131
Jesson, David 181, 188, 192
Johnson, Boris 1–2, 185, 194–5, 197
Joint Committee of the Four Secondary Associations 39
Jones, Gareth 110
Jones, Ken 2, 30
Joseph, Keith 159
    GCSE 160
    secondary school reform 161–3
junior technical schools 6–9, 11, 17, 19–20

'Keep the grammar schools campaign' (Birmingham) 132
Kelly, Ruth 175
Kent County Council 182, 187–8, 190
Kidbrooke (comprehensive girls' school) 30–1
Kilfoyle, Peter 171
King, Horace 79
King Edward VI grammar school (Birmingham) 179, 188, 192
Kinnock, Neil 156
Knole Academy 187
Kogan, Maurice 118

Labour opposition 29, 43, 52, 63, 83, 119, 124, 126, 128, 140–1, 144, 147, 156, 166, 168–9, 171, 193
Labour Party 1–2, 15, 22, 25–6, 50, 59, 69, 103, 143, 145, 172, 174, 180, 201 n.57
    "comprehensive schools for all" policy 51
    Conference 25, 52
    dogmatism 54
    Educational Advisory Committee 32
    Learning to Live (1958) 48–9, 52
    opposition within 90–103
    Policy for Secondary Education, The (1951) 25
    radicalism 98
Ladyman, Stephen 174
Lane, David 123
Laws, David 189
Lawson, Nigel 162
Lee, Herbert 61–2

Leicestershire experiment/scheme 2, 44, 54, 58, 65–8, 70–1, 76, 82–4, 91, 121
Letwin, Oliver 161
Liberal Party (subsequently Liberal Democrats) 89, 184, 186–7, 189–91, 194
Linstead, Hugh 23
Llewellyn, Ed 179
Lloyd, Geoffrey 2, 30, 46–50, 53–4, 58–62, 82–3, 85–6, 197
    Five Year Plan 50, 54
    vacillating approach 61
Lloyd George, David 7
London Conservative Women's Conference 30
London County Council 23, 25, 30–1, 72
London School of Economics 181
London Schools Plan 24, 30–1
Longden, Gilbert 47–9, 93, 98–9, 106, 110, 115, 143–4
Lowe, Roy 2, 30, 82

MacArthur, Brian 121
MacGregor, John 163
Macleod, Iain 69–70
Maclure, Stuart 166
Macmillan, Harold 28, 40–1, 46–7, 57–8, 60, 62, 70
    housing policy 33–4
    National Economic Development Council 72
Maitland, John 39, 47
Major, John 2, 165, 172, 176
    'choice and diversity' 166–9, 172
    Policy Unit 168–9
    statements on selection 165–6
Manchester Grammar School 90, 167
Manchester Guardian (newspaper) 29, 45
Mandler, Peter 83, 108, 209 n.95, 212 n.90
Marks, Kenneth 128, 141
Marsden, Dennis 108
Mary Datchelor grammar school 152
Marylebone Grammar school 152
Mason, Stewart 65, 67, 71
Maude, Angus 30, 99, 110–14, 117, 120–2, 127, 129, 133, 146, 149
Maudling, Reginald 81

Maxwell-Fyfe Committee on Party Organisation (1947) 203 n.25
May, Theresa 1–2, 191–4, 197
  pro-grammar school policy 185
McCartney, Robert 182, 185
McCulloch, Gary 30, 82
McIntosh, John 183
McLoughlin, Patrick 179
Miles, Alice 178–9
Miliband, David 174–5
Ministry of Education 21, 23, 25–6, 58, 60, 62, 68–9, 83, 108, 122, 197, 206 n.117
  partnership 18
  ultra-pragmatic spirit 63
Miscampbell, Gordon 156
Monday Club 142, 154
Moore, Donald 52
Moore, Royston 93, 115, 117
More, Jasper 97
Morgan, Nicky 190–2
Morrison, Charles 123, 127–8
Moss, Reginald 42
Moyle, Arthur 39
Mundella grammar school (Nottingham) 142
Mulley, Fred 149–51
multilateral school 5, 10, 17, 20–4, 55

National Advisory Committee (NAC) on Education (Conservative Party) 92, 99–100, 104, 110, 115–16, 118, 121, 130, 147, 203 n.25, 210 n.30
National Association of Labour Teachers 22, 29
National Association of Schoolmasters 139
National Centre for Social Research 181
National Council for Educational Standards (NCES) 140, 153
National Curriculum 163
National Education Association 140
National Health Service 50
National Union of Teachers (NUT) 15, 46, 137, 139, 165
New Labour (1997–2010)
  ballots and new restrictions 173–5
  city academies 174
Newport Borough Council 70

Newport Education Committee 69
New Society (magazine) 108
Newsom, John 67
'Newsom children' 96
Newsom Report (1963) 73–7, 86
  Boyle and 75–6
  and CSE exam 84
  cultural and linguistic shortcomings 74
  intelligence and ability 74
  positive discrimination 74
Newton, Lord 77, 79
Nonconformists 6
non-selective schools 96, 98, 142, 156, 160, 163, 179, 191–3
  future of 131
  selective schools and 85, 119, 146, 148, 153–4, 167, 179, 191
  senior schools 82
North of England Conference 94, 139
Norwood, Cyril 11
Norwood Report (1941) 11–12
nursery schools 139–40, 171
  expansion programme 132–3, 144
  provision 132, 135

Observer, The (newspaper) 192
Office for Fair Access (OFFA) 197
Office of the Schools Adjudicator (OSA) 189
Ofsted reform 183
O' Leary, John 169
Onslow, Cranley 141
open enrolment 155, 162–3
Ottaway, Richard 184
outreach programmes 188, 191
over-subscribed schools 187
Oxford University 90, 97, 181, 197

Parents' Charter 156
parents/parental choice 124, 138, 142, 154, 156, 159, 172, 195
  education system and alienating parents 170
  parent power 149
  rights 148–9
  selection process 68
  voucher system 137, 159
Partridge, Wickham 53
part-time education 63
Patten, John 166–7

Pawsey, James 156
Pedley, Richard 120
Pedley, Robin 42, 65, 82–3
Pickthorn, Kenneth 26, 49, 77
Pile, William 135
Pitman, James 39, 47
Plowden, Lady Bridget 80, 140
Plowden Report (1967) 107
polytechnics 99, 147, 172
'Poor Law complex' 156
post-primary education 7, 9, 20
Potts, Edward Maynard 143
Powell, Enoch 47, 76, 117
Powell, Lucy 192
Prentice, Reginald 88, 145
Prescott, John 175
Price, Christopher 122, 124
primary education/schools 6–7, 17, 19, 24, 29, 43, 49, 57, 86, 106, 116, 130, 132–4, 139, 171, 176, 193
Prior, Jim 105
pro-comprehensive campaigners/policy 31, 33, 35, 39, 41–3, 47, 95, 142, 190, 198
progressive educational establishment 121, 140, 194
progressivism 12, 15, 41, 51, 75, 114, 140, 163
public schools 5, 14, 25, 27, 29, 50, 52, 89, 101, 104, 106, 118, 183
   co-operation policy 90
   eminence 14
   Fleming Report (1944) 15
   integration 14, 49, 90
   'question' 13–15, 44–6, 90
Public Schools Commission Report (1968) 104
pupil, types 7, 11–12, 17, 52, 81, 83
Pupil Premium policy 183, 188–9, 192–3

Queen Elizabeth Grammar School (Faversham) 194
Queen Elizabeth's school (Barnet) 167
Queen Elizabeth school (Penrith) 167
Quennell, Joan 78
Quinton, Anthony 197

Raison, Timothy 144
Rees, Merlyn 79–80

Renton, David 77
Rickover, Hyman 72
Ridley, Nicholas 159
Ripon grammar school 174
Rippon, Geoffrey 111
Robbins Committee 93, 137
Robbins Report (1963) 72
Roseveare, Martin 35
Rotherham 64
Royal Assent 155, 171
Royal Grammar School (High Wycombe) 181
Rumbelow, Helen 178–9
Russell Group universities 197

Salisbury, Lord 6
Sanders, Nicholas 157–8
Sanderson, Michael 30
Sapsted, Jimmy 129
'Save our School' campaigns 141
School Admissions Code 183, 186, 189
school building programme 41, 47, 75, 96, 112, 123, 132
school leaving age, raising of 13, 17–19, 24, 33, 65, 67, 76, 91, 109, 132–4, 151, 201 n.34
School Standards and Framework Act (1998) 173, 194
Schools that Work for Everyone (2017) 191, 193
secondary education 5–7, 14, 18, 21, 34, 42–3, 48–51, 71–2, 76, 80–1, 85, 98, 102, 114, 118, 120, 146, 154, 158
   fee-paying in 19
   mode of assessment 16
   multilateral school 10
   population 86
   raising standards 178
   replacement programme 134
   separatist system of 96
   uniform pattern 126
secondary modern schools 5, 7–8, 10–11, 19–21, 35–6, 38, 42–3, 48–9, 51, 53–5, 59–60, 63, 66–7, 72–4, 85, 88, 96, 100, 111, 113–15, 147
   academic specialisms 56
   advanced courses 52
   Code for Public Elementary Schools 9
   curriculum and goals 21, 34

degree of choice 120
development 32–3, 72
extension 61
external examinations 36–7, 67
and GCE 37
notion of 10
secondary school reorganization 58, 71, 76, 78, 81, 84, 86–7, 92, 95, 99, 109–10, 119, 135–6
bipartisan consensus 118
educational considerations 126
provision 132
Secondary Schools Examinations Council 37, 67
Seldon, Anthony 182
selective schools 20, 36, 44, 51, 81–2, 109, 131, 142, 160, 166–7, 169, 177, 182, 185–7
contextual admissions 193
positive signals for 185–7
proposed expansion 187–90
Sevenoaks annexe proposal 189–90
Sexton, Stuart 149, 160
Shaw, Arnold 119
Sheffield Hallam University 181
Shephard, Gillian 167–70, 172
Short, Edward 110, 114–15, 124, 132, 134–5
Circular 10/70 141
Education Bill (1970) 115, 117, 119, 121, 123, 125, 128
Short, Renee 120, 128
Silkin, Samuel 135
Simon, Brian 2, 30, 81–2
Skeffington, Arthur 31
Slater, Harriet 77
Smieton, Mary 66–7
Smith, Jacqui 175
Soames, Nicholas 184
social engineering policies 187–9, 191, 198
socialism 23–4, 91
social mobility 22, 186, 192
Spearing, Nigel 156
specialist colleges/schools 174, 178
Blair policy for 181
in technology and languages 169
specialization for schools 166, 170
Special Place examination 16–17, 19
Spectator (magazine) 138

Spencer, Raine 53
Spens Report (1938) 9–10, 14
Spens, Will 9, 14
Squire, Robin 168
stand-alone grammar schools 174
state education 50, 75, 197
bureaucracy and over-centralised system 183
drive in 50–5
and independent schools 1, 45
and media establishment 167
selective 2, 27, 180, 184, 194 (*see also* selective schools)
standards 176
Stewart, Michael 45, 77, 81, 86
St John-Stevas, Norman 141, 147–9, 151–6
St Olave's school (Orpington) 218 n.16
Strand grammar school 141
Sunak, Rishi 195
Sutton Coldfield Girls School 157–8
Sutton Trust 181, 188, 193, 198
Swingler, Stephen 33, 52
Swinton Committee 33
Szamuely, Tibor 117

Talbot, Vincent 100–2
Tameside dispute and reorganization 147, 150–1, 157–8
Taylor, William 61
Teachers' Superannuation Bill 28, 33–4
teacher training 74–5, 130, 198
colleges, expansion 51, 93
reform 159, 163
techniques 74
Tebbit, Norman 162
technical schools 8, 22–3, 30, 32–3, 36, 38–9, 47, 50, 53, 56, 58, 67, 78, 81, 83. *See also* grammar schools
high schools (as recommended by Spens Report) 9–10
junior 6–9, 11, 17, 19–20
Technische Hochschulen 198
Thatcher, Margaret 2, 118, 119, 149–51, 154–5, 165, 172, 185, 204 n.33, 214 n.67
economic reality 144–6
as flexible minister 125–39
in opposition 119–25

politics of distraction 139–44
  stance on academic qualifications 133–4
Thatcherism (in education)
  early dilemmas 155–9
  Joseph period (1981–6) 159–61
  National Curriculum 155
  per capita funding 161–3
  secondary school reform 161–3
Thompson, Kenneth 63, 66–7, 69, 73, 77
Thorneycroft, Peter 46–7
Thornton, Malcolm 154, 159
Thorpe, Jeremy 145
three-tier comprehensive system 100, 104
Tiley, Arthur 61
Times Educational Supplement 55, 108, 145
Times, The (newspaper) 90–1, 114, 121, 131, 140, 152, 165–7, 175, 177–8
Timms, Stephen 175
Timothy, Nick 192
Tomlinson, George 25
Tory Reform Committee 41
Trades Union Congress (TUC) 75
tripartite system 3, 8, 11, 20, 22, 25–6, 30, 33, 36, 47, 53, 59, 79–83, 87–9
Truss, Liz 195
Tulloch, Margaret 187
Turner, Barbara 92–3
Turner, James 188
two-tier systems 91

union militancy 144–5
United States Congress 72
universities 1, 17, 29, 45, 53, 72, 93, 101–2, 137, 172, 177, 181, 192–3, 197–8. *See also specific university*
Urban Aid Programme 140
Urton, William 61–2
Ussher, Victor 128–9

Vaizey, John 145
van Straubenzee, William 123, 128, 147–8, 150, 159
Victorian philanthropy 5
Vignoles, Anna 192–3
vocational education 5, 8, 78, 83, 172, 184, 197–8

voluntary schools 133, 143, 149, 166
Vosper, Dennis 49

Walden, George 168
Walker, Gordon 108
Walker, Peter 111, 113
Wallington and Carshalton Times 142
Warren, K. G. 107
war-time coalition government 7
war-time developments (Butler) 12–15
Welby, Justin 1
Wellington College 182
Wessex Provincial Area Council 98
West, Anne 182
West Riding Education Committee 31–2
Whitelaw, William 162
White Papers 15–19, 51, 55–8, 60, 62, 65, 75–6, 84, 85–6, 139–40, 165
  Secondary Education for All (1958) 27, 82, 197
  lack of clarity 62
  policy 58–9, 62, 66, 68
  Education: A Framework for Expansion (1972) 139–40
  Better Schools (1985) 160
  Choice and Diversity (1992) 166
  Self-Government for Schools (1996) 170
  Higher Standards, Better Schools For All (2005) 175
Wilkinson, Ellen 22
Willetts, David 176–81, 183, 195
Willey, Frederick 67, 79
Williams, Paul 59
Williams, Shirley 128, 151
Williams, Tom 87
Williamson, Gavin 195
William Tyndale Junior School 151
Wills-Pope, Brian 176
Wilshaw, Michael 188
Wilson, Harold 81, 85–6, 115, 125, 147, 149, 154
Wilson, Percy 99
Winant, John G. 13
Wolverhampton Grammar school 116
Woodcock, George 75

Yom Kippur war 144

Zahawi, Nadhim 195